Romantic Literature

John Gilroy

Longman
is an imprint o

PEARSON

Harlow, England •
Sydney • Tokyo •
Cape Town • Madı

 York Press

YORK PRESS
322 Old Brompton Road, London SW5 9JH

PEARSON EDUCATION LIMITED
Edinburgh Gate, Harlow CM20 2JE. United Kingdom
Tel: +44 (0)1279 623623   Fax: +44 (0)1279 431059
Website: www.pearsoned.co.uk

First edition published in Great Britain in 2010

© Librairie du Liban *Publishers* 2010

The right of John Gilroy to be identified as author
of this work has been asserted by him in accordance
with the Copyright, Designs and Patents Act 1988.

ISBN 978-1-4082-0479-5

British Library Cataloguing in Publication Data
A CIP catalogue record for this book can be obtained from the British Library

Library of Congress Cataloging in Publication Data
Gilroy, John, 1946-
  Romantic literature / John Gilroy.
    p. cm. -- (York notes companions)
  Includes bibliographical references and index.
  ISBN 978-1-4082-0479-5 (pbk. : alk. paper) 1. English literature--19th
century--History and criticism--Handbooks, manuals, etc. 2. English
literature--18th century--History and criticism--Handbooks, manuals, etc. 3.
Romanticism--Great Britain--Handbooks, manuals, etc. 4. Literature and
society--Great Britain--History--19th century. 5. Literature and
society--Great Britain--History--18th century. I. Title.
  PR457.G56 2010
  820.9'145--dc22
                                        2010008347

10 9 8 7 6 5 4 3 2 1

14 13 12 11 10

Phototypeset by Carnegie Book Production, Lancaster
Printed in Malaysia, CTP-KHL

Contents

Contents

Part One
Introduction

In his Preface to *Poems* (1853), Matthew Arnold describes as almost a form of sickness the self-referential character of modern Victorian poetry. Its morbidly introspective preoccupations lead him to remark that 'the dialogue of the mind with itself has begun'. Today, however, we expect that the 'modern' work of literature will provide this personal voice; that originality and freshness of response will in some way replace old forms and rules with writing that is accessible, revealing what is going on inside the author's head, instead of primarily describing the world outside.

It was during the Romantic period that the life of the writer began to come under the same kind of scrutiny as the work. First called to many people's minds when thinking of the poet Percy Bysshe Shelley, for example, are the circumstances of his death. He was drowned when his small boat encountered a storm off the north-west coast of Italy, and his body was washed ashore with a copy of John Keats's poems open in his pocket. He was cremated on the seashore by Lord Byron and the adventurer Edward Trelawney, and Byron snatched his heart out of the flames. This well-documented story inevitably led readers to think of Romantic poets like Shelley in terms of an enduring public image (that of the youthful and tragic Romantic exile) based on legendary episodes in their careers. A predominant notion of the Romantic poet is still popularly that of a subjective, introverted, young and storm-tossed

1

figure, perhaps dying young in pathetic, or in the case of Byron fighting for the cause of Greek independence, heroic circumstances.*

As virtual inventor of the 'Romantic hero' figure, in the celebrated verse-tales of his early years of fame (see Part Four: 'Heroes and Anti-heroes'), it was Byron who recognised the limitations of making a cult of the value, and even the grandeur, of the individual sensitive soul. As the chapter on 'Heroes and Anti-heroes' shows, Byron was to turn away from the popular image of heroism with which he was associated, realising that although writing can be a valuable form of action, it must not be made a substitute for other kinds of action. He understood that working directly in the world to build a republic or going to fight in the cause of liberty is of more importance than the self-regard which, in its subscription to the myth of the writer-hero, can sometimes lead to destructiveness.

In *Don Juan* (1819–24), Byron engages directly with the real world, leaving behind the melancholy egotism of *Childe Harold* (1812, 1816 and 1818) and the heroes of the verse-tales and, in so doing, escapes the kind of morbidity that Matthew Arnold objects to in modern literature. By the middle of the nineteenth century, continental Romanticism was tied up with nationalism, and individual self-assertion took the form of glorying in the strength and power of the hero. Nietzsche, Wagner and Hitler have all been described as 'Romantics', and Oceanus's remark in Keats's *Hyperion* (1820), '''tis the eternal law / That first in beauty should be first in might', is a reminder that certain elements of Romanticism could be enlisted in the cause of dangerous ideologies.

The stereotyped version of the Romantic poet is a patchwork made up of very different figures. William Blake, a poet of the city, and William Wordsworth, a poet of nature, were innovative writers, physically dissimilar from the iconic images of the younger Romantics. Even in his youth, although a sympathiser, Wordsworth was not an active participant in the French Revolution of 1789, and in his greatest poetry he is not a rebel at all. In 'Resolution and Independence' (published in *Poems in Two Volumes*, 1807) he places, or displaces, the

---

* Although Byron was active in the campaign, he actually died in bed from a fever which he contracted at Missolonghi in 1824.

notions that literary men sometimes have of themselves, the sense of the artist as bohemian rebel with or without a cause, when he remarks on the deaths of young contemporaries (Robert Burns at thirty-seven, Thomas Chatterton at seventeen), 'We poets in our youth begin in gladness; / But thereof comes in the end despondency and madness' (ll. 48–9). After his encounter with the old leech-gatherer, a man 'bent double' in age, yet still cheerfully responsive to the poet's questions, he realises the falsehood of an obsessive self-indulgence: 'I could have laughed myself to scorn, to find / In that decrepit Man so firm a mind' (ll. 144–5).

The diversity in Romantic literature led A. O. Lovejoy to write of the need to discriminate among many different 'Romanticisms'.[1] Romanticism can involve a taste for nature and common life, or a taste for the extraordinary, the supernatural and grotesque. It can describe the local colour of one's native country, but equally the exoticism of foreign parts. It may either exalt simplicity or revolt against it. It can admire particularity in describing a landscape or move away from the material world altogether. To the English reader, the work of Blake, Wordsworth, Byron and Shelley might suggest that the Romantics belong on the side of the political Left. Yet it can be equally obvious from some European perspectives that Romanticism can be a right-wing movement, beginning with the resistance of France's conservative neighbours to the French Revolution, and linked with a Catholic religious revival.

Samuel Taylor Coleridge, the most theoretical of the English Romantics, links poetry with the new philosophy of Kant,* and reflects the inwardness of the contemporary religious revival in his sense of the poet as a prophet, of being even God-like, in the importance he attaches to the role of the creative Imagination (see Part Four: 'Imagination, Truth and Reason'). His views are developed after twenty years of a

---

* Immanuel Kant's concept of Pure Reason (*Critique of Pure Reason*, 1781) is that of a faculty which enables us to 'think' certain ideas, like 'freedom', without 'understanding' what such ideas could possibly mean. In this sense, poetry, while it might give us intimations of what cannot be 'understood', nevertheless communicates something acknowledged to be no less 'real'. In *The Prelude* (1805) Wordsworth defines Imagination as 'absolute strength / And clearest insight, amplitude of mind, / And reason in her most exalted mood' (XIII.168–70).

bitter, divisive war in Europe and, in this context, it was deeply consoling, for writers and readers alike, to make art and the ideal seem to be more important and valid than reality. The concept of Romantic Imagination, for which Coleridge provided the essential definitions, has to be seen in this sense as a post-war phenomenon.

Wordsworth, who writes in his epic poem *The Prelude* (1805) of the growth of his own mind, is probably the most prominent English figure reflecting the Romantic subjectivism of a period often referred to as the 'age of Wordsworth'. Traditionally, epics had been written on national or universal themes. Yet Wordsworth does go on to write about his nation after completing *The Prelude*, in his sonnets and in *The Excursion* (1814). The real-life subjects of his *Lyrical Ballads* collection (1798) fit in with a previous taste in poetry rather than establish a new one. But in these Wordsworth does not write as a simple man. Although he employs the ballad form and deals with elemental situations, his poems are not remotely like the folk ballads of tradition. They are a thoughtful man's poems *about* simplicity. In poems which deal with figures from common life, Wordsworth shifts his emphasis from the poor subjects themselves to place it instead on the way he responds to them. Similarly, the landscape of 'Tintern Abbey', the last poem in the collection, is not presented as the busy, even industrialised, scene which it was in Wordsworth's time, but as unpeopled, and therefore very different from the populated landscapes of George Crabbe in *The Village* (1783) or of Burns in 'The Cotter's Saturday Night' (1786), or the countryside of William Cowper in *The Task* (1785), or even the churchyard of Thomas Gray's 'Elegy written in a Country Church-Yard' (1751).

It has to be stressed, however, that not all Romantic literature is about introversion and self-communication. Crabbe, Cowper and Burns write about the natural world in an objective and radically simple manner. Though Burns was explicitly radical in his politics and the others not necessarily so, all reflect in their various ways the sentiments of the last two decades of the eighteenth century. This was a period of great upheaval, in the shape of the American and French Revolutions, which attracted much favourable comment from the radical intellectuals of the day. Sophisticated writers become interested in the popular ballad form with its simple metres and vocabulary, its universal themes of love and death, and its links with the common people. The concerns of daily life among the lower orders in society become the subjects of literatures making a point of contrasting what they are doing with poetic conventions and earlier traditions. 'By such examples taught', writes Crabbe, 'I paint the cot, / As truth will paint it, and as bards will not'.[2] The Prophetic Books of Blake, too, share something of the radical simplicity of primitive literature. Their main literary model is the Old Testament, and the simple free-verse form of their sentences is without any of the subjective feelings of the storyteller.

The chapters which follow set out to explore the diversity and range of Romantic-period literature. Although now distant from us, it seems somehow still more intimate to our concerns than other literature historically closer, that of the 1930s, for instance. Concepts of rights, of freedom and equality which it enshrines, together with its quest to find new psychological depths that give identity to the individual and meaning to human life, have a peculiarly modern resonance.

It is important to understand a period's history as much as possible, both for its own intrinsic interest, and as an essential background for the writing it produced (see Part Two: 'A Cultural Overview'). The chapters in Part Three: 'Texts, Writers and Contexts' look first of all at 'writing in revolution', setting an agenda not only for exploring the literature of an age of social and political revolution, but also with the additional purpose of examining a literature which was itself in a state of revolution. A discussion of the pamphlet wars and Revolution controversy of the 1790s, as seen through the writings of its prominent contributors, is followed by a chapter on the place of the natural world in Romantic writing, and then chapters on dramatic writing, verse narrative, fiction and travel writing. Part Four: 'Critical Theories and Debates' explores topics central to the period, such as imagination, religion, the concept of Romantic 'heroism', and the decline of civilisations. Part Five provides timelines, detailed further reading and some useful electronic resources.

The scope of Romantic-period prose extends from the imaginative excesses of the gothic novel, in the writing of Horace Walpole (*The*

Castle of Otranto, 1764), William Beckford (*Vathek*, 1786), Ann Radcliffe (*The Mysteries of Udolpho*, 1794) and Matthew Lewis (*The Monk*, 1796), to the political debate of 'Jacobin' fiction, in works such as William Godwin's *Caleb Williams* (1794). A genuinely innovative conception, such as Mary Shelley's *Frankenstein* (1818), combines both the gothic and the novel of ideas, while domestic and social concerns appear in the novels of writers such as Fanny Burney (*Cecilia*, 1782), Susan Ferrier (*Marriage*, 1818) and especially Jane Austen, whose six major works are pre-eminent in their handling of manners and social issues in the first quarter of the nineteenth century. Rivalling Byron's stature and influence, Walter Scott, in his prolific Romantic fiction of regional and national manners, virtually invented the historical novel with *Waverley* (1814), while Thomas Love Peacock's 'satirical-conversation' novels, such as *Nightmare Abbey* (1818), make use of dramatic form and dialogue to provide a satirical perspective, not only on prominent literary figures, but also on the 'crotchets', cults and fads of the time. In addition to fiction, the period abounds in the distinctive prose of Romantic polemicists and essayists such as William Cobbett, Thomas De Quincey, William Hazlitt and Charles Lamb, and the letters of major writers such as Keats and Coleridge have made, in their own right, important contributions to literary criticism.

Many benefits which make up the fabric of contemporary society and are now more or less taken for granted have their origins in the Romantic period. Shelley, a modern figure out to improve the humanity of the state system, argued for an extension of the franchise, universal suffrage, more frequent parliaments and the equalisation of constituencies. His pre-Marxist labour theory of value argues for a distinction to be made between estates and unearned income, and what a man earns by his talents, and that this should be an absolute principle of organising incomes and produce in society. In addition to such details in programmes for social reform, many of which have been adopted since Shelley's time, the Romantic period saw the emergence of the women's movement, and women writers of the Romantic period, although by and large neglected until the latter years of the twentieth century, are now recognised as having made contributions of central importance to the cultural, political and aesthetic developments of the age.* Writers such as Mary Wollstonecraft and Helen Maria Williams (1761–1827),[3] for example, were key eyewitnesses to events in revolutionary France, while Mary Wollstonecraft is not only the most prominent writer in the earliest years of feminist thought, but also a distinctively new kind of travel writer. Her daughter, Mary, by William Godwin, would later write *Frankenstein*, the most famous and enduring of Romantic novels. In addition to the gathering momentum for the enfranchisement of women, the period also witnessed the abolition of slavery and the establishment of animal rights. At the very heart of Romantic doctrine is a democratic idealism proclaiming the dignity of man and the world's potential for happiness rather than despair.

Perhaps something of the relevance and intimacy sustained by Romantic-period literature in the present day concerns the special immediacy with which it is often thought to express the 'essential passions of the heart'. The phrase is used by Wordsworth in his Preface to *Lyrical Ballads* to explain why he chose to write about low and rustic life, and in a selection of the 'language really used by men'. He argues that such conditions make a good subject for poetry because, together, they express the deepest and most permanent human experiences that will survive the fashionable and ephemeral interests of the day. Wordsworth here argues primarily against the kind of poetry of his own day, which he considered to be superficial in its human content and overly artificial in its style. But the claim he makes for his poetry is a large one and suggests that it offers stability and a permanence beyond the reach of historical change.

The Romantic period, though, was one of enormous change. Wordsworth's taste for the landscape of the Lake District, and his

---

*   In their anthology, *Romantic Poetry and Prose* (Oxford: Oxford University Press, 1976), the editors, Harold Bloom and Lionel Trilling, included only Dorothy Wordsworth as the token female Romantic writer. Duncan Wu, the editor of *Women Romantic Poets: An Anthology* (Oxford: Blackwell, 1997), includes twenty-seven poets in a volume of over 600 pages.

particular attitudes to the natural world which have tutored our own current ones, were not shared by the dominant literary culture of the century before him. Concepts such as the 'essential passions of the heart' perhaps need to be debated in order to discover whether they can survive from one historical period to another. Do more recent notions, shaped by the very different circumstances of the present century and the last one, correspond with Wordsworth's account of such 'passions'? Even with the help of historical knowledge, it is important to find in Romantic literature relevant contemporary meanings, and this process always underlines the fact that the literature of its own time inevitably differs to a degree from what can be made of it today.

John Gilroy

Notes

1   See A. O. Lovejoy, 'On the Discrimination of Romanticisms', in M. H. Abrams (ed.), *English Romantic Poets: Modern Essays in Criticism* (Oxford: Oxford University Press, 1975), pp. 3–24.
2   Crabbe, *The Village*, I.53–4.
3   Helen Maria Williams, *Letters Written in France* (1790).

Part Two
A Cultural Overview

Romantic literature reflects in innumerable ways the radical social and political upheavals of its age. The French Revolution of 1789 brought to an end the reign of King Louis XVI and Marie Antoinette. The king was executed in January 1793, after being found guilty of treason by the new National Convention, and the execution of his queen followed in October of the same year. England's monarch at this time was George III who had acceded to the throne in 1760. His recurrent bouts of insanity led to his being replaced in 1811 by his son George, Prince of Wales, who acted as Regent (the 'Regency period') before becoming King George IV on his father's death in 1820. It was during the early years of George III's reign that England lost control of its former colonies in North America. The American War of Independence, conducted with French military support, came to an end in 1783, and the Declaration of Independence (1776) led to the formation of the United States of America. The principles of democratic and representative government, which had motivated the uprising in America, were those which were to inform the revolution in France.

William Wordsworth, whose voice is probably the most central to the literature of the times, was only nineteen, Samuel Taylor Coleridge seventeen. William Blake, at thirty-two, was coming into his poetic maturity, and his illuminated poem, *A Song of Liberty*,* written before the outbreak of war between England and France on 1 February 1793, is typical of the contemporary sense of imminent change and exhilaration. It describes the birth of the flaming spirit of revolution later named as 'Orc',[†] and his conflict with the tyrannical sky-god, later to be called 'Urizen'.[‡] The poem ends with the Spirit of Revolution breaking up the ten commandments, or the prohibitions against political, religious and moral liberty, and the bringing in of a free and joyful world to Albion (England):

2. Albion's coast is sick, silent; the American meadows faint!
3. Shadows of Prophecy shiver along by the lakes and the rivers and mutter across the ocean. France, rend down thy dungeon! [...]
10. The speary hand burned aloft, unbuckled was the shield, forth went the hand of jealousy among the flaming hair, and hurl'd the new born wonder thro' the starry night [...]
17. All night beneath the ruins; then, their sullen flames faded, emerge round the gloomy king,
18. With thunder and fire, leading his starry hosts thro' the waste wilderness he promulgates his ten commands, glancing his beamy eyelids over the deep in dark dismay,
19. Where the son of fire in his eastern cloud, while the morning plumes her golden breast,
20. Spurning the clouds written with curses, stamps the stony law to dust, loosing the eternal horses from the dens of night, crying:
    'Empire is no more! and now the lion and wolf shall cease.'

---

*   An appendix to *The Marriage of Heaven and Hell* (1793).
†   Probably from 'orchis', Greek for 'testicle', and symbolic, in Blake's mythology, of sexual revolution.
‡   'Urizen' meaning possibly 'your reason'; or 'horizon', in the sense of limits being put upon imaginative possibility. See Milton, *Paradise Lost*, VII. 225–31. A bronze statue of Blake's 'Newton', inspired by Milton's lines, stands in the forecourt of the British Library (Euston Road) in London.

Blake's free verse* is itself a demonstration of the liberty he celebrates. Milton, by writing in blank verse,† had attempted to recover his epic poem *Paradise Lost* (1667) from what he calls 'the modern bondage of rhyming'.¹ Blake, in his address 'To the Public' (*Jerusalem*),² writes that blank verse is 'as much a bondage as rhyme itself' and that 'Poetry Fetter'd, Fetters the Human Race!'

The excitement of revolution and its promise of liberty is also evident in Coleridge's early poem 'Destruction of the Bastille', a fragment, like the 'stone' from amidst 'the dust / Of the Bastille' which Wordsworth 'pocketed' as a 'relick' on his way through Paris in 1791³ (see Part Four: 'Forms of Ruin'). As Blake instructs France to 'rend down' its dungeon, Coleridge commands Tyranny to depart from its coasts:

Heard'st thou yon universal cry,
And dost thou linger still on Gallia's shore?‡
Go, Tyranny! Beneath some barbarous sky
Thy terrors lost, and ruin'd power deplore!
What tho' through many a groaning age
Was felt thy keen suspicious rage,
Yet Freedom rous'd by fierce Disdain
Has wildly broke thy triple chain,
And like the storm which Earth's deep entrails hide,
At length has burst its way and spread the ruins wide.

In the final couplet, like the volcanic activity which was interesting contemporary vulcanologists such as Sir William Hamilton,§ and artists such as Joseph Wright,¶ freedom has overwhelmed tyranny. The poem

---

* Verse written in irregular line lengths, lacking rhyme and the regular syllabic stress pattern of traditional metre.
† Lines of iambic pentameter which are unrhymed.
‡ Coleridge uses the Latin word for Gaul (France).
§ Sir William Hamilton, British Ambassador to the court of Naples (1764–1800), studied local volcanic activity and earthquakes, and wrote a book on Pompeii.
¶ Joseph Wright of Derby (1734–97) painted many works inspired by the eruptions of Mount Vesuvius he had witnessed.

anticipates a fertile future emerging like growth from the productive soil of a volcano's eruption. As 'Liberty [...] / Shall throb in every pulse, shall flow thro' every vein', the once oppressed peasant 'views his harvests rise'. In the last stanza, Coleridge envisages the wider spread of liberty, 'Till every land from pole to pole / Shall boast one independent soul!' He prays that England, as first to throw off the chains of absolute monarchy, might always stand as an example to countries such as France in their own pursuit of freedom:

> And still, as erst, let favour'd Britain be
> First ever of the first and freest of the free!

Wordsworth describes how, on their summer vacation, arriving in France as Englishmen on the Feast of the Federation (13 July 1790), he and his friend Robert Jones had been 'hospitably' received by the celebrating French, 'As their forerunners in a glorious course': *The Prelude* (1805), VI.411–12. In the 'Destruction of the Bastille' (1789–91), Coleridge remembers England's own 'Glorious Revolution' (1688) when the unpopular King James II was replaced by King William and Queen Mary. In the year before the Bastille fell, Whig political clubs were formed all over England to celebrate this centenary, and the French Revolution of the following year brought together many groups of much more radical activists, who now worked in sympathy with them. Those who wanted parliamentary reform joined forces with figures who had been raised in the tradition of religious dissent, itself with its foundations in reformist and opposition politics and, in addition, there emerged groups of working-class radicals who met in organisations such as the London Corresponding Society and began to influence political life.

In his carefully meditated retrospective account of the French Revolution in Books IX and X of *The Prelude*, Wordsworth distinguishes among the different types of people all looking towards a shared prospect of 'happiness unthought of' (X.708). In language which possibly reflects the craze for the novel activity of ballooning,* he writes of how even 'inert' people (as in inert gas)† '[w]ere rouz'd', whereas those already endowed with 'lively natures' were positively 'rapt away', like the contemporary balloonists he had probably witnessed in France, caught up from the ground and taken into the heady and rarefied upper atmosphere. First of all, there were people who had always been visibly active in their planning:

> They who had fed their childhood upon dreams,
> The play-fellows of Fancy, who had made
> All powers of swiftness, subtlety, and strength
> Their ministers, used to stir in lordly wise
> Among the grandest objects of the sense,
> And deal with whatsoever they found there
> As if they had within some lurking right
> To wield it;

And then there were those who, although none the less committed, had been more privately at work with their schemes:

> They too, who, of gentle mood
> Had watch'd all gentle motions, and to these
> Had fitted their own thoughts, schemers more mild,
> And in the region of their peaceful selves.

---

* The first manned balloon ascent, in a Montgolfier hot-air balloon, was that of Pilâtre de Rozier and the Marquis d'Arlandes from the Bois de Boulogne on the western outskirts of Paris, 21 November 1783. The first ascent in a hydrogen balloon was that of Jacques Charles and Noel Robert on 1 December 1783 from the gardens of the Tuileries in Paris. Wordsworth would almost certainly have observed balloon flights during his periods of residence in France, as well as in England. See 'There's something in a flying horse / There's something in a huge balloon' (Prologue to 'Peter Bell, a Tale').

† The so-called 'pneumatic chemists', among them Wordsworth's contemporaries Joseph Priestley and Henry Cavendish, were doing important work on the nature and composition of gases.

Both kinds of revolutionary figures

> Did now find helpers to their hearts' desire,
> And stuff at hand, plastic as they could wish,
> Were call'd upon to exercise their skill,
> Not in Utopia, subterraneous Fields,
> Or some secreted Island, Heaven knows where,
> But in the very world which is the world
> Of all of us, the place in which, in the end,
> We find our happiness, or not at all. (ll. 708–28)

British Reactions

The opposition Whig party in England and its leader, Charles James Fox, hailed events in France as being in the spirit of their own ideals of individual liberty, but after Edmund Burke's warnings in his *Reflections on the Revolution in France* (1790) (see Part Three: 'Writing in Revolution'), more and more prominent Whigs moved to join the Tories. The opposition became increasingly powerless against William Pitt, the prime minister, who was able to legislate as he wished, in defence of what the Tories believed to be in the best interests of the country. France had begun to assume imperial aspirations and this would prepare the way for Napoleon's rise to power by the end of the 1790s. Although the Terror ended with the execution of Robespierre in July 1794, there was no change in the general policies of the Republic which, with its aggressive military ambitions, had the ultimate aim of uniting Europe under a single emperor.

As the 1790s progressed, England developed a cultural insularity which saw the foundation of organisations such as the Association for Preserving Liberty and Property against Republicans and Levellers (1792), and the setting up by George Canning, in 1797, of a newspaper, *The Anti-Jacobin*, whose stratagem was to attack the works and ideas of the radicals and support Pitt's government in its struggle against France and the Revolution. Exactly contemporary with the writing of *Lyrical*

Ballads (it ran for thirty-six issues between November 1797 and July 1798), the memory of *The Anti-Jacobin* has survived mainly because of the poetry with which the editors supported their pages of controversy. The cartoonist James Gillray was employed by Canning to produce plates based on the newspaper's work, one of which, 'The New Morality' (1798), attacking liberal writers, among them Robert Southey, Samuel Taylor Coleridge and Charles Lamb, accompanies Canning's poem of that title in the final edition. England had a tradition of freedom of expression by which literature was able to form and influence public opinion. 'The New Morality', however, uses poetry to attack what it sees as misguided French philanthropy, whose concept of 'Universal Man' runs contrary to the virtues of patriotism:

> —No—through the extended globe his feelings run
> As broad and general as the unbounded sun!
> No narrow bigot *he*;—*his* reason'd view
> Thy interests, England, ranks with thine, Peru!
> France at our doors, he sees no danger nigh,
> But heaves for Turkey's woes the impartial sigh;
> A steady Patriot of the World alone,
> The friend of every country—but his own.[4]

As national opinion swung behind government opposition to radical sympathisers, the radicals themselves were placed in a difficult situation. Their principles separated them from the majority of their educated peers, while their own social position led them to a purely abstract conception of 'the people', keeping them from the ranks of the masses who were to become the foundation of radical English politics in future times. While they were isolated on two fronts at home, the French Revolution itself increasingly failed to provide them with any kind of reasonable alternative. In May 1794, on the arrest of prominent radical reformers, including Thomas Hardy (not to be confused with the Victorian poet and novelist) and John Thelwall of the London Corresponding Society, Pitt suspended Habeas Corpus, allowing the government to hold suspected agitators without trial. Although Hardy and Thelwall and their arrested sympathisers were acquitted, the government's response to an attack on the king's carriage as he went to open parliament in October 1795 was to introduce the Treasonable Practices and Seditious Meetings Acts (known as the 'Gagging Acts'). These acts proved to be highly effective and, from the middle of the decade, the radical movement was forced to retreat underground.

The Romantic literature of the 1790s inevitably owes much of its revolutionary character to the spirit of these times, but in the context of deteriorating relations between Britain and France, a conservatism begins to be reflected in the work of some of its prominent writers. Coleridge, in the mid-1790s, was an active lecturer in support of the radicals' cause, and a campaigning journalist against the war with France, but his poem, 'Fears in Solitude', written on 28 April 1798, at a time when there were strong rumours that France might be about to invade England, shows him turning away from the hopes of political liberty raised by the French Revolution, and towards a celebration of the village of Nether Stowey in Somerset, where he was currently living with his wife and child. 'We have been too long / Dupes of a deep delusion!' he writes, going on to find consolation in the beauty of his immediate surroundings, from which he then extends his thoughts outwards, towards the love of his native country.

The poem takes inspiration from the sentiments associated with Burke in his conservative *Reflections*. For Burke, the 'selfish and mischievous ambition' of radical ideologues, 'turbulent, discontented men of quality', is their 'profligate disregard of a dignity which they partake with others'. Burke argued that people should begin to love, first of all, what he calls the little 'platoon' that they belong to, the family, the hearth, the home and village, and then develop outwards from this basis towards a love for their native land. One particularly well-loved place might become, therefore, representative of the whole nation.

In 'Fears in Solitude', Coleridge addresses first his country:

O native Britain! O my Mother Isle [...]
Whatever makes this mortal spirit feel
The joy and greatness of its future being!

There lives nor form nor feeling in my soul
Unborrowed from my country! O divine
And beauteous island! (ll. 182, 190–4)

The poem concludes with a paean to the little plot of ground from which this wider, universal celebration emanates:

And now, belovéd Stowey! I behold
Thy church-tower, and, methinks, the four huge elms
Clustering, which mark the mansion of my friend;*
And close behind them, hidden from my view,
Is my own lowly cottage, where my babe
And my babe's mother dwell in peace! With light
And quickened footsteps thitherward I tend,
Remembering thee, O green and silent dell!
And grateful, that by nature's quietness
And solitary musings, all my heart
Is softened, and made worthy to indulge
Love, and the thoughts that yearn for human kind. (ll. 221–32)

Burke had written, 'To be attached to the subdivision, to love the little platoon we belong to in society, is the first principle (the germ as it were) of public affections. It is the first link in the series by which we proceed towards a love to our country and to mankind.'[5] The phrasing anticipates the title of Book VIII of *The Prelude*, 'Retrospect.—Love of Nature leading to Love of Mankind', where Wordsworth in a development which parallels that of Coleridge, describes 'the way that led [him] on / Through Nature to the love of Human Kind' (VIII.387–8).

Although Wordsworth and Coleridge associated with prominent radical figures, their work in the late 1790s began to move more towards the subjective and imaginative, while the purpose behind their cooperative venture, *Lyrical Ballads* (1798) (see Part Three: 'Revolution, Reaction and the Natural World'), to appeal to the common man 'in a selection of language really used by men' (Preface to *Lyrical Ballads*, 1802), was

---

* Wordsworth at nearby Alfoxden.

actually difficult to achieve. As Kelvin Everest points out, Romantic poetry in its radical dimension was not able to reach the mass of the common people, who were prevented by their lack of education from a knowledge of the English literary tradition, while in the political climate of the time, the actual readership for such a publication was likely to be alienated from it.[6] Living in the Quantocks in 1797, Wordsworth, Coleridge and Dorothy Wordsworth experienced hostility from the rural community for their harmless activities which were perceived as suspicious, as well as from the government's Home Office spy system, which sent an agent into Somerset to report on them. In one of these reports, the agent writes to his superior in language which has a decidedly sinister inflection:

> I think this will turn out no French affair, but a mischiefuous gang of disaffected Englishmen. I have just procured the Name of the person who took the House! His name is *Wordsworth* a name I think known to Mr. Ford.[7]

This hostility is particularly ironic for being levelled at Wordsworth and Coleridge in the very year in which they were composing *Lyrical Ballads*. Their best intentions towards the people were actually resulting in antagonism *from* the people.

Writers and Their Audience

The problem of the audience for Romantic literature is centrally important to an understanding of both its creation and reception. Although *Lyrical Ballads* was intended to have a broad democratic appeal, its sales were never particularly high, unlike those of Byron's verse-tales fifteen or so years later. These sold by the tens of thousands, as Byron, conscious of market demands, was able to exploit the wartime situation in which travel was made impossible by the British blockade. It was naval power which got Byron himself through the Mediterranean, and the sales of *Childe Harold* and the verse-tales meant that he was able to achieve much more successfully what Wordsworth identified as the role for a poet, 'a man speaking to men' (Preface to *Lyrical Ballads*, 1802). Yet, as Philip Martin has argued, Byron's approach to his readership verged on the cynical, as his verbal dexterity, combining with his aspirations for a fashionable reputation, achieved an audience 'that allowed him to slip comfortably into easy habits of writing'.[8]

Percy Bysshe Shelley's politics were the dominating concern of his life, yet sometimes, through a lack of audience awareness, he failed to be as effective as he might otherwise have been. His sonnet 'England in 1819' ('An old, mad, despised, and dying king'), while earnestly taking up the cause of the people against the political repression of the Regency, invites questions about the sophistication of the readership it seeks. The deployment of words such as 'sanguine', 'liberticide', 'illumine', 'tempestuous' and 'senate' for parliament seems rather to be reinforcing the very class differences that the sonnet sets out to discredit. The rise of the publisher during the Romantic period also altered the relationship of writer and audience. It was partly Blake's need to keep an intimate connection with his readers that motivated him to take on himself the entire responsibility for his printed and illustrated texts. But such painstakingly time-consuming production methods, individually engraving poems and painting them by hand, were unable to compete and, as Kelvin Everest has pointed out, large sales were to become increasingly an indication of success. The result was that writers were often provided with what he calls 'an unhappy register of their public standing and influence'.[9]

Blake, Wordsworth and Coleridge lived through a period of immense political optimism as well as an equally intense period of disappointment and savage government suppression. The second-generation Romantics, living also within the shadow of the French Revolution, but without having experienced its terrors or the dangerous reactions it provoked, often came to regard the earlier models of radicalism as apostates and turncoats. Wordsworth, growing towards middle age, became Distributor of Stamps for the county of Westmorland,* Coleridge wrote

---

* Sheets of stamped paper, issued by the Treasury, upon which legal documents were written and newspapers printed. The day-to-day business of issuing them and receiving payment was handled by sub-distributors. Wordsworth was required to act as an intermediary between them and the Treasury.

right-wing journalism, Blake retreated into the private obscurities of his Prophetic Books, and Southey, Coleridge's partner in their youthful 'Pantisocracy' scheme to set up a utopian community in America, was appointed Poet Laureate in 1813, leading to his sycophantic celebration of monarchy in *A Vision of Judgement* (1821). Wordsworth himself was in the unenviable situation of having had his work dismissed by criticism from contemporaries who thought he was too radical, and then by his younger contemporaries who thought that he was not radical enough.

The Young Romantics and Reform

In the immediate aftermath of the Napoleonic wars, the younger generation of Romantic poets, still inspired by the best principles of the French Revolution, were able to transfer their idealism to issues of social reform in their own times. A figure such as Byron, however, originally associated with reform, turned away from politics in the years of his first celebrity, as the Holland House Whigs, with whom he was involved, became more pro-establishment and therefore less congenial to his own revolutionary ideas.[*] It is perhaps possible to see, in the proud and detached heroes of his verse-tales, something of the situation of the poet himself, a figure beyond obligation to society (see Part Four: 'Heroes and Anti-heroes'), cherishing a private sense of wrong, and alienated from the values of the public who bought his works and made him a celebrity.

In his verse-drama *Prometheus Unbound* (1820), Shelley presents two semichoruses of 'Furies' who mock the hero, using the French Revolution as an example of human hopes disappointed:

> *Semichorus I*
> See a disenchanted nation
> Springs like day from desolation;

---

[*] Byron joined the Cambridge Whig Club in 1807 and became associated with the Holland House Whigs, reformers presided over by Lord Holland, who included the popular poets of the day, Samuel Rogers and Thomas Campbell.

To truth its state is dedicate,
And freedom leads it forth, her mate;
A legioned band of linkèd brothers
Whom love calls children—

Semichorus II
'Tis another's:
See how kindred murder kin:
'Tis the vintage-time for death and sin;
Blood, like new wine, bubbles within:
Till Despair smothers
The struggling world, which slaves and tyrants win. (I.567–77)

Aligned with the persuasions of some earlier Romantic writers, *Prometheus Unbound* represents Shelley's belief that reform can only be truly established through a change in mental perception. In his sonnet 'To the Republic of Benevento',* inspired by the failure of a nationalist insurrection near Naples,† Shelley writes:

Man who man would be,
Must rule the empire of himself; in it
Must be supreme, establishing his throne
On vanquished will, quelling the anarchy
Of hopes and fears, being himself alone. (ll. 10–14)

Shelley's emphasis on the individual recalls William Hazlitt's experience of hearing Coleridge preach in January 1798: 'Mr Coleridge rose and gave out his text, "And he went up into the mountain to pray, *himself alone*".'[10] In Hazlitt's account, the 'poetical and pastoral excursion' in the sermon was no doubt informed by Coleridge's own experience of

---

* This was written in 1821 and published posthumously by Mary Shelley as 'Political Greatness'.
† Led by the 'Carbonari', an early nineteenth-century manifestation of the Risorgimento (the 'Resurgence') dedicated to the unification of Italy, and with which Byron was actively involved.

turning from external revolution to nature as a means of effecting change, an internal revolution through a withdrawal from society, rather than a political one which, like that in contemporary France, all too often resulted in bloodshed:

He talked of those who had 'inscribed the cross of Christ on banners dripping with human gore.' He made a poetical and pastoral excursion – and to show the fatal effects of war, drew a striking contrast between the simple shepherd boy, driving his team afield, or sitting under the hawthorn, piping to his flock, 'as though he should never be old', and the same poor country lad, crimped, kidnapped, brought into town, made drunk, at an alehouse, turned into a wretched drummer boy, with his hair sticking on end with powder and pomatum, a long cue at his back, and tricked out in the loathsome finery of the profession of blood.

The younger generation of Romantics came to prominence during the Regency, a time of great indulgence and moral licentiousness, but equally one of political oppression under the right-wing, post-war government of Lord Liverpool. Two of Liverpool's ministers, singled out for particular critical attention by Byron and Shelley, are Viscount Castlereagh, the Foreign Secretary, and Lord Eldon, the Lord Chancellor. Castlereagh, who earlier in his career had been involved in the suppression of the Irish rebellion of 1798, was one of the architects of the Congress of Vienna, concerned with the restructuring of Europe after the defeat of Napoleon in 1815. Various nationalist movements had arisen in Europe among those who felt that their interests had been marginalised in the 'fencing' of France by buffer states, and both Shelley and Byron would become involved in such political manoeuvrings. They were both supporters of the Italian Carbonari movement, and Byron himself would die while fighting for the cause of Greek independence from Turkey. In the course of an attack on Southey, whom he regarded as a renegade, Byron in *Don Juan** attacks Castlereagh for

* Written in 1818, published in 1833.

his role in the Irish uprising, and his condoning of the Austrian control of Italy:

> Cold-blooded, smooth-faced, placid miscreant!
> Dabbling its sleek young hands in Erin's gore,
> And thus for wider carnage taught to pant,
> Transferr'd to gorge upon a sister shore;
> The vulgarest tool that tyranny could want,
> With just enough of talent, and no more,
> To lengthen fetters by another fix'd,
> And offer poison long already mix'd.
> > (*Don Juan*, Dedication, stanza 12)

As Hamlet makes his mother Gertrude a personification of 'frailty', Shelley, in one of his most powerful political poems, 'The Mask of Anarchy' (1819), makes Castlereagh the embodiment of 'Murder':[*]

> I met Murder on the way—
> He had a mask like Castlereagh—
> Very smooth he looked, yet grim;
> Seven bloodhounds followed him. (ll. 5–8)

Shelley's use of 'mask', in the sense of fraud or false show, reflects upon the title of the poem with its courtly associations of 'masquerade', a form of masked entertainment or public event staged as a compliment to a monarch or aristocrat. The poem attacks the establishment by using its own language, just as Blake, for example, might interrogate terms like 'pity' or 'mercy' to demonstrate how, in contemporary society, that which is often called good can sometimes mask evil.[†] As a means to making a populist appeal, Shelley employs a balladic verse form, usually

---

[*] 'Frailty, thy name is woman!' (*Hamlet*, I.ii.146). Shelley effectively says, 'Murder, thy name is Castlereagh.'
[†] See Blake, 'The Human Abstract' (*Songs of Experience*, 1794): 'Pity would be no more, / If we did not make somebody Poor; / And Mercy no more could be, / If all were as happy as we.'

devalued by the genteel and polite, and similar in its way to that of Blake's *Songs*, while his use of the term 'Anarchy' would have had a disturbing resonance for conservative readers in 1819, appalled by the prospect of mob insurrection* or by the executions of their class allies in France. Following Castlereagh in the 'ghastly masquerade' (l. 27) is Lord Eldon, whose 'erminèd gown', a symbol of purity, is a cloak for his 'Fraud' (l. 14), and whose tears, which he was famous for shedding in public, become the crocodile tears of the hypocrite. Shelley had his own personal reasons for the attack on Eldon, by whom he had been refused custody of his children by his first wife, Harriet:

> Next came Fraud, and he had on
> Like Eldon, an erminèd gown;
> His big tears, for he wept well,
> Turned to mill-stones as they fell.
>
> And the little children, who
> Round his feet played to and fro,
> Thinking every tear a gem,
> Had their brains knocked out by them. (ll. 14–21)

The year of 'The Mask of Anarchy', 1819, is the subject of Shelley's sonnet 'England in 1819', which, like *Caleb Williams*, the novel written by his father-in-law William Godwin (1794), presents a savage indictment of 'things as they are'[11] in contemporary English society. In his verse-tale *Julian and Maddalo* (written 1819, published 1824; see Part Three: 'Romantic Verse Narrative'), Shelley's persona, Julian, looks to the future with optimism, but in the conclusion to his sonnet Shelley adopts a hesitant tone, as he imagines that the social and political evils of the times 'Are graves from which a glorious Phantom *may* / Burst to

---

* 'The Mask of Anarchy: Written on the Occasion of the Massacre at Manchester', was inspired by the events at St Peter's Field, Manchester (16 August 1819), where an estimated 60,000 to 80,000 people who had gathered to hear the radical 'Orator' Henry Hunt were charged by the militia, resulting in loss of life and injury. The massacre became known as the 'Peterloo' massacre, in ironic reference to the recent battle of Waterloo (1815).

illumine our tempestuous day' (my emphasis). This deliberate withdrawal from a statement of absolute conviction is a characteristic of the Romantic mode, comparable in its way to Wordsworth's determined effort to avoid assertiveness in 'Tintern Abbey'[12] – 'To them I may have owed another gift' (l. 37), 'If this / Be but a vain belief' (ll. 50–1), 'And so I dare to hope' (l. 66).

Of the 'Romantic positives',[13] 'hope', termed by M. H. Abrams one of the 'high Romantic words',[14] had taken the most damaging blows. Shelley's Demogorgon, in *Prometheus Unbound*, speaks of the need 'to hope till Hope creates / From its own wreck the thing it contemplates',[15] but the period's sense of tragic loss and disappointed expectations is captured well by Friedrich's painting *The Wreck of the 'Hope'*, with its central image of a ship overwhelmed by shelves of crushing ice.[16] In England, the painter J. M. W. Turner wrote a fragmentary poem, 'The Fallacies of Hope', to provide himself with titles with which to illustrate his own paintings on the theme.[*]

Abrams argues that, in the light of recent historical events, the mission of Romantic writers 'was to assure the continuance of civilization by reinterpreting to their drastically altered condition the enduring humane values'. Their only way to achieving this end, he writes, was by setting out 'to reclaim and to bring to realization the great positives of the Western past'.[17] For Abrams, these positives of life, love, liberty, hope and joy could be maintained by writers 'making whatever changes were required in the theological systems by which these values had earlier been sanctioned'.[18] This was indeed the route pursued by the first-generation poets, Blake, Wordsworth and Coleridge, whose work is largely based on an inherited biblical tradition. The values to which the second-generation Romantics, Shelley, Keats and Byron, were drawn, however, lay in the classical past. Athenian democracy was a model for social reform, and the more liberated world of paganism provided their alternative to the moral restrictiveness of Christianity.

---

[*]   Turner also made use of quotations from Byron's poems in the titles of his pictures.

Class Conflict

Shelley, Keats and Byron died young and in exile. Their cosmopolitanism and their celebration of the alternative cultures of Italy, Greece and the Orient (the Middle East), demarcate them from the Lake School, whose provincialism, as he sees it, is made the object of Byron's satire in *Don Juan*.[19] Yet although, as poets, they are usually taken together as a group, their similarities are probably more obvious retrospectively, as in their own time they were seen as distinct from each other. In terms of their shared interests in the classics, for example, Byron and Shelley, with their public-school training, were privileged by comparison with Keats, who had no knowledge of Greek, and who picked up most of his information from books such as Lemprière's Classical Dictionary. Keats had left school at the age of fifteen to pursue his career as an apothecary and to train as a surgeon. Harsh contemporary reviews of his poetry are predicated on an often shared condescension, regarding him as trespassing beyond his own class in writing on topics which by rights should have been closed off to him.

In a savage review of *Endymion* in *Blackwood's Edinburgh Magazine*, John Gibson Lockhart cruelly dismisses Keats, advising, 'It is a better and a wiser thing to be a starved apothecary than a starved poet; so back to the shop Mr. John, back to "plasters, pills, and ointment boxes," &c.'[20] Keats's friend and fellow-poet Leigh Hunt, the editor of *The Examiner*, is also made a target of Lockhart's abuse, in his case as much for his radical principles* as for his poetry. But the attacks are made on the same basis of class and social position as those on Keats, which were themselves partly motivated by Keats's association with Hunt and his radical circle. Whereas Southey, in his Preface to *A Vision of Judgement*, placed Byron in a 'Satanic school of poetry', Lockhart places Keats and Leigh Hunt in a different one. In an article for *Blackwood's* in October 1817, Lockhart (signing himself, 'Z') writes:

---

* The brothers John and Leigh Hunt, as editors of *The Examiner*, were sentenced to two years' imprisonment in 1813 for an attack on the Prince Regent.

It is strange that no one seems to think it at all necessary to say a single word about another new school of poetry which has of late sprung up among us. This school has not, I believe, as yet received any name; but if I may be permitted to have the honour of christening it, it may henceforth be referred to by the designation of The Cockney School.[21]

Lockhart, describing Leigh Hunt as the Cockney School's 'chief Doctor and Professor', sees him as 'a man certainly of some talents' but also as one of 'exquisitely bad taste, and extremely vulgar modes of thinking and manners in all respects'. With the typically superior tone he adopts in his dismissal of Keats, Lockhart pronounces Hunt as 'a man of little education [who] knows absolutely nothing of Greek, almost nothing of Latin'.[22] Byron's own assessment of Keats reveals an identical class-consciousness, as when, in writing to his publisher John Murray, Byron would have him believe that he can't recall Keats's name, referring to the *Edinburgh*'s praise of 'Jack Keats or Ketch or whatever his names are'.[23] Byron's social placing of Keats is with the low-life figure of the notorious Jack Ketch, a hangman under Charles II.

Keats's early death was widely believed to be the consequence of the attacks on him in the reviews, as Byron famously wrote in *Don Juan*:

> John Keats, who was killed off by one critique,
> Just as he really promised something great,
> If not intelligible, without Greek
> Contrived to talk about the gods of late,
> Much as they might have been supposed to speak,
> Poor fellow! His was an untoward fate.
> 'Tis strange the mind, that very fiery particle,
> Should let itself be snuffed out by an article.[*] (Canto XI.60)

Shelley, too, wrote *Adonais* (1821), as an elegy for Keats, on the same understanding that the critical reviews had contributed to his death.

---

[*] Byron refers to the review by John Wilson Croker in the *Quarterly Review*, xix (April 1818), pp. 204–8.

The major reviews had immense power and represented a north-south divide. The two Scottish publications, the Whig *Edinburgh Review* and the Tory *Blackwood's*, rivalled the London-based *Quarterly Review* and *London Magazine*. The *London Magazine*, edited by John Scott, included work by eminent essayists such as William Hazlitt, Charles Lamb and Thomas De Quincey, and the Romantic essay proved to be the ideal form in which, amidst the proliferation of partisan writing in the reviews and in the increasing number of newspapers, topical issues could be addressed. Radical figures such as Hunt and Hazlitt produced a more political version of the genre, while Charles Lamb's engaging blend of sentiment and irony in the *Essays of Elia* anticipates the nineteenth-century novel in the hands of similar writers such as Dickens. The importance of the contemporary reviews and magazines, and the levels of emotion they were able to generate, is best illustrated by John Scott's death in a duel to which Lockhart had challenged him over a criticism of methods in *Blackwood's Magazine*.

In addition to criticism levelled at Keats for his encroachment onto the jealously guarded territory of classical themes and subjects, there was another kind of objection to his work, implicit in Lockhart's term 'cockney', and broadening to reflect the Romantic period's central concerns with the natural world and urban life. In his Preface to the *Lyrical Ballads*, Wordsworth writes of 'the encreasing accumulation of men in cities' and the gradual blunting of sensibility being brought about by the 'uniformity of their occupations'. The changes in society caused by the shift from an agrarian to an industrial economy resulted in the kind of rural depopulation and physical dilapidation described in Oliver Goldsmith's *The Deserted Village* (1770). This ever-hastening trend is concurrent with a strong emergence and development of natural description in poetry, ranging from that which belongs to the school of the 'picturesque', exploiting the aesthetic possibilities of new rural landscapes, to the elegiac and politically motivated poetry of nature, of the kind in which John Clare protests against enclosure and the transformation of the rural landscape (see Part Three: 'Revolution, Reaction and the Natural World').

To the privileged upholders of literary taste, the 'cockney' Keats was a city-dweller, but his residence in Hampstead made him, more specifically, a suburbanite. The suburbs of a city, such as London's Hampstead, although coming to be seen in the Romantic period as fashionable and desirable places to live, were associated with a long tradition of trade, criminality and prostitution. Byron, in one of his letters to Murray, implies these associations when he writes that, in his opinion, Keats 'took the wrong line as a poet – and was spoilt by Cockneyfying and Suburbing'.[24] The more contemporary sense of the suburb is also carried by Byron's letter, in which he sees Keats aspiring, as a social climber, to a more genteel life in the suburbs, as well as being an upstart in his illegitimate literary attempts, described in the same sentence as no more than 'versifying Tooke's Pantheon and Lempriere's Dictionary'.[25]

In addition to being part of the radical 'Leigh Hunt' circle, Keats in his early poetry was also seen to be influenced by what the reviews thought of as the regrettable artifice of Leigh Hunt's own poetry of nature and comfortable suburban domesticity. Lockhart writes of Hunt:

> He is the ideal of a Cockney Poet. He raves perpetually about 'green fields,' 'jaunty streams,' and 'o'er-arching leafiness,' exactly as a Cheapside shop keeper does about the beauties of his box on the Camberwell road. Mr Hunt is altogether unacquainted with the face of nature in her magnificent scenes; he has never seen any mountain higher than Highgate-hill, nor reclined by any stream more pastoral than the Serpentine River.[26]

These remarks point to the comparatively tame landscapes of Hunt, as seen in the light of a taste formed by the larger Romantic aesthetics and philosophical conceptions of Wordsworth's poetry. From this point of view, the poetry of Hunt and Keats seems to reflect the prettiness of the suburban garden rather than the sublime prospects of the Wordsworthian vision. That Keats seems to indulge in a form of poetical gardening, therefore, associates him with the kind of middle-class city-worker who, by escaping to a 'countrified' life in the suburbs, is able to imitate the habits of the more affluent landowner who could afford to go in pursuit of the picturesque or tend his own estate. The perceived vulgarity of the

'Cockney' school was seen in its implication that the 'natural world' of the suburbs could produce the same high-minded morality as nature in its more expansive vistas. The following extract from Keats is typical of the verse which the contemporary reviews had in mind:

> But might I now each passing moment give
> To the coy muse, with me she would not live
> In this dark city, nor would condescend
> 'Mid contradictions her delights to lend.
> Should e'er the fine-eyed maid to me be kind,
> Ah, surely it must be whene'er I find
> Some flowery spot, sequestered, wild, romantic,
> [...] Where on one side are covert branches hung,
> 'Mong which the nightingales have always sung
> In leafy quiet; where to pry, aloof,
> Atween the pillars of the sylvan roof
> Would be to find where violet beds were nestling,
> And where the bee with cowslip bells was wrestling.
> There must be too a ruin dark and gloomy,
> To say 'joy not too much in all that's bloomy'.[27]

Keats's 'suburban' poetics, although it was attacked by contemporary arbiters of literary taste, anticipated that 'respectable' Victorian sensibility which, like the parallel Biedermeier period in Germany, turned to a comfortable and comparatively secure domestic mode of living in the face of an ever more turbulent world (see Part Three: 'Romantic Fiction').

The 'encreasing accumulation of men in cities' leads, in the Romantic period, to an urban experience of psychic dislocation and detachment, remarked upon in *The Prelude* by Wordsworth, who remembers that as a schoolboy his understanding was baffled by reports of how, in London, 'men lived / Even next-door neighbours, as we say, yet still / Strangers, and knowing not each other's names' (VII.118–20). Writing of an experience which occurred later, when he was a resident in London, it is as though, in the passive construction of the sentence which begins his account of it, Wordsworth's feelings seem to be detached from his actual self: 'O Friend! One feeling was there which belong'd / To this great City' (VII.593). On this particular occasion, as he walks in the 'overflowing Streets' (l. 596) and the face of everyone he passes seems to be a mystery to him, he experiences that very sense of separateness which had so perplexed him as a child. His unseeing self makes his fellow-beings into a 'second-sight procession' (ll. 600–1) which, in another image possibly taken from ballooning, 'glides / Over still mountains' (ll. 601–2) with no 'ballast' (l. 603) to hold it down. His encounter with a blind beggar, 'Wearing a written paper, to explain / The story of the Man, and who he was' (ll. 613–14), is an appropriate chastisement to his self unseeing. The blind beggar, in turning 'sightless eyes' (l. 621) upon him, obliges Wordsworth to undergo the same experience of being 'looked at' without really being noticed. In language which reflects a religious (Methodist) sense of being 'Abruptly […] smitten' (l. 610) and 'admonish'd' (l. 622) by this encounter, Wordsworth realises that detachment is no longer an option, and that the life of our fellow men is a shared responsibility.

William Blake, in 'London', from *Songs of Experience* (1794), begins his poem, too, with himself as a detached observer, wandering the city streets to 'mark' (in the sense of 'remark' or notice) the 'Marks of weakness, marks of woe' in every face he meets. But the controlling, observing eye ('I […] mark') of the first stanza is swiftly replaced by the main verb at the end of the second, making Blake the passive recipient of cries he has no other choice but to 'hear'. The leisurely iambic tetrameter of stanza one, appropriate to the spectator who prefers to remain detached, gives way to the second stanza's urgent trochaic rhythm which, as the poem proceeds, contributes to a sense of Blake's involvement in, and shared degree of responsibility for, the urban blight from which he had initially tried to maintain his distance. The 'youthful Harlot's curse' at the conclusion of 'London' reflects on the criticism to which Hunt's and Keats's verse was subjected as part of the 'cockney' school. The longstanding reputation of the suburbs for prostitution encouraged critics, hostile to their work, to associate its eroticism with the kind of suburban debasement affronting genteel society.

New Worlds: Romantic Expatriates

The eroticism which characterises so much of the poetry of the later Romantics was part of their principled opposition to contemporary British society. Byron's scandalous celebrity, Shelley's racy Genevan lifestyle and the adolescent sensuality of Keats, seen by Christopher Ricks as a purposive strategy to embarrass,[28] is a reminder of their comparative youth. In middle and later years, Wordsworth and Coleridge are drawn towards biblical traditions and, in Coleridge's case, to the cloudy metaphysics of Germanic philosophy. Keats, Shelley and Byron, on the other hand, are part of what Marilyn Butler refers to as 'The Cult of the South',[29] reflected in Keats's yearning for 'a beaker full of the warm South' and for 'Dance, and Provençal song, and sunburnt mirth!'[30] The exuberance of youth contributes to their sense of how the Imagination works. Their concept is not, as for Wordsworth and Coleridge, that of a faculty which works hand-in-glove with memory, but one operating instead with spontaneity and the instantaneous, as illustrated by Keats's 'if Poetry come not as naturally as the leaves to a tree it had better not come at all',[31] or the conflation of sexual climax, death and creativity in the moment of annihilation with which Shelley concludes his 'Epipsychidion' (1822):

> We shall become the same, we shall be one
> Spirit within two frames, oh! Wherefore two?
> One passion in twin-hearts, which grows and grew,
> Till, like two meteors of expanding flame,
> Those spheres instinct with it become the same,
> Touch, mingle, are transfigured; ever still
> Burning, yet ever inconsumable:
> In one another's substance finding food,
> Like flames too pure and light and unimbued
> To nourish their bright lives with baser prey,
> Which point to Heaven and cannot pass away:
> One hope within two wills, one will beneath

Two overshadowing minds, one life, one death,
One Heaven, one Hell, one immortality,
And one annihilation. (ll. 573–87)

Several powerful traditions are represented in the literature of the Romantic period. There is what Jerome J. McGann calls the poetry of imaginative desire, quoting Keats: 'What mad pursuit? What struggle to escape? / What pipes and timbrels? What wild ecstasy?'[32] There is the literature of common life, the writings of an age of revolutions and of societies in transition, and there are also romantic literatures which McGann describes as 'philological',[33] including the whole interest of the period in ancient forms of religion and myth, as well as in the occult, in orientalism, and enchantment. The subject is rich, and further explored in the chapters to follow.

Notes

1   See Milton's prose preface ('The Verse') to *Paradise Lost*, Book I.
2   See *Jerusalem: The Emanation of the Giant Albion*, Plate 3. *Jerusalem* was written and illustrated between 1804 and 1820.
3   See *The Prelude*, IX.63–7.
4   L. Rice-Oxley (ed.), *Poetry of the Anti-Jacobin* (Oxford: Basil Blackwell, 1924), p. 176.
5   Edmund Burke, *Reflections on the Revolution in France*, ed. Conor Cruise O'Brien (Harmondsworth: Penguin, 1968), p. 135.
6   Kelvin Everest, *English Romantic Poetry* (Milton Keynes: Open University Press, 1990), p. 73.
7   J. Walsh to J. King, 15 August 1797: quoted in Juliet Barker, *Wordsworth: A Life* (London: Viking, 2000), p. 190.
8   Philip W. Martin, *Byron: A Poet before his Public* (Cambridge: Cambridge University Press, 1982), p. 96.
9   Everest, *English Romantic Poetry*, p. 69.
10   William Hazlitt, *My First Acquaintance with Poets* (1823).
11   William Godwin, *Things as they Are: or The Adventures of Caleb Williams*, ed. Maurice Hindle (Harmondsworth: Penguin, 1988).
12   'Lines Written a Few Miles above Tintern Abbey', *Lyrical Ballads* (1798).

13   Hazlitt, 'The Romantic Positives', in *My First Acquaintance with Poets*, pp. 427–31.

14   M. H. Abrams, *Natural Supernaturalism: Tradition and Revolution in Romantic Literature* (New York: Norton, 1971), p. 431.

15   *Prometheus Unbound*, IV.573–4.

16   Caspar David Friedrich, *The Wreck of the 'Hope'*, sometimes called *The Sea of Ice* (1823–4).

17   Abrams, *Natural Supernaturalism*, pp. 430–1.

18   Ibid., p. 431.

19   See the Dedication to *Don Juan*, stanza 5.

20   *Blackwood's Edinburgh Magazine*, ii (August 1818), p. 524.

21   Ibid., ii (October 1817), p. 38.

22   Ibid.

23   Leslie A. Marchand (ed.), *Byron's Letters and Journals*, 13 vols (London: John Murray, 1973–94), vol. 7, p. 217.

24   Ibid., vol. 8, p. 102.

25   Andrew Tooke, *Tooke's Pantheon of the Heathen Gods and Illustrious Heroes* (1698).

26   *Blackwood's Edinburgh Magazine*, ii (October 1817), p. 39.

27   'To George Felton Mathew', ll. 31–52.

28   See Christopher Ricks, *Keats and Embarrassment* (Oxford: Oxford University Press, 1976).

29   Marilyn Butler, *Romantics, Rebels and Reactionaries: English Literature and its Background 1760–1830* (Oxford: Oxford University Press, 1981), ch. 5, 'The Cult of the South: The Shelley Circle, its Creed and its Influence'.

30   'Ode to a Nightingale', ll. 15, 14.

31   Keats, Letter to John Taylor, 27 February 1818: *The Letters of John Keats*, ed. H. E. Rollins, 2 vols (Cambridge, Mass.: Harvard University Press, 1958), vol. 1, pp. 238–9.

32   Jerome J. McGann (ed.), *Romantic Period Verse* (Oxford: Oxford University Press, 1994), p. xix.

33   Ibid., p. xxi.

Part Three
Texts, Writers and Contexts

Writing in Revolution: Burke, Paine and Wordsworth

At the heart of the Romantic movement is the French Revolution, and the ten years that followed the fall of the Bastille in Paris in 1789 are often referred to as the Revolutionary Decade in Great Britain. It was a period which produced seminal texts by writers such as Edmund Burke, Thomas Paine, William Godwin and Mary Wollstonecraft (see Part Three: 'Romantic Travel Writing'), whose opinions inspired some of the most important work of the Romantics in poetry, fiction and non-fictional prose. Historically, wars had been fought by people on behalf of monarchies, but both the American war, leading to the Declaration of Independence in 1776, and the revolution in France were democratic uprisings in which the people, the lower and middle classes, fighting on their own behalf, were rising up against the aristocracy, and asserting the rights of man. The excitement and enthusiasm of the times took on a religious fervour, as the prospect of change was often interpreted as the coming to pass of biblical prophecies with their promise of a millennial period of universal peace and happiness. Robert Southey who, with his fellow 'Lake School' poets, William Wordsworth and Samuel Taylor Coleridge, had lived through the revolutionary times, remembered it in precisely this way as he reflected on his own radical youth from the more reactionary standpoint of his later years. Only those persons who had experienced it at first hand, he wrote, could 'conceive or comprehend [...] what a visionary world seemed to open upon those who were just entering it. Old things seemed passing away, and nothing was dreamt of but the regeneration of the human race'.[1] In *The Excursion* (1814), Wordsworth, too, in the figure of the Solitary (a version of his own earlier revolutionary self), recalled 'Saturnian rule / Returned,—a progeny of golden years / Permitted to descend and bless mankind. / —With promises the Hebrew Scriptures teem'.[2]

In Britain, the events in France were greeted with enthusiasm by those who believed the French were following the system of constitutional monarchy, established by the 'Glorious Revolution', which had placed William of Orange on the English throne in 1688. Constitutional monarchy differs from absolute monarchy in that the sovereign's power is limited by a written or unwritten constitution. When Wordsworth, with his friend Robert Jones, arrived in France on their summer vacation walking tour in 1790, they found themselves swept up in the celebration of the Feast of the Federation, commemorating the beginning of the revolution a year previously. The people had fêted them because 'we bore a name / Honoured in France, the name of Englishmen, / And hospitably did they give us hail / As their forerunners in a glorious course' (*The Prelude*, VI.409–12).* A few months after the fall of the Bastille, the Society for Commemorating the Revolution in Great Britain was addressed by Richard Price (1723–91), a Unitarian minister, in London. The Unitarians were Protestants who denied the doctrine of the Trinity (three persons in one God) and were associated with rationalism and dissent (see Part Four: 'Faith, Myth and Doubt'). Price delivered his address ('A Discourse on the Love of Our Country', 4 November 1789)[3] at the Unitarian meeting house in the Old Jewry, in which he asserted that the English had been 'made an example to other kingdoms' and had become 'the instructors of the world'. What is noticeable about Price's address is the characteristically biblical register in which he talks of the French Revolution. In the Gospel of St Luke, Simeon, who had been promised by the Holy Ghost that he would not die until he had seen the saviour of the Gentiles, exclaimed on witnessing the baby Jesus, with his mother and St Joseph at the Temple, 'Lord, now lettest thou thy servant depart in peace [...] For mine eyes have seen thy salvation' (Luke 2:29–

---

* All references to *The Prelude* are to the edition of 1805 unless otherwise stated.

30). Price quotes these words (the 'Nunc Dimittis') which follow on from his remark, 'What an eventful period is this! I am thankful that I have lived to it [sic].' With an allusion perhaps to Psalm 42, 'As the hart pants after the water brooks, so panteth my soul after thee, O God', Price proclaimed, 'I have lived to see the rights of men better understood than ever; and nations panting for liberty, which seemed to have lost the idea of it.' After sharing in the benefits of the Glorious Revolution, Price declared, he had been 'spared to be a witness to two other Revolutions, both glorious', by which he meant the American as well as the French, and looked forward to 'a general amendment beginning in human affairs'.

Conservative Opinion

Price's 'Discourse' heralded what was to become known as the Pamphlet War, in which supporters and opponents alike of the revolution in France argued their case and created in the process some of the finest polemical writing of the Romantic period. One of the most powerful oppositional voices was that of the great statesman and political theorist Edmund Burke, whose *Reflections on the Revolution in France* (November 1790)[4] was directly provoked by Price's address. At the time of its publication, the King of France, Louis XVI, and his queen, Marie Antoinette, together with their children, had been forcibly removed by the mob from the Palace at Versailles and brought to Paris where they were imprisoned. The *Reflections*, which by September 1791 had gone through eleven editions, is a tour de force of rhetorical style. Burke's strategy was to appeal to the emotions and sentiments of his reader. He writes with a sense of personal outrage at what is being done in the name of liberty in France.

Although the drift of English Romanticism would tend to be in the opposite direction from the position Burke adopted, it is his highly charged personal tone which makes him an essentially Romantic writer. Instead of writing detachedly, by distancing himself from the events he deplores, Burke at one point vividly recreates the scene of the king and queen's abduction, inviting the reader to witness it in all its horror. He describes the seizing of the royal family and its attendant massacres, which left 'the most splendid palace in the world [...] swimming in blood [...] and strewed with scattered limbs and mutilated carcases'. Burke writes of Louis XVI that on this occasion, 'As a man, it became him to feel for his wife and children.' This is an echo of the moment in Shakespeare's *Macbeth* where the weeping Macduff, learning of the murder, at Macbeth's behest, of his wife and children and being urged by Malcolm to 'Dispute it like a man', replies, 'I shall do so; / But I must also feel it as a man' (*Macbeth*, IV.iii.219–21). Burke argues that the monarchy and the established government constitute a system which cannot be 'better adapted to preserve a rational and *manly* freedom' (my emphasis). Of the king he writes, 'I am very sorry to say it, very sorry indeed, that such personages are in a situation in which it is not unbecoming in us to praise the virtues of the great.' 'Virtue' is derived from the Latin *virtus*, whose fundamental meaning is 'manliness', cognate with *vir*, 'man'. And it is the moral issue of what 'manliness' means which is at the heart of Shakespeare's play. When Lady Macbeth urges Macbeth to murder Duncan by implying a cowardice in his delay, Macbeth replies, 'I dare do all that may become a man; / Who dares do more is none' (I.vii.46–7). By daring to do more than is becoming to a man, Macbeth is implying that, in some pervertedly heroic sense, he might transcend the status of the common man. Yet, at the same time, by daring to do more than a man might dare, Macbeth becomes *inhuman*. He ceases in that sense to be a man, becoming instead a butcher. And Burke's bloody account of the Versailles episode reminds us not only of one of Shakespeare's bloodiest plays, but also of the issues at stake in his own contemporary society. For Burke, the new revolutionary principles are predicated on a ruthless inhumanity.

The abduction is prefigured by Burke's remark that after a day of 'confusion, alarm, dismay' the king and queen 'lay down, under the pledged security of public faith, to indulge nature in a few hours of respite'. It is this natural process of sleep which, reminiscent of Macbeth's brutal murder of the sleeping Duncan, is disturbed by the 'centinel' who cries out to the queen to 'save herself by flight'. Generally speaking, characters in Shakespeare's plays who are unable to sleep are irredeemable. Lady Macbeth becomes incapable of sleep, and Macbeth himself, after the murder of Duncan, exclaims 'Methought I heard a voice cry, "Sleep no more! / Macbeth does murther sleep"' (II.ii.32–3). Recalling Robespierre's massacres of royalist and other prisoners in September 1792, from which he finds himself distanced (echoing *Hamlet*, I.ii.147) by no more than 'a little month' (*The Prelude*, X.65), Wordsworth in Paris, and alone in his room at night, 'seem'd to hear a voice that cried, / To the whole City, "Sleep no more"' (X.76–7). In the allusion to *Macbeth*, Wordsworth recognises, in Robespierre's actions, Macbeth's ruthlessness in furthering his aims. 'It is necessary', Robespierre had written, 'to annihilate both the internal and external enemies of the republic or perish with its fall',[5] and Wordsworth's echoes of both *Hamlet* and *Macbeth* remind us of plays in which the natural order has been disturbed by regicide, the central incident in each. Even in the process of murdering it, Macbeth acknowledges sleep as 'nature's second course, / Chief nourisher in life's feast' (II.ii.36–7),* and Burke in the *Reflections* considers the French Revolution's offensive against royalty as essentially an offence against nature itself.

In this connection, both Burke's and Wordsworth's echoes of Shakespeare reflect a characteristic tendency of their age towards what would become known in time as 'Bardolatry'. Shakespeare is everywhere in Romantic literature, for the reason, as Rupert Christiansen points out, that in the latter half of the eighteenth century, in the great move of European taste towards the primitive and sincere, 'What had seemed naïveté, even crudity, could now be regarded as truth to Nature, while [Shakespeare's] irregularities evinced his powers of feeling and imagination, not his inability to be lucid and courtly.'[6]

In a celebrated passage of his text Burke recalls seeing the queen, Marie Antoinette, 'then the dauphiness', at Versailles 'sixteen or seventeen years' previously. She is apotheosised in Burke's memory as a heavenly 'vision', a sacred figure to whose defence he imagines 'ten

---

* Macbeth implies either the second mode of existence or the second course of a meal. Pudding appears to have been the first course at dinner, the joint or roast being the 'second'.

thousand swords must have leaped from their scabbards'. Now, in her 'fall', he recognises that 'the age of chivalry is gone'. This celebrated utterance underlines Burke's understanding of France as the original source of the concept of chivalry, 'a nation of gallant men [...] of men of honour and of cavaliers'. The words 'chivalry' and 'cavalier', from the French *cheval* (horse), suggest the knightly qualities which, in literary history, revered the place of women in society. In what Burke calls this 'new conquering empire of light and reason' which has replaced them, 'All the decent drapery of life is to be rudely torn off.' The clothing metaphor is appropriate to Burke's description of Marie Antoinette's being obliged to fly 'almost naked' from her 'bed', as the old decencies are outraged and the 'murder of a king, or a queen, or a bishop, or a father' ('Regicide, and parricide, and sacrilege') becomes 'only common homicide'. We are reminded again of Shakespeare in Burke's phraseologies. 'On this scheme of things,' he writes, 'a king is but a man; a queen is but a woman; a woman is but an animal; and an animal not of the highest order.' For King Lear, 'unaccommodated man', denied his customary trappings, 'is no more but such a poor, bare, fork'd animal' (III.iv.97–8), and Burke's elegiac 'the age of chivalry is gone', the repetitive 'The unbought grace of life [...] is gone! It is gone', and his 'Never, never more, shall we behold that generous loyalty to rank and sex', recall the world of kingly respect and authority which vanishes with the death of Cordelia, as lamented in Lear's words, 'Thou'lt come no more, / Never, never, never, never, never' (V.iii.308–9).

The name 'Cordelia', in the meaning attached to it in Shakespeare's tragedy, derives in part from *cor*, the Latin word for 'heart'. The heart likewise becomes in Burke's *Reflections* the seat of that 'moral imagination' which raises us 'to dignity in our own estimation', something 'which the heart owns, and the understanding ratifies'. The foregrounding here of feeling, the 'heart' before reason, recalls Coleridge's remark on Wordsworth's writings, the excellence of which, he says, 'I no sooner felt than I sought to understand.'[7] For Burke, the new 'barbarous philosophy' is the 'offspring of cold hearts and muddy understandings'. Once again the issues raised by *Macbeth* are recalled. To the individual no longer able to discriminate between moral good and moral evil, as is the case with the eponymous hero of that play, the world becomes muddy and inscrutable. Duplicity is the keynote of *Macbeth*. In every point all service is 'twice done, and then done double' (I.vi.15), so that ultimately life itself is reduced to confusion and meaninglessness, 'a tale / Told by an idiot [...] Signifying nothing' (V.v.26–8). 'Confusion now hath made his masterpiece', exclaims Macduff on finding the murdered Duncan, and the murky contents of the witches' cauldron stand in as a metaphor for that confusion, where what is 'fair' and what is 'foul' ('Fair is foul, and foul is fair', I.i.11) in the moral order can no longer be distinguished. It is precisely this confusion which Burke identifies as the legacy of the French Revolution:

> The most wonderful things are brought about in many instances by means the most absurd and ridiculous; in the most ridiculous modes; and apparently, by the most contemptible instruments. Everything seems out of nature in this strange chaos of levity and ferocity, and of all sorts of crimes jumbled together with all sorts of follies.

Burke and the Sublime

The 'strange chaos' upon which Burke remarks is taken up later in the *Reflections*, where he asks of France 'what sort of a thing must be a nation of gross, stupid, ferocious, and at the same time, poor and sordid barbarians, destitute of religion, honour, or manly pride, possessing nothing at present, and hoping for nothing hereafter?' The unsettling phrase 'what sort of a thing' is meant to denote something monstrous and uncouth, reminding us of Milton's 'Chaos' and his strange creation of the personified 'Death' in Book II of *Paradise Lost*: 'The other shape, / If shape it might be called that shape had none / Distinguishable in member, joint, or limb, / Or substance might be called that shadow seemed, / For each seemed either' (I.666–70). What sort of a thing, we ask, might this be? These are the very lines that Burke quotes, in his celebrated *A Philosophical Enquiry into the Origin of our Ideas of the Sublime and Beautiful*, to illustrate 'Obscurity' as a source of the sublime. Published in 1757, and therefore more than thirty years before his *Reflections*, Burke's *Enquiry* explored the nature of the aesthetic responses we make when we experience something as either sublime or beautiful. The sublime, according to Burke 'the strongest emotion which the mind is capable of feeling' (Part 1, Section VII), is always predicated upon our feelings of terror. 'Indeed terror is [...] the ruling principle of the sublime' (Part 2, Section II). Burke's essay defined sublimity as follows:

> Whatever is fitted in any sort to excite the ideas of pain, and danger, that is to say, whatever is in any sort terrible, or is conversant about terrible objects, or operates in a manner analogous to terror, is a source of the *sublime*.
>
> (Part 1, Section VII)

In his *Philosophical Enquiry* Burke's concern with terror, and its frisson of 'pain' and 'danger', was purely aesthetic. By the time he came to write his *Reflections on the Revolution in France*, the word 'terror' had taken on a new meaning for him. For Robespierre, the architect of 'The Terror' and the September massacres, the 'first political maxim should be that one guides the people by reason, and the enemies of the people by terror [...] Terror is only justice that is prompt, severe, and inflexible; it is thus an emanation of virtue [...]'.[8] But it becomes clear from the *Reflections* that when Burke imagines the summary justice of the guillotine, his earlier aesthetic of terror becomes insupportable to him. Burke shrinks with horror from a society where manners, civilisation and learning 'will be cast into the mire, and trodden down under the hoofs of a swinish multitude'. He appears to look back on that aesthetic world to which his *Enquiry* contributed so much when, perhaps with an eye to the concept of picturesque beauty, he imagines, in the 'groves' of the revolutionary French academies, not a pleasing vista with a distant eyecatcher to lend enchantment to the view, but one where 'at the end of every visto, you see nothing but the gallows' (see Part Four: 'Romantic Travel Writing').

Burke's argument throughout his *Reflections* is that, by adhering to traditions, 'an inheritable crown; an inheritable peerage', the 'inheriting privileges, franchises, and liberties, from a long line of ancestors', we are essentially following what is appropriate to our own natures. Such inheritances are not to be seen as impositions but rather as the natural accretion of centuries which have evolved with our human development to provide for our needs. 'We procure reverence to our civil institutions', says Burke, 'on the principle upon which nature teaches us to revere individual men; on account of their age, and on account of those from whom they are descended.' In a sentence reflecting an Augustan balance,* he writes: 'Thus, by preserving the method of nature in the conduct of the state, in what we improve we are never wholly new; in what we retain we are never wholly obsolete.' What Burke calls 'superadded ideas, furnished from the wardrobe of a moral imagination' are therefore necessary 'to cover the defects of our naked shivering nature', and it is important for his conception of society that the mysteries surrounding those elements which inspire obedience and reverence are not investigated or openly revealed. They must forever remain obscure in order to maintain their authority as the 'pleasing illusions' which make 'power gentle, and obedience liberal', encouraging the 'sentiments which beautify and soften private society'. Nature and the human heart constitute for Burke 'the great conservatories and magazines of our rights and privileges'.

William Godwin and Mary Wollstonecraft

In this context, Burke's use of the term 'magazine' is interesting, as one of its meanings is a store for ammunition and gunpowder. In his

---

* In England the Augustan period was roughly the first half of the eighteenth century. Its prominent writers (e.g. Pope, Swift, Addison) admired the literature produced by Virgil, Horace and Ovid under the Roman emperor Augustus (27BC – AD14). A favoured form was the couplet which provided a structural balance: 'Willing to wound, and yet afraid to strike, / Just hint a fault, and hesitate dislike' (Pope, 'Epistle to Arbuthnot'). This influence can be detected in Romantic literature in a line such as Shelley's 'The hand that mocked them, and the heart that fed' ('Ozymandias'), and in the titles of Jane Austen's novels, *Pride and Prejudice*, *Sense and Sensibility*.

novel *Things as they Are; or The Adventures of Caleb Williams* (1794), the philosophical anarchist and political opponent of Burke, William Godwin, employs the term when referring to the 'secret' locked up in the trunk of one of his protagonists, Ferdinando Falkland. In the story Falkland, who is the personification of chivalry, commits a murder for which he allows another to be unjustly blamed and hanged. His chivalric profile protects him from any suspicion. Any, that is, except for that of his servant-companion, Caleb Williams, who believes that Falkland's locked trunk may contain incriminating revelations. When there is a fire one night at Falkland's house, Caleb decides to break into the trunk: 'I snatched a tool suitable for the purpose, threw myself upon the ground, and applied with eagerness to a magazine which enclosed all for which my heart panted.' When Falkland appears unexpectedly, with eyes emitting 'sparks of rage', the lid of the trunk falls and his 'secret' remains intact. In Godwin's novel the trunk becomes a central symbol. Falkland's chivalric 'mystery' is locked away, out of sight. His sense of honour and the people's inability to see anything other than 'good' in him are threatened in this episode by the revolutionary 'fire' which is endangering the house. The contents of Falkland's 'magazine' are therefore explosive because once revealed they will show him for what he truly is. Prior to Godwin, Burke had used the term in the *Reflections* to express his anxiety, for his own conservative reasons, that what is necessary for our moral good, the 'magazines of our rights and privileges', will be '*exploded*' (my emphasis) by the French Revolution 'as a ridiculous, absurd, and antiquated fashion'.

Within a month of the publication of Burke's *Reflections*, Mary Wollstonecraft, who would later marry Godwin and give birth to Mary, the author of *Frankenstein* (see Part Four: 'Heroes and Anti-heroes') and future wife of Shelley, published her response to Burke in *A Vindication of the Rights of Men* (1790).[9] With an allusion to his *Enquiry* on the sublime and the beautiful, she takes issue with Burke's rhetorical register as a disguise of reality; 'for truth in morals', she writes, 'has ever appeared to me the essence of the sublime; and, in taste, simplicity the only criterion of the beautiful'. To form our judgements exclusively on 'our *feelings*' for what we regard as the beauties of the past and its traditions is misleading – 'the ivy is beautiful, but, when it insidiously destroys the trunk from which it receives support, who would not grub it up?' She asserts that civilisation had in fact been stopped in its progress by inheritance, 'hereditary property – hereditary honours', and that man had been changed into an artificial monster 'by the station in which he was born'. Property, as Mary Wollstonecraft understands it, has therefore come to be confused with propriety, two very similar words in English. Unless a person has property, he cannot be expected to be a person of propriety or moral worth. True happiness, she insists, 'can only be enjoyed by equals' and charity 'is not a condescending distribution of alms, but an intercourse of good offices and mutual benefits, founded on respect for justice and humanity'. In this sense she shares the opinion of a poet such as William Blake who, in 'The Human Abstract' (*Songs of Experience*, 1794), denounces 'pity' and 'mercy' as parasitical upon real social evils:

> Pity would be no more,
> If we did not make somebody Poor:
> And Mercy no more could be,
> If all were as happy as we.

Blake argues that it is the obligation of each of us to rectify society's ills, and then the so-called virtues on which we pride ourselves will simply wither away and become redundant. On Burke's principles, as Mary Wollstonecraft points out, for no other reason than that it was adopted by our 'ignorant forefathers', slavery ought never to be abolished and we must therefore 'term an atrocious insult to humanity the love of our country'. She effectively turns Burke's emphases on feeling and the human heart against him; 'he has lost his heart of flesh who can see a fellow-creature humbled before him, and trembling at the frown of a being, whose heart is supplied by the same vital current, and whose pride ought to be checked by a consciousness of having the same infirmities.'

Radical Reaction

By far the most sustained and devastating attack on Burke's *Reflections* was Thomas Paine's *Rights of Man: Being an Answer to Mr. Burke's Attack on the French Revolution* (March 1791).[10] Paine, who was born in Thetford, Norfolk, had been active in the American revolutionary war and in the year of its inception (1776) had published *Common Sense*. In the kind of pithy utterance one associates later with William Blake, 'Government, like dress,' he argued there, 'is the badge of lost innocence; the palaces of kings are built upon the ruins of the bowers of paradise.' The *Rights of Man* is dedicated to the first American President, George Washington, and, after he published its second part in 1792, Paine was accused of treason and fled England for France, where he became a citizen and a member of the French Convention. Originally a friend of Burke, Paine was implacably opposed to him during the Revolution controversy of the 1790s. He avoids the emotive rhetoric of the *Reflections*, 'a frenzy of passion' as he describes it, writing instead in a plain and accessible prose. This, in the judgement of Pitt's government, together with its wide circulation and the promotion of its ideas by the London Corresponding Society (one of the many radical groups of the time), made the *Rights of Man* a very subversive document. 'There never did,' writes Paine, 'there never will, and there never can exist a parliament, or any description of men, or any generation of men, in any country, possessed of the right or the power of binding and controuling posterity to the "*end of time*".'

Like Mary Wollstonecraft, Paine takes issue with Burke over the question of hereditary rights and property: 'The vanity and presumption of governing beyond the grave, is the most ridiculous and insolent of all tyrannies. Man has no property in man; neither has any generation a property in the generations which are to follow.' On the basis of the American Declaration of Independence, Paine argues from the principle of men's equality at birth, and in answer to Burke's assertion that constitutional right was something conferred by tradition he writes: 'The continual use of the word *Constitution* in the English Parliament, shows there is none; and that the whole is merely a form of Government without a Constitution, and constituting itself with what powers it pleases.'

In the second part of *Rights of Man*, Paine engages with Burke over the question of monarchy. Where Burke talked in terms of the 'decent drapery' of life and of ideas 'furnished from the wardrobe of a moral imagination' as part of his collective metaphor pointing up the necessity to keep the sources of authority hidden from the public gaze, Paine employs the same figure in dispelling the mystery. What is called monarchy, he writes, 'always appears to me a silly, contemptible thing. I compare it to something kept behind a curtain, about which there is a great deal of bustle and fuss, and a wonderful air of seeming solemnity; but when, by accident, the curtain happens to be open, and the company see what it is, they burst into laughter.' For Paine, the virtue of 'the representative system of government' is that 'Whatever are its excellences or its defects, they are visible to all.' It exists, he writes, 'not by fraud and mystery [...] but inspires a language, that, passing from heart to heart, is felt and understood.' It will be recalled that, in precisely this way, Burke had privileged feeling before understanding when he had talked of established ideas of government as those 'which the heart owns and the understanding ratifies'. It is evident that Burke and Paine argue from identical premises but in an entirely different direction from each other. Burke insists that it is because of, and appropriate to, our nature that we have the institutions we inherit, while Paine argues that we have them in flat opposition to it. Like Mary Wollstonecraft, Paine, when questioning his principles in contemplating government, turns Burke's emphasis on the 'feeling' human heart against him. '"Ten years ago," says he, "I could have felicitated France on her having a government, without enquiring what the nature of that government was, or how it was administered." Is this the language of a rational man? Is it the language of a heart feeling as it ought to feel for the rights and happiness of the human race?'

Thus, for Paine, monarchy is a mode of government that 'counteracts nature'. In contrast, 'the representative system is always parallel' with its 'immutable laws [...] and meets the reason of man in every part'.[11] In her *Vindication of the Rights of Men*, Mary Wollstonecraft remarks upon

Burke's apparent blindness to the sufferings of the dispossessed while being emotionally devastated by the plight of the French royal family. 'Misery, to reach your heart, I perceive, must have its cap and bells; your tears are reserved, very *naturally*, concerning your character, for the declamation of the theatre, or for the downfall of queens.'[12] With an eye to Burke's construction of the Versailles episode in terms of Shakespeare's *Macbeth*, Paine, too, sees his mode of presentation as one 'very well calculated for theatrical representation' to produce 'a weeping effect'. He goes on to remind Burke that 'he is writing History and not *Plays*'. The sense that with his 'spouting rant of high-toned exclamation' Burke is concerned 'for the sake of show' and the superficies of things rather than their realities, lies behind one of the most celebrated of Paine's remarks on him in *Rights of Man*: 'He is not affected by the reality of distress touching his heart, but by the showy resemblance of it striking his imagination. He pities the plumage, but forgets the dying bird.' This memorable metaphor recalls Pope's *Windsor Forest* (1713), where the death of a shot pheasant is made less significant in Pope's scheme of things than the opportunity it offers for a description of its iridescent plumage:

> Ah! What avail his glossy, varying dyes,
> His purple crest, and scarlet-circled eyes,
> The vivid green his shining plumes unfold,
> His painted wings and breast that flames with gold?

One of Paine's central arguments in the *Rights of Man* is that Burke fails to distinguish between persons and principles. It is not the person of Louis XVI which, for the French, had become the issue, but the despotism he stood for. For Paine it is, in fact, to the credit of the Revolution that in seizing the king it has maintained its idealistic principles:

> What Mr Burke considers as a reproach to the French Revolution (that of bringing it forward under a reign more mild than the preceding ones), is one of its highest honours. The revolutions

that have taken place in other European countries, have been excited by personal hatred. The rage was against the man, and he became the victim. But, in the instance of France, we see a revolution generated in the rational contemplation of the rights of man, and distinguishing from the beginning between persons and principles.

Paine argues that in his comprehensive acceptance of the inherited rights of authority, 'Mr Burke must compliment every government in the world, while its victims who suffer under them, whether sold into slavery, or tortured out of existence, are wholly forgotten.'

The Testimony of Individual Experience

William Wordsworth made his second visit to France in 1791 between the ages of twenty-one and twenty-two and at the height of the revolutionary activity. He stayed from November until December 1792 and, prior to this, was resident in London at various stages throughout 1791, associating with prominent radical and dissenting figures, such as Samuel Nicholson, an acquaintance of one of his cousins. With Nicholson, Wordsworth attended the meeting house at the Old Jewry to hear Joseph Fawcett's lectures. Fawcett was considered by Godwin to be one of his 'principal oral instructors',[13] and the meeting house was where Richard Price in 1789 had delivered the sermon that had sparked off the revolution controversy. Both Wordsworth and Nicholson were likely to have been acquainted at this time with the prominent radical publisher, the Unitarian Joseph Johnson, whose bookshop became a meeting place for many liberal intellectuals of the day. William Godwin, for example, met both Thomas Paine and Mary Wollstonecraft at one of Johnson's dinners in November 1791. Burke's *Reflections*, Wollstonecraft's *Vindication of the Rights of Men* and Paine's *Rights of Man* were all available by March 1791, and it was likely that by the spring of that year Wordsworth was reading them. In Book IX of *The Prelude*, he writes: 'Like Others I

had read, and eagerly / Sometimes, the master Pamphlets of the day'
(IX.95–6) and, given the circles in which he was moving at this time,
his political persuasions were most likely to have been inclined in
Paine's direction. Ultimately, Wordsworth's opinions were formed by
his own direct experience of events in France. His belief in political
revolution as a means to the betterment of mankind was shaken by
Robespierre's 'Terror' which began with the September massacres (3–
7 September 1792). After the execution of the king in January 1793
he transferred his allegiance, as *The Prelude* recounts, to the rational
philosophy of William Godwin, whose *Enquiry Concerning Political
Justice*, published the following year, he saw as the best means to
fulfilling his idealism (X.806–11). It was only when Godwin proved
equally inadequate as a compensation that Wordsworth turned back to
the natural world, the original source of his inspiration, encouraged
by the sustaining agency of both his sister, Dorothy, and his poetical
collaborator, Samuel Taylor Coleridge (X.905–16).

Books IX and X of *The Prelude*, entitled 'Residence in France' and
'Residence in France: The French Revolution' respectively, describe the
turbulent progress of the birth of the French Republic and Wordsworth's
participation in some of its stormiest episodes. Having initially, as a
student, visited France in the earliest stages of the Revolution,
Wordsworth recalls in Book IX how, to some extent, the sense of himself
as a tourist was still with him as he 'sported with the dust / Of the
Bastille […] And from the rubbish gathered up a stone / And pocketed
the relick in the guise / Of an Enthusiast' (IX.63–7). On such occasions
'Affecting more emotion than [he] felt', Wordsworth goes on to describe
how a painting of Mary Magdalene by Charles Le Brun had much more
recompensed his 'Traveller's pains' (IX.75). He presents himself as a
spectator of events, coming upon them, in terms reminiscent of Paine's
remarks on Burke's 'theatrical' sense of the Revolution, as though he
had 'abruptly pass'd / Into a theatre, of which the stage / Was busy with
an action far advanced' (IX.92–4). For a time, he had mixed in company
whose social niceties scrupulously avoided 'all discourse, alike / Of good
and evil' that was associated with the pros and cons of revolutionary
principles. But gradually such society, he recalls, grew tedious and he

'withdrew / Into a noisier world; and thus did soon / Become a Patriot; and my heart was all / Given to the People, and my love was theirs' (IX.119–25).

The term 'Patriot' meant, at this time, a sympathiser with the Republican cause, a friend of the people and an anti-monarchist. At the beginning of Book IX, Wordsworth describes how his upbringing in the English Lake District had already prepared him for the democratic principles he was encountering in France. In that 'poor District' no one had been 'vested with attention or respect / Through claims of wealth or blood' (IX.217, 224–5). Similarly, at Cambridge, he had experienced something 'Of a Republic, where all stood thus far / Upon equal ground [...] And wealth and titles were in less esteem / Than talents and successful industry' (IX.229–30, 234–5). It was inevitable, in Wordsworth's thoughts, that someone like himself and 'tutor'd thus' should 'hail / As best the government of equal rights / And individual worth' (IX.242, 246–8).

In October 1792, Wordsworth returned to Paris from Orléans, where he had been living, cheered with the hope that now that France had defeated the Prussian army at Valmy on 20 September, and declared itself a Republic on 22 September, the violent course of the Revolution, as witnessed in the massacres only 'a little month' previously (X.75), would be halted. But his vivid sense of the world in which he was involved in Paris, as has already been noted, brought to his mind at night Macbeth's cry, 'Sleep no more!' Wordsworth also seems to pick up on the predominantly tactile imagery of *Macbeth* ('unseamed', 'munch'd', 'thick and slab', 'sticking on his hands', 'blanket of the dark') when, of the September massacres, he describes how, in his disturbed imagination, he 'felt and touch'd them' (X.66). It was as though the dreadful violence of the Revolution, so disturbingly close to him, could be almost physically experienced.

The word 'revolution', etymologically, is originally associated with the motion of the stars and planets. The *Oxford English Dictionary* defines it as 'The action or fact, on the part of celestial bodies, of moving round in an orbit or circular course; the apparent movement of the sun, stars, etc., round the earth.' When Burke in his *Reflections* introduces Marie Antoinette as the 'delightful vision' he first remembered seeing, he constructs his description of her in cosmological terms. The dauphiness is a radiant sun or planet who 'surely never lighted on this orb, which she hardly seemed to touch'. Burke remembers how he saw her 'just above the horizon, decorating and cheering the elevated sphere she just began to move in, – glittering like the morning-star [...]'. In language which recalls the medieval geocentric cosmology, and entirely appropriate to the chivalric world of his vision, Burke exclaims, 'Oh! What a revolution! And what an heart must I have, to contemplate without emotion that elevation and that fall!' Whereas Richard Price, like Simeon in the New Testament, had been joyful to have lived to see the advent of a new world, Burke laments the disappearance of the old one, and regrets that he 'should have lived to see such disasters fallen upon [the queen] in a nation of gallant men'. Again he uses his words advisedly. 'Disaster' is a derivation from 'Dis-astro: ill-starred. An unfavourable aspect of a star or planet' (*Oxford English Dictionary*). Marie Antoinette's fall is therefore to be compared in Burke's terminology to those dire events which were once believed to follow on from cosmic disorders bringing catastrophe to human affairs. Shooting stars (literally, 'disasters') and comets were among such disorders, as in Calphurnia's words, 'When beggars die there are no comets seen; / The heavens themselves blaze forth the death of princes' (*Julius Caesar*, II.ii.30–1).

In Paris, and in an apprehensive state of mind, Wordsworth describes how 'the fear gone by / Press'd on me almost like a fear to come' (X.62–3) and the cyclical processes of 'revolutions', such as described above by Burke, leads him on to a disturbing consideration of the likely course of the French 'revolution' in a scheme where all things have a natural recurrence:

> no Star
> Of wildest course but treads back his own steps;
> For the spent hurricane the air provides
> As fierce a Successor; the tide retreats
> But to return out of its hiding place

In the great Deep; all things have second birth;
The earthquake is not satisfied at once. (1850 version, X.78–84)

Prior to his return to Paris in the October of 1792, Wordsworth had been in Blois and Orléans. His love affair with Annette Vallon during the period of his stay in France would result, in December of that year, in the birth of their child, Caroline, and it was while he was living in Orléans that Wordsworth consorted with members of the French military who were disaffected with the course the Revolution was taking. These were figures, as he describes them in Book IX, 'well-born', the 'Chivalry of France', and all ruled by one spirit, with the exception of 'only one', he adds, 'hereafter to be nam'd'. This group of aristocratic opponents who had no fear 'of bad becoming worse, / For worst to them was come' (IX.131–9) had in their midst Michel Beaupuy, the exception to whom Wordsworth refers. Beaupuy, an officer who, unlike the others all 'bent upon undoing what was done' (IX.136), was a committed republican, became probably the most influential figure Wordsworth would encounter before his meeting for the first time with Coleridge in Bristol in 1795. The friendship between Wordsworth and Beaupuy, who was killed in action during the French invasion of Germany in 1796, was comparatively brief, from February until July 1792, but Beaupuy's influence upon Wordsworth's republican sentiments was such that had it not been for his compulsion to return to England for 'want of / Funds' (X.191–2), he imagines himself as having doubtless 'made a common cause / With some who perish'd' (X.195–6). In actuality, the experience of the Revolution made the polemics of Burke and Paine in the pamphlet war realisable for Wordsworth. On one occasion, as he accompanied Beaupuy in the French countryside, he encountered a 'hunger-bitten' (IX.511) child whose predicament causes Beaupuy to exclaim, ''Tis against *that* / Which we are fighting' (IX.518–19). Wordsworth adds that 'I with him believed / Devoutly that a spirit was abroad / Which could not be withstood' (IX.519–21). He was convinced that the best principles of the republican cause, if followed to their conclusion, would inevitably result in the abolition of such poverty. What, in

Godwin's philosophy, would be described as 'necessity', is also at work in Wordsworth's thoughts as, on his return from France, he hears of impediments to the progress of the anti-slavery campaign which had been initiated by Thomas Clarkson and William Wilberforce in 1787. He was not, he recalls, unduly perturbed, in that he had 'laid this faith to heart, / That, if France prosper'd […], this most rotten branch of human shame, / […] Would fall together with its parent tree' (X.222–7). The concept of 'necessity' implied simply that if man followed his reason, his condition would inevitably improve. Both Burke and Paine, as previously described, had contested the means by which man's happiness was to be achieved, and had argued from their respective positions about what sorts of things were appropriate to his nature and to his reason. In his recollection of his discourses 'in solitude' with Beaupuy (IX.327), Wordsworth recounts their conversations, which seem to have devolved upon the Burke–Paine controversy, namely:

> the end
> Of civil government, and its wisest forms,
> Of ancient prejudice, and chartered rights,
> Allegiance, faith, and law by time matured,
> Custom and habit, novelty and change,
> Of self-respect, and virtue in the Few
> For patrimonial honour set apart,
> And ignorance in the labouring Multitude. (IX.328–35)

The 'labouring Multitude' brings to mind the 'swinish multitude' of Burke's *Reflections*, and Wordsworth is remembering his radical self at this time as very much under the influence of Beaupuy's enthusiasm.

The Revolution controversy, placing an obligation upon everyone to take sides, reflects a common feeling in Romantic-period writers that their own age of change and crisis was one of momentous and unprecedented significance in the history of mankind.

Extended Commentary: Wordsworth, *The Prelude* (1805), Book IX, lines 436–504

The first version of *The Prelude* was completed thirteen years after the height of Wordsworth's revolutionary fervour, and one of its great strengths, as a work of literature in the Romantic 'confessional' mode, is the candour with which it reveals, in hindsight, the true state of Wordsworth's mind at separate stages of his intellectual development. He does not attempt to conceal that he affected more emotion than he felt when, as a tourist, he had 'sported with the dust / Of the Bastille' (IX.63–4) and had pocketed a souvenir, while his mention of a youthful 'Dejection taken up for pleasure's sake' (VI.482) is not beyond a wry self-mockery to be found elsewhere in his poems. In this passage from Book IX, Wordsworth is recalling the walks and discourse that he shared with Beaupuy, his 'patriot Friend' (IX.553), listening to his political opinions, yet at the same time, in the midst of his conversations, candidly admitting that his thoughts were often elsewhere. His 'frequent walk' (IX.439) with Beaupuy would be along the Loire or in the 'wide Forests of the neighbourhood' – in other words, amidst the very landscapes which gave birth to the romance tradition in France. The high woods 'over-arch'd with open space / On every side' (IX.441–2) recall the 'pillared shade / High overarched' and occupied by the post-lapsarian Adam and Eve in *Paradise Lost* (IX.1106–7). For Wordsworth, it was 'A solemn region', made more solemn in his recollection, and as the Miltonic allusion implies, by how the paradisiacal promise held out by France would be betrayed and lead to a corresponding 'fall' in a country which was at this time 'innocent yet / Of civil slaughter'.

From this point, the verse-paragraph, as far as line 480, consists of three extended sentences whose purpose is to reflect the movements of Wordsworth's mind as he 'wander'd on' with his 'rever'd companion'. The processes of thought are intimately tied in with the peripatetic activity and the 'earnest dialogues' which accompanied it, as well as with the operations of his discursive imagination when often, as Wordsworth tells us, from these earnest dialogues he 'slipp'd in thought / And let remembrance steal to other times'. The 'slippage' refers to a relaxation of his earnestness, a mild admission of his culpability in failing to keep focused with Beaupuy on the serious issues of debate. Yet there is also a sense that by giving Beaupuy the 'slip' in this way he was able to indulge a heart-warming and imaginative engagement with the romantic suggestiveness of the beautiful part of France in which he finds himself. He thinks of the forests as the former home of hermits in an age of faith. His creative imagination makes, from the distant sounds of horses' hooves, the sound of 'Angelica, thundering through the woods / Upon her Palfrey, or that gentler Maid / Erminia, fugitive as fair as She'. Angelica and Erminia are the heroines respectively of Ariosto's *Orlando Furioso* (1516) and Tasso's *Gerusalemme Liberata* (1575), familiar to Wordsworth through his studies of Italian under his tutor, Agostino Isola, at Cambridge. As recalled in the second of his lengthy sentences, he would see in his mind's eye 'a pair of Knights / Joust underneath the trees' or sounds of merriment and music would conjure up for him, as though from Spenser's *Faerie Queene* (1596), 'Satyrs in some viewless glade, with dance / Rejoicing o'er a Female in the midst'. Intensely imagined episodes of this kind 'did often', Wordsworth writes, 'in this way / Master my fancy'. He looks back to the age of chivalry and romance literature, allowing his heart to feel the power of its imaginative resonance.

In the third sentence of the verse-paragraph, Wordsworth goes on to describe how, on their walks, he and Beaupuy might encounter a convent, 'a roofless pile', in the kind of pleasantly situated spot that in former times would have invited pleasing thoughts of melancholy. Such a place has already been described in Book II of *The Prelude*, in the account given of a childhood horse-riding expedition to Furness Abbey. It is a beautiful spot from which, with a deliberate echo in this verse-paragraph, Wordsworth takes his leave with 'thundering hoofs' (II.122–44; see IX.451–3). Unlike the ruined Furness Abbey, the 'Dismantled' convent is the result, not of the 'reverential touch of Time', but of 'violence abrupt'. The atheist Revolution's abrupt severance with its past is what Burke fears most when he reflects on the slow evolution of Church and State and the displacement of due reverence by destruction.

There is the anticipation of a natural pause at the end of line 475 where we might have expected the sentence to end – 'I could not but bewail a wrong so harsh'. But its continuation with, 'And for the matin Bell to sound no more / Griev'd, and the evening taper, and the Cross' etc. permits Wordsworth's regret to linger poignantly as 'music dwells / Lingering – and wandering on as loth to die' in his sonnet 'Inside of King's College Chapel, Cambridge'.

From his 'heart-bracing colloquies' with Beaupuy on pressing republican issues, therefore, Wordsworth honestly admits that he relaxed (compare Blake: 'Damn Braces: Bless Relaxes') into another world of imaginative possibility, and this 'In spite of real fervour' (for Beaupuy's position) as well as of that, he acknowledges, which might have been 'Less genuine and wrought up within myself'.

The beginning of the next verse-paragraph, one long sentence from lines 480 to 502, recalls Beaupuy pointing out some celebrated sites and buildings dating from the time of King Francis I, the 'Site / Of Romorentin, home of ancient Kings', the 'imperial Edifice of Blois', and a 'rural Castle […] where a Lady lodg'd'. With an echo of how he had 'slipp'd in thought' from Beaupuy's conversation, Wordsworth says that her name has 'now slipp'd / From [his] remembrance'. Based on historical fact, the story surrounding these places is of a romantic attachment between King Francis and the 'Lady' (possibly Anne de Pisseleu d'Heilly) during which it was their custom to signal to each other 'By cressets and love beacons, intercourse / 'Twixt her high-seated Residence and his / Far off at Chambord on the Plain beneath'. As in the previous verse-paragraph where Wordsworth, in a sequence of lines without end-stops, mimics his thought processes as they wander away into the realms of Romance literature, so here the verse pattern reflects a similar dwelling on this beautiful 'Tradition of the Country'.

As *The Prelude* was written several years after the walks he had taken with Beaupuy, Wordsworth, in the light of the Revolution controversy and the political stances adopted by Burkeans and Paineites, is now able to make a balanced judgement of his own position in the debate. He is attracted to what Keats might describe as 'Huge cloudy symbols of a high romance'.[14] The story of Anne and King Francis captures his imagination as 'on these spots', he writes, 'with many gleams I look'd / Of chivalrous delight'. 'Even' in such a setting, though with less regret than he felt for the loss of 'the peaceful House / Religious' (because, to himself as a young republican, the monarchy was much more at fault than the Church) — 'Even here', writes Wordsworth, his 'Imagination', which 'At times' led him to righteous indignation against 'Kings' and 'their vices', was exactly the faculty to 'mitigate the force / Of civic prejudice, the bigotry, / So call it, of a youthful Patriot's mind'. Wordsworth's construction is a triumph of syntax. His balanced phrasing captures perfectly the dichotomy within his thoughts. Part of his temperament is still attracted to the chivalric past of Burke's *Reflections*, to the age of 'Kings' whose 'better deeds', he acknowledges, are balanced against their 'vices'. Yet, while admitting that republicanism in a 'youthful Patriot's mind' can often be a source of 'prejudice' and 'bigotry', he justifies his own 'virtuous wrath and noble scorn' for those things that Paine had attacked in *Rights of Man*. The passage reveals how the political thought of the French revolutionary period is demonstrably at work in the recollection of a major Romantic poet whose 'chivalrous delight' in the history of France implies 'not the less' his 'Hatred of absolute rule, where will of One / Is law for all'.

In the 1850 version of *The Prelude*, Wordsworth includes a passage on Burke (Book VII, 'Residence in London', ll. 512–43), certainly not written before 1820, in which he recalls witnessing his performance in parliament. He is celebratory of Burke's philosophy in a way that would have been at odds with the political persuasion of his younger self and indicates his increasing conservatism as he advances in years. He addresses the 'Genius of Burke' who

> the majesty proclaims
> Of Institutes and Laws, hallowed by time;
> Declares the vital power of social ties
> Endeared by Custom; and with high disdain,
> Exploding upstart Theory, insists
> Upon the allegiance to which men are born.

Wordsworth describes the revolutionary times as 'big / With ominous change, which, night by night, provoked / Keen struggles, and black clouds of passion raised' and asks:

> Could a youth, and one
> In ancient story versed, whose breast had heaved
> Under the weight of classic eloquence,
> Sit, see, and hear, unthankful, uninspired?

By this point in his career, Wordsworth finds in Burke a more sympathetic politics. The stress which he places upon 'repeated experience and regular feelings' in the Preface to *Lyrical Ballads* sits more happily, even in 1800, with Burke than with Paine. Even as early as the 1805 *Prelude*, Wordsworth's thoughts were developing in that direction. While he acknowledges in the passage from Book IX (above) that the youthful patriot can be guilty of 'civic prejudice' and 'bigotry', he seems to realise that his 'Imagination' is overheated when 'potent to enflame' to 'virtuous wrath' and 'noble scorn'. There is a hint that Wordsworth recognises his own tendency towards a youthful wrongheadedness in the arch use of 'virtuous' and 'noble'. It was that dangerous fire of youthful idealism which the imagination was also called upon to 'mitigate'. The passage does seem to dwell on what has passed and gone, and it is the paragraph's flourishing conclusion – 'chivalrous delight'– that directs our thoughts, though not exclusively, towards Burke.

Notes

1   Edward Dowden (ed.), *The Correspondence of Robert Southey with Caroline Bowles* (Dublin: Hodges, Figgis & Co.; London: Longmans, Green & Co., 1881), p. 52

2   Wordsworth, *The Excursion*, III.761–4.

3   Quotations are taken from *The Norton Anthology of English Literature*, ed. S. Greenblatt, 8th edn (New York and London: Norton, 2006), vol. 2, pp. 149–52.

4   Quotations are taken from *The Norton Anthology of English Literature*, 8th edn, vol. 2, pp. 152–8.
5   P. H. Beik (trans. and ed.), *The Documentary History of Western Civilisation: The French Revolution* (London: Walker & Co., 1971), p. 283 (cited hereafter as Beik, *French Revolution*).
6   Rupert Christiansen, *Romantic Affinities: Portraits from an Age, 1780–1830* (London: The Bodley Head, 1988), p. 225.
7   S. T. Coleridge, *Biographia Literaria*, ch. 4.
8   Beik, *French Revolution*, p. 203.
9   Quotations are taken from *The Norton Anthology of English Literature*, 8th edn, vol. 2, pp. 159–63.
10   Quotations are taken from *The Norton Anthology of English Literature*, 8th edn, vol. 2, pp. 163–7 unless otherwise stated.
11   Thomas Paine, *Rights of Man*, ed. Henry Collins (Harmondsworth: Penguin, 1969), pp. 204–5.
12   Mary Wollstonecraft, *Political Writings*, ed. Janet Todd (Oxford: Oxford University Press, 1994), p. 14.
13   See Nicholas Roe, *Wordsworth and Coleridge: The Radical Years* (Oxford: Clarendon Press, 1988), p. 24.
14   Keats, Sonnet: 'When I have fears'.

Revolution, Reaction and the Natural World: Wordsworth and Coleridge, Clare and Blake

In Book IX of *The Prelude*, William Wordsworth recalls how his 'subservience from the first / To [...] Nature's single sovereignty' (IX.236–7) convinced him that, at the time of its outbreak, the French Revolution 'seemed nothing out of nature's certain course' (IX.252). He looked upon events in France as the achievement of those things he had always, from childhood, felt to be true and right. As the story progressed, however, and the French who 'now, become oppressors in their turn' had changed 'a war of self-defence / For one of conquest' (X.792–4), he found himself returning to those virtues upon which his original convictions had been built, of which he now felt more sure than ever. The natural world was their embodiment, and he pays tribute to it at the conclusion of Book II:

> If in this time
> Of dereliction and dismay, I yet
> Despair not of our nature; but retain
> A more than Roman confidence, a faith
> That fails not, in all sorrow my support,
> The blessing of my life, the gift is yours,
> Ye mountains! Thine, O Nature! Thou hast fed
> My lofty speculations; and in thee,
> For this uneasy heart of ours I find

A never-failing principle of joy,
And purest passion. (II.456–66)

As we have seen, Edmund Burke, in his *Reflections on the Revolution in France* (1790), took nature as the premise from which to argue against the Revolution, while Thomas Paine in *Rights of Man* (1791) made nature the principle by which to support it. Burke's essentially conservative standpoint differs from Paine's in that he thinks of Nature as something established by God in his dispensation for man at the beginning of time (*natura naturata*).* Paine's position has more in common with a progressive view, looking at nature as a process and working towards something yet to be realised (*natura naturans*).† As one of the most prominent first-generation Romantics who had lived through the revolutionary years, Wordsworth moved gradually towards the more conservative and retrospective views of Burke, to find in the feelings rather than in reason, in rustic life, in the natural world and other forms of cultural primitivism, a sounder and a more solid base upon which to construct a better future for society. Samuel Taylor Coleridge, too, reflecting this pattern in Wordsworth, writes in 'France: An Ode' (1798) from personal experience, and converts political concepts of slavery and liberty into metaphors of the mind in its relationship with nature.

In the first stanza of 'France: An Ode', the elements of the natural world, 'waves', 'forests', 'clouds' and 'sun', are invoked to bear witness to the poet's worship of liberty, a liberty which he now believes he had misplacedly lodged in political revolution. The language of militarism is converted from revolutionary activity to the benevolent natural scene. A 'march' becomes not that of soldiers, but a march of the clouds 'no mortal may control!' (l. 2); 'homage', the kind paid only by the 'ocean waves' to 'eternal laws'; and the 'solemn music of the wind' (l. 8) an 'unconquerable sound' (l. 14). Whereas, in *The Prelude*, Wordsworth marks the outbreak of war between France and Britain (1793) as the time when he experienced 'Change and subversion from this hour'

* Literally 'nature natured', or nature as it is.
† Literally, 'nature naturing', or in process.

(X.234), Coleridge identifies his similar moment of crisis in 1798, when the French invasion of Switzerland had brought him to recognise that freedom cannot be won or imposed by external power. In the final stanza of the poem he asserts that revolution by a people who are enslaved in their perceptions, whose minds are confined by the limits of their physical senses, simply replaces one form of slavery with another:

> The sensual and the dark rebel in vain,
> Slaves by their own compulsion! In mad game
> They burst their manacles, and wear the name
> Of freedom graven on a heavier chain! (ll. 85–8)

Essential liberty, as Coleridge now realises, resides in the power of his own being to unite with, and so repossess, the natural world:

> And then I felt thee on the sea-cliff's verge,
> Whose pines, scarce travelled by the breeze above,
> Had made one murmur with the distant surge!
> Yes, while I stood and gazed, my temples bare,
> And shot my being through earth, sea, and air,
> Possessing all things with intensest love,
> Oh Liberty, my spirit felt thee there! (ll. 99–105)

The poem concludes with enfranchised perception expressed as an act of spontaneous love. As Nicholas Roe writes: 'These final lines of Coleridge's "Ode" are his most confident assertion of the One Life as a redemptive possibility that might replace his former hopes that France would "compel the nations to be free".'[1]

New Concepts of the Material World

If Burke conceived of Nature as fixed and permanent, representing the conservative values to which Wordsworth and Coleridge were increasingly inclined, the Jacobinical ideas associated with figures such as the early Godwin and Tom Paine were more influential on younger Romantics, and formed around notions of a dynamic natural world in the process of perfecting itself. H. W. Piper in *The Active Universe*[2] makes a detailed study of how French materialist thought, at first influential on Wordsworth and Coleridge, was transmitted to second-generation Romantics including Byron, Keats and Shelley. He describes how the reaction against a Newtonian, mechanical, view of the universe began in mid-eighteenth-century France, where a world view developed which saw systems of inert matter coming to be replaced by systems involving active forces. The biological sciences began to produce facts for which mechanics had no explanation, and phenomena such as growth, reproduction, chemical action and electricity, all objects of investigation during the period, seemed to contradict the assumption that matter was inert. The ideas, he writes, that 'all matter was living, organic and animal, that all natural objects, as organized forms of matter, had their own life and sensibility, and that the whole organization of the natural world was capable of intelligent purpose (whether expressed in evolution* or in a provident interest in mankind) were all widely diffused in pre-Revolutionary France'.[3]

During the period in which he was living there (1791–3), Wordsworth became familiar with a variety of radical contemporary ideas and was personally involved with many of their exponents. The concept of natural forms as organised bodies, endowed with powers of sensation and reflection, occurs throughout his major poetry. In Book IX of *The Excursion* (1814), the character of the Wanderer speaks of 'An *active* Principle' which 'subsists / In all things, in all natures; in the stars / Of azure heaven, the unenduring clouds, / In flower and tree, in every pebbly stone / That paves the brooks, the stationary rocks, / The moving waters, and the invisible air' (IX.3–9). According to Piper, Shelley, too, who was widely read in the French materialist tradition, 'expresses all the leading ideas of the movement – that matter is "alive", that there is a pervading spirit co-eternal with the universe, that all things are governed by Necessity, and that they work out the will of the pervading

---

*   Piper (p. 193) points out that Keats's lines in *Hyperion*, II.206–28 make his poem 'almost the first recorded statement of the doctrine of evolution by natural selection'.

spirit in an evolution of nature and man towards perfection'.[4] Shelley's idea of matter as alive rather than inert is to be found in his early poem *Queen Mab* (1813), where, in terms which are very close to those of Wordsworth, he writes:

> Throughout this varied and eternal world
> Soul is the only element, the block
> That for uncounted ages has remained
> The moveless pillar of a mountain's weight
> Is active, living spirit. Every grain
> Is sentient both in unity and part. (IV.139–44)

His notion of man's perfectibility, as being conterminous with that of the material world, links man closely to his natural environment and looks towards a millennial prospect which will be a perfection of society as well as of the physical world:

> Spirit of Nature! Thou
> Life of interminable multitudes;
> Soul of those mighty spheres
> Whose changeless paths through heaven's deep silence lie;
> Soul of that smallest being.
> The dwelling of whose life
> Is one faint April sun-gleam;—
> Man, like these passive things,
> Thy will unconsciously fulfilleth:
> Like theirs, his age of endless peace,
> Which time is fast maturing,
> Will swiftly, surely come;
> And the unbounded frame, which thou pervadest,
> Will be without a flaw
> Marring its perfect symmetry. (III.226–40)

Shelley's phrase, 'Will swiftly, surely come', reflects the concept of Necessity, through which it was believed that man's progress, in sympathy with the natural world, would be one of steady and inevitable improvement. Piper points out that Volney, whose book *Les Ruines* (1791)* was immensely influential during the revolutionary period, was one among several contemporary theorists who believed that the natural world took a providential interest in mankind. He 'taught that "the secret power which animates the universe" had made man the architect of his own destiny through his sensibility to pleasure and pain, and that man must necessarily become happy'.[5]

Another radical figure, John Stewart,† and one with whom Wordsworth became acquainted in Paris, believed that 'atoms experienced "sufferings and enjoyments" and that a multiplied state of these formed "the patient feeling of a whole system" or "mode"'. Man was one of these modes or systems and men were 'the instruments of nature in its moral motion, formed to procure well-being or happiness to all animated matter'.[6] In a theory of natural philosophy extending to a rule of conduct, Stewart believed that, as all organised 'forms' of nature were alive and capable of feeling, it followed that 'Man must "do no violence to any part of animate matter"'.[7] Sentiments such as these lay behind the fight for animal rights, which began to gather momentum in the Romantic period,[8] as well as of such contributions to *Lyrical Ballads* (1798) as *The Ancient Mariner*‡ and 'Lines Left upon a Seat in a Yew-Tree'.§ The fourth book of Wordsworth's *Excursion* accentuates much of this contemporary ideology, including necessity and, most essentially, through man's sympathy with it, the moral efficacy of the natural world:

---

* Volney's *Ruins of Empire* is the book from which Frankenstein's Creature 'obtained a cursory knowledge of history'.

† He was known as 'Walking Stewart' because of the immense feats of pedestrianism which had taken him from India, through the Middle East and the whole of Europe. He was the acquaintance of many important radical figures of the day, including Thomas Paine. Thomas De Quincey, a close friend, records that Wordsworth was 'captivated by his eloquence' (See Piper, *The Active Universe*, p. 68.)

‡ 'He prayeth well who loveth well / Both man and bird and beast'; 'He prayeth best who loveth best, / All things both great and small' (ll. 645–8).

§ '[H]e, who feels contempt / For any living thing, hath faculties / Which he has never used [...] thought with him / Is in its infancy' (ll. 48–51).

For the Man—
Who […] communes with the Forms
Of nature, who with understanding heart
Both knows and loves such objects as excite
No morbid passions, no disquietude,
No vengeance, and no hatred—needs must feel
The joy of that pure principle of love
So deeply, that, unsatisfied with aught
Less pure and exquisite, he cannot choose
But seek for objects of a kindred love
In fellow-natures and a kindred joy. (IV.1207–17)

Lyrical Ballads (1798)

Lyrical Ballads with a few other poems is the result of a year-long collaboration between Wordsworth and Coleridge, and was published anonymously in 1798. In the Preface to the second edition of 1800, Wordsworth describes how part of his own purpose in contributing to the volume was to attempt, in the light of a rapidly changing society, to re-educate the sensibilities and demonstrate how 'the human mind is capable of being excited without the application of gross and violent stimulants'. In his own recollection of their joint enterprise, Coleridge recalls that Wordsworth's part in the division of labour between them was to direct the mind to nature, to 'the loveliness and the wonders of the world before us', not only by removing from our eyes 'the film of familiarity', but also by making us attuned to the sounds for which we have 'ears that hear not'.[9] Christ uses the 'eyes to see, ears to hear' terminology frequently and, in the use of this language, Coleridge acknowledges the 'importance' of a subject about which Wordsworth himself is emphatic,* and gives an almost religious status to their mutual purpose.

Observational accuracy is a characteristic of poems in the collection which prominently feature the natural world. Wordsworth writes, 'I

---

* 'The subject is indeed important!' (Preface).

have at all times endeavoured to look steadily at my subject; consequently, I hope that there is in these poems little falsehood of description'.[10] But the poems respond equally to nature's voices, the 'sounding cataract',[11] the song of the nightingale,[12] the 'still, sad music of humanity [...] of ample power / To chasten and subdue' ('Tintern Abbey', ll. 92–4), the 'thousand blended notes' of 'Lines Written in Early Spring'. This particular poem is a reminder that, in *Lyrical Ballads*, nature's presence elicits, in whatever form it takes, a positive response from Wordsworth and Coleridge. Their only negative response is in their sense of what man himself has done or is capable of doing. In its historical context, *Lyrical Ballads* is the product of its authors' reaction to disillusion with the French Revolution, and in 'Lines Written in Early Spring', it is the shadow of man falling across the peaceful setting which causes the poet grief and bewilderment at how the natural world can produce a being who preys upon his kind.

Although it tells a tale of sorts and is written in a variation of the ballad metre,* the poem bears out Wordsworth's remark in his Preface that 'the feeling therein developed gives importance to the action and situation, and not the action and situation to the feeling'. It presents an 'active' natural world which, in the light of Wordsworth's nature philosophy, lends more than a simple fancifulness to his 'faith that every flower / Enjoys the air it breathes' (ll. 11–12). All natural things are in harmony and cooperative. The birds' notes are 'blended', the twigs spread themselves out 'To catch the breezy air'. As in 'Anecdote for Fathers' where the 'careless mood' (l. 33) of the five-year-old boy contrasts with that of an adult who can only 'think, and think, and think again' (l. 14), the imponderable activity of the birds ('Their thoughts I cannot measure', l. 14) is set against the poet's own grief-laden cerebration: 'thoughts' (l. 4), 'think' (l. 7), 'think' (l. 19), 'thoughts' (l. 21). The poet's responsiveness to nature's attempt to 'link' his 'human soul' to 'her fair works' (stanza 2) is compromised by thoughts of 'Man's inhumanity to man',[13] bringing a poignant dirge-like tone ('sad', 'griev'd', 'wreathes', 'lament') to the 'Early Spring' promise of the title.

---

* Ballad Metre (as in *The Rime of the Ancient Mariner*) is commonly 4-stress, 3-stress. Here Wordsworth provides three 4-stress lines and a final 3-stress one.

'Lines Written a Few Miles above Tintern Abbey', the loco-topographical poem at the conclusion to the first edition of *Lyrical Ballads*, represents, in its welcome return to nature, Wordsworth's reaction to the revolutionary times in which he had been so recently and disturbingly involved. Its prolix subtitle, 'On Revisiting the Banks of the Wye during a Tour, July 13, 1798', points immediately to the tradition of 'picturesque' travel. Tourists at a much-visited spot such as this one* would take up a station from which to admire the view, carefully noting the time and date of their observations among other circumstantial details, common in 'picturesque' title-pages (see Part Four: Romantic Travel Writing). At first sight, therefore, this is a poem which sets up expectations that all the conventional approaches to landscape and the language of their expression will be recognised. As the poem progresses, however, it becomes something altogether different, removing the emphasis from the busy eye of the first eighteen lines, with their liberal use of the demonstrative pronoun ('this dark sycamore', 'these plots of cottage ground', 'these orchard tufts'), to place it instead on a landscape of the mind where the eye is finally 'made quiet' (l. 48).

Wordsworth had first come to the Wye Valley in 1793, when compelled to leave both France and his love, Annette Vallon, who was carrying his child, and had walked across southern England and into the West Country. The quiet return in the company of his sister Dorothy which the poem describes is significant in recalling the political events and the emotional turmoil he had experienced five years previously.

Although 'Tintern Abbey' is a poem about a companionable visit to a pleasant spot, its landscape for Wordsworth, Tom Paulin argues, is ominous and tragic, as well as beautiful.[14] Paulin's reading of 'Tintern Abbey' is important, and takes its direction from the poem's subtitle and the significance of the date it records. On 13 July 1793, five years to the day before 'Tintern Abbey' was written, the radical French

---

* Wordsworth was familiar with the work of the Reverend William Gilpin, including his *Observations on the River Wye, & Several Parts of South Wales &c. Relative Chiefly to Picturesque Beauty; Made in the Summer of the Year 1770* (1782).

politician Marat had been assassinated by Charlotte Corday,* and within a day of this date, four years previously, the French Revolution itself had begun.† Marat's death led to Robespierre and the Terror, and Wordsworth had himself experienced the fear of that time at first hand. The 13th of July was therefore a date full of revolutionary significance for him.

Paulin points to specific words and phrases in 'Tintern Abbey' which, he believes, lend support to his idea that Wordsworth, suffering from post-revolutionary survivor's guilt ('more like a man / Flying from something that he dreads') is experiencing 'flashbacks' to his urban life in revolutionary France ('the din / Of towns and cities'). His guilt about abandoning Annette combines with that of being a fellow-traveller with a ruthless political creed, whose ideology has been replaced by tyranny. Paulin believes that Wordsworth is unable to enjoy simple pleasure in the pastoral landscape that the poem describes because of the emotional baggage he brings to it. This is reflected in words which take on particular revolutionary overtones: 'plots' (l. 11), 'copses' for 'corpses' (l. 13) 'sick' in 'sycamore' (l. 10), even the ricochet of gunfire in the hard consonants of 'sounding cataract' (l. 77). Additional landscape features have possible similar connotations. The 'tall rock' (l. 78) might suggest the Tarpeian Rock from which, in antiquity, traitors to republican Rome were thrown, while 'The mountain' (l. 79) may have more recent political connotations for Wordsworth in being the name, in the French National Assembly, for the upper section of the chamber occupied by the revolutionary Jacobins.‡

Paulin makes out a case for 'Tintern Abbey' being an example of how the subconscious codes language in a way not necessarily recognised by the superego.§ Echoes of *Hamlet* and *Macbeth* in 'the fretful stir /

---

* Jacques-Louis David produced a famous painting of this event in which the figure of Marat, murdered in his bathtub, is made to look like a secular *pietà*.
† 14 July 1789.
‡ Leaders of The Mountain were Maximilien Robespierre, Georges Jacques Danton and Jean Paul Marat. They dominated a powerful political organisation called the Jacobin Club.
§ In Freud's terms, that part of the psyche which, at an unconscious level, blocks what it considers unacceptable to the conscious mind.

Unprofitable, and the fever of the world' (ll. 53–4)* suggest that Wordsworth's ostensibly tranquil re-visit poem ('Five years have passed') conceals a subtext of serious melancholy, while the political overtones are compounded further by the presence within the poem of the blind republican poet Milton. There are seven direct references to eyes or blindness in 'Tintern Abbey' (as well as 'cataract'), while the term 'half-extinguish'd thought' (l. 59) recalls Milton's Samson, 'But he, though blind of sight, / Despised, and thought extinguished quite'.[15] As Milton uses blindness as a metaphor for living in a monarchist state, Wordsworth may here be identifying himself with Samson. Additionally, words such as 'lofty', 'dim', 'sublime', and the term 'evil tongues' can all be traced to *Paradise Lost*, as can Wordsworth's 'light of setting suns', which recalls Lucifer who 'fell [...] and with the setting sun / Dropped from the zenith like a falling star' (I.743–5). Paulin concludes that it is Milton who has the last word in 'Tintern Abbey', with Dorothy Wordsworth in her 'solitary walk' (l. 136) inevitably recalling Adam and Eve who, 'Through Eden took their solitary way' (XII.648–9). If, therefore, the landscape of 'Tintern Abbey' is Wordsworth's and Dorothy's Eden, then Wordsworth's alter ego, Paulin would argue, is Adam, mourning the loss of his innocence.

In 'Tintern Abbey', Wordsworth substitutes a redemptive power in the natural world for the promise of a revolution which has since degenerated into bloodshed and imperialism. Using the language of the French materialist philosophy whose influence had helped him to emerge from a false political dream, he writes that he owes to the landscape's active, sentient 'forms of beauty' (l. 24), not only those 'sensations sweet' (l. 28) which have led to his 'tranquil restoration' (l. 31) but also, more significantly,

---

* 'How weary, stale, flat, and unprofitable / Seem to me all the uses of this world!' (*Hamlet*, I.ii.133–5). 'Duncan is in his grave; / After life's fitful fever he sleeps well' (*Macbeth*, III.iii.22–3). In Book X of *The Prelude*, Wordsworth had quoted from *Macbeth* when, in Paris, and removed by only 'a little month' from the September massacres, he 'seem'd to hear a voice that cried, / To the whole City, "Sleep no more"' (ll. 65, 76–7). See *Macbeth*, 'Methought I heard a voice cry, "Sleep no more!"' (II.ii.32).

feelings too
Of unremembered pleasure; such, perhaps,
As may have had no trivial influence
On that best portion of a good man's life;
His little, nameless, unremembered acts
Of kindness and of love. (ll. 31–6)

Wordsworth is saying that whenever he has performed an act of kindness, maybe one so small that he can no longer even remember it, his action has been influenced directly by these natural 'forms'. Nature for Wordsworth is a *moral* force, and the language of 'Tintern Abbey' suggests that the 'mighty world / Of eye and ear' (ll. 206–7) that 'never did betray / The heart that loved her' (ll. 123–4), is a kind of replacement for the deity itself. He describes nature as:

The anchor of my purest thoughts, the nurse,
The guide, the guardian of my heart, and soul
Of all my moral being. (ll. 110–12)

When he goes on to describe how also 'owed' to 'These forms of beauty' is his 'serene and blessed mood' (l. 42) enabling him to 'see into the life of things' (l. 50), Wordsworth means exactly the life of *things*, by which the material universe, active and providential on our behalf, can predispose us to the good. As Shelley would later write in *Queen Mab*:*

And the minutest atom comprehends
A world of loves and hatreds; these beget
Evil and good: hence truth and falsehood spring;
Hence will and thought and action, all the germs

---

* In Shelley's poem, Queen Mab, the Fairy Queen, awakens the soul of the sleeping Ianthe and, in a series of visions, shows her how a glorious future is open to men if they will abandon their evil ways and live according to the laws of reason and love. She is the same Queen Mab who is dismissed as fanciful and deceptive by Mercutio in *Romeo and Juliet* (I.iv.53–94), but who arguably reveals through dreams 'things true' (I.iv.52).

Of pain and pleasure, sympathy or hate,
That variegate the eternal universe. (IV.145–50)

Wordsworth's sense of this energy in matter is communicated
syntactically in the lines where he acknowledges 'A motion and a spirit,
that impels / All *thinking* things, all objects of all *thought* / And rolls
through all things' (my emphases: ll. 101–3).

Lyrical Ballads, primarily concerned with nature, systematically replaces
a concept of revolution through politics with a no less revolutionary, self-
established natural order. In 'Lines',[16] Dorothy Wordsworth is invited to
'Make haste' (l. 11) and 'with speed' (ll. 14, 38) 'resign' her 'morning
task', rather than pursue it (l. 11). She is instructed to 'bring no book'
(ll. 15, 39), and give her day over to 'idleness' (ll. 16, 40). Wordsworth's
'Lines' are intended to confront a society whose values are based solely on
study, diligence and industry. The French revolutionary calendar* is
replaced here with a 'living Calendar' by which Wordsworth and his sister
'regulate' their own chronology: 'We from today [...] will date / The
opening of the year' (ll. 19–20). They will obey 'laws' which their own
'hearts' have made (l. 29) and dance to their own tune ('We'll frame the
measure† of our souls / They shall be tuned to love', ll. 35–6). Their new
calendar, rather than recording days, weeks and months, will acknowledge
the sweet 'minute' (l. 2) the 'hour of feeling' (l. 24) and the sensual
'moment' (l. 25), while enslavement to 'joyless forms' (l. 27) will give
way to 'the blessed power that rolls / About, below, above' (ll. 33–4), the
language of 'Tintern Abbey' here used in a playful context.

In 'Expostulation and Reply', Wordsworth presents himself as
someone open to the 'impressive'‡ powers of nature (ll. 21–2), in
altercation with an interlocutor who, as the Advertisement to the 1798
edition remarks, was a friend 'somewhat unreasonably attached to
modern books of moral philosophy'. The poem begins,

* The Calendar of Reason with which the French Revolution replaced the Gregorian
  Calendar until its restoration in 1805.
† A 'measure' is a dance.
‡ The language of stanzas 5 and 6 reflects the sensationalist philosophy of John Locke and
  David Hartley, who conceived of the mind as passive and open to sense 'impressions'
  through which it gradually built up its understanding of the world.

'Why William, on that old grey stone,
'Thus for the length of half a day,
'Why William, sit you thus alone,
'And dream your time away?

'Where are your books? That light bequeath'd
'To beings else forlorn and blind!
'Up! Up! And drink the spirit breath'd
'From dead men to their kind.'

As the poem continues, the light-hearted difference between the two opponents recalls, earlier in the decade, the much more serious political debate between Burke and Paine, here arguing on the rights of man. In his *Reflections*, Burke had written:

We are afraid to put men to live and trade each on his own private stock of reason; because we suspect that this stock in each man is small, and that the individuals would do better to avail themselves of the general bank and capital of nations, and of ages.[17]

Paine replied:

I am contending for the rights of the *living*, and against their being willed away, and controlled and contracted for, by the manuscript assumed authority of the dead; and Mr Burke is contending for the authority of the dead over the rights and freedom of the living.[18]

In 'Expostulation and Reply', William's natural spontaneity and instinctiveness ('When life was sweet I knew not why', l. 14) are at odds with an unwholesome 'spirit breath'd / From dead men' as their bequest to the living. Again, the poem's celebration of nature, of 'things forever speaking' (l. 26), replaces revolutionary political debate with its own form of quiet radicalism.

Although, in terms of its contents, *Lyrical Ballads* has been shown to have much in common with contemporary magazine literature[19] and that, in order to make money out of it, Wordsworth obviously thought that he had made concessions to popular taste, Marilyn Butler has argued that the date of its publication was the most significant issue. She writes that there was nothing in Wordsworth's collection that could not have been written a decade earlier, and had it been published then, it would hardly, apart from its merit, have attracted attention. However, its subject matter, its simplicity of language and its democratic appeal to 'common life' (Preface) made *Lyrical Ballads* an inflammatory publication in a time of government suppression. 'As it was', Butler writes, 'literary excellence was an additional offence. It made Wordsworth readable, and therefore more dangerous.'[20] Wordsworth's language of natural description is certainly very accessible, avoiding the kind of tutored diction which had been employed to describe the natural world through much of the previous century. The clear, predominantly monosyllabic, opening of 'Lines' is typical:

> It is the first mild day of March:
> Each minute sweeter than before,
> The red breast sings from the tall larch
> That stands beside our door.
>
> There is a blessing in the air,
> Which seems a sense of joy to yield
> To the bare trees, and mountains bare,
> And grass in the green field.

The final line here, drawing attention to what elsewhere Wordsworth celebrates as the 'common growth of mother-earth',[21] accentuates the importance of the 'common' as it is used in his poetry. In one episode of *The Prelude*, he recalls how, wandering alone through the streets of London, and detached to the point where he was 'beyond / The reach of common indications' (VII.608–9), a salutary encounter with a blind beggar rebukes the poet's indifference to his fellows. Such is the importance Wordsworth usually attaches to the 'common' that, as *The Prelude* passage implies, to put ourselves beyond its reach is to put ourselves beyond the reach of the only thing that can save us.

John Clare and 'the Poetry of Earth'

Lyrical Ballads was the culmination of a growing emphasis in poetry on cultural primitivism and the value of the common, of which the revival of interest in the ballad tradition was itself an example. But the 'experiments', as Wordsworth describes his poems in the 1798 Advertisement, suggests an educated and conscious endeavour to subscribe to this taste, while the magisterial prose of the 1800 Preface demonstrates the distance between his own voice and that of the true 'peasant poet'. The eighteenth century saw a vogue for such people, including Stephen Duck, 'the Thresher Poet', Mary Collier, the 'Poetical Washerwoman', the 'milkmaid' poet Anne Yearsley, and Robert Bloomfield, the 'farmer poet' (see Part Three: 'Romantic Verse Narrative'). The two most celebrated figures in this line were the Ayrshire ploughman Robert Burns and the Northamptonshire peasant poet John Clare.

Both Burns and Clare, however, occupy a complex cultural position and belong to a broader circle than their designation as simply 'peasant' poets would suggest. After the success of the Kilmarnock edition of his poems in 1786, Burns was admitted to the sophisticated Edinburgh literary world, while his best compositions have become firmly established as part of an international song tradition. His second song editor, George Thomson, commissioned a whole group of British composers to set his songs to music, and in Europe, Pleyel, Haydn, Beethoven, Weber and Hummel produced chamber settings for his songs which often started life as simple folk melodies. Clare, like Burns, was musical. He played the fiddle and was the first serious collector of English folk material, gathering and transcribing several hundred songs.[22] He shared the same publisher as Keats,[*] who even drafted lines from 'Lamia' onto the back of a note Clare had sent to

---

[*]   John Taylor, of Taylor and Hessey, publishers.

Taylor. The two poets never met, but they did exchange views and books.[23] Clare, as a worker in the fields, distinguished his own intimate knowledge of the natural world from that of Keats, whose 'descriptions of scenery', he writes, 'are often very fine but as it is the case with other inhabitants of great cities he often described nature as she appeared to his fancies & not as he would have described her had he witnessed the things he describes'.[24] Keats, in turn, on being shown Clare's poem 'Solitude' (1821), observed that 'the Description too much prevailed over the Sentiment'.[25] But as Jonathan Bate remarks, 'For Clare [...] description is sentiment.'[26] Clare's descriptions of the natural world are largely localised, being confined to the immediate environs of Helpston where he lived, but with their concepts of liberty, equality, fraternity and, above all, feeling, they share much that is central to the Romantic period.

Wordsworth, before being 'call'd forth / From the retirement of [his] native hills' had never dreamt, as he writes in *The Prelude*, 'of aught / More grand, more fair, more exquisitely fram'd / Than those few nooks to which my happy feet / Were limited' (XI.224–30). Unlike that of Wordsworth, Clare's experience never really extended beyond the landscape of within a few miles' radius from his birthplace, but he shares with Wordsworth a deep love of place, and that same bond of fellowship with which Wordsworth was 'early tutor'd [...] / To look with feelings of fraternal love / Upon those unassuming things, that hold / A silent station in this beauteous world' (XII.49–52). Although many of Wordsworth's formative moments were part of nature's ministry of fear and took place in settings of natural sublimity, the basis on which the reputation of his poetry is built is equally one of his love for, and identification with, the commonplace features of the natural world. John Constable, who shared with Wordsworth and Clare a deep attachment to locality, and who was a correspondent of Wordsworth's, focused on the common things of nature for his inspiration as an artist: 'The sound of water escaping from mill-dams, old rotten banks, shiny posts and brickwork – these scenes made me a painter – and I am grateful.'[27] Clare's lines from 'The Moorhen's Nest' (*c.* 1812–31) reflect an identical responsiveness to the small-scale and often disregarded, itemising the visual objects but at the same time investing them with the feeling of his much-used 'I love':

A gate whose posts are two old dotterel trees,
A close with molehills sprinkled o'er its leas,
A little footbrig with its crossing rail,
A wood-gap stopped with ivy-wreathing pale,
A crooked stile each path-crossed spinney owns,
A brooklet forded by its stepping stones,
A wood-bank mined with rabbit-holes—and then
An old oak leaning o'er a badger's den
Whose cave-mouth enters 'neath the twisted charms
Of its old roots and keeps it safe from harms,
Pickaxes, spades, and all its strength confounds
When hunted foxes hide from chasing hounds.
Then comes the meadows where I love to see
A flood-washed bank support an aged tree. (ll. 67–80)

Clare's situation as an agricultural worker contributes to his awareness of the smallest goings-on in nature, many of which are observed, not from the superior vantage-point of the picturesque tourist or landscape artist, but from his physical position literally at ground level. In the intimacy it holds with the natural world, Clare's best poetry is reminiscent of the prose writings of the American naturalist Henry David Thoreau, whose acute observational eye leads to such journal entries as, 'I had no idea there was so much going on in Heywood's meadow',[28] a line that could almost have been written by Clare himself.

Where Coleridge and Wordsworth find a freedom in nature ('Oh Liberty! My spirit felt thee there')[29] that had been denied to them by political revolution, Clare in his nature poetry describes a landscape of loss and exclusion that had both deeply personal as well as political implications. As he grew into manhood, the 'open field' system, allowing a shared ownership to rural communities and making the freedom of his sort of childhood possible, was gradually being replaced by a process of economics-dictated 'enclosure'. Much of the land once held in common, permitting him to wander at will and develop his familiarity with the minutest natural details, was now closed off, so that in a poem like 'The Moors' (1827), words like 'commons' and 'little' have taken on a new and regrettable significance for him. The common people have disappeared from the land they once held in common, and 'Each little path [...] Where little flowers bloomed round' has been 'stopped' by people who privilege economics and proprietorship over genuine freedom:

> Moors losing from the sight, far, smooth and blea,
> Where swopt the plover in its pleasure free,
> Are vanished now with commons wild and gay
> As poets' visions of life's early day [...]
> Fence now meets fence in owners' little bounds
> Of field and meadow, large as garden grounds,
> In little parcels little minds to please
> With men and flocks imprisoned, ill at ease. (ll. 37–50)

For Clare, 'Enclosure like a Bonaparte let not a thing remain',[30] so that the natural world was increasingly a reminder of political tyranny rather than of freedom:

> There once were lanes in nature's freedom dropt,
> There once were paths that every valley wound—
> Enclosure came and every path was stopped;
> Each tyrant fixed his sign where paths were found,
> To hint a trespass now who crossed the ground.[31]

These lines, described by Clare's London patron Admiral Lord Radstock as 'radical slang',[32] point to a strong democratic sentiment in Clare, reflecting principles of the revolutionary decade which had by this time (1821), for Wordsworth and Coleridge, long been commuted into conservatism. In 'The Lament of Swordy Well' (composed 1821–4, published 1835), Clare makes the enclosed land speak for its own rights as territory that, in pre-enclosure times, had offered communally supportive hospitality to animals and men alike:

> There was a time my bit of ground
> Made freemen of the slave;
> The ass no pinar'd dare to pound
> When I his supper gave;
> The gypsies' camp was not afraid,
> I made his dwelling free,
> Till vile enclosure came and made
> A parish slave of me. (ll. 177–84)

The word 'parish' for Clare is double-edged, in having not only the positive implications of belonging to a community, but also the negative sense of being thrown on the parish (as Clare's father was), being made the recipient of Poor Relief and deprived of one's freedom. The revolutionary principles of fraternity and liberty (*fraternité, liberté*) are therefore very immediate issues in Clare's poetry. Whereas nature should stand for freedom, it has been turned into a mode of imprisonment, and in the manner of John 'Walking' Stewart who had afforded 'rights' to all organised forms of nature, Clare identifies not just with the rights of all living things such as animals and birds, but with the natural topography itself as being in every way his equal. In 'The Lamentations of Round-Oak Waters' (composed 1818, published 1835), he finds as much an 'equal' (*égalité*) in the speaking stream which identifies with his sorrow, as Robert Burns a 'fellow mortal' in the mouse whose nest he disturbs.[33] Clare's comparable poem, 'Field Mouse's Nest' (*c.* 1832–7), free from Burns's attached moral sentiments, exemplifies the way in which his poetry refuses to discriminate among natural phenomena by placing the beautiful before the grotesque, or privilege one thing over another. In addressing a fallen elm tree as 'Friend not inanimate', Clare transmits to the natural world the sentiments which had informed the best principles of the French Revolution, for, as Jonathan Bate remarks, the word 'friend' is suggestive of radical philanthropy. Clare, who spent almost thirty years confined in lunatic asylums, had good reason to sympathise with the vulnerability of creatures* as well as of the landscapes on which his poetry so often focuses. The systematic defamiliarisation of a natural world upon which his identity was dependent, and with which he was so emotionally involved, appears to have induced a psychosis, supporting, albeit tragically, Wordsworth's conviction of 'How exquisitely the individual Mind [...] / to the external world / Is fitted, and how exquisitely too [...] / The external world is fitted to the mind'.[34]

William Blake and the Limits of the Natural World

In a letter to Dr John Trusler (1799), Blake wrote, 'The tree which moves some to tears of joy is in the Eyes of others only a Green thing that stands in the way.'[35] One of Blake's marginal commentaries on his 1815 edition of Wordsworth's poems reads, 'You shall not bring me down to believe such fitting and fitted I know better & Please your Lordship.' For Blake, Wordsworth's consciousness of his own responses to nature implied a separation between the self and the universe.† Commenting on Wordsworth's 'The Influence of Natural Objects',‡ Blake writes, 'Natural objects always did & now do weaken, deaden and obliterate imagination in me.' As Northrop Frye comments, 'Blake criticized Wordsworth sharply for ascribing to nature what he should have ascribed to his own mind and for believing in the correspondence of the human and natural orders.'[36] For Blake, Wordsworth's 'mighty world / Of eye and ear', and the details of nature which so delighted the eyes and ears of a poet like Clare, are a form of sensual imprisonment, confining man to what he saw as a barren world of objects and materialism. He is not interested in what Clare sees as beauty in the

---

* Jonathan Bate remarks that in his many poems about the nests of birds, the 'vulnerability of the nest [...] becomes an analogue for the vulnerability of his own being-in-the-world': Jonathan Bate, *The Song of the Earth* (London: Picador, 2000), p. 158. A good example is 'The Pettichap's Nest'.

† See William Hazlitt, who remarked of Wordsworth, 'It is as if there were nothing, but himself and the universe' (*The Round Table*).

‡ The skating scene, later incorporated into *The Prelude*, Book I.

elusive pettichap or the solitary snipe,* he writes in *The Marriage of Heaven and Hell* (1793):

> How do you know but ev'ry Bird that cuts the airy way,
> Is an immense world of delight, clos'd by your senses five?
>
> (Plate 6)

For Blake, as a mystic, it was important to transcend the material world, the visible evidence of man's original transgression, through what he called the 'supreme delight' of his 'fourfold vision'.[37] In his Introduction to *Songs of Experience* (1794), 'The starry floor / The watry shore' are the limits of man's fall, which are 'giv'n thee till the break of day'. In other words, the natural world, for Blake, is not something given as a gift to be celebrated, but something 'giv'n' in the sense of imposed, until earth's 'fallen light' can be renewed. Blake makes use of nature as a symbolist and a revolutionary. 'Where man is not', he writes, 'nature is barren.'[38] In 'Holy Thursday' from *Songs of Innocence* (1789), the river, the flowers, the wind and thunder are all prominent in the lyric, but they have a purposive function which gives them a significance beyond being simply natural phenomena.

'Holy Thursday' records an annual service in Lent, when children attended St Paul's Cathedral to give thanks to the patrons and founders of their charity schools. Their colourful procession ('red & blue & green'), strictly regimented ('two & two') by 'Grey-headed beadles', gradually begins to lose its regimentation as the river simile replaces their 'walking' with its 'flow'. Where the River Thames gliding 'at his own sweet will' would be sufficient of itself as a touching or majestic sight for Wordsworth,[39] in Blake's poem, the presence of the children, who 'like Thames waters flow', begins to take on the power of an inundation. And from this sense of an irresistible flood, their simple pairings develop into 'multitudes', and then into 'thousands' as they raise 'the voice of song' first, 'like a mighty wind', and then as 'thunderings'. Blake, through this developing sequence of natural images, gives an overwhelming potency to innocence and thus raises an

* See 'The Pettichap's Nest' and 'The Snipe'.

82

awareness of the rights of children in a society which traditionally denies them a voice. One of Blake's few illustrations to Shakespeare ('Pity'), illustrates the part of his soliloquy where Macbeth, hesitating to murder Duncan, imagines that if he were to do so,

> pity, like a naked new-born babe,
> Striding the blast, or heaven's cherubin, hors'd
> Upon the sightless couriers of the air,
> Shall blow the horrid deed in every eye,
> That tears shall drown the wind. (I.vii.21–5)

In Shakespeare's image, the weak, defenceless baby, suddenly endowed, like the children in Blake's lyric, with enormous strength, represents the power of innocence, for which the elements at their most forceful are the appropriate metaphors.

Blake's concept of innocence is imaged as something primordial, and the natural world contributes to the deliberate naivety and simplicity of his *Innocence* lyrics. Blake is writing songs *of* innocence, rather than the hymns by contemporaries which, from the superior assumptions of the adult perspective, were written *for* children, such as Christopher Smart's *Hymns for the Amusement of Children* (1775), Charles Wesley's *Hymns for Children* (1763), and Isaac Watts's *Divine and Moral Songs for the Use of Children* (first dated edition 1715). Blake, opening up avenues for the imagination rather than closing down options, writes 'happy songs' that 'Every child may joy to hear',[40] and conscripts the energy of the natural world to symbolise that joy. Innocence, for Blake, is to be alive to the world. He does not subscribe, as Wordsworth, Shelley and others do, to the active universe of French materialist thought, but, being from a dissenting background, responds more to imagery which is grounded in a biblical tradition, that of visions and emblems, as well as to the medieval, gothic style with which he became familiar when making pencil sketches of the royal tombs in Westminster Abbey.* The lyrical poetry of *Songs of Innocence and of Experience* is a series of engraved,

---

* Apprenticed to the engraver James Basire, Blake was employed at an early age to make drawings of the royal tombs in Westminster Abbey.

interrelating words and images, making use of the organic natural forms which gothic art imitated. 'Grecian Art is Mathematic Form,' he writes, 'Gothic is Living Form',[41] and the plates of the lyrics are a reflection of the free forms and flowing lines of living, natural things.

The *Innocence* lyrics present a world in which, as in the painting *Peaceable Kingdom* (1834) by the American artist Edward Hicks (1780–1849), adults and children, different races, predatory animals and domestic ones, live in harmony together within a nurturing and enclosing natural environment. S. F. Bolt, in a seminal essay, 'The Songs of Innocence' (1947),[42] has shown how Blake went to great lengths to achieve the self-contained and peculiar naivety of these poems. He ensures that natural descriptions are almost devoid of the use of adjectives which 'inevitably introduces the personality of the observer'. So, for example, Wordsworth himself contributes loneliness to the cloud in 'Daffodils', but in Blake's poems, where adjectives do appear, they are used simply to define characteristics which are typical of the things they describe. Birds in 'Nurse's Song' are 'little', sheep in 'The Lamb' are 'wooly', woods in 'Laughing Song' are 'green'. There is a sense, too, that in his 'happy songs' Blake is stating that writing is *against* the song. The 'rural pen' of the Introduction to *Innocence* has 'stain'd the water clear'. In 'A Memorable Fancy' (*The Marriage of Heaven and Hell*), Blake, in the terms of his own mythology, writes of how he 'was in a Printing house in Hell & saw the method in which knowledge is transmitted from generation to generation'. The editors of the Norton Anthology note that here he 'allegorizes his procedure in designing, etching, printing and binding his works of imaginative genius'.[43] These then, as Blake himself writes, 'were receiv'd by Men […], and took the forms of books & were arranged in libraries'. Nature, in a poem from *Innocence* such as 'Laughing Song', effectively abandons the written word to communicate itself in the simple expressive utterance of its refrain, 'Ha, Ha, He':

> When the green woods laugh with the voice of joy
> And the dimpling stream runs laughing by,
> When the air does laugh with our merry wit,
> And the green hill laughs with the noise of it.

When the meadows laugh with lively green
And the grasshopper laughs in the merry scene,
When Mary and Susan and Emily,
With their sweet round mouths sing Ha, Ha, He.

When the painted birds laugh in the shade
Where our table with cherries and nuts is spread
Come live & be merry and join with me,
To sing the sweet chorus of Ha, Ha, He.

Read in the context of 'improving' verse, which made use of living creatures such as ants and bees to encourage work and industry,* Blake's handling of the ant and the glow-worm in 'A Dream' (*Innocence*) is quietly subversive. In his dream he hears the cry of a lost and 'heart-broke' emmet [ant]:

O my children! Do they cry,
Do they hear their father sigh.
Do they look abroad to see,
Now return and weep for me.

Its lament is heard by a glow-worm, one of Wordsworth's 'unassuming things, that hold / A silent station in this beauteous world', who is made to say:

I am set to light the ground,
While the beetle goes his round:
Follow now the beetle's hum,
Little wanderer hie thee home.

In other words, the conventionally 'busy' ant, 'Troubled wildered and

---

* See, for example, John Bunyan's divine emblem 'Upon the Pismire' [an ant] based on Proverbs 6:6: 'Go to the ant, thou sluggard; consider her ways and be wise', or Isaac Watts's 'Against Idleness and Mischief': 'How doth the little busy bee / Improve each shining hour'.

forlorn / Dark benighted travel worn', is saved and put on the right path by the light of the 'idle' glow-worm. And furthermore, Blake's dream, 'Where on grass methought I lay', shows him as already adopting the glow-worm's procedure of doing nothing very much.

Natural objects serve the same symbolic purpose in *Songs of Experience*, although, in this darker world, the happy piper of the Introduction of *Innocence* is replaced in the *Experience* Introduction by the more severe figure of 'the Bard', invoking the masses to return to grace, in a time of political turbulence (1794). If, in *Innocence*, the natural world is represented by images of harmony and reciprocity, it is used in *Experience* to polarise and introduce division and apartness. Thus, 'My Pretty ROSE TREE' seems to be a lyric about jealousy and the complexities of possessive love. 'A Poison Tree' makes use of imagery from the Garden of Eden, but tells a darker story of a friendship which turns out to be something else, a tale of self-loathing projected onto another. 'The Sick Rose' carries a web of meanings which seem to imply sexual knowledge, the 'storm' of existence and, perhaps, the Fall seen as the collapse of the English Commonwealth, when happiness, the bed of 'crimson joy', was replaced by monarchy's repression.

For Romantic writers such as those examined above, nature became a special focus for inspiration, offering, through the scientific enquiries of the age, a new understanding of creation, and of man's place within it. As well as providing a source of fulfilment sufficient in itself, or of consolation in a time of political disillusion, the natural world could also, as it did for Blake, suggest the power of the Imagination to transcend its material limits.

Extended Commentary: Blake, 'The Tyger' (*Songs of Experience*, 1794)

In probably the most famous lyric from *Songs of Experience*, the polarity exists in the distinction the reader is invited to consider between the compassionate God of mercy, the creator of 'The Lamb' in the *Songs of*

Innocence, and the fearsome God of justice, maker of 'The Tyger'. The 'deeps or skies' invite speculation on heaven and hell which, in the context of this lyric, reflects Blake's radical reassessment of orthodox teachings about the Creator. As with the other lyrics from the collection, Blake engraved, decorated and coloured the plate by hand, and the poem is a very interesting example of how, in the *Songs*, text and image relate to each other. Blake ensures that a reader of these lyrics would also be looking, contemporaneously, at a picture, and in this particular poem there is a peculiar incongruity between the fearsome tiger described in the text and the often innocuous-looking image in variants of the plate. The cuddly creature, in some versions wearing a smile on its face, seems to belong more to the world of childlike innocence than to the dangerous 'forests of the night' of *Experience*. The poem shares the expressiveness of the other songs, which, in their visual detail and simple rhythms, suggest that Blake wanted them remembered and passed on, focusing on their orality, the spoken tradition in poetry which preceded the written form.

At first sight, and this was clearly Blake's intention, *Songs of Innocence and of Experience* looks like a child's picture-book. As many critics have shown, Blake worked within a tradition of such writing, but did so in order to subvert it, challenging those writers whose intention was to shape and control children's minds through books of instruction and improvement, and allowing the child instead to engage imaginatively with texts which were open-ended and uncertain of reference.

Since it was written, it is true to say that 'The Tyger' has become as much the property of children as other classic texts directed specifically at them. The primitive quality which it shares with Henri Rousseau's* 'tiger' pictures, makes it visually memorable, while its insistent trochaic metre lends it perfectly to recital by children in exactly the same way as a nursery rhyme like 'Twinkle, twinkle, little star'.[44] Blake shares the immediacy of his responsiveness to the natural world with John Clare. The opening of Clare's 'The Pettichap's Nest' (1835), 'Well, in my many walks I rarely found / A place less likely for a bird to form / Its nest', carries the same 'presence' of something observed at once, rather than

---

* Henri ('Le Douanier') Rousseau (1844–1910), French primitive painter.

'recollected in tranquillity'.* 'Tyger Tyger' brings the creature immediately before our eyes, just as, later in the poem, as Frankenstein with his Creature, we watch it as it comes alive, 'And when thy heart began to beat'.

The 'Modern Prometheus' of Mary Shelley's story is a reminder, however, that Blake's use of the natural world in 'The Tyger' takes its revolutionary purpose beyond the common observation of poets such as Clare, and into the more universal territories of myth and politics (see Part Four: Faith, Myth and Doubt). Prometheus, the creator (Prometheus Plasticator), is embedded into the second stanza of 'The Tyger' ('What the hand, dare sieze [sic] the fire?'), as Blake begins to speculate on the nature of creators and the creative process.† As well as the myth of Prometheus in stanza 2, Blake includes that of Daedalus and Icarus, and the fall of Lucifer. Daedalus, constructor of the Cretan labyrinth, shares with Prometheus the role of craftsman or maker. He warned his son, Icarus, that since the wings he had made on which they would both escape from the labyrinth were held together by wax, they should avoid flying too near to the sun. Icarus disobeyed and fell to the sea. In common with Prometheus, therefore, who rebelled against Jupiter, Icarus represents rebelliousness, and shares his fall with Lucifer ('When the stars threw down their spears'),‡ who was cast out from heaven for refusing to serve God ('Non serviam'). In a complex cluster of mythic allusion and meaning, Blake creates a combination of suffering, creativity, rebellion, and imaginative 'Energy'.[45]

The 'fearful symmetry' of the tiger, as well as pointing to its symmetrical black and tawny stripes, may involve, too, the Burkean categories of sublimity and beauty. The tiger is a creature of beauty, but one which also inspires fear. Burke, in his essay on the sublime and the beautiful, discusses the horse as just such a creature which, in different contexts, can be a 'useful beast, fit for the plough' or, when its *neck is clothed with thunder*

---

* Wordsworth: 'Poetry [...] takes its origin from emotion recollected in tranquillity', Preface to *Lyrical Ballads*.

† For a fuller discussion of the Prometheus myth, see Part Four: 'Heroes and Anti-heroes'.

‡ See Urizen's lament: 'The stars threw down their spears & fled naked away. / We fell' (*The Four Zoas*, V.64:27–8), an allusion to the war in Heaven in *Paradise Lost* and the Book of Revelation.

and it '*swalloweth the ground with fierceness and rage*' can inspire the 'terrible and the sublime'.[46] Burke's *Reflections on the Revolution in France* (1790) reveal his later anxieties about 'terror', for him 'the ruling principle of the sublime'.[47] In France, as Christine Kenyon-Jones has remarked, accounts of the Revolution and its 'Terror' frequently compared the French republicans to predatory beasts. *The Times* of 7 January 1792 claimed that 'now loose from all restraints' the French were 'more vicious than wolves or tigers', while in the same newspaper on 26 July 1793, Marat's eyes were described as resembling 'those of the tyger cat'.[48] In his memorable description of the tiger 'burning bright, / In the forests of the night', Blake's revolutionary sympathies may have led him to think of England's Commonwealth and, in particular, of Andrew Marvell, Milton's Latin Secretary during the Protectorate. In the poem, 'Bermudas' (composed 1653–4, published 1681), Marvell's lines, 'He hangs in shades the orange bright / Like golden lamps in a green night', anticipate the tiger's golden eyes that Blake may have in mind, while its tawny coat in the green forest recalls, too, Marvell's lines in 'Upon Appleton House' (first published 1681): 'The tawny Mowers enter next; / Who seem like *Israelites* to be, / Walking on foot through a green sea'. The 'burning' tiger may also be suggesting the flame-like pattern and colour of its coat. In the poem, fire is prominently featured in the 'furnace' from which the smith (Roman, Vulcan; Greek, Hephaestus), with 'hammer' and 'anvil', creates forms from inchoate material. Blake, we must assume, as himself an artist and creator, identifies with the kind of energy and creativity he so admires in the mythic figures he has included in the poem. Milton's Satan (Lucifer) was, in his reading of *Paradise Lost* (1667), the hero of the epic (see Part Four: 'Heroes and Anti-heroes'). His inclusion of Daedalus anticipates Stephen Dedalus, in Joyce's *Portrait of the Artist as a Young Man* (1916) who, as an aspiring 'Romantic' artist himself, must 'fly by the nets' of Irish nationalism, language and religion 'to forge in the smithy of [his] soul' what he describes as 'the uncreated conscience of my race'. 'I will not serve', he says, echoing Lucifer's words, 'that in which I no longer believe.'

It is this heroic energy which leads Blake to question the division which the orthodox make between Christ and the Devil. Rather than our being obliged to reconcile an infinitely merciful with an infinitely terrible God, Blake suggests that we should abandon this concept and begin to think of Jesus and Lucifer as one and the same. Christ, in Blake's conception, is not the 'pale Galilean'[49] of orthodox belief, but an imaginative revolutionary and, like his tiger, full of beauty and energy. 'Deeps' and 'skies' are not, therefore, to be seen as divorced from each other and in endless opposition. There should instead, Blake thinks, be a 'Marriage of Heaven and Hell' to make up the kind of unity he presents in the *Innocence* lyrics.

On the basis of this construction, therefore, the disparity in 'The Tyger' between text and plate makes sense. Blake is saying that prophetic, imaginative, artistic people have always been in danger of being looked upon with fear by the orthodox, and especially by those in society who have a vested interest in keeping *things as they are*.* 'The tygers of wrath are wiser than the horses of instruction', he writes,[50] and, to compound this conception, Romantic art has several examples of horses being attacked by terrifying predatory beasts. George Stubbs's *White Horse frightened by a Lion* is one example,† while the French Romantic Eugène Delacroix (1798–1863) did several paintings on this theme. The pale horse of orthodoxy will always be afraid of the 'tigerish' spirit. Blake's own illustrations of 'The Tyger' (of which there are several variants) are often far from terrifying. As well as being sometimes made to look innocuous, the 'tyger' is painted, not as the text depicts it, 'In the forests of the night', but in broad daylight, under a blue sky. In 'Auguries of Innocence',‡ Blake writes:

> We are led to Believe a Lie
> When we see not Thro the Eye,
> Which was Born in a Night to perish in a Night,
> When the Soul Slept in Beams of Light.
> God Appears & God is Light

---

* *Things as they Are; or The Adventures of Caleb Williams*, William Godwin's indictment of English society in his novel of 1794.

† George Stubbs (1724–1806).

‡ Composed between 1801 and 1805 but not published until 1863.

To those poor Souls who dwell in Night,
But does a Human Form Display
To those who Dwell in Realms of day. (ll. 125–32)

The implication of Blake's image for 'The Tyger' is that, if seen for what they truly are, society's imaginative figures are not terrifying at all. Although enlightened, they are harmless. In the change from 'Could frame' (l. 4) to the rhetorical 'Dare frame' of the final line, Blake moves to answer his own question. The 'immortal hand or eye' belongs to any creative visionary. Blake himself as framer, forger (as in a smithy) and creator advises his readers not to be frightened out of their wits by people they may mistakenly think of as tigerish. He is saying to them that, as a visionary poet, and an artist himself, he is really no more to be feared than the 'pussy-cat' tiger, the image on the plate. In such original and engaging poetry, Blake makes his symbolic approach to the natural world revolutionary, at a time when nature was often being employed as a form of reaction to revolution.

Notes

1   Nicolas Roe, *Wordsworth and Coleridge: The Radical Years* (Oxford: Clarendon Press, 1988), p. 233.
2   H. W. Piper, *The Active Universe: Pantheism and the Concept of Imagination in the English Romantic Poets* (London: Athlone Press, 1962).
3   Ibid., p. 25.
4   Ibid., p. 165.
5   Ibid., p. 22.
6   Ibid., pp. 70–1, quoting Stewart.
7   Ibid., p. 71.
8   See D. Perkins, *Romanticism and Animal Rights* (Cambridge: Cambridge University Press, 2003). Christine Kenyon-Jones, *Kindred Brutes: Animals in Romantic-Period Writing* (Aldershot: Ashgate, 2001).
9   S. T. Coleridge, *Biographia Literaria*, ch. 14.
10 Preface to *Lyrical Ballads*.
11 'Lines Written a Few Miles above Tintern Abbey', l. 77.
12 Coleridge, 'The Nightingale'.

13   Compare Robert Burns, 'Man was Made to Mourn: A Dirge' (1784), stanza 7.

14   'Paulin on Wordsworth: The Secrets of "Tintern Abbey"', BBC Four, 2002. See also Tom Paulin, *Crusoe's Secret: The Aesthetics of Dissent* (London: Faber, 2005), pp. 138–63.

15   *Samson Agonistes*, l. 1687.

16   'Lines Written at a Small Distance from My House and Sent by My Little Boy to the Person to Whom They Are Addressed'.

17   Edmund Burke, *Reflections on the Revolution in France*, ed. Conor Cruise O'Brien (Harmondsworth: Penguin, 1968), p. 183.

18   Thomas Paine, *Rights of Man*, ed. Henry Collins (Harmondsworth: Penguin, 1969), p. 64.

19   See Robert Mayo, 'The Contemporaneity of the *Lyrical Ballads*', *Publications of the Modern Language Association of America*, 69 (1954), pp. 486–522.

20   Marilyn Butler, *Romantics, Rebels and Reactionaries: English Literature and its Background 1760–1830* (Oxford: Oxford University Press, 1981), p. 61.

21   'Peter Bell', stanza 27.

22   See George Deacon, *John Clare and the Folk Tradition* (London: Sinclair Browne, 1983).

23   See Mina Gorji, *John Clare and the Place of Poetry* (Liverpool: Liverpool University Press, 2008), p. 2.

24   J. W. and Anne Tibble, *The Prose of John Clare* (London: Routledge & Kegan Paul, 1951), p.223.

25   See Jonathan Bate, *John Clare: A Biography* (London: Picador, 2003), p. 189.

26   John Clare, *Selected Poems*, ed. Jonathan Bate (London: Faber, 2003), p. xvii.

27   Quoted in Kenneth Clark, *Civilisation: A Personal View* (London: John Murray, 1969), p. 281.

28   Bradford Torrey and Francis H. Allen (eds), *The Journal of Henry D. Thoreau*, 2 vols (New York: Dover Publications, 1962), vol. 1, p. 148.

29   Coleridge, 'France: An Ode'.

30   'Remembrances', in John Clare, *Selected Poems*, p. 134.

31   'The Village Minstrel', in John Clare, *Selected Poems*, pp. 36–7.

32   See Bate, *John Clare: A Biography*, p. 219.

33   'To a Mouse: on turning her up in her nest with the plough, November 1785'.

34   William Wordsworth, *The Poetical Works of William Wordsworth*, ed. E. de Selincourt and Helen Darbishire, 6 vols (Oxford: Clarendon Press, 1949), vol. 5, p. 339.

35 William Blake, letter to Dr John Trusler, 23 August 1799: *The Letters of William Blake, and Related Documents*, ed. Geoffrey Keynes, 3rd edn (Oxford: Clarendon Press, 1980), p. 9.

36 Northrop Frye, *Fearful Symmetry: A Study of William Blake* (Princeton: Princeton University Press, 1947), p. 39.

37 S. Foster Damon, *A Blake Dictionary: The Ideas and Symbols of William Blake* (Brown University Press, 1988), p. 436.

38 *The Marriage of Heaven and Hell* (Plate 10).

39 'Composed Upon Westminster Bridge, September 2, 1802'.

40 Introduction, *Songs of Innocence*.

41 'On Virgil'.

42 Margaret Bottrall (ed.), *William Blake: Songs of Innocence and Experience* (Basingstoke: Macmillan, 1970), pp. 114–22.

43 Stephen Greenblatt (ed.), *The Norton Anthology of English Literature*, 8th edition (New York and London: Norton, 2006), vol. 2, p. 117.

44 'The Star' from *Rhymes for the Nursery* (1806) by Jane Taylor (1793–1824).

45 See 'Energy is Eternal Delight', *The Marriage of Heaven and Hell*, Plate 4, 'The Voice of the Devil'.

46 Edmund Burke, *A Philosophical Enquiry into the Origin of our Ideas of the Sublime and Beautiful*, ed. Adam Phillips (Oxford: Oxford University Press, 1990), p. 60. Burke is quoting Job 39:19, 24 (misquoted).

47 Ibid., p. 54.

48 Kenyon-Jones, *Kindred Brutes*, p. 46.

49 Swinburne, 'Hymn to Proserpine'.

50 *The Marriage of Heaven and Hell*, Plate 9.

Dramatic Writing: Walpole, Southey and Byron

The Romantic period is not usually known for the prominence of its theatre, and the Romantic poets' desire to write plays has often been regarded as a misapplication of their talents. Yet interest in drama was intense during these years and extended into many areas of life not immediately associated with playwriting and theatre-going. Parliamentary proceedings, electioneering, royal and legal processions, public executions, art exhibitions and military spectacle all involved theatricality of one kind or another, and the age saw an upsurge in different forms of performance, not simply main-piece dramas, but musical interludes, pageant, farce, pantomime and melodrama.

Spoken drama was permitted by patent granted to the two major London playhouses, Drury Lane and Covent Garden, while the Stage Licensing Act (1737) ensured that all plays were submitted to the Lord Chamberlain's Office for censorship. The theatre was not, at this time, the respectable venue for an attentive playgoing public, but had long been associated with various forms of disorderly and immoral conduct, as well as being suspiciously regarded by government as an alternative meeting place for dissident political activity. Playhouses which did not have a royal patent were known as 'minors', catering for alternative forms of popular entertainment and extending beyond the central area of London. William Wordsworth, in *The Prelude*, refers to one of these, 'Half-rural Sadler's Wells', where 'more than once' he took his seat to see 'Singers, Rope-dancers, Giants and Dwarfs, / Clowns, Conjurors, Posture-masters, Harlequins, / Amid the uproar of the rabblement, / Perform their feats' (VII.288, 293–6).

The theatres themselves operated a system of audience stratification where the box, the gallery and the pit ensured that class differences were observed and reinforced. During the revolutionary decade of the 1790s the tendency was for these divisions to crumble, just as distinctions between the drama of the patent theatres and that of the minors also began to erode. As a consequence of the new order in society, the fashionable world inclined to drift away from the playhouses, and private theatricals became popular among members of the upper classes, who believed that legitimate theatre was under threat from the kind of entertainment to which Wordsworth refers above.

During the Romantic period the nature of theatre was such that performance was only part of a playgoer's experience. Dancers, singers, musicians, set designers, visual artists and creators of mechanical special effects all contributed to ensure that a play was a multi-media event.

Serious theatre involved the staging of Shakespeare, the Restoration and early eighteenth-century dramatists, as well as prominent mid-century playwrights and some contemporaries. Shakespeare's reputation, as can be seen from the numerous allusions to him in Romantic literature,[*] was rapidly developing into the 'bardolatry' of a period which, in the work of William Hazlitt, Samuel Taylor Coleridge, Charles Lamb and John Keats, produced some of the finest criticism of his plays. Censorship meant that drama involving politics could be seriously cut or even banned,[†] but historical plays, such as Byron's *The Two Foscari* (1821), discussed below, offered dramatists the opportunity to remove sensitive material to different eras or contexts, while gothic drama, reflecting the peculiarly stressful temper of the times, covered all kinds of extreme situations, inviting debate over a range of social and political issues.

---

[*] See Part Three: 'Writing in Revolution'; 'Romantic Verse Narrative'; 'Romantic Fiction'; and Part Four: 'Imagination, Truth and Reason'; 'Heroes and Anti-heroes'.
[†] Byron's *Cain* (1821), for example.

Theatrical productions also fostered the demand for texts of plays in performance, and the Romantic period is distinguished for producing dramas which lent themselves more to being read than performed. These so-called 'closet dramas' enabled writers to experiment with different forms and subject materials. Byron's *Cain* (1821), for example, was not intended for performance and its subject matter was considered too blasphemous to be admitted onto the stage. *Cain* takes the unprecedented step of actually referring to Jehovah by name, instead of taking some form of substitute deity as the target of its attack. It also steers away from a slavish adherence to Shakespearean tragedy by being a three-act drama in blank verse, written instead for the imagination of the reader. 'I am trying an experiment', Byron writes of it, 'which is to introduce into our language – the *regular* tragedy – without regard to the Stage – which will not admit of it – but merely to the *mental* theatre of the reader.'[1] In his verse-drama *Manfred* (1817), the 'action' is confined mainly to the protagonist's mental struggles (and presumably, Byron's)* over his guilt about an incestuous relationship with his sister ('I loved her, and destroy'd her', II.ii.117). Byron subtitles his work 'A Dramatic Poem', and the plays of the major Romantic poets, such as Wordsworth's *The Borderers* (1797), Percy Bysshe Shelley's *Prometheus Unbound* (1820) and *The Cenci* (1820) and Coleridge's *Remorse* (1813), all tend towards a lyrical register.

Joanna Baillie: Plays on the Passions

The Scottish dramatist Joanna Baillie, much admired by Byron, had published in 1798 a series of Plays on the Passions,[2] to which she appended a lengthy 'Introductory Discourse' setting out a programme for drama which would concentrate on 'feelings', where 'irregular bursts, abrupt transitions, sudden pauses, and half-uttered suggestions, scorn all harmony of measured verse, all method and order of relation'.[3] One is reminded here of such components in Captain Wentworth's

---

*   Byron had a close relationship with his half-sister, Augusta Leigh, whose third daughter, Medora, may have been the offspring of their incestuous affair.

urgent, heartfelt letter of declaration to Anne Elliot in *Persuasion* (1818), and of Anne's suspicion of her would-be lover, Mr Elliot, in whom 'There was never any burst of feeling'[4] (see Part Three: 'Romantic Fiction').

In Jane Austen's novel, outbursts such as Wentworth's are no longer a sign of disorder, but rather of an emotional spontaneity to be celebrated. Joanna Baillie's psychological drama is primarily concerned with the effects of monomania, a single-minded obsession, on the individual. In her tragedy *De Monfort*, the eponymous hero's ruling passion is hatred. Baillie is interested in the small 'beginnings'[5] of such passions which, in a character like De Monfort, can first be identified and then traced in his temperament to account for the tragedy he is responsible for bringing about. Baillie here anticipates Coleridge in his 'character criticism' approach to Shakespeare's drama where, for example, Hamlet's reluctance to murder the praying Claudius is not, as Dr Johnson had assumed, an indication of Hamlet's 'fiendishness' (in wanting to deny Claudius salvation), but rather, according to Coleridge, a sign of his procrastinating character. Dr Johnson, in Coleridge's view, is wrong in his interpretation because he has not understood that the way in which Hamlet is likely to act (or in this case, not act) is detectable from the beginning: 'Of such importance is it to understand the germ of a character.'[6]

Baillie's interest is in the passions which, motivating human activity, 'carry on a similar operation in the breast of the monarch, and the man of low degree'.[7] This subject, she believes, is 'equally interesting to all'. Like Joanna Baillie, Wordsworth in *Lyrical Ballads* (published in 1798, the same year as *Plays on the Passions*) sets out to explore, in what William Hazlitt calls his 'levelling' muse,[8] the 'essential passions of the heart'. Wordsworth believes that by tracing the primary laws of our common nature, 'a class of Poetry would be produced, well adapted to interest mankind permanently'.[9] Both Wordsworth and Baillie reflect the strong democratic processes at work in the revolutionary decade, and Wordsworth shares Baillie's interest in how expression of the passions can dictate an individual's speech patterns. In his 'Note' to 'The Thorn' he writes that 'Words, a Poet's words more particularly, ought to be weighed in the balance of feeling and not measured by the space which they occupy upon paper.' For Wordsworth, 'Poetry is passion' and he points out how, under the pressure of emotion, people will often 'cling to the same words' and depend on the 'repetition of words which appear successfully to communicate [their] feelings'. In their mutual 'democratic' concern to exploit the language of feelings held in common, and in their belief in an essentially expressive medium, both Baillie and Wordsworth reflect the politics and the aesthetics which lie at the heart of the Romantic period.

In their attempt to reconstruct the dramatic literature of the age, Joanna Baillie's Plays on the Passions focus on the minute details of a character's temperament. As a playwright, Baillie echoes the 'picturesque' principles of landscape composition when she compares traditional tragic heroes, in all the grandeur of their conception, to the view of 'distant mountains' which we see in outline, but 'the varieties of whose roughened sides, shaded with heath and brush wood, and seamed with many a cleft, we perceive not'[10] (see Part Three: 'Romantic Travel Writing'). Her focus on the 'little attended to' and often overlooked 'bursts of passion' which are 'marked by shades so delicate'[11] is reminiscent of the kind of detailed attention given to the natural world by Romantic poets such as Coleridge, Wordsworth or John Clare (see Part Three: Revolution, Reaction and the Natural World). It also indicates her desire to take drama away from the stylised gestures and attitudes taken up by actors in the large theatres, as a way of assisting distanced members of an audience to follow the play. A critic such as Charles Lamb shares this distaste for the way in which actors can, and often do, come between the audience and the play's writer. Hamlet's 'transactions between himself and his moral sense', his 'solitary musings' and 'silent meditations', are ruined by 'a gesticulating actor, who comes and mouths them out before an audience, making four hundred people his confidants at once'. What we see upon the stage 'is body and bodily action; what we are conscious of in reading is almost exclusively the mind, and its movements'.[12] Joanna Baillie, who writes that 'even the smallest indications of an unquiet mind [...] will set our attention as anxiously upon the watch, as the first distant flashes of a gathering storm',[13] not only anticipates Byron's ambition to create 'the *mental* theatre of the reader' but also Coleridge's remark that to watch the acting of Edmund Kean 'is like reading Shakespere by flashes of lightning'.[14] Kean's emotionally expressive acting style and intense energy leads Charles Lamb to comment that 'It is difficult for a frequent play-goer to disembarrass the idea of Hamlet from the person and voice of Mr. K.' The mind's 'free conceptions', he believes, must not be 'cramped and pressed down' by 'the province of acting', where 'eye, and tone, and gesture' are impediments to 'that delightful sensation of freshness, with which we turn to those plays of Shakespeare which have escaped being performed'. Yet Romantic writers, including Lamb, were fascinated by actors like Kean, whose presences were the perfect outward expression, not only of the drama of contemporary society, but also of the lives of a beginning 'celebrity' culture, embodied in figures such as Byron, himself a member of the Drury Lane Management Committee.

There are many and various reasons as to why Romantic writers were drawn to the stage. Partly it was to do with the dazzling stage-presence of the actor. Prestige and attention also accompanied theatrical success. There was the prospect of financial reward, the lure of the Shakespearean revival of the time, as well as the social cohesiveness of the theatre in an age which was becoming more fragmented and divided. Practically all the Romantic poets persisted in their quest for theatrical success and, insofar as they did so, the literature of the theatre must be regarded as central, not peripheral, to the Romantic period.

Closet Drama

Horace Walpole completed his tragedy *The Mysterious Mother* four years after the publication of *The Castle of Otranto* in 1764. He has the privilege, therefore, of initiating two important genres, the gothic novel and the gothic drama (see Part Four: 'Faith, Myth and Doubt'). Fifty copies of *The Mysterious Mother* were printed for private circulation at Walpole's own press at Strawberry Hill, but apart from contemporary 'closet' readings, the play was not performed in public until more than two hundred years later.*

* At the Citizens Theatre, Glasgow, 2001.

Involving an explosive mixture of power and transgressive sexuality, *The Mysterious Mother* anticipates the same kind of dark world of tyranny and incest to be found in Shelley's tragedy *The Cenci*. Its tragic heroine, the Countess of Narbonne, had been separated from her then returning husband for many months. By a fatal accident which had befallen him, she had been prevented from a much-anticipated sexual reunion, and put herself in the place of a young woman, Beatrice, with whom her unwitting son, Edmund, not quite sixteen, had made an assignation. This 'bed trick' produced Adeliza, who had been brought up among a school of orphans as a 'ward' of the Countess, while she herself banished Edmund on the pretext of his supposed sexual misdemeanours with Beatrice. The Countess, who now lives with her secret as a usurper of Edmund's rightful place in Narbonne, encounters him again when, sixteen years later, he returns with a soldier-friend to lay claim to his inheritance. The Countess, aware of the affection Edmund develops for Adeliza, but deceived into thinking that his friend, Florian, is the wooer, encourages the marriage which Benedict, a villainous monk, solemnises. The full details of the story are not revealed to the audience until the horrified Countess reveals to Edmund that he has married a sister who is also his daughter. In the denouement, the Countess stabs herself, Adeliza is borne off to a nunnery and Edmund flees back to the wars to offer himself up to death.

In his Prologue, Walpole, aware of his disturbing ('horrid, not polite', l. 2)[15] material, cites respectable, classical precedents for its themes in the drama of Euripides and Sophocles. He associates his own 'muse' (l. 1) with that of Shakespeare, whose 'Invention' (l. 10) in the creation of Hamlet's and Banquo's ghosts, and his obedience to 'Nature' (l. 10) rather than to rules, makes him a sharer in the wider political freedoms associated with all 'Britons' (l. 9). Milton's artless or untutored Shakespeare, whom he describes in his poem 'L'Allegro' as 'Fancy's child',[16] anticipates this Romantic construction of the bard, the 'expressive' Shakespeare who, in Wordsworth's phrase, had 'unlocked his heart' in his sonnets.[17] In true Romantic fashion, Walpole appeals to his reader-audience's 'feeling' (l. 34) as the measure of a play's success, while he distinguishes his own drama from the more formal, rule-bound, practice of French theatre.

The Mysterious Mother employs many of the external properties that have since come to be associated with 'gothic' drama: the 'awful silence', 'antique towers' (I.i.1–3), the peasant who advises 'go not to the castle' (I.i.20). But the play itself is remote from the incidentals of dramatic action or the gratuitous gloom of the 'graveyard' school.* Like *Hamlet*, which begins upon the outer battlements, before retreating into the claustrophobic world of its eponymous hero's mind, Walpole's play commences on 'A platform', turning away almost immediately towards the Countess and her psychological drama of anguish, guilt and self-division.

The atmosphere of *The Mysterious Mother* is sexually charged. The Countess's 'nuptial rites' with the Count 'Had with the sting of pleasure taught her passion' (I.i.192), and exceeding even Gertrude's sexual appetite in her haste to remarry within a month of Hamlet's father's death (*Hamlet*, I.ii.153), the Countess has put herself in Beatrice's place on the very night of her husband's fatal accident. Edmund, too, 'A lusty youth, his father's very image' (I.i.110) and, like his mother, sexually voracious, is no more dissuaded by his father's death that day from satisfying his 'opening passion's swelling ardour' (II.i.11) with, as he thinks, 'Beatrice's melting beauties' (II.i.27). Even his companion, Florian, 'of morals loose enough' (II.i.24), seems dismayed at Edmund's filial heedlessness, only to elicit Edmund's query, 'Wouldst thou have turned thee from a willing girl, / To sing a requiem to thy father's soul?' (II.i.31–2). It is not difficult to see why Coleridge might have been led to describe *The Mysterious Mother* as 'the most disgusting, detestable, vile composition that ever came from the hand of man', or why the more heterodox Byron should have called it 'a tragedy of the highest order, and not a puling love play'.[18]

In the midst of this disturbed set of relationships are figures who are either celibate or orphaned, and even Peter, the porter of the castle, who

---

* A lugubrious vogue set by Edward Young in his poem, 'The Complaint, or Night Thoughts on Life, Death and Immortality' (1742–4). A similar poem, 'The Grave' (1743) by Robert Blair, joined it in popularity and frequently between the same covers.

should be the guardian of its domestic security, reveals to Florian that he, too, had lusted after Beatrice: 'she ne'er would look on me, / Or we had saved full many a woful day!' (I.i.115–16).

Beyond the complex, incestuous coupling of a mother and son, Walpole's play seems to offer no conception of secure and dependable family alliances. Although the Hamlet–Gertrude affinity is inevitably called to mind, Walpole complicates matters even further by introducing, in the Edmund–Adeliza attraction, a problematic father and daughter liaison. After the death of the Abbess, who has been a mother-figure to her, Adeliza tells the Countess that Edmund's overtures 'Sound like the precepts of a tender parent' (III.i.137). Walpole's own biography has possibly played its part in his formulation of this tangled web. His own powerful father, the British prime minister Sir Robert Walpole,* may lie behind the 'apparition' of the dead Count, whose retributive gaze of patriarchal opposition, with 'eyes like burning stars' (II.i.223), opposes the problematic sexuality of the son.

In his Postscript to the play, Walpole describes his purposes in constructing the character of the Countess. Lamenting its comparative decline since the age of Shakespeare, he considers drama as being not only 'void of nature', but also (anticipating Joanna Baillie), without 'the power of affecting the passions' (p. 69). He therefore tries to 'raise the character of the criminal' by invoking his audience's sympathy for the Countess's passionate longing for her husband. 'Her very fondness' for him becomes 'in some measure the cause of her guilt', and is therefore perhaps more understandable 'than if she had coolly meditated so foul a crime' (p. 66). Walpole suppresses the story until the last scene, in order that the audience may be prejudiced in her favour and that 'a whole life of virtue and penance might in some measure atone for a moment, though a most odious moment, of a depraved imagination' (pp. 66–7). The Countess's praises are frequently sung by others. Peter the porter remarks

---

* Sir Robert Walpole was prime minister from 1721 until 1742. Horace Walpole was rumoured to have been the product of an adulterous relationship of his mother's, but also bore a strong resemblance to one of his father's illegitimate children. His reputation for effeminacy is reflected in Coleridge's remark that 'No one with a spark of true manliness, of which Horace Walpole had none' could have written *The Mysterious Mother*.

to Florian that 'Such virtue never dwelt in female form' (I.i.102), and even the villainous monk, Benedict, admiring her religious devotion, says 'This woman was not cast in human mould' (I.i.152). The Countess's own estimation of her worth is expressed to Edmund in gendered terms, echoing the speech of Elizabeth I to her troops at Tilbury in 1588:[*] 'Though frail my sex, I have a soul as masculine / As any of thy race', while Edmund's response in his soliloquy is equally gendered:

> Commanding sex!
> Strength, courage, all our boasted attributes,
> Want estimation; ev'n the pre-eminence
> We vaunt in wisdom, seems a borrowed ray,
> When virtue deigns to speak with female organs. (III.i.320–4)

The suspenseful structure of the play is designed by Walpole to build admiration for the character of the Countess and to act as a buffer against the final revelation of her terrible secret. His purpose is to insist that the heroine's feelings and virtues should be treated in a way which is gender-blind, that criminal sexuality should not be allowed to obscure the Countess's admirable qualities, any more than if she were a male where sexuality is able to be kept discreet from personality.

The transgressive nature of *The Mysterious Mother* kept it literally 'under wraps' in Walpole's own time. Lady Diana Beauclerk produced seven illustrations of the play, with its characters posed in various sentimental postures, and these could be viewed by select friends of Walpole who happened to visit the 'Beauclerk Closet' within the 'Beauclerk Tower' at Strawberry Hill. Walpole placed a copy of the play in the drawer of a writing table within the 'closet', so that this hiding of an unspeakable secret at the heart of a 'mystery' comes to anticipate many such secrets contained in similar mysterious 'rooms' in nineteenth-century Romantic and Victorian literature.[†]

---

[*] 'I have the body of a weak and feeble woman, but I have the heart and stomach of a king.'

[†] For example, Heathcliff's room in Emily Brontë's *Wuthering Heights* (1847), and the Red Room and Rochester's attic in Charlotte Brontë's *Jane Eyre* (1847).

Political Drama

In 1794, Robert Southey wrote his three-act play, *Wat Tyler*, inspired by the Peasants' Revolt of 1381,* an account of which Thomas Paine had included as a footnote to the second part of *Rights of Man* (1792). Paine writes a partisan version of the rebellion and finds, in Tyler, a historical English precedent for the kind of Jacobin revolutionary at work in contemporary France. Southey had given the manuscript of his play to his brother-in-law Robert Lovell, who in turn had given it to the radical publisher Samuel Ridgeway. Ridgeway, who was serving a term in Newgate prison, had offered to publish it without attaching Southey's name, but because of the political climate of the day he decided against it. The year, 1794, saw the treason trials of the leaders of the London Corresponding Society,† and the government's measures against all forms of dissident activity made it dangerous to publish the kind of inflammatory material that Southey had written. *Wat Tyler* did not surface until 1817 when, in February of that year, a pirated edition was published by Sherwood, Neely and Jones. Its clear intention was to embarrass Southey who, then Poet Laureate, had publicly disavowed his earlier radical principles. How the play came into the hands of the publishers is unclear, and Southey's attempt to prevent its publication failed after Lord Eldon's decision that its seditious content made it exempt from copyright protection.

The immediate aftermath of Napoleon's fall was an even more turbulent time for England than the revolutionary 1790s, and the prospect of civil war was a real one. Disaffection which had been to some extent restrained during the war years re-emerged in protests over

---

* 'The Peasants' Revolt' was the most famous among several popular insurrections in the Middle Ages. It was led by Wat Tyler who, during his negotiations with Richard II, was attacked and killed by the Lord Mayor of London and one of the King's knights. In spite of the King's assurances to the rebels that their demands would be met, he reneged on his promise and Tyler's two associates also, Jack Straw and John Ball, were subsequently pursued, captured and beheaded.

† A society which debated parliamentary reform. Its leaders were Thomas Hardy, John Horne Tooke and John Thelwall.

taxation and workers' rights, and new radical groups, led by prominent figures such as William Hone and Richard Carlile, were agitating for reform. Southey's play was therefore of immense topical relevance in the context in which it eventually appeared, and it was eagerly seized on by reformers, not only as a demonstration of the principles at work behind popular democratic movements, but also as a way of attacking Southey for betraying their cause and, as a Tory spokesman, impeding reform and advocating the transportation of dissenters. By 1827, seventeen editions of *Wat Tyler* had appeared, including one by Hone, in which Hone quotes, as typical of Southey's reactionary sentiments, an extract from his 'last article against Reform in the last *Quarterly Review*':

> If the opinions of profligate and mistaken men may be thought to reflect disgrace upon the nation, of which they constitute a part, it might verily be said, that England was never so much disgraced as at this time.

The controversy over *Wat Tyler* brought Southey into confrontation with Byron, whose maiden speech in the House of Lords* had argued against the transportation of Luddite frame-breakers in Nottingham. In the Dedication of *Don Juan* (begun 1818), Byron attacks Southey as the most renegade of the Lake Poets, by contrasting him with the republican poet Milton, who, as a Puritan, had hated Charles I but did not, after the Restoration, become an opportunist and praise Charles II:

> *He* deign'd not to belie his soul in songs,
> Nor turn his very talent to a crime—
> *He* did not loathe the sire to laud the son,
> But closed the tyrant-hater he begun. (*Don Juan*, ll. 79–80)

In his Preface to *A Vision of Judgement* (1821), his laureate tribute to George III written on the King's death, Southey makes an oblique

---

* 27 February 1812.

reference to Byron as leader of a 'Satanic School' of poetry, having already incurred his wrath by spreading rumours of a 'League of Incest' among Byron, Percy Bysshe Shelley, Mary Godwin (Shelley) and Claire Clairmont at Geneva in 1816.[19] In an Appendix to *The Two Foscari* (1821) Byron writes that he is not ignorant of 'Southey's calumnies [...] which he scattered abroad on his return from Switzerland against me and others', and in the Preface to his own satire on Southey's poem, *The Vision of Judgment* (1822), he writes, 'The gross flattery, the dull impudence, the renegado intolerance, and impious cant, of the poem by the author of "Wat Tyler", are something so stupendous as to form the sublime of himself – containing the quintessence of his own attributes.'

In 1817 Coleridge defended Southey's expression of youthful principles (which they had once both shared)* and to which he referred as Southey's 'boyish *leaning*' in the play '(far more to the honour of his heart than to the impeachment of his understanding)'.[20] In his Preface to *Wat Tyler* published in 1837[21] Southey acknowledged the play as representing a legitimate stage in his development, and that he felt no reproach in having written it or any more shame for 'having been a republican, than of having been a boy'. The play begins with a May festivity. Young people, including Alice, Tyler's daughter, and Piers, her suitor, dance around a maypole, while Tyler and his friend, Hob, look on. The setting is similar to the ones described in the opening lines of Oliver Goldsmith's *The Deserted Village* (1770), and of Blake's poem, 'The Ecchoing Green' (1789). The older generation presides over the younger while, in both poems, there are dark implications for the survival of rural innocence. Shakespeare's tragedy *Romeo and Juliet* is also recalled where Tyler and Hob, like old Capulet and Montague, reminisce about their younger days together:

> TYLER: Aye, we were young,
> No cares had quelled the heyday of the blood:

---

* Coleridge and Southey had planned in 1794 to emigrate to America together and to set up a utopian community called Pantisocracy. It was to be based on the best principles of the French Revolution, but the scheme failed to materialise.

We sported deftly in the April morning,
Nor marked the black clouds gathering o'er our noon,
Nor feared the storm of night. (I.i.21–4)

As Tyler's conversation with Hob progresses, their mutual resentment over the government's taxation 'to fill their armies, / And feed the crows of France' (I.i.56–7) is ominously linked, in the gathering storm clouds image, to England's current war (declared in 1793). Hob's question, 'Of what service is the state?' (I.i.73) reflects a theme that runs through much of Southey's political writing, as well as that of many contemporary radicals, including William Godwin who in 1794 published *An Enquiry Concerning Political Justice*, in which he discusses the redundancy of governments and envisages a society based wholly upon reason. Tyler echoes Godwin's belief that power is itself corrupting and that the State is the obstacle to the universal adoption of the French Revolution's 'liberty, equality and fraternity':

TYLER: Who should pay for
The luxuries and riots of the court?
Who should support the flaunting courtier's pride,
Pay for their midnight revels, their rich garments,
Did not the state enforce?—Think ye, my friend,
That I, a humble blacksmith, here at Deptford,
Would part with these six groats—earned by hard toil,
All that I have!—to massacre the Frenchmen,
Murder as enemies men I never saw,
Did not the state compel me? (I.i.74–83)

Tyler sets up what is often accepted as the Romantic opposition between the natural world and the human, and recognises, as William Blake does, the need to put justice in the place of parasitical so-called virtues such as mercy and pity:*

---

* Compare Blake, 'The Human Abstract' (*Songs of Experience*, 1794): 'Pity would be no more, / If we did not make somebody Poor: / And Mercy no more could be, / If all were as happy as we.'

TYLER: Nature gives enough
For all; but Man, with arrogant selfishness,
Proud of his heaps, hoards up superfluous stores
Robbed from his weaker fellows, starves the poor,
Or gives to pity what he owes to justice!' (I.i.114–18)

The young idealistic Piers equates happiness with virtue (I.i.98–106) but, in their exchange, the embittered Tyler can see that virtue is no proof against the ravages of poverty: 'Thou art yet young: the blasting breath of want / Has not yet froze the current of thy blood' (I.i.109). Southey here alludes to Thomas Gray's 'Elegy' (1751) where the poet, musing on the disadvantaged occupants of a churchyard, describes how 'Chill Penury' was responsible for their 'destiny obscure' and 'froze the genial current of the soul'. In mid-century, Gray here raises the spectre of revolution but, unlike Southey in the revolutionary 1790s, he is content to sidestep it and simply lay it to rest. He abandons protest, drawing instead analogies with the natural world in lines now famous simply for the beauty of their imagery:

Full many a gem of purest ray serene,
The dark unfathom'd caves of ocean bear:
Full many a flower is born to blush unseen,
And waste its sweetness on the desert air. (ll. 53–6)

And he also achieves it by making the inequalities in society an irrelevance in the face of death the leveller:

The boast of heraldry, the pomp of pow'r,
And all that beauty, all that wealth e'er gave,
Awaits alike th'inevitable hour.
The paths of glory lead but to the grave. (ll. 33–6)

Southey is concerned with the needs of the poor who rebel against their masters. He believes, as would Shelley later, that if the quality of life is so bad, then reform involving, if necessary, public disorder, is not only justified but also absolutely required as a moral duty. When Tyler murders the Tax-gatherer in an act of outraged retaliation for his indecent examination of Alice, Hob cries out: 'We have broke our chains, we will arise in anger, / The mighty multitude shall trample down / The handful that oppress them.' The lines anticipate those of Shelley's 'The Mask of Anarchy' (1819):*

> Rise like Lions after slumber
> In unvanquishable number—
> Shake your chains to earth like dew
> Which in sleep had fallen on you—
> Ye are many—they are few. (xci)

John Ball, the priest who has been imprisoned for the exercise of his true Christianity and who advocates seasoning with mercy the justice called for by the mob (II.i.117–18), reminds them:

> Though your proud oppressors spared not you,
> Show you excel them in humanity.
> They will use every art to disunite you;
> To conquer separately, by stratagem,
> Whom in a mass they fear;—but be ye firm;
> Boldly demand your long-forgotten rights,
> Your sacred, your inalienable freedom.
> Be bold—be resolute—be merciful. (ll. 118–25)

Shelley's advice is identical. Invoking the 'old laws of England [...] Children of a wiser day', he advocates, in defence of them, a passive resistance in the face of government violence:

---

* 'The Mask of Anarchy' was written in response to the 'Peterloo' massacre at St Peter's Field, Manchester in 1819. A cavalry charge was ordered to disperse a crowd which had gathered to hear a radical orator, Henry Hunt, speak on parliamentary reform. Fifteen people died and hundreds were injured.

Stand ye calm and resolute,
Like a forest close and mute,
With folded arms and looks which are
Weapons of unvanquished war,

And let Panic, who outspeeds
The career of armèd steeds
Pass, a disregarded shade
Through your phalanx undismayed. (ll. 319–26)

Southey's play calls into question the evils and hypocrisies of an establishment which is more concerned with the perpetuation of its power than with the dispensation of justice. The 'war of honour' (I.i.190) which, in the words of the Tax-gatherer, is 'a glorious war [...] and must be supported' (I.i.189–90), brings to mind Falstaff's questioning of what he calls simply the empty word, 'honour' (*1 Henry IV*, V.i.134). The Archbishop's appeal to 'divinity [...] the sacred privilege of kings' (II.ii.18–19) is exposed as meaningless when invoked as a means to consolidate oppression, and Tresilian's accusation of 'plain John Ball' (II.i.129) as someone opposed to 'the sacred rights of property' (III.ii.31) recalls Godwin's indictment in *Caleb Williams* (1794) of a people so conditioned that when Caleb, to prevent a fire from spreading, orders them to pull down an adjacent house, 'They seemed astonished at a direction which implied a voluntary destruction of property.'[22]

Wat Tyler's rhetorical power well demonstrates the potential of Romantic political drama to represent public concerns in this medium. John Ball's prophecy, when he is made to speak eloquently of a democratic future, is an example:

There will be a time when this great truth
Shall be confessed—be felt by all mankind.
The electric truth shall run from man to man,
And the blood-cemented pyramid of greatness
Shall fall before the flash. (ll. 64–8)

The new science of electricity provides here a means to unify and vitalise an enervated society. It recalls Shelley, as a child at Field Place, remembered by his sister, Hellen, as practising 'electricity upon us'. In spite of her terror, she kept silent while 'with as many others as he could collect, we were placed hand-in-hand round the nursery table to be electrified'.[23] The 'blood-cemented pyramid of greatness' calls to mind the setting of Shelley's political sonnet 'Ozymandias' (see Part Four: 'Forms of Ruin'), where the 'level sands' are made symbolic of an equal society in which invidious distinctions between oppressor and oppressed have been abolished. As with so much of the hope invested in the Romantic revolutionary period, Wat Tyler's defiant, even heroic, speech (III.ii.101–14) expresses only an imagined future. It is the perjured King Richard who concludes the play: 'Let the blood-reeking sword of war be sheathed, / That the law may take vengeance on the rebels' (III.ii.117–18). As with other political dramas of the period such as Wordsworth's *The Borderers* (1797) and Shelley's *The Cenci* (1820), *Wat Tyler* presents a bleak view of power and its abuses.

Historical Drama

Historical drama in the Romantic period was often employed by playwrights as a means of circumventing censorship and displacing issues of national concern within different eras and contexts. *The Two Foscari* (1821), one of two dramas written by Byron inspired by Venetian history,* portrays the conflict between the machinery of state and the private freedom of the individual, an issue of central importance to the Romantic period. In *Wat Tyler*, John Ball calls for justice with mercy but, in *The Two Foscari*, Byron demonstrates that justice and mercy cannot be thus reconciled. The play has two tragic characters, The Doge himself, Francis Foscari, and his son, Jacopo. Already in exile for a previous offence, Jacopo, unable to imagine life apart from his beloved city, has opened a treasonous correspondence with the Duke of

---

* The other, *Marino Faliero* (1820), was the only play of Byron's to be performed in his lifetime. It was made into an opera by Donizetti in 1835.

Milan 'in the full knowledge / That it would fall into the senate's hands, / And thus he should be re-conveyed to Venice' (I.i.296–8). In the play, the city's prevailing air of claustrophobic gloom is sustained by the imprisoned Jacopo, for whom, like Byron's own Prisoner of Chillon, 'all earth, except his native land, / To him is one wide prison' (I.i.290–1).* Jacopo's wife, Marina, acts as a compassionate mediator between her suffering husband and the implacable Doge, who puts his service to the state before all personal interest and human pity. The Foscari family are themselves pursued by the vengeance of the patrician Loredano, who believes that the elder Foscari has been responsible for the poisoning of both his father and his uncle.

Byron gives no indication of the Doge's innocence or guilt by supplying any historical background information, and therefore it is impossible to determine whether Loredano is acting out of justifiable revenge, or is motivated by some inscrutable purpose. In a letter to John Murray in which he states his belief that, 'if understood', his plays 'will in time find favour (though *not* on the stage) with the reader', Byron writes that what he seeks to show in '"The Foscari's" is the *suppressed* passions'.[24] As with Joanna Baillie's plays on the passions, Byron's interests seem to lie less in the '*dramatic*'[25] and more in his characters' feelings and motivations which invite a reader's investigation. In its repeated appearance throughout the play, 'The Question' (I.i.2), as used by the ruling Council of Ten to mean the torture of its prisoners, comes to signify an interrogative role which readers must apply to the dramatic proceedings.

Byron's reference to the 'suppression' of passions suggests hidden motivations extending beyond the simpler 'dramatic' pursuit of Francis Foscari by Loredano, and the relationship between the Doge, his son and his son's wife take the play closer to the territory of Walpole's closet drama than the more familiar world of revenge tragedy. The Doge expresses his emotions for Venice in language which suggests the kind of love normally reserved by a man for a woman. Traditionally, a Doge of Venice 'wedded' the city to the sea by casting a ring into the waters

---

* See Byron, *The Prisoner of Chillon*: 'And the whole earth would henceforth be / A wider prison unto me' (ll. 322–3) and Hamlet's, 'Denmark's a prison' (II.ii.243).

of the Adriatic,* and for Foscari, Venice, with her 'diadem' and 'gems' is his 'queen of ocean', his 'Lady of Lombardy' (II.i.18–20). This feminised role of the city in the Doge's life puts a particular inflection on the intimate nature of his dialogue with his son's wife. Her name, Marina, suggests her symbolic association with the sea, while the Doge's immovable position on treason to the state obliges him to assert his patriarchal authority in enforcing his son's defeat. At the conclusion of his lyrical paean to the Venice of his youth (I.i.96–121), 'I was a boy then', his guard's response to Jacopo is 'Be a man now: there never was more need of manhood's strength' (I.i.121–3). It is Loredano who, in the play, acts out a 'manly' role which the overshadowed Jacopo is unable to do. For him, Venice is the mother from which he is unwilling to be separated, and to whom he keeps returning. In this Oedipal situation, Jacopo seeks to usurp his father's role, while Francis usurps that of his son, to take the place of his wife. The Doge, who rejects Marina's plea that he might intervene on Jacopo's behalf ('I found the law; I did not make it', II.i.395) speaks with the disinterested voice of Shakespeare's Angelo in *Measure for Measure*,[26] and this identification so completely with paternal authority suggests that he is effectively consenting to the substitution of himself in his son's place.

Byron's heterodox stance is underlined in the Doge's response to Marina's accusation of his inhumanity to Jacopo: 'I forgive this, for / You know not what you say'. The echo of Christ's words from the cross† secularises Jacopo's role as willing victim of his father's politics by putting him in the situation of Christ, the willing victim of his own Father's sacrifice.‡ Shortly afterwards, the Doge becomes the Old Testament Abraham when, in conversation with Loredano, he announces that he has observed 'the welfare of the state' with veneration 'like / A priest's for the high altar, even unto / The sacrifice of my own blood'.§

---

*   See 'This ducal ring with which I wed the waves' (II.i.81).

†   'Father, forgive them; for they know not what they do' (Luke 23:34).

‡   'For God so loved the world, that he gave his only begotten Son, that whosoever believeth in him should not perish, but have everlasting life' (John 3:16).

§   Abraham is commanded by God to make a sacrifice of his son, Isaac (Genesis 22:1–19).

In the Doge's response to Marina in Act II (ll. 333–66), Byron sets out his own conception of a hostile, determinist universe in which man, who thinks he exercises his control, is simply at the mercy of blind fortune:

> So, we are slaves,
> The greatest as the meanest—nothing rests
> Upon our will; the will itself no less
> Depends upon a straw than on a storm;
> And when we think we lead, we are most led,
> And still towards death, a thing which comes as much
> Without our act or choice, as birth, so that
> Methinks we must have sinned in some old world,
> And *this* is hell. (ll. 357–65)

This speech, with its echoes of Hamlet's speculations on will and fate,[*] represents the dark obverse of Romantic idealism, similar in its attitude to the position adopted by Maddalo, the Byronic persona of Shelley's poem *Julian and Maddalo* (written 1819, published 1824), who opposes Julian's belief in the power of the will to bring about change (see Part Three: 'Romantic Verse Narrative'. In the face of the Doge's unyielding behaviour, Marina offers the alternative option of pity. Her stance is reflected in the role adopted by the compassionate senator, Barbarigo, who, attempting to 'mitigate' Loredano's hatred 'To milder thoughts' (I.i.374–5), exhorts him to 'be human!' (V.i.160). Yet if Marina's charity is her moral virtue, she also suggests an unbreakable cycle of vengeance when she reminds Loredano, 'I have some sons, sir, / Will one day thank you better' (III.i.268–9). Byron is sceptical about power. The lesson he takes from history, and no less from recent events, is that one form of power is simply exchanged for another. In *Childe Harold* (1818) he proclaims the 'blood of earth' shed in Roman and Napoleonic times alike as the 'universal deluge, which appears / Without an ark for wretched man's abode, / And ebbs but to reflow!' (IV.xcii). In *The Two*

---

[*] 'Our wills and fates do so contrary run / That our devices still are overthrown, / Our thoughts are ours, their ends none of our own' (*Hamlet*, III.ii.211–13).

Foscari he deals directly with the temptations of power in his presentation of two senators who, invited to view the proceedings of the Council of Ten against the Doge, are revealed, through their conversation together, to be making their semblance of duty a cloak for their personal ambition:

> SENATOR: Let us view them: they,
> No doubt, are worth it.
>
> MEMMO: Being worth our lives
> If we divulge them, doubtless they are worth
> Something, at least to you or me.
>
> SENATOR: I sought not
> A place within the sanctuary; but being
> Chosen, however reluctantly so chosen,
> I shall fulfil my office.
>
> MEMMO: Let us not
> Be latest in obeying the Ten's summons.
>
> SENATOR: All are not met, but I am of your thought
> So far—let's in.
>
> MEMMO: The earliest are most welcome
> In earnest councils—we will not be least so. (ll. 88–97)

The Doge's privileging of power before his obligations to his son are contained in his response to Marina's appeal to his feelings as a father: 'I have other duties than a father's; / The state would not dispense me from those duties' (II.i.184–5). But his nemesis arrives with the death of Jacopo, when his stoical profile crumbles and he throws himself upon his dead son's body. Marina's response is:

> Aye, weep on!
> I thought you had no tears—you hoarded them
> Until they are useless; but weep on! He never
> Shall weep more—never, never more. (IV.i.215–18)

Her echo of King Lear's words over the body of his daughter* indicate that Doge Foscari, instead of being regarded as victim, must be seen to share Lear's responsibility for the tragedy he has brought about by his own folly. His own 'deference due even to the lightest word / That falls from those who rule in Venice' (II.i.298–9) is undercut by Loredano's cynicism, when he responds to Barbarigo's reservations over the Doge's deposition, 'But will the laws uphold us?' with 'What laws?—The Ten are laws; and if they were not, / I will be legislator in this business' (IV.i.36–8). In his haste to depose Foscari immediately upon the death of Jacopo, Loredano, the Council's spokesman, uses the Doge's own logic against him:

> The feelings
> Of private passion may not interrupt
> The public benefit; and what the state
> Decides today must not give way before
> Tomorrow for a natural accident. (ll. 266–70)

The Doge's immediate death, on his fall from power, comes when he hears the tolling bell of St Mark's proclaiming his successor. The *suppressed* passions' are now allowed to surface, but they are too late to save him, as Doge Foscari has allowed himself no existence beyond his consuming office of state.

Living in Venice during the Austrian occupation, Byron had first-hand experience of the vicissitudes of power, making the city 'which was once a tyrant', as Shelley writes to Thomas Love Peacock, 'now the next worse thing, a slave'.[27] Byron seems to have identified with the Venetian Doges as aristocrats and lonely figures, behind whose

---

* 'Thou'lt come no more, / Never, never, never, never, never' (V.iii.308–9).

apparent power was concealed the real authority of the Council of Ten. In 1843 Giuseppe Verdi was invited to Venice by Count Mocenigo, a descendant of the family whose palace Byron had rented there. In the following year he wrote for the Venetian opera house, La Fenice, his opera, *I due Foscari*, based on Byron's play. Verdi's life experience was similar to Byron's in that in the space of three years he lost both his wife and two children, to an extent becoming, like Byron's alter ego, the Corsair, 'Warp'd by the world in Disappointment's school'.[*] Verdi, whose own love for his native Bussetto matches Jacopo's for Venice, sees the younger Foscari as a victim. In *The Two Foscari*, Byron projects himself into the roles of tragic characters who are thus defined by political and historical circumstances. His identification with figures who, like himself, are exiled, explains his own fascination with people such as Napoleon and Jacopo Foscari, and his attraction in this play to Foscari's sense of belonging, seems somehow inevitable in the context of the serial dislocations of his own comparatively brief life.

Walpole, Southey and Byron reflect in their various ways the extensive, engaging and versatile drama of the Romantic period, exploring a range of theatrical possibilities in the private passions, in the more public arena of political issues and in the larger stage spectacles of historical events.

Extended Commentary: Walpole, *The Mysterious Mother* (1768), V.i.312–420

In Act V of Walpole's play, dramatic irony heightens audience suspense, as the newly married Edmund and Adeliza, innocent of their circumstances, kneel as her 'children' before the Countess and ask for her blessing. The filial bonds between parents and children, in King

---

[*] See Byron, *The Corsair* (1814), l. 253. In 1848 Verdi produced his opera *Il Corsaro* based on the poem.

Lear's terms 't'intrinse t'unloose' (II.ii.75),* are ruptured as the Countess, instead of joining hands, demands of her son that he 'loose that hand' (l. 314). Her terrible reversal of regular feelings, 'hell has no venom / Like a child's touch' (ll. 315–16), reflects the crippled society over which she presides, one in which her 'blessing' becomes a 'curse' (ll. 393–4) and where Edmund's 'curse' on her will seem more like 'piety' (l. 331). Confronted with his fatally wounded mother and the swooning Adeliza, Edmund's realisation of something untouchable inhibits any kind of normal response: 'For both I tremble, dare not succour either' (l. 385).

The Countess's revelation, withheld until this point, makes particular demands upon the audience. Either we acknowledge that desire and active sexuality, natural to her as a woman, allow a sympathetic understanding of her predicament, or we see that excessive desire as inimical to the normative values associated with the family, and therefore as something tragic. Later Romantic writers would make identical challenges to reader response. In 'Lamia', for example, Keats invites readers to decide against or in favour of the female figure. Given that the name 'Lamia' (a dangerous vampire) is conferred upon her exclusively by a male character in the poem, Keats seems to be asking us if we are willing simply to accept that name, inviting us to consider whether it is woman and the sexual act which kills the hero, Lycius, rather than his own male taboos and fears.

Edmund's 'dreadful apprehension' (l. 366) of his mother's secret as gradually revealed sits well with intimations, throughout the play, of an emotional entanglement between them. The 'burning zeal' (l. 258) with which he kisses her hand in Act III recalls the 'zeal' of the discussion that, 'getting beyond its wonted barrier', generates in Robert Wringhim a symbolic, if not a literal, bastard in Hogg's *Confessions*[28] (see Part Three: 'Romantic Fiction'). The Countess's reference to Edmund as 'devoted victim' (l. 319) possibly implies more than simply the destiny to which he has been fated, and a displacement anxiety, shared by both mother and son, is expressed first in Edmund's, 'ha! is not that my lord? / He shakes the curtains of the nuptial couch, / And starts to find a son there'

* Too intricately involved to be unloosed.

118

(ll. 332–4), then shortly afterwards, in the Countess's exclamation, 'Almighty pow'r!' (l. 341), at what she supposes is an apparition of the Count.

In her own terms the Countess is a 'monster' (l. 321), a 'fury' (l. 330) and a 'tiger' (l. 339), yet in the Postscript, Walpole makes the point that, although he could not lessen her guilt 'without destroying the subject itself', his belief is that 'her immediate horror and consequential repentance were essential towards effectuating her being suffered on the stage'. Edmund, in refusing to strike his mother dead, takes the moral line when he exclaims, 'I dare not punish what you dared commit' (l. 382), but it is the Countess who evokes the more complex audience reaction.

With a series of allusions to Shakespeare deployed in the final stages, Walpole invites thematic comparisons with his own tragedy. In response to Benedict's 'Who did this deed?' (l. 388), the dying Countess replies, 'Myself' (l. 389). Here she is made to echo Desdemona's reply, 'Nobody; I myself', to Emilia's 'O, who hath done this deed?' in *Othello* (V.ii.123–4). Benedict is thus cast in the role of Iago, while something of Desdemona's moral worth inevitably reflects upon the Countess. And just as Othello's 'I have no wife' (V.ii.97) is echoed by Edmund's response to Benedict – 'My wife! / Thou damning priest! I have no wife' (ll. 398–9), Othello, as practised upon by Iago, invites comparison with Edmund as a man more sinned against than sinning. On the other hand, Benedict's triumphant remark to Florian, 'Who was the prophet now? / Remember me!' (ll. 402–3), calls to mind the Ghost in *Hamlet*'s 'remember me' (I.v.91), and accentuates his villainous role, since the Ghost speaks to Hamlet of rectifying what is clearly 'rotten in the state of Denmark' (I.iv.89), while Benedict, far from improving a bad situation, is out to compound the chaos he has created. The play is subtle, and complex in the range of response it demands from its audience.

Walpole constructs, in the Countess–Edmund–Adeliza triangle, an unholy threesome, reminiscent of Satan, Sin and Death, the parody of the Holy Trinity in *Paradise Lost*. In Milton's poem, 'Sin', born of Satan, springs from his head. In then coupling with him, she gives birth to 'Death' who, in turn, goes on to couple with his mother. This is tantamount to saying that indulging in familiarity with sin begins to give pleasure. The abandonment of the self to sin breeds death, and death lusts after the sin that engendered it. Walpole's trinity is not so unerringly conceived, but similar blasphemous implications are present, and of the kind to keep a drama like *The Mysterious Mother* firmly within the closet. The Countess's dying words repeat those of Christ on the cross, ''tis accomplished' (l. 395). The New Testament frequently uses the marriage metaphor, and in their Latin form, the words 'consummatus est' have been construed to imply the consummation of Christ's own marriage with his people. In the controversial, sexualised context of Walpole's play, consummation, as incest, gives to the Countess's words a particularly impious resonance. Edmund, too, as an albeit unwitting participant in the Countess's 'luxurious fancy' (l. 351), has already been made to echo the last words from the cross as, kneeling before his mother in Act III, he says to her, 'Madam, behold your son' (l. 267).[*]

The conclusion of the play echoes the enormity of the final events in *King Lear*. When Lear enters with Cordelia dead in his arms, he refers to the horrified, unmoving bystanders as 'men of stones' (V.iii.258). 'Had I your tongues and eyes,' he exclaims, 'I'ld use them so / That heaven's vault should crack'. Shakespeare presents his audience with a grouping in which we are meant to imagine the king and his daughter as a kind of secular *pietà*,[†] the central objects in a mausoleum, surrounded by statues or 'men of stones'. In *The Mysterious Mother*, the Countess, about to reveal to Edmund her secret, says 'let thy blood / Curdle to stone!', while Florian, who comes across the horror-stricken Edmund before his dead mother, is 'stiffened with amazement' (l. 405). Here, too, a final tableau is presented whereby the two figures are 'petrified' in the presence of a tragic figure. Edmund once more imagines his father's retribution, 'ha! 'tis my father calls! / I dare not see him' (ll. 407–8), and in his reference to the dismal scene as 'this theatre of monstrous guilt', he includes himself as well as his mother and Adeliza.

---

[*] 'When Jesus therefore saw his mother and the disciple standing by, whom he loved, he saith unto his mother, Woman, behold thy son!' (John 19:26).

[†] The body of Jesus on the lap of his mother after his deposition from the cross. The most famous representation is that of Michelangelo in St Peter's Basilica in the Vatican.

Byron's concept of closet drama as *'mental* theatre' calls to mind the essentially psychological drama of *Hamlet*, whose eponymous hero's term for his own head is 'this distracted globe' (I.v.97). As commentators have pointed out, an audience watching the play in the Globe theatre would have detected a triple pun.* Perhaps Walpole, as well as referring to the spectacle of the tragedy, acknowledges through Edmund's words the transgressive nature of the drama he has written, a 'theatre of monstrous guilt', to be kept well and truly out of public view.

Notes

1   Leslie A. Marchand (ed.), *Byron's Letters and Journals*, 13 vols (London: John Murray, 1973–94), vol. 8, p. 210.
2   Joanna Baillie, *A Series of Plays: In Which it is Attempted to Delineate the Stronger Passions of the Mind* (1798; Oxford and New York: Woodstock Books, 1990).
3   Ibid., p. 31.
4   Jane Austen, *Persuasion*, ch. 18.
5   Baillie, *Plays on the Passions*, p. 64.
6   Jonathan Bate (ed.), *The Romantics on Shakespeare* (Harmondsworth: Penguin, 1992), p. 320.
7   Baillie, *Plays on the Passions*, p. 42.
8   William Hazlitt, *The Spirit of the Age* (1825), 'Mr Wordsworth'.
9   Wordsworth, Preface to *Lyrical Ballads* (1800).
10   Baillie, *Plays on the Passions*, p. 29.
11   Ibid., pp. 59–60.
12   Charles Lamb, 'On the Tragedies of Shakespeare, Considered with Reference to Their Fitness for Stage Representation', in Stephen Greenblatt (ed., *The Norton Anthology of English Literature*, 8th edn (New York and London: Norton, 2006), vol. 2, pp. 493–6.
13   Baillie, *Plays on the Passions*, pp. 10–11.
14   Samuel Taylor Coleridge, *The Table Talk and Omniana of Samuel Taylor Coleridge*, ed. T. Ashe (London: George Bell, 1884), p. 25.
15   All references are to Paul Baines and Edward Burns (eds), *Five Romantic Plays, 1768–1821* (Oxford: Oxford University Press, 2000).
16   Milton, 'L'Allegro' (1631).

*   'Globe' also as microcosm.

17 Wordsworth, 'Scorn not the Sonnet'.

18 Peter Sabor (ed.), *Horace Walpole: The Critical Heritage* (London: Routledge & Kegan Paul, 1987), pp. 147–8.

19 Leslie A. Marchand (ed.), *Byron's Letters and Journals*, 13 vols (London: John Murray, 1973–94), vol. 6, p. 76.

20 *Courier*, 18 March 1817.

21 Robert Southey, *The Poetical Works of Robert Southey Collected by Himself in Ten Volumes* (London: Longman, Orme, Brown, Green & Longmans, 1837–8), vol. 2.

22 William Godwin, *Caleb Williams*, vol. 1, ch. 6.

23 Quoted in Richard Holmes, *Shelley: The Pursuit* (London: Weidenfeld & Nicolson, 1974), p. 17.

24 Marchand (cd.), *Byron's Letters and Journals*, vol. 8, p. 218.

25 Ibid.

26 See *Measure for Measure* (II.i.17–31).

27 Percy Bysshe Shelley, *The Letters of Percy Bysshe Shelley*, ed. Frederick L. Jones, 2 vols (Oxford: Clarendon Press, 1964), vol. 2, p. 43.

28 See James Hogg, *The Private Memoirs and Confessions of a Justified Sinner*, ed. John Carey (Oxford: Oxford University Press, 1981), p. 12.

Romantic Verse Narrative: Keats, Shelley and Coleridge

Until the eighteenth century, despite the developing role of fiction, almost all imaginative writing, narrative and descriptive, was in verse. In the Romantic period, the long narrative poem was still predominant, and prose did not really begin to supplant it until the era of the great Victorian novel. Many of the best-known achievements in British Romantic poetry are in narrative form. The typical pre-Romantic eighteenth-century poem, for example James Thomson's *The Seasons* (1730), or Thomas Gray's 'Elegy' (1751), or Oliver Goldsmith's *The Deserted Village* (1770), was perhaps descriptive or reflective and did not, as such, have a 'story' to tell. It is in the Romantic period itself that verse narrative came to its greatest prominence and had its most memorable successes.

The rise of the novel in the eighteenth century clearly has something to do with this. Although the genre was proliferating, poetry still had a higher status than prose fiction, which was regarded as rather a low and frivolous form by the high-minded critical establishment. In Chapter 5 of *Northanger Abbey* (1818), Jane Austen mounts a vigorous page-long defence against 'contemptuous censure' of the novel, and in Chapter 14, she makes it a mark of Henry Tilney's discernment that he responds to Catherine Morland's 'gentlemen read better books' with 'The person, be it gentleman or lady, who has not pleasure in a good novel, must be intolerably stupid.' Opinion, nurtured by deference to a long tradition of classical poetry and drama, regarded fiction as something that could be written by hacks or even, as in the case of the gothic novel, by women. The gothic's readership, mainly middle-class women like Catherine Morland, was open to the censure of moralists and guardians of virtue. So the incorporation of narrative into the poetic mainstream made the tale element more acceptable, perhaps even more respectable, than if it were in prose-fiction form.

The reading public in Britain was also expanding rapidly and the critical reviews of the period, such as the influential *Edinburgh Review* founded in 1802 (see Part Two: 'A Cultural Overview'), were catering for a taste in reading which was spreading beyond a narrow elitist readership. By 1818 the *Edinburgh Review*'s initial print run of 800 copies had increased to a circulation of 14,000, with each copy being read by a dozen people, on average. Many of the great publishing houses, such as in England Longman (Wordsworth's publisher) and John Murray (Byron's), and in Scotland Constable (Scott's) and Blackwood, were first and foremost commercial enterprises, which, along with their counterparts in the developing industries like engineering and textiles, were out to increase their profits in the widening markets of the day. As well as having much critical success, therefore, many of the verse narratives of the period were, as a consequence of marketing, commercially successful, sometimes on a grand scale. Writers like Walter Scott, Thomas Moore and Byron found the writing of verse-tales particularly lucrative. Scott, a widely read poet before he became a novelist, earned £600 for *The Lay of the Last Minstrel* (1805), Moore received an advance of £3,000 for *Lalla Rookh* (1817), both astonishing amounts of money in their time, while Byron's *The Bride of Abydos* (1813) sold 6,000 copies in one month and *The Corsair* (1814) 10,000 copies in a single day. Even by the standards of modern-day literary 'blockbuster' sales, such success would be difficult to parallel.

Yet Scott's poetry, Moore's *Lalla Rookh*, even the verse-tales of Byron are now hardly read at all outside of academic circles. And just as the context in which such poems were written and celebrated passes inevitably into history, so the reasons for their popularity have to be investigated and largely reconstructed. In fact verse narrative, for over a hundred years an important literary genre, is now little practised by poets and neglected by critics, and by 1940 might be said to have been virtually dead. The last 'story' poems of length to be written by accomplished poets were Victorian ones, elaborately plotted tales such as Robert Browning's *The Ring and the Book* (1868–9), Alfred Lord Tennyson's *Maud* (1855–6) or Matthew Arnold's *Sohrab and Rustum* (1853). The Victorian period, however, is usually defined as the great age of the novel. With a few exceptions, such as those mentioned, poets seem to have been content to leave storytelling to fiction writers, acknowledging that novels, with their freer rhythms and their lack of formal restraints, are perhaps a more suitable genre in which to tell tales of length and complexity.

The plot or the storyline of a narrative poem, as with other forms of poetry, is often of secondary importance to the ways in which the poet makes use of language. The story being told might be a familiar, perhaps even a legendary one, and our feelings of suspense or of simple curiosity about how things are going to turn out, which are raised in a good prose story, are often less important to readers of narrative poetry than the pleasure given by the rhythms, the imagery and the resonances of words, which cannot be entirely and satisfactorily explained by reference to the events being described. Thus from the Romantic narrative poem what we tend to remember is often the visual or auditory imagery, the 'music' rather than the story itself, so that there always seems to be at the heart of the verse tale a lyrical impulse.

The Ballad Tradition

Among the narrative poems of interest to a period which placed emphasis upon forms of cultural primitivism was the ballad, with its strong folk idiom. Ballads, often about the fates of individuals and building towards an exciting conclusion, are a type of dramatic narrative poetry with a self-contained plot and a small number of characters. Because of their restriction originally to musical forms and presentation, they can also be termed the most lyrical category of narrative verse. The 'lyrical ballad' of William Wordsworth and Samuel Taylor Coleridge acknowledges both the narrative and the musical characteristics of the form, and even today we refer to the words of ballads (songs) as 'lyrics'. In his Preface to *Lyrical Ballads* (1798), Wordsworth said that the inward or 'expressive' quality of this particular collection of poems would take precedence over the mimetic or strictly 'ballad' element, the 'tale' which effectively imitates action in the external world. The poems would be distinguished from 'the popular poetry' of the day because 'the feeling therein developed gives importance to the action and situation, and not the action and situation to the feeling'. By the popular poetry of the day, Wordsworth had in mind the gothic ballads of poets such as Gottfried Bürger,* whose work is probably included among what he calls in the Preface the 'deluges of idle and extravagant stories in verse', which he believed were contributing to the debasement of a genuine poetic sensibility. Discussing Bürger in a letter to Coleridge in 1798, Wordsworth remarks that 'incidents are among the lowest allurements of poetry', and of how in Bürger's poems, although he remembers the 'hurry of pleasure' from reading about 'incidents', he has no recollection of 'delicate or minute feelings'.[1]

Among other narrative verse forms inherited by the Romantics was Epic, the highest of what were known as the 'kinds' of poetry, and the genre to which all major poets aspired. In epic poetry a high value is placed upon heroism, and the epic hero stands for something beyond his own individual concerns to represent a shared world view. Even Milton, the last great writer of epic in English, is able to assume in *Paradise Lost* (1667) a collective assent to the biblical account of creation in Genesis. Although the English Romantic poets showed appropriate respect for the epic and saw themselves as under an obligation to attempt it, their lack of any homogeneous world view made for difficulties in their relationship towards it as a genre. From among the six canonical Romantic poets only two narrative poems might be said to have achieved something of epic status, Byron's *Don Juan* (1818–24) and Wordsworth's *The Prelude* (1805).

---

* Gottfried Bürger (1747–94): German poet whose ballads with their energy and supernatural content were very influential in Early European Romanticism.

Byron's *Don Juan* is one of the lengthiest and the most ambitious of Romantic narrative poems which, in a letter to Thomas Medwin, Byron himself called 'an epic as much in the spirit of our day as the Iliad was in Homer's'.[2] Yet although he obviously considered *Don Juan* an epic and consistently makes references to that tradition throughout the poem, it is his own sceptical individualism which subverts the form, making it instead a means of revealing his own sensitive and complicated personality. Similarly, when Wordsworth's epic narrative *The Prelude* is referred to by Coleridge as a 'prophetic Lay', 'An orphic song', 'A song divine',[3] it is its lyrical rather than its epic qualities which are being singled out. In the same vein, in the first of two abortive attempts to write an epic narrative, John Keats instructs his muse to abandon *Hyperion*'s tale of the warring Titans altogether, exclaiming 'For thou art weak to sing such tumults dire: / A solitary sorrow best befits / Thy lips, and antheming a lonely grief' (III.3–6). Here he effectively asserts that his own talent is for writing lyric and not epic poetry.

Although he attempts to write epic, Keats found his particular strength in romance narrative. This differs from the epic in that its pretensions are more moderate. Less elevated in tone and not necessarily lengthy, its emphasis is not on the historical mission of a personality, but rather on his individuality and on the colourful, fabulous events in which he becomes involved. Whereas in epic, there is a shared belief in everything miraculous and outside of human experience, in romance narrative the supernatural is understood as being essentially no more than a fairytale element. The hero of the epic is defined wholly by what he does, and by his behaviour in the situations in which he becomes involved. There is no psychological analysis as such, whereas in romance narrative an individual's character might be analysed and his emotions described in detail. In his own romances Keats often examines conflicting situations after the open-ended manner of Shakespeare, who is his ultimate inspiration. And like a dramatist he allows his characters to act out their conflicts without intervening as an author to tell us what to think.

In the Romantic period the more aspiring among the new numbers of literate people wanted verse narrative but they also wanted instruction.

This, however, had to be in a form appropriate to their perceptive abilities. In other words, they often wanted a simple moral or a reflection. And they did not want this necessarily to interfere with the plot, the 'tale' the poem was telling. One innovative feature of the Romantic verse-tale is the way it frequently sets up narrative expectations of this kind only to subvert them, or shift the onus of responsibility for interpretation away from the author and on to the reader. Robert Burns, for example, subtitles his celebrated 'Tam O'Shanter' (1791) 'A Tale'. The story is of drunken Tam who, benighted while returning home late from a market-day drinking session, stumbles across a coven of witches celebrating a witches' sabbath and is then made the terrified object of their pursuit. Given that Tam's horse 'Maggie', in the course of the witches' chase, 'left behind her ain gray tail', the subtitle 'A Tale' takes on a particular irony. Burns's provision of a moralising conclusion to the 'tale' is an ironic simplification of a marvellous and somewhat inexplicable story into a straightforward, and by his readers anticipated, warning against drinking and wenching. In Wordsworth's poem 'The Idiot Boy', Johnny, the subject of the title, is invited by his mother to give an account of his night wanderings: 'And, Johnny, mind you tell us true'. Johnny's response, however, is of a different order: '(His very words I give to you,) / "The cocks did crow to-whoo, to-whoo, / And the sun did shine so cold."'4 Poems such as 'Simon Lee', 'Anecdote for Fathers' and 'We are Seven'5 leave us with similarly enigmatic statements or open-ended conclusions from which readers are invited simply to make meanings for themselves. In fact Wordsworth sometimes addresses his readers directly. In 'Simon Lee', in his assumption of a genteel readership ('O gentle reader'), and speaking in the language of 'politesse' ('I hope you'll kindly take it'), he salutes those expectations of a simple moral conclusion which his poem is not going to supply.

Romance Narrative

In *The Eve of St Agnes* (1819), Keats creates a romance world of make-believe, where habitual distinctions between reality and illusion no longer seem applicable. St Agnes was a thirteen-year-old Christian martyr whose symbol was the lamb and, according to legend, a girl who went supperless to bed on St Agnes' Eve (21 January) would have a vision of her lover. In the poem, Madeline follows these directions and, as she sleeps, is duly visited by Porphyro. His arrival, however, is fraught with peril as his family and Madeline's, like the Montagues and Capulets in *Romeo and Juliet*, are enemies. The promise of sexual fulfilment is thus always compromised by the possibility of its prevention, while the icy setting at the opening of the poem and the life-denying presence of the aged beadsman, a medieval retainer employed to say prayers for the threatening household, represent the frigid alternative for Madeline. The life of Porphyro is endangered by the 'blood-thirsty' (l. 99) opponents of his quest, yet when the 'argent revelry', first heard as music, eventually 'burst in' (l. 37) they are 'Numerous as shadows' (l. 39), of whom the narrator says, 'These let us wish away' (l. 41). Their 'reality', in other words, seems no more actualised than the 'woofed phantasies' in which we are later told that Madeline is herself 'entoil'd' (l. 288). The poem's strategy is to represent unstable versions of what might be taken as 'real'. Ideas of repressed desire on the very threshold of fulfilment are partially allowed to surface, only to sink back into the realms of the subconscious, rather as the struggling so-called 'Giants' of Michelangelo are reclaimed by, even as they appear to be escaping from, the marble blocks which imprison them. Thus Keats's 'carved angels, ever eager-eyed', are almost bursting from their stone 'cornice' (ll. 34–5). Porphyro, 'with heart on fire' (l. 75), sinks 'pale as smooth-sculptured stone' (l. 297) before Madeline. Music, later 'yearning like a God in pain' (l. 56), moves the aged beadsman momentarily to tears, before he subsides again into a cold isolation, while the would-be eloquence of Madeline's heart is suppressed 'As though a tongueless nightingale should swell / Her throat in vain, and die, heart-stifled, in her dell' (ll. 206–7).

A poem with which Keats was familiar, and indeed borrowed from in *The Eve of St Agnes*, was Coleridge's *Christabel* (1816). Part of Coleridge's purpose in this poem seems to have been to articulate liminal or subconscious motivations, allowing taboo or potentially harmful emotions, or transgressive issues involving sexual desire and fulfilment, to surface and be given a form of harmless expression. In Part 1 of Coleridge's work, the central character, Christabel, goes to the woods to pray by an oak tree. Here she has an encounter with Geraldine, who claims to have been abducted by a band of warriors. Geraldine is pitied and taken home by Christabel, where, that night, Geraldine, whose appearance is partly that of a serpent woman, seems to involve her in some form of sexual initiation. In Part 2, Sir Leoline, the father of Christabel, now infatuated with Geraldine, undertakes to reunite her with her own father, Lord Roland de Vaux of Tryermaine. The two men had once been friends, but have long since become estranged from each other. Sir Leoline employs Bracy the Bard as his emissary to Lord Roland, but Bracy demurs because of a dream he has had of Christabel caught in the toils of a 'bright green snake'. After a short and enigmatic third section, the poem breaks off and remains a fragment. In the brief Part 3, Coleridge describes how a father, burdened by excessive love for his child, can find himself sometimes inexplicably expressing his emotions in 'words of unmeant bitterness'. Such psychologically authentic episodes are here acknowledged, and the writing of *Christabel* seems to have served the purpose of somehow working off all kinds of questionable impulses without actually bringing them to realisation – as Coleridge himself puts it, 'To dally with wrong that does no harm' (*Christabel*, l. 669). In his poem 'The Pains of Sleep' (1803), he talks of his awareness of a series of obscure and unspeakable feelings which have come to him in nightmares and which he clearly understands to lurk below the surface of his consciousness. Without the benefit of the language in which a later science of psychology would explain such experience, the poem speaks of 'Desire with loathing strangely mixed', of 'Deeds to be hid which were not hid' and of 'The horror of [such] deeds to view / To know and loathe, yet wish and do!'

In his own poem Keats, in a similar way, seems to be marking Madeline's transition from a state of innocence to one of experience by incorporating a sexual agenda under the guise of a richly sensuous and highly wrought romance narrative. As in *Christabel*, where the vampiric nature of the Geraldine/Christabel relationship stands in for Christabel's sexual initiation, Porphyro arrives a 'famish'd pilgrim' (l. 339) in his quest for Madeline. Various sexual symbolisms are associated with him. His name suggests that it may have been inspired by 'porphyre', an obsolete word for a serpent. His 'lofty plume' (l. 110), recalls the 'sable plumes' of the helmet which, after crushing his son Conrad to death, enables Manfred to make sexual advances on Isabella in Horace Walpole's gothic novel, *The Castle of Otranto* (1764).

In order to 'access' Madeline, Porphyro must first encounter Angela, a version of Juliet's Nurse. Like *Romeo and Juliet*, *The Eve of St Agnes* involves lovers threatened by inimical forces. Angela's name suggests her Christian allegiances, as does Christabel's name in Coleridge's poem, and Angela's role in relation to Porphyro's 'stratagem' (l. 139) for Madeline is that of guardian 'angel'. She takes the conventional view that he 'must needs the lady wed' (l. 179). As Christabel is herself responsible for admitting Geraldine into the castle, Madeline too seems to realise, subconsciously, that in order to admit Porphyro she must first sideline Angela. Anticipating Lucy Westenra's complicity with the Count in Bram Stoker's *Dracula* (1897), she 'Rose like a mission'd spirit, unaware: / [...] and down the aged gossip led / To a safe level matting' (ll. 93, 95–6). Porphyro's urgent desires are imaged in a chromatic display. Thought, 'a full-blown rose' (l. 135), makes 'purple riot' (l. 136) in his heart, anticipating his encounter with the sleeping Madeline. On the threshold of experience and as yet 'Blinded alike from sunshine and from rain', Madeline, it seems, 'As though a rose should shut, and be a bud again', will be unable to put off her new-found knowledge.

In the fragmentary form in which *Christabel* exists, it may be that Coleridge is suggesting a censoring factor at work, permitting his conscious self to restrain his poem's more transgressive elements. It is possible that the name 'Bracy' suggests such restraint, and that Coleridge, the poet, is himself Bracy the Bard.* In *The Eve of St Agnes*, and from the orthodox point of view, the motives of Keats's Porphyro are more than suspect. Instead of observing the fasting associated with St Agnes' Eve (51), he appeals to Madeline's senses, setting up for her a

---

* Compare William Blake's 'Damn braces: Bless relaxes' (*The Marriage of Heaven and Hell*, Plate 9).

banquet which reflects the close association between food and the erotic, playing 'Close to her ear' (l. 293) 'an ancient ditty, long since mute' (l. 291). In her somnolent condition Madeline recalls that 'sweet tremble in mine ear' (l. 308) and we are here reminded of where Satan in *Paradise Lost* is discovered by Gabriel, 'Squat like a toad, close at the ear of Eve' (IV.800). In dreams, as analysed by Freud, the ear is often vaginal and the 'predatory' Porphyro's first sight of Madeline, as she undresses, recalls the moment in Book IX where we see Satan, on his first sight of Eve, disarmed of his malice by her beauty. For the moment, he stands 'Stupidly good' (l. 465), but a recollection to his grim purpose is carried in the line: 'But the hot hell that always in him burns' (l. 476). The situation finds its counterpart in Porphyro, who initially 'grew faint' (l. 224) at Madeline's Eve-like presence ('She knelt, so pure a thing, so free from mortal taint', l. 225), but finds that 'Anon his heart revives' (l. 226) and he is freed to advance his 'stratagem'.

That Man's sexual consciousness, a sign of his fallen condition in *Paradise Lost*, is present as a concept in Keats's poem, is suggested by Madeline who, as 'tongueless nightingale' (l. 206), recalls the rape of Philomel by Tereus.* Porphyro, secreted in Madeline's closet 'That he might see her beauty unespied' (l. 166), has parallels with Iachimo in *Cymbeline* who, concealing himself in a trunk in order to spy upon the sleeping Imogen, notes that she has been 'reading late / The tale of Tereus; here the leaf's turn'd down / Where Philomele gave up' (II. ii.44–5). In the blood-red light of the 'casement', Madeline undresses. Between four and five months later Keats would write both 'La Belle Dame Sans Merci' and his verse narrative 'Lamia' (the name meaning 'vampire'), and the sexual associations of the vampire myth, contained in both, are already present in *The Eve of St Agnes*. 'Porphyro grew faint', the poem tells us. Is it possibly at the sight of 'her silver cross' (l. 221)

---

* Procne's husband, King Tereus of Thrace, lusted after her sister, Philomel, and having raped her, cut out her tongue to prevent her from revealing the deed. However, Philomel wove her story into a tapestry and Procne in revenge having killed their son, Itys, served him as a dish to Tereus who unwittingly ate him. The Olympian gods changed Procne into a nightingale (whose song of mourning is for the loss of her son), Philomel appropriately into a swallow (which has no song) and Tereus into a hoopoe, a crested bird.

for, as she 'unclasps her warmed jewels one by one' (l. 228), including presumably the cross, 'Anon his heart revives' (l. 226)? The 'Solution sweet' of stanza 36 leads Madeline to exclaim as a 'vamped' creature dependent upon her lover, 'my heart is lost in thine'. Together, 'like phantoms' (l. 361) and alerting a wakeful 'bloodhound' (l. 365) they journey to the home Madeline is promised 'o'er the southern moors' (l. 351).

For the second-generation Romantic poets Byron, Shelley and Keats, the southern lands of Greece and the Mediterranean represented a form of sexual liberalism denied, for example, to the beadsman who 'Northward [...] turneth' (l. 19) to a life of deprivation (see Part Four: 'Faith, Myth and Doubt'). As with some of the verse narratives already mentioned, Keats refuses to supply a satisfyingly conventional conclusion to his tale. We never learn whether the 'lovers' (l. 371) ever reached their 'home'. Keats distances us from the immediacy of the breathless suspense of their departure and all we are told is that the events of the story happened 'ages long ago' (l. 370). We might suggest that for Keats (and consistent with the pattern of his developing philosophy), the inadequacy of being 'Blissfully haven'd both from joy and pain' (l. 240) makes the 'storm' (l. 371) into which they fled, like the 'tempests' of Shakespeare's Sonnet 116, symbolise the necessary experiences of the 'storms' of life itself.

Philosophical Verse Narrative

Shelley's *Julian and Maddalo*, written in early 1819, is contemporary with *The Eve of St Agnes* and is subtitled 'A Conversation'. The conversation takes place between Count Maddalo, a version of Lord Byron, and Julian, who represents in some ways Shelley himself. They argue, from their respective points of view, about man's future, Julian optimistically, Maddalo more pessimistically. In the course of the debate, and in an attempt to bolster his side of the argument, Maddalo takes Julian to a madhouse in the lagoon, where they listen to the melancholy tale of one of its inhabitants, the Maniac.

In the prose preface to the poem Shelley describes Maddalo as a man 'of the most consummate genius', a potential 'redeemer of his degraded country', but who has 'an intense apprehension of the nothingness of human life'. Julian, we learn, is 'passionately attached to those philosophical notions which assert the power of man over his own mind, and the immense improvements of which, by the extinction of certain moral superstitions, human society may yet be susceptible'. Here we find Shelley's own verse-narrative characterisations corresponding to the satirical portraits of Mr Cypress (Byron) and Scythrop Glowry (Shelley himself) in Thomas Love Peacock's novel *Nightmare Abbey* (see Part Three: 'Romantic Fiction').

The poem is based on the period during August 1818, when Shelley was visiting Byron and his young daughter Allegra at Byron's palace, the Palazzo Mocenigo, on the Grand Canal in Venice. Allegra was Byron's natural child by Mary Jane Clara ('Claire') Clairmont, Mary Shelley's stepsister. She had been raised by Claire, under Shelley's care, from her birth on 12 January 1817, until she was sent to Byron in Venice on 28 April 1818, hence the reference in line 155 to the 'six months or so' of Julian's separation from the child. Shelley tells us in the preface that Julian is conjectured by his friends to have some good qualities 'in spite of his heterodox opinions', adding, with a wry look at his notoriously humourless self, that 'Julian is rather serious'.

The poem opens with a description of the marine landscape of the Venetian Lido (now a built-up resort) where, during their time together, Shelley and Byron would ride the 'level sand' (l. 12) and hold their conversations. Julian declares, 'I love all waste and solitary places; where we taste / The pleasure of believing what we see / Is boundless, as we wish our souls to be' (ll. 14–17). The language recalls the 'lone and level sands' which 'boundless and bare' stretch 'far away' at the conclusion of Shelley's sonnet, 'Ozymandias', which was published in January 1818. There, as here, the topography is politicised and has a close relationship to the democratic ('level') future to which Shelley looked forward; a future freed ('boundless') from all social and political constraints as he saw them (see Part Four: 'Forms of Ruin').

Returning at sunset from one of their rides, the talk between Julian and Maddalo 'grew somewhat serious'. Although 'pleasing', it is also 'forlorn' (ll. 39–40) and brings to Julian's mind, significantly for Shelley's theme as the poem develops, the fruitless debates of the fallen angels in Book II of *Paradise Lost*, who 'reasoned high / Of providence, foreknowledge, will and fate, [...] And found no end, in wandering mazes lost' (II.558–61). Julian 'Argued against despondency' (l. 48), but 'pride' made Maddalo 'take the darker side', leading Julian to deduce from this display of Byronic egotism that Maddalo's 'sense that he was greater than his kind / Had struck [...] his eagle spirit blind / By gazing on its own exceeding light' (ll. 48–52).

This 'light' of the Romantic egotist now gives way to the light of a sunset over the lagoon. In the description which follows (ll. 53–85), reminiscent of the Venetian pictures of Shelley's contemporary, J. M. W. Turner, the beautiful landscape of Italy (the 'Paradise of exiles', l. 57) is transformed 'as if the Earth and Sea had been / Dissolved into one lake of fire' (ll. 80–1). Although memorable as a set piece, this passage is by no means a gratuitous interruption to the narrative. The dissolution of all material objects by the transforming light of the setting sun anticipates Julian's assertion later in the poem that the mind has power to change all circumstances, no matter how apparently intractable they might be.

In context, this passage, by presenting a form which is not so easily transfigured by the light of the sunset, contributes importantly to the developing debate. The 'deformed and dreary pile' of the madhouse, the home of the 'Maniac' whose story makes up the long central section of the poem, is something which resists such aesthetic transfiguration, and thus stands as a symbolic obstacle to Julian's claims for the transfiguring power of thought. Maddalo points it out to him. Julian looks, 'and saw between us and the sun' (98), a bell tower 'In strong and black relief' (l. 106). Here we are reminded of a similar ominous object, the 'strange shape' of the ship of death in Coleridge's *Ancient Mariner*, which, while 'The western wave was all a-flame [...], drove suddenly / Betwixt us and the sun' (ll. 175–6). The sound of the asylum's tolling bell, as Maddalo indicates, is calling 'the maniacs each one from his cell / To vespers' (ll. 110–11), leading Julian to offer one of his 'heterodox opinions': 'As much skill as need to pray / In thanks or hope for their dark lot have they / To their stern maker' (ll. 111–13). To this Maddalo adds his own view of the human condition, '"And such,"—he cries, "is our mortality / And this must be the emblem and the sign / Of what should be eternal and divine!"' (ll. 120–2).

By this stage in the narrative, therefore, the entire city of Venice, so recently made glorious by the light of the sun, has sunk into a deep 'gloom' (l. 137), both literally and figuratively. The sense here is in some ways akin to that fall from joy to dejection associated in particular with the Romantic temperament and to be found, for example, in Shelley's own 'Stanzas written in Dejection', in Coleridge's 'Dejection: An Ode', in the 'melancholy fit' of Keats's 'Ode on Melancholy' and in Wordsworth's 'Resolution and Independence' – 'As high as we have mounted in delight / In our dejection do we sink as low'.[6] Although Julian is at risk of seeing things from Maddalo's point of view, it is clear that, as the poem continues, his optimism begins to gain ground.

In the palace on the following morning, Julian amuses himself in 'rolling billiard balls about' (l. 157) with Maddalo's child ('A lovelier toy sweet Nature never made', l. 144) and, when Maddalo appears, the conversation of the previous evening resumes. Julian now indicates the carefree child as lending support to his own optimistic side of the debate. As 'blithe, innocent and free' (l. 167), she is a type of that which he imagines could be the condition of the whole race of man were he to exercise the power of his mind to bring about change: '—it is our will / That thus enchains us to permitted ill [...] if we were not weak / Should we be less in deed than in desire?' (ll. 170–6). He resists Maddalo's belief that man is a 'passive thing' (l. 161) only, and says:

> We know
> That we have power over ourselves to do
> And suffer—what, we know not till we try;
> But something nobler than to live and die—
> So taught those kings of old philosophy
> Who reigned, before Religion made men blind. (ll. 184–9)

Here we see the relevance to the argument of the billiard balls game. Newton's first law of motion had stated that a body must continue in a state of rest unless acted upon by some external force. From Maddalo's point of view, therefore, the mind is simply, like the billiard ball, a passive recipient of action upon it, whereas for Julian the mind is an agent for change: 'Where is the love, beauty and truth we seek / But in our mind?' (ll. 174–5). Maddalo's response to Julian, however, is simply to say, 'You talk Utopia' (l. 179).

Maddalo hopes to cure Julian of his 'beautiful idealisms' by introducing him to the forlorn figure of the Maniac: 'I knew one like you / Who to this city came some months ago / With whom I argued in this sort, and he / Is now gone mad' (ll. 195–8). What follows is the Maniac's lengthy soliloquy, a sequence of fragments separated by lines of asterisks. It requires careful attention, but its contents essentially support neither Julian nor Maddalo in their respective arguments. The Maniac does not give Julian's exclusive autonomy to the mind: 'I know / That to myself I do not wholly owe / What now I suffer, though in part I may' (ll. 320–2). On the other hand, unlike Maddalo, he will refuse to vent his hatred and his scorn upon the world, allowing 'the full Hell' within him to 'infect the untainted breast / Of sacred nature with its own unrest' (ll. 351–3). There is much more to be said on the soliloquy, but essentially the Maniac, while not exactly bearing out Julian's hopes for humanity, does not support Maddalo either in his deeply pessimistic arguments about the human condition.

As a consequence of the Maniac's story, and unlike the endless speculations of Milton's fallen angels 'in wandering mazes lost', Julian and Maddalo's own ego-centred debate, 'was quite forgot' (l. 520) and they are now in fact 'agreed' (l. 525) on the origins of the maniac's ills. Insofar as the expression of his sufferings 'in measure' (metre), would be a kind of 'poetry' (l. 542), Julian and Maddalo are together in their belief that some form of creativity can emerge from apparent evil. Julian remembers Maddalo's remark: 'Most wretched men / Are cradled into poetry by wrong, / They learn in suffering what they teach in song' (ll. 544–6).

In the final stages of the poem Julian is tempted to remain in Maddalo's grand palace, reverencing the cultural heritage of Venice and nurturing his own sensibilities. However, his return to London implies that he has communal values, and it is only after 'many years' (l. 583) that he returns to Venice. Maddalo is 'travelling far away / Among the mountains of Armenia' (ll. 586–7), but Julian is received by Maddalo's child who is now a woman, 'a wonder of this earth / [...] Like one of Shakespeare's women' (ll. 590–2).* He questions her about the fate of the Maniac, in response to which she supplies a brief outline of what has since happened to him. The woman had apparently come again, 'but after all / She left him' (ll. 605–6). Julian persists in his questioning and receives the reply, 'And was not this enough? / They met—they parted'. When still he persists, Julian says, 'she told me how / All happened—but the cold world shall not know'.

Here the poem ends enigmatically, raising a reader's expectation that the narrative will be brought to a satisfying conclusion, but then challengingly inviting further speculation on what additional information the narrator might be withholding. As in many comparable verse-tales of this period, readers must supply the purpose of the story for themselves. One clue to Shelley's approach might be found in his final remarks on the Maniac in the Preface. There we read: 'His story, told at length, might be like many other stories of the same kind: the unconnected exclamations of his agony will perhaps be found a sufficient comment for the text of every heart.'

So maybe Maddalo's daughter was right. Like Shakespeare, who perhaps has two sets of readers, those who respond and those who do not, she is implying that to wear one's heart on one's sleeve is to expose oneself far more to misunderstanding than sympathetic concern. If we have hearts, Julian appears to be saying, we can identify with the Maniac's tale and do not have to be told. If we are not moved, then we have not understood, revealing ourselves simply as cold worldlings.

The form of this poem is consistent with its content. The Maniac's fragmented speech, which according to Julian is 'in its wild language' (l. 541) a form of 'poetry' (l. 542), seems jarringly distinct from the urbane heroic couplets in which it is contained and in which the poem, as a whole, is written. It may be that Shelley, flattering Byron's delight

---

* See, for example, Miranda in *The Tempest*: 'O you wonder' (I.ii.427).

in the Augustan poets by using their most employed verse form, is using it himself in such a way as to suggest an alternative to the restrictions it imposes. We know that Keats incurred the wrath of the critical establishment, including Byron, by mocking the heroic couplet's dominant rhythm in which, he said, the Augustans mistook a 'rocking horse' for 'Pegasus'.[7] Shelley's poem, although it adheres strictly to the heroic couplet form, is allowed, structurally, the kind of freedom for which Julian argues in much broader terms against Maddalo. The opening fourteen lines without an end stop are a good example, where the tight heroic couplet form is fully operative, yet allowed a fluidity at one with the marine landscape and its 'ever shifting sand'.

The Romantic Ballad

As mentioned above, the ballad was a popular form of narrative verse in the Romantic period. A developing interest in primitivism, emerging via Pastoral and the influential philosophy of Jean-Jacques Rousseau, viewed civilisation, sophistication and the conscious control of reason as unreliable guides, compared with the more simple and dependable emotions of humble cottage-dwellers or the members of primitive tribes. The poetry of the Romantics drew widely for inspiration on the materials of folk narrative ballads, lyrical folk songs, broadside ballads and chapbooks. Collections of ballad material such as those of Bishop Percy in his *Reliques of Ancient English Poetry* (1765) were widely influential. Their mixture of pastoral dialogues, ballad imitations, historical songs and even forgeries mingled with the appeal of the ballads of Bürger, the gothic novel and the fabricated Celtic world of Macpherson's 'Ossian',* predisposing writers born, like Coleridge, in the 1770s to place a special value on the supernatural and on simple tales and diction. Coleridge's *Ancient Mariner* owes its intense supernaturalism, otherworldliness and, in its original form, its archaisms,

---

*   James Macpherson (1736–96) claimed to have discovered an epic poem on the subject of the mythical Irish hero, Fingal, written by his son, Ossian. He published a collected *Works of Ossian* in 1765, but its authenticity was questioned.

to traditional ballads. Its moral didacticism, too, as expressed in the simplicity of the final 'message', 'he prayeth best, who loveth best', belongs to the world of the Broadsides.* But Coleridge in *The Ancient Mariner* was not just copying ballad rhetoric, he was essentially developing the tradition both in the intensity of his concentration on a simple, central situation and in his use of a symbolic narrative imagery.

The ballad tells of how a ship set sail from a harbour, which may have been suggested by the small harbour of Watchet in Somerset, and heads south to cross the Equator towards Antarctica. The Mariner's inexplicable shooting of a friendly albatross which has begun to accompany the vessel, brings disaster upon the voyage. Coleridge had read everything possible in the way of sea-going literature, but even so, the voyage of this ship is a curiously enigmatic affair. We are never told its name, or the name of its captain or any of the crew. It is an important ship because it has a complement of two hundred men ('four times fifty living men'), almost three times as many as Captain Cook on the *Endeavour*. We are never told the purpose of its voyage, or where it is bound, or if it is a naval or a merchant vessel. Eventually, after much suffering and the death of the entire ship's company, the Mariner is returned to his home country by the agency of spirits who drive the ship back towards its harbour. Before landing, the Mariner encounters a boat containing a hermit, who 'shrives' him of his sins, but there is a sense that the Mariner's real salvation has taken place, long before, at sea when he redeems his wilful act by a spontaneous blessing of nature's 'happy living things'. Like Cain's in the Old Testament, the Mariner's fate is forever to wander the earth, telling his story as a warning to whomever he judges to be in need of it.

The Rime of the Ancyent Marinere, to give it the title in its original form, was published anonymously in the *Lyrical Ballads* collection of 1798. In 1797, Coleridge was living at Nether Stowey at the foot of the Quantock Hills, a few miles away from William and Dorothy Wordsworth. Late one November afternoon, the three of them set out on a walking tour and, according to Wordsworth, talked of writing a

---

* Many ballads were written on a single sheet of paper and were known as 'Broadside ballads'. They were sold by itinerant hawkers in streets and at fairs.

poem to be sent to the *New Monthly Magazine* in order to 'defray' their expenses.[8] Wordsworth had been reading an account in 'Shelvock's *Voyages*'[9] of the sighting of albatrosses at Cape Horn, and suggested to Coleridge the central act of the Mariner killing one of these birds. Throughout the summer of 1797 Coleridge had been working on ballad poems, but *The Ancient Mariner* was the one that developed most quickly. When the trio returned from their walk, about three hundred lines of it had been written and, by the following March, it was completed. When the second edition of *Lyrical Ballads* appeared in 1800, Coleridge had revised the poem, removing many of the original archaic words and phraseologies, and he kept on revising it until it was eventually collected with his poems in *Sibylline Leaves* (1817). Now, published for the first time under his own name, it included a prose 'gloss' in the margin, another voice as it were, commenting on the action of the narrative and providing a further perspective on events.

The Ancient Mariner has more in common with the ballad tradition than the other poems in the *Lyrical Ballads* collection. For the most part, Coleridge retains the four-stress/three-stress ballad metre in four-line stanzas, but he also provides variations in the line numbers and introduces a variety of pauses, repetitions and rhyme patterns. The usual effect of ballad metre is to give a sense of progression and inevitability to the narrative, but in *The Ancient Mariner*, in the 'beat' of the poem, there is an additional sense that it was conceived in the course of a walk rather than within the confines of a study.

In the first edition of *Lyrical Ballads*, the poem was at the beginning of the collection and Wordsworth's 'Tintern Abbey' at the end. This, too, Wordsworth claimed, had been entirely composed on a walk: 'I began it upon leaving Tintern, after crossing the Wye, and concluded it just as I was entering Bristol in the evening, after a ramble of 4 or 5 days with my sister.'[10] In *My First Acquaintance with Poets* William Hazlitt recalled the peripatetic habits of Coleridge and Wordsworth respectively. The one he called 'dramatic', the other 'more lyrical'. Hazlitt continues:

Coleridge has told me that he himself liked to compose in walking over uneven ground, or breaking through the straggling branches of a copse-wood; whereas Wordsworth always wrote (if he could) walking up and down a straight gravel-walk, or in some spot where the continuity of his verse met with no collateral interruption.[11]

In the light of Hazlitt's remarks, there is a connection here to be made between the nature of the two 'framing' poems of *Lyrical Ballads* and the walking habits of their authors. 'Tintern Abbey' certainly has the kind of stately progression consistent with what Hazlitt has to say about Wordsworth's habitual mode of composition, whereas the hypnotic rhythm of *The Ancient Mariner* reflects Coleridge's more effortful and purposive movements as he made his way across the Quantock Hills on that November afternoon: 'Day after day, day after day, / We stuck, nor breath nor motion' (ll. 115–16). It is possible in this poem that was partly composed 'on the hoof' to hear the sound of footsteps in such lines.

A virtual industry has grown up around *The Ancient Mariner* and there are numerous critical interpretations of it. One among many approaches is to see it as a form of veiled autobiography, where Coleridge is possibly describing the unhappiness of his own love life. The albatross becomes associated in this connection with one of the women in his experience: his wife Sara, or Dorothy Wordsworth perhaps, or Sara Hutchinson. The Mariner's sufferings are a version of the terrors of Coleridge's opium addiction and his physical and mental breakdown. He is eventually 'rescued' through his work and friendships, and his isolation, similar to the Mariner's, could be the reason that induced him throughout his life to tell his own story. He is indeed remembered for his wonderful talk, *Table Talk*, his 'conversation poems' and lectures.

The poem has also been read, in probably the most traditional interpretation, as a form of Christian allegory. The Mariner commits a sin in shooting the albatross, a wilful act of unreason for which he has to atone through suffering. He then, through the agency of the 'Hermit good', is returned to the harbour of his redemption and restored to the community of the 'kirk' and the 'wedding feast'. The prose gloss, which Coleridge appended to the 1817 version of the poem, lends support to this kind of interpretation, although the spirit world it describes is not specifically a Christian one, but one which establishes a much broader, neo-Platonic, magically hermetic context where everything symbolically participates in other levels of being. Within this world, abstractions are given a form of concrete presence and the spiritual is made absolutely as real as the material. Thus, the ship can be moved on either by the breeze or by the spirits, the sun can be obscured by mist or by the 'bars' of the spectral ship.

Coleridge attached to the head of the poem a Latin epigraph from the *Archaeologiae Philosophicae* (1692) of Thomas Burnet, a writer of great interest to the Romantics,* which begins: 'I can easily believe that there are more invisible than visible beings in the universe.' In this sense, *The Ancient Mariner* has also been construed as a paradigm of the Romantic Imagination, with the eponymous hero a kind of visionary who, having accessed a higher form of 'truth', is obliged to wander for evermore through what Coleridge in his poem 'Dejection' called that 'cold world allow'd / To the poor loveless ever-anxious Crowd'.[12] Thus, like a modern-day Romantic poet, he is condemned to tell his story to those who, devoid of imagination in a world of 'objects, still beheld / In disconnection dead and spiritless',[13] are truly the inhabitants of a 'Nightmare LIFE-IN-DEATH' (l. 194) experience.

The Ancient Mariner is also a story of great human tragedy. Many people die because of the Mariner's action: 'Four times fifty living men / [...] dropped down one by one' (ll. 216, 219). A modern approach to the poem is to see the Mariner's remorse, his sense of guilt and his compulsion to tell his story over and over again as symptomatic of what might now be called, 'post-traumatic stress disorder'. Two hundred or

* In his *The Sacred Theory of the Earth* (1681–9) Thomas Burnet argued that the world we now inhabit, originally created as perfect and beautiful, is the result of man's wickedness and that the wild and desolate regions of the earth are evidence of God's wrath with his creation. Burnet's work, although essentially theological, had the effect of drawing attention to those elements of landscape which were often associated with the aesthetics of the Sublime.

so years before the syndrome was recognised, Coleridge has somehow perceived the Mariner's predicament as a form of Romantic pathology. The same, it could be said, is true of George Crabbe's poem 'Peter Grimes' (1810), which has many echoes of Coleridge's ballad. Its justly famous descriptions of the Suffolk tidal reaches, like those of the 'rotting sea' (l. 240) in the 'Mariner', are a kind of psychological landscape reflecting the isolation of Grimes in his guilt, while his paranoia, his 'projection' of culpability and his need to talk incessantly, have similarly modern resonances.

In another epigraph to his poem, Coleridge refers to 'how the Ancient Mariner cruelly, and in contempt of the laws of hospitality, killed a Sea-bird and how he was followed by many and strange Judgements'.[14] This emphasis on hospitality is there from the outset in the presence of the 'Wedding-Guest'. There is a sense carried throughout the poem that, like guests at a wedding feast we, as guests of the world we inhabit, should behave as such. The Mariner's cruel act of hostility against the albatross results in his total exclusion from a community of 'Old men, and babes, and loving friends / And youths and maidens gay!' (ll. 608–9). The extremity of this exclusion is accentuated by the silence of even one of his closest relatives, that of his 'brother's son', who standing 'knee to knee' said 'nought' to him (ll. 341–4).

Finally, in some ways, we can think of the Mariner's sin as an ecological transgression and of the poem as a form of green parable. As recipients of the 'tale' we, like the Wedding-Guest, are made morally responsible for what happens. Through our collective thoughtlessness, through our technology and our exploitations of the natural world, we damage it, and the poem's 'message' becomes consequently an urgent one for our times. Just as the Mariner warns the Wedding-Guest, Coleridge seems to be issuing a warning to his readers. If we persist in being inhospitable to nature, nature may, in the end, become inhospitable to us. *The Ancient Mariner* is one of the most celebrated of all Romantic verse-tales, a combination of lyrical resonance and sophisticated balladic technique with which the simple prose narrative struggles to compete.

Verse-narrative, represented by the three examples above, allowed for an extraordinary range of forms, topics and settings, and is as typical of this period of literary history as the shorter, expressive lyric poem with which Romantic poetry is perhaps more often associated.

Extended Commentary: Coleridge, *The Rime of the Ancient Mariner* (1817), lines 1–40 and 610–17

The typical Shakespearean comic perspective is to see life as a series of plays within plays or concentric circles. Each of the inhabitants of a particular circle takes the one it occupies as reality and laughs at the inhabitants of the others for their perceived ignorance. Outside each circle, however, is a larger one, and it is only in dreams or under the pressure of various psychic urgencies, or through art perhaps, that a door is opened and the further ranges of reality are made 'real'. What the traveller journeying through that door encounters may be attractive or frightening, or both. Having glimpsed these regions in which often unknown depths of his own nature are revealed to him, he may return to the comparative safety of the ordinary world of appearances, often forgetting what has been seen and experienced. A play such as *A Midsummer Night's Dream* (see Part Four: Imagination, Truth and Reason), like *The Ancient Mariner*, full of strange places and events and set, as is Coleridge's poem, in the context of a wedding, involves four groups of characters. Two of these groups are the geniuses of their respective places and only on the rarest of occasions move to the margins of other ones. But two of the groups, the 'lovers' and the 'mechanicals', journey back and forth between settings with surprising, bizarre and sometimes dangerous consequences. Shakespeare's scene placing of 'Athens, and a wood near it' is significant here as, to an Elizabethan audience, Athens would have stood in for 'Reason', while 'wood' retained something of its medieval meaning of 'mad' ('here am I, and wode [pronounced 'wood'] within this wood', II.i.192). In *A Midsummer Night's Dream* madness is always near reason, and the play invites us to define the meanings we might want to give to these terms in a variety of contexts.

Coleridge's poem opens as a Wedding-Guest is stopped by a Mariner. We are not told why he is selected as 'one of three', apart from the inscrutable 'explanation' provided by the Mariner himself towards the end of the poem: 'That moment that his face I see, / I know the man that must hear me' (ll. 588–9). It is urgent for this Wedding-Guest as 'next of kin' (l. 6) to be present at events. He demands a reason for the Mariner's intervention ('Now wherefore?'), then appeals from the familiar world of obligations and social commitments (stanza 2) to be allowed to go on his way. After all, the last thing anyone would want while hurrying, late, to a wedding would be for an ancient mariner to accost him with 'There was a ship' (l. 10)! Two worlds are here in conflict with one another.

The present indicative of the first line has the effect of removing the Mariner from a recognisable historical narrative in which we might expect to hear something of his circumstances, just as the present participle, 'the children walking', of Blake's 'Holy Thursday' makes them, without an explanatory context, an immediate presence.[15] In Coleridge, the Mariner simply looms and is there.

The world of the 'tale' now intrudes upon 'reality'. Even though the Wedding-Guest is released from the 'skinny hand' of the Mariner, he is held by his 'glittering eye' and, as though charmed to the spot, 'stood still' (l. 18). He is removed, in other words, from the familiarity of the wedding, the great type of order in society, and put into the situation of 'a three years child' who is made the recipient of a story. In the same kind of way Porphyro with Angela in *The Eve of St Agnes* is described as a 'puzzled urchin' with an 'aged crone / Who keepeth clos'd a wond'rous riddle-book, / As spectacled she sits in chimney nook' (stanza 15).

As the tale commences (l. 21), the Wedding-Guest is obliged ('He cannot chuse but hear', l. 18) to enter the Mariner's world. However, in stanza 8, familiar experience still competes with the Mariner's narrative for domination.

Higher and higher every day,
Till over the mast at noon—
The Wedding-Guest here beat his breast,
For he heard the loud bassoon.

Its attempt to maintain a presence is finally overwhelmed in stanza 10:

The Wedding-Guest he beat his breast,
Yet he cannot chuse but hear;
And thus spake on that ancient man,
The bright-eyed Mariner.

The Wedding-Guest is presented with the vivid, almost childlike, cut-out shapes and movements associated with the classroom of the three-year-old. We are reminded of the simple movements of a 'Captain Pugwash' episode:

The ship was cheered, the harbour cleared,
Merrily did we drop
Below the kirk, below the hill,
Below the light house top.

The Sun came up upon the left,
Out of the sea came he!
And he shone bright, and on the right
Went down into the sea.

As well as the simplicity and arresting strange powers of visualisation here, there is also a hint of menace in 'Out of the sea came he!' Beauty, strangeness and fear are increasingly the experience of the Wedding-Guest as he makes that gradual transition, by way of the Mariner's story, from a normative world of logic and empiricism to one of imaginative 'truth'. This is the habitual awareness of the child and indicates the possibilities which the Romantics saw in childhood for recovering the wonders lost, as Wordsworth described it, to the 'earthly freight' of 'custom'.[16]

The conclusion of the poem returns the Wedding-Guest from his experience of that world as 'one that hath been stunned' (l. 622). But the Mariner continues to occupy it. All his misfortunes seem predicated on his acts of will or on his rational, conscious attempts to 'know' or interrogate it. It is only when, in an act of spontaneous 'love' (l. 284) for creation that he blesses the 'happy living things' (l. 282), and does so 'unaware' (l. 287), that we see his true redemption to have taken place, not at the hands of the holy hermit, but at sea. His renewed kinship with creation is to him even 'sweeter than the marriage-feast' (l. 601) and presumably also to the 'sadder' and 'wiser' Wedding-Guest who turns 'from the bridegroom's door' (l. 621).

Lines 610–17

The Mariner's parting words to the Wedding-Guest are delivered in the form of a moral conclusion which, in the light of the tale itself, has often puzzled commentators. It is certainly true that the Broadside ballad was given to imposing a crude moralism on sensational narratives, yet the Mariner's sentiments are not of this kind. To reflect on them is to be aware of how the profundity of the message is carried by their simplicity. Coleridge's own comments, too, throw light on the ending of a poem which has consistently called 'reasoning' into question. Late in his life he responded to the poet Anna Barbauld's objection that the poem lacked a moral:

> I told her that in my own judgment the poem had too much; and that the only, or chief fault, if I might say so, was the intrusion of the moral sentiment so openly on the reader as a principle or cause of action in a work of pure imagination. It ought to have had no more moral than the *Arabian Nights'* tale of the merchant's sitting down to eat dates by the side of a well and throwing the shells aside, and lo! A genie starts up and says he *must* kill the aforesaid merchant *because* one of the date shells had, it seems, put out the eye of the genie's son.

The emphases on the words *must* and *because* in the passage suggest that trying to fit the merchant's situation to the genie's 'logic' is no more appropriate than the futile attempts of the Mariner's crew to apply a syllogistic logic to the kind of events which elude it in lines 91–102. In this sense, *The Ancient Mariner*, like Burns's 'Tam O'Shanter', or Shelley's *Julian and Maddalo*, encourages its readers to explore beyond the 'moral' or the 'explanation'. Coleridge calls his poem 'a work of pure imagination', a faculty of mind which, in the Romantic period, owes its definition to him more than anyone.[17] The poem itself is a demonstration of the Imagination's unifying, or 'coadunating'* powers at work. One example will have to suffice:

> Still as a slave before his lord,
> The OCEAN hath no blast;
> His great bright eye most silently
> Up to the Moon is cast—
>
> If he may know which way to go;
> For she guides him smooth or grim.
> See, brother see! How graciously
> She looketh down on him.

The calm sea, as ever under the moon's gravitational influence, lies as a prostrate slave before its lord. But here the iniquity of slavery, a major political issue of the time, is converted to a benevolent reciprocity between the masterful, yet gracious, moon, and the sea in a *willing* obeisance to it. Science, politics and the natural world are imaginatively present in a seamless weld, with Imagination's symbol, the 'great bright eye' of the moon, reminding us of that 'glittering eye' of the 'bright-eyed mariner', and of how an encounter with this kind of 'madness' ('greybeard loon!') can lead us to the truth of higher reason.

---

* Coleridge's term which means to bring things to a state of oneness: co-ad-unate.

Notes

1   Letter to S. T. Coleridge: *The Letters of William and Dorothy Wordsworth*, ed.
     E. de Selincourt, 8 vols (Oxford: Clarendon Press, 1967; repr. 2004), vol. 1
     (revised by Chester Shaver), *The Early Years, 1787–1805*, p. 234.
2   Quoted in Byron, *Don Juan*, ed. T. G. Steffan, E. Steffan and W. W. Pratt
     (Harmondsworth: Penguin, 1973), p. 588.
3   S. T. Coleridge, 'To a Gentleman' (1817).
4   'The Idiot Boy', *Lyrical Ballads* (1798).
5   *Lyrical Ballads* (1798).
6   'Resolution and Independence', stanza 4.
7   Keats, 'Sleep and Poetry', ll. 181–7.
8   Mary Moorman, *William Wordsworth: A Biography*, 2 vols (Oxford:
     Clarendon Press, 1957–65), vol. 1, p. 348.
9   George Shelvocke, *A Voyage Round the World by way of the Great South Sea*
     (1726).
10   Fenwick Notes: notes by Wordsworth, compiled in 1843 by Isabella
     Fenwick: *The Fenwick Notes of William Wordsworth*, ed. Jared Curtis
     (London: Bristol Classical Press, 1993), p. 15.
11   William Hazlitt, *Selected Writings*, ed. Ronald Blythe (Harmondsworth:
     Penguin, 1970), p. 60.
12   'Dejection: An Ode', ll. 300–1.
13   William Wordsworth, *The Poetical Works of William Wordsworth*, ed. E. de
     Selincourt and Helen Darbishire, 6 vols (Oxford: Clarendon Press, 1949),
     vol. 5, p. 402.
14   S. T. Coleridge, *The Complete Poetical Works of Samuel Taylor Coleridge*, ed.
     Earl Leslie Griggs, 2 vols (Oxford: Clarendon Press, 1956), vol. 1, p. 186.
15   Blake, 'Holy Thursday', in *Songs of Innocence*, l. 2.
16   Wordsworth, 'Ode: Intimations of Immortality from Recollections of early
     Childhood', ll. 125–7.
17   See S. T. Coleridge, *Biographia Literaria*, ch. 13.

Romantic Fiction: Hogg, Peacock and Austen

Division

There are many stories throughout the nineteenth century which take as their subject the theme of the fragmented and divided self. It appears in the work of major writers such as Edgar Allan Poe, Mrs Gaskell, Charles Dickens, Robert Louis Stevenson, Oscar Wilde, Henry James and Joseph Conrad,[1] and seems to have been something of a preoccupation. There were precedents in the Romantic period. William Godwin's *Caleb Williams* (1794), for example, had described a symbiotic relationship between his two main characters, Falkland and Williams, and Caleb Williams himself is a fragmented personality taking on the roles of outlaw, beggar, farmer, Jewish writer and hunch-backed watchmaker in his attempt to escape from Falkland, his persecutor (see Part Three: Writing in Revolution). Almost a quarter of a century later, Mary Shelley in *Frankenstein* (1818), the novel she dedicated to William Godwin, her father, had presented an enduring image of a divided self in the shape of her main protagonist, Dr Frankenstein and his Creature (see Part Four: Heroes and Anti-heroes).

In the literature of antiquity, the division within man as a part-spiritual, part-corporeal being is thought to lie behind all those fables describing relationships and couplings between gods and mortals as, for example, Europa and the Bull, Cupid and Psyche, and Leda and the

Swan. Thus, in *Frankenstein*, a novel which draws importantly on classical mythology, the repulsive form of the Creature serves to remind Dr Frankenstein, the 'Modern Prometheus', of the creaturely limitations that he wants to abolish. As in Percy Bysshe Shelley's concept of the gap between inspiration and composition,[2] Frankenstein's ambitions are compromised by the 'hideous' form into which they are resolved. Mary Shelley warns of the potential destructiveness that often lurks behind the triumphs of Romantic idealism.

The Romantic period was preoccupied with ideas about division and self-division. In *The Prelude*, William Wordsworth remembers a time in the development of his own imagination when 'Thus strangely did I war against myself' (XI.74). In *The Four Zoas* (1797), William Blake describes Albion's 'fall into Division & his Resurrection to Unity',[3] not, in this case, in terms of the traditional Fall of Man from the Garden of Eden, but as a fall from wholeness into a state of alienation from his own being. The period also reflects a quest for unity and integration through the agency of what Samuel Taylor Coleridge would call the 'coadunating' imagination (see p. 149, footnote, above), the faculty which reconciles opposites to bring everything into a state of 'oneness'. In a letter to his radical acquaintance, John Thelwall, Coleridge expresses his yearning for a transcendental sense of the 'One Life', as he calls it: 'the universe itself, what but an immense heap of *little* things? [...] My mind feels as if it ached to behold and know something *great*, something *one* and *indivisible*'.[4]

It is important to understand, therefore, that the nineteenth century inherited from the Romantic period an extensive literature on the subject of division and fragmentation, and to this it made its own contribution, introducing new social issues peculiar to its times. A rapidly changing society, as the later Condition of England writers would document,* had the effect of fragmenting not only traditional communities but also the individual lives of those who, displaced from the land as a consequence of the industrial revolution and labouring in the new workplaces, were becoming estranged from their work as well as from each other. Instead of

---

* Thomas Carlyle coined the phrase in his pamphlet, *The Condition of England Question* (1839).

being regarded as people, workers might now, for example, be described as 'hands'. In Dickens's *Hard Times* (1854), the schoolboy 'Bitzer', the product of a 'Utilitarian' education,* famously defines a horse as a 'graminivorous quadruped'. He reduces the horse, or the idea of the horse as a whole creature, to what Coleridge might call 'a heap of little things': 'Forty teeth, namely twenty-four grinders, four eye teeth, and twelve incisive', and so on. Bitzer himself has clearly become an embodiment of a mechanistic and alienating system whose effect, in the long term, as Dickens sees it, is to fragment everything, including people, into 'bits'.

Contributing also to this sense of alienation and self-division, and closely allied to the developing emphasis the nineteenth century would place upon work, was the separation of the public from the private realm. As early as 1800, Wordsworth had noted as a disturbing development 'the encreasing accumulation of men in cities'.[5] As the world became more complex and demanding, with political events and technological processes less easy to assimilate or to understand, the tendency, at least among the more middle and well-to-do classes, was to retreat and to cultivate an environment over which it was felt some authority might still be asserted. Dickens's *Great Expectations* (1860–1) introduces a character, Wemmick, whose official persona in the city contrasts with one of domestic decency and tenderness after working hours. In the evening he raises the drawbridge of his little 'castle' at Walworth and, retreating into a cosy world of fireside security, lovingly cares for his elderly father. In Germany the 'Biedermeier' period, following the end of the Napoleonic wars, witnessed the same kind of impulse, realised not only in literature but also in the visual arts, and extending to such things as domestic decor and furnishing.† This reaction in the early nineteenth century to an

---

* A philosophy which judges the moral worth of something only insofar as it is seen to contribute to general utility. Its major proponents were Jeremy Bentham (1748–1832), James Mill (1773–1836) and John Stuart Mill (1806–73).

† The ideal interior of the Biedermeier period focused on practicality and convenience. Its style refuted the pomposity typical of Napoleonic days, preferring to focus on enhancing the bourgeois family world and a comfortable social position. Furniture tended to occupy all available space. As well as fixed pieces, there were, typically, easy-to-move 'incidental' tables, screens, richly upholstered divans, armchairs and chairs, and glass showcases containing copious *objets d'art*.

increasingly troublesome and intractable external world is, to a large extent, or perhaps even a greater one, still with us, and manifested in such growth industries as the garden centre and the home beautiful, catering for territory over which it is still seen as possible for the individual to have a measure of control.

'Two truths are told': Divided Selves

James Hogg's novel *The Private Memoirs and Confessions of a Justified Sinner* involves both external and internal divisions. Historically, it looks back to a society of religious and political conflict in late seventeenth-century Scotland, yet published towards the end of the Romantic period in 1824, it looks ahead to later Victorian novels in its dealings, not only with issues of property and inheritance, but also, like many of them, with doubles and various forms of psychological self-division. Structurally, the novel is itself divided, in being the same story twice-told. The first of its accounts is a tale told 'from tradition' and narrated, following a particular convention, from the point of view of a supposed 'Editor' ('The Editor's Narrative'). The second is the same story, but this time told in his own words, by the so-called 'justified sinner', a suicide, whose grave has been opened a hundred years after his death, revealing, with the remains of his corpse, a pamphlet containing his 'Private Memoirs and Confessions'. The final section of the book, describing the discovery and exploration of the suicide's grave, is a sort of 'gothic' coda to an extraordinary sequence of events, in which Hogg not only incorporates verbatim an actual account of a grave opening he had witnessed a year previously and published in *Blackwood's Magazine*,[6] but also, rather like the director Alfred Hitchcock's briefly intervening in his own films, making an appearance himself as the real 'Ettrick Shepherd'.* For reasons of this kind

---

* James Hogg, born at Ettrick, Scotland, and largely self-educated, was a shepherd by trade. Known as 'The Ettrick Shepherd', he was a self 'divided', like his 'ploughman' compatriot Robert Burns, between on the one hand his humble existence and, on the other, his participation in the sophisticated Edinburgh literary society of his times. He is the subject of a late poem by Wordsworth, the elegy 'Extempore Effusion on the Death of James Hogg' (1835).

Hogg has been credited with anticipating aspects of modernist and postmodernist fiction and, in fact, it was the French novelist André Gide who, in the earlier twentieth century, was responsible for rescuing the *Confessions* from comparative neglect. Perhaps the longstanding historical alliance between Scotland and France had something to do with the particular way in which Hogg's novel recommended itself to the mind of a prominent French writer, but whatever may have been the case, the story Hogg tells is powerfully, at times unpleasantly, disturbing, and extraordinarily difficult to paraphrase.

Initially, in the first part of the book, we are given an account of a disastrous marriage between the old laird of Dalcastle, George Colwan, and a pious young woman of strict Calvinist leanings, Rabina Orde. The match is almost Chaucerian in its farcical beginnings.* The laird's irreligion, his coarseness, his flirting and drinking scandalise his new wife and very quickly lead to a separation. While he moves into quarters in the lower part of his house, 'The upper, or third story of the old mansion-house, was awarded to the lady for her residence.' Hogg implies, therefore, the traditional opposition between the flesh and the spirit, and the marital arguments become in this way symbolic of the divisions in Man's nature. While Rabina, aloft, occupies her time in extended doctrinal debates with her religious mentor, the Reverend Robert Wringhim, George ('old Dal'), receives visits from a 'fat bouncing dame', Arabella Logan.

Two sons, however, are born from the marriage between George and Rabina. The first, also named George, inherits his father's animal spirits, indulging in various sports and games and frequenting taverns and brothels. But the second son, Robert, given Wringhim's surname, is brought up under his mother's regime as a strict and dour Calvinist. The two brothers do not in fact meet until much later in life when, despite his attempts to be friends, George finds that Robert is relentlessly inimical to him, stalking his every move and accusing him of moral turpitude in the language of his implacable fanaticism: 'George became utterly confounded; not only at the import of this persecution, but how in the world it came to pass that this

* See, for example, 'The Merchant's Tale'.

unaccountable being knew all his motions, and every intention of his heart, as it were intuitively.'

As events turn out, George Colwan is murdered one night outside a tavern where he has been consorting with his riotous friends. Drink-fuelled arguments have led to his being challenged to a duel by one of them, supposedly a man called Drummond, who then, suspected of George's murder, flees into exile abroad. Bel Calvert, a prostitute who had earlier been 'entertaining' Drummond, has witnessed the murder and has watched as two figures, one of whom in every way inexplicably identical to Drummond but who, she knows, cannot possibly be him, arranges for his shadowy companion, lurking in a dark alleyway or 'wynd', to give George his death blow. 'Old Dal' shortly afterwards dies of sorrow for the death of his son, and his estates pass into the hands of Robert Wringhim and his mother. Arabella Logan, outraged by this and convinced by Bel Calvert's story that Robert was the dark figure who murdered George, makes a journey with her to the lands of Dalcastle to confront Robert and accuse him of the murder of his brother. To their astonishment, however, they see Robert walking along in the company of a young man who appears to be the 'dead' George Colwan. The 'Editor's Narrative' draws to an end with Bel Calvert's bewilderment expressed in her remark, 'we have nothing but our senses to depend on, and if you and I believe that we see a person, why, we do see him. Whose word, or whose reasoning can convince us against our own senses?' Mrs Logan and Bel Calvert together set about Robert, who mysteriously calls out for help to one 'Gil-Martin'. No help is forthcoming, however, and the two women decide to let Robert go: 'We could easily put an end to thy sinful life, but our hands shall be free of thy blood.' As the Editor's Narrative concludes, the reader is left with a suspicion that Robert Wringhim has some mysterious double who is a shape-changer and can impersonate whoever he wishes at will. The Editor at this point announces that he will now present 'readers' with an 'original document of a most singular nature'. This of course turns out to be Robert's 'Confessions', exhumed from his grave, and the narrative we have just been given is told all over again, but from Robert's point of view.

The story in essence is of Robert's puritanical upbringing to the point where he is assured by his spiritual 'father', the Reverend Wringhim, of his 'justification': that no matter how sinful his actions on this earth, he is guaranteed salvation. Elated at this news, Robert tells of how he 'bounded away into the fields and the woods, to pour out my spirit in prayer before the Almighty for his kindness to me'. Prior to this moment he has described how he has eliminated opposition to himself by lying about people or framing them, and this state of mind, within the psychological framework of the novel, engenders what William Blake might have called an 'emanation' of himself. This turns out to be the 'demonic' figure, Gil-Martin, who then comes into his life and for whose aid we remember him calling at the end of the Editor's Narrative. The rest of the 'Confessions' traces the systematic demise of Robert who, under Gil-Martin's influence, now begins to eliminate people by murdering them, including his brother and, it would seem, although the 'Confessions' part is equivocal about this, his mother and an innocent girl into the bargain.

Although Hogg's novel is telling a story about things as they happen in the world of external events, its strategy is to present a divided psyche in the person of Robert, for whom George represents his carnal and Gil-Martin his spiritual self. Robert confesses that, 'against the carnal portion of mankind, I set my face continually', but Gil-Martin's function is to lead him constantly into situations where that repressed self is given expression. Thus, he is astonished to hear from Gil-Martin about episodes of his drunken debauchery of which he has no knowledge, and which he has obviously suppressed, and it becomes clear from the developing history that in his 'spiritual' self he is responsible for the murder of his brother and his father, while in his 'carnal' self he has disposed of his mother and the girl. Supporting this pattern, sometimes Gil-Martin is 'seen' as George, at other times as the Leader of the 'elect' upon earth and, as Robert's life becomes increasingly hellish and tormented and moves towards his eventual suicide, Gil-Martin, his role redundant, fades away from the story. His once 'majestic' face now 'haggard' recalls the 'haggard, emaciated' face of Falkland, Caleb Williams's double in Godwin's novel. In Mary Shelley's, it recalls the physically reduced state of its eponymous 'hero', Frankenstein, whose various destructions of brother, maidservant, father, best friend and wife are finally revealed to have been simply versions of the *self*-destruction which is all that is finally left to him to carry out.

Consistent with the Romantic period's laying stress upon new democratic forms of society, on community and relationship, and on the replacement of retribution by forgiveness, Hogg's novel deploys numerous examples of how 'division' can be healed and the divided self reintegrated. During one episode in the Editor's Narrative, George Colwan experiences a transcendental moment of Coleridgean 'oneness' as, on an early morning walk, he becomes aware of a reciprocity between himself and the glorious aspects of nature. It is only when he allows himself to think negatively of his brother that this sense of 'wholeness' disintegrates and vengefulness once more destroys his peace. Later, as we have seen, Mrs Logan and Bel Calvert refuse to take vengeance on Robert, and there are many such later instances where a generosity of spirit provides some hope for the dark world that this novel presents.

One evening, in his protracted flight from Gil-Martin, Robert fetches up at the house of a weaver. The weaver is suspicious of him and receives him 'ungraciously', telling him 'of a gentleman's house at no great distance, and of an inn a little further away'. The weaver's wife, however, 'who sat with a child on her knee' exclaims, 'You are a stranger, it is true, but *them* that winna entertain a stranger will never entertain an angel unawares.' The episode has distinct echoes of the Christmas story, the Virgin Mary and the Christ child, and it also calls to mind the conclusion of William Blake's lyric, 'Holy Thursday':[7] 'Then cherish pity, lest you drive an angel from your door.' Blake's point in *Songs of Innocence* is that 'pity' should no longer be a gift which the polite classes bestow upon the so-called deserving poor, but rather something that those classes must learn to 'cherish' at their peril of neglecting it. As the neglected children of the poem become more real and familiar to them, so the traditional 'pity' will become more of a stranger.

Confessions of a Justified Sinner is a novel of major importance in the handling of 'division' in Romantic literature, but it also raises other issues which are central to the period. One is the status of subjective and objective reality. As readers of Hogg, we are constantly being asked to decide between what is real and what is apparent. When Wordsworth, for example, talks of 'a life that breathes not' and of 'Powers there are / [...] Which the gross world no sense hath to perceive, / Nor soul to dream of',[8] it may be remote from our own cognitive experience but, nevertheless, we do not believe that he is telling us something untrue. A poet such as John Keats consistently interrogates his own grasp of 'reality': 'Surely I dreamt to-day, or did I see / The wingèd Psyche with awakened eyes?'[9] In 'Ode to a Nightingale' he asks uncertainly, 'Was it a vision, or a waking dream?— / Fled is that music—Do I wake or sleep?' In Emily Brontë's *Wuthering Heights* (1847), Mr Lockwood's sense of 'the real' is disturbed when, awaking from his dream about Catherine Earnshaw at Wuthering Heights, he finds that Heathcliff, at the window, is actually talking to the very subject of the dream. As Ellen Dean's narrative proceeds, Lockwood becomes aware that his 'real' self has somehow been incorporated into the old woman's 'fireside tale' of which he is now being made the recipient.

In its shaping of 'reality', Hogg's novel occupies a strange hinterland between Hamlet's assertion that 'There are more things in heaven and earth [...] / Than are dreamt of in [...] philosophy' (I.v.166–7) and Gertrude's statement to Hamlet on the (to her) invisible Ghost, 'yet all that is I see' (III.iv.133). We recall Bel Calvert's 'We have nothing on earth but our senses to depend on', but the disparities between the Editor's Narrative and the Confessions proper constantly call into question our ability to decide between what is real and what is not. To borrow a line from *Macbeth*, 'Two truths are told' (I.iii.127). Unlike the conventional gothic novel of the kind written by Ann Radcliffe, in which the mysterious is systematically demystified as the narrative unfolds, Hogg's novel begins in the familiar light of day, but becomes progressively more obscure. As readers we are encouraged to think of the book as a straightforward story, only to find that, as we attempt to make analogues and resemblances from the details being supplied, we become as hopelessly entangled in the narrative as Robert Wringhim in the web of the loom at the weaver's cottage. When we turn to the author, James Hogg, for enlightenment we find, in Part 3, that he has abandoned his author's privilege and stepped into the fiction himself. We have, therefore, no authoritative view on which we can depend. Bel Calvert describes to Mrs Logan that one of the mysterious figures she has witnessed '*was extremely like Drummond.* So like was he […]'. Yet just a little earlier, at Bel's trial, Mrs Logan had exclaimed that '*Like* is an ill mark.'

Romantic literature frequently describes the journey rather than its completion. As such it lays stress on the life of the creative process itself. William Blake's *Songs of Innocence and of Experience* (1794) function dialectically, never allowing their reader to take up a comfortable position in a single point of view: 'He who binds to himself a joy / Does the winged life destroy'.[10] In this sense Hogg's novel maintains its dynamic, endlessly shifting its ground and carries its reader forward, 'not merely or chiefly by the mechanical impulse of curiosity,' as Coleridge writes of the work of imagination, 'or by a restless desire to arrive at the final solution, but by the pleasurable activity of mind excited by the attractions of the journey itself'.[11]

The Romantic Satirical Novel

Thomas Love Peacock's *Nightmare Abbey* (1818) is, in its way, a counterpart of William Hazlitt's *The Spirit of the Age, or Contemporary Portraits* (1825), in which Hazlitt takes a broad survey of the Romantic period through a discussion of its most prominent representatives. Peacock's novel, though, is a topical satire on the age, written with the intention, he says, of bringing 'to a sort of philosophical focus a few of the morbidities of modern literature'.[12] James Hogg's *Confessions*, in this respect, would perhaps have fallen into the category of the disturbing and pathological kind of writing which Peacock believes is exemplified in the work of Byron amongst others. The last Canto of *Childe Harold* is exactly contemporary with the writing of *Nightmare Abbey*, and its ranging reflections on ruins and decay encourage, for Peacock, a subjective and gloomy introspection (see Part Four: 'Forms of Ruin'):

We wither from our youth, we gasp away—
Sick—sick; unfound the boon—unslaked the thirst,
Though to the last, in verge of our decay,
Some phantom lures, such as we sought at first—
But all too late,—so are we doubly curst.
Love, fame, ambition, avarice—'tis the same,
Each idle—and all ill—and none the worst—
For all are meteors with a different name,
And Death the sable smoke where vanishes the flame. (IV.cxxiv)

Unlike Wordsworth, writes Hazlitt, Byron does not describe 'a daisy or a periwinkle, but the cedar or the cypress',[13] and in *Nightmare Abbey* he actually becomes 'Mr Cypress', who sings his song in the familiar register of *Childe Harold*, the fourth Canto of which, Peacock remarked, was 'really too bad'.[14] Mr Cypress's song begins:

There is a fever of the spirit,
The brand of Cain's unresting doom,
Which in the lone dark souls that bear it
Glows like the lamp in Tullia's tomb:
Unlike that lamp, its subtle fire
Burns, blasts, consumes its cell, the heart,
Till, one by one, hope, joy, desire,
Like dreams of shadowy smoke depart.

When the song concludes, Mr Glowry, the proprietor of Nightmare Abbey, exclaims 'Admirable', and says to the assembled company, 'Let us all be unhappy together.' As a rejoinder, the more light-hearted and companionable Mr Hilary calls for 'a catch'. With echoes of the 'catch' sung in *Twelfth Night* (II.iii.58–71), this particular one, with its refrain of a 'bowl' of 'good wine', is sung as an antidote to Byronic gloom, just as Sir Toby, Sir Andrew and Feste's catch is sung to confound Malvolio's lugubrious brand of life-denying puritanism.

Peacock calls *Nightmare Abbey* 'a comic romance', feeling it necessary '"to make a stand" against the "encroachments" of black bile',[15] and amusing himself 'with the darkness and misanthropy of modern literature, from the lantern jaws of which I shall endeavour to elicit a laugh'.[16] As one of the four 'humours' upon whose equitable balance the health of the body was said to depend, the presence of 'black bile' in the literature of the day was a symptom of disease in the nation. Peacock's becomes a voice to counter the sort of writing which, as a result of post-Napoleonic disillusionment, had developed a debilitating inwardness that endangered society's wellbeing. This is certainly how Shelley saw things in his Preface to *The Revolt of Islam* (1818). The sympathies connected with the French Revolution, he writes, 'extended to every bosom', but 'such a degree of unmingled good was expected, as it was impossible to realise'. The 'melancholy desolation' of 'cherished hopes' had resulted in a 'gloom and misanthropy' which had 'tainted the literature of the age with the hopelessness of the minds from which it flows'. In his belief that literature can and does affect the health of a country, Peacock looks back to figures such as Pope who, throughout his work, makes a correlation between healthy writing and a good society. It looks forward also to a writer like George Orwell, who in *Politics and the English Language* (1946) reveals how certain uses of language can have far-reaching and often dangerous consequences for a nation's moral health. Thus, although Peacock emphasises its comedy, *Nightmare Abbey* has a serious purpose, setting out to heal with morals, as Pope said of satire, not necessarily what it 'hurts' with wit,[17] as its tone is much too spirited and light-hearted for that, but rather to raise awareness of how it is possible for 'distempered ideas', with 'ample time and space to germinate into a fertile harvest of chimaeras', to create diseases that infest society.

This emphasis on the healing aspect of writing has parallels with Peacock's contemporary, John Keats. In transmitting from his study of medicine to poetry his 'idea of doing some good for the world',[18] Keats reminds us of how often Romantic writers, rather than escape into the ivory towers of their own personal idealisms, concern themselves closely with their community. Wordsworth once told a visitor from America that 'although he was known to the world only as a poet, he had given twelve hours thought to the conditions and prospects of society, for one to poetry'.[19]

In *Nightmare Abbey*, the hero of the story, Scythrop Glowry, Peacock's good-humoured version of his friend Shelley, retreats into a tower as the consequence of a disappointment in love. Here he begins to 'devour romances and German tragedies' and develops a *'passion for reforming the world'*. Peacock parodies Shelley's style when Scythrop, 'his cogitative faculties immersed in cogibundity of cogitation', invites his new love, Marionetta Celestina O'Carroll (based on Shelley's first wife, Harriet Westbrook), to open a vein in each other's arms and drink the blood 'as a sacrament of love'. 'Then we shall see', he says, 'visions of transcendental illumination, and soar on the wings of ideas into the space of pure intelligence.' Shelley's notions of acquainting 'the more select classes of poetical readers with beautiful idealisms of moral excellence'[20] find their counterpart in the 'seven copies' only of the transcendental 'treatise' which Scythrop manages to sell – a joke at the expense of Shelley's pamphlet of 1812, *Proposals for an Association of Philanthropists*.

Yet Scythrop/Shelley is not there simply to be the object of criticism. Like all good satirists, Peacock can recognise the virtues of his targets as well as their shortcomings. When Glowry, Scythrop's father, talks of how the minds of women are 'are always locked up, and vanity and interest keep the key', Scythrop's enlightened reply is, 'But how is it that their minds are locked up? The fault is in their artificial education, which studiously models them into mere musical dolls, to be set out for sale in the great toy-shop of society.' Here he anticipates Melanie, heroine of Angela Carter's novel *The Magic Toyshop* (1967), who, confronted by the manipulative Finn and his puppet *'sylphide'*, recognises that 'the doll was herself'.[21] In this connection, Marionetta's name in Peacock's novel (marionette, a puppet) is relevant. She evokes in response to her question, 'What would you have, Scythrop?' his declaration, 'You, for the companion of my studies, the partner of my thoughts, the auxiliary of my great designs for the emancipation of mankind.' We are reminded by Scythrop's words of Shelley's own enlightened views, as he was one of the few men of his generation who found intellectual companionship in women at a time when women had absolutely no rights in society whatsoever. Shelley, of course, would marry the daughter of Mary Wollstonecraft, author of *A Vindication of the Rights of Woman* (1792), although Mary Shelley, sadly, never knew her mother.

Apart from his versions of Byron in Mr Cypress or Shelley in Scythrop, Peacock has a cast list of contemporaries who are satirised for their various 'crotchets'. Although it might be misleading to draw too specific a correspondence between some of the characters and their obsessions, it is clear that among the more prominent figures in the story is Coleridge in the person of Mr Flosky (from Greek, meaning 'a lover of shadows'). In his youth, we are told, Flosky had been 'an enthusiast for liberty, and had hailed the dawn of the French Revolution as the promise of a day that was to banish war and slavery, and every form of vice and misery, from the face of the earth'. However, 'Because all this was not done, he deduced that nothing was done [...], that the overthrow of the feudal fortresses of tyranny and superstition was the greatest calamity that had ever befallen mankind, and that their only hope now was to rake the rubbish together, and rebuild it without any of those loop-holes by which the light had originally crept in.' In the dialogues where he appears, Flosky is made to exemplify the notorious obscurity of his thought for which Byron, with probably the *Biographia Literaria* (1817) in mind, would satirise him in the Dedication* to *Don Juan*:

> And Coleridge, too, has lately taken wing,
> But like a hawk encumber'd with his hood,—
> Explaining metaphysics to the nation—
> I wish he would explain his explanation. (ll. 13–16)

'Mystery was [Flosky's] mental element', we are told, and at one point in a conversation with Marionetta '(*Mr Flosky suddenly stopped: he found himself unintentionally trespassing within the limits of common sense.*)' When, during another exchange, Marionetta is trying to extract from

---

* Written in 1818, published in 1833.

Mr Flosky's excessive wordiness the reasons for Scythrop's unhappiness, she resorts to straight talking. The dialogue, which Peacock sets out in the form of a dramatic episode, reads as follows:

MARIONETTA: Will you oblige me, Mr. Flosky, by giving me a plain answer to a plain question?

MR. FLOSKY: It is impossible, my dear Miss O'Carroll. I never gave a plain answer to a question in my life.

MARIONETTA: Do you, or do you not, know what is the matter with my cousin?

The strategy she adopts is identical to that of Rosencrantz who, with a plain and monosyllabic question, tries to elicit from the equivocating Hamlet the location of the murdered Polonius: 'What have you done, my lord, with the dead body?' (IV.ii.5). We are reminded here perhaps of how Coleridge, as one of the period's greatest critics of Shakespeare, would later famously identify with Hamlet, the type of the Romantic artist, and a figure like himself torn between his obligations to the world and a dark inward sense of an inadequacy to his tasks: 'I have a smack of Hamlet myself, if I may say so.'[22]

Equally satirised is the fashionable reader, Mr Listless, who finds that 'modern books are very consolatory and congenial' to his feelings. A 'delicious misanthropy and discontent, that demonstrates the nullity of virtue and energy' puts him, he says, 'in good humour with myself and my sofa'. As an occupant of the sofa, Mr Listless calls to mind the famous opening of William Cowper's *The Task* (1785), 'I sing the sofa', though his particular brand of effete sensibility is a travesty of Cowper's man of feeling. It corresponds more closely with Peacock's 'accurate description of [the] pensive attitude' he shows being adopted by Scythrop when Scythrop 'placed the ball of his right thumb against his right temple, curled the forefinger along the upper part of his forehead', and 'rested the point of the middle finger on the bridge of his nose'. Perhaps the pensive posture is anticipated in Wordsworth's slightly self-mocking 'For oft, when on my couch I lie / In vacant or in pensive mood',[23] and Peacock's tendency, in highlighting the self-regarding solipsism of the age, is to put his stress rather upon conversation, sociability and the kind of 'association' William Godwin defined as being 'of unquestionable advantage', namely an 'unreserved communication, especially among persons who are already awakened to the pursuit of truth'.[24]

In fact, the Romantic period is as much about gatherings, colloquies, friendships and collaborations as it is about solitude and introspection, and Peacock's critique of his contemporaries reaches a comical denouement when the mysterious Celinda, Marionetta's rival for Scythrop's affections, makes her appearance as a 'supernatural' figure before the assembled cast. As this follows upon their collective discussion of ghosts, a general panic ensues, during which they all make their individual exits from various doors and windows. Peacock is making the point that instead of a mutually supportive and collective intelligence, it is the 'every man for himself' mentality which ironically unites this odd collection of characters with their various 'crotchets' or obsessions. One detects the classicist Peacock's agreement with Mr Hilary, that the contrast of 'this mystifying and blue-devilling of society' with 'the cheerful and solid wisdom of antiquity' is too forcible not to strike anyone 'who has the least knowledge of classical literature'. A similar clarity of perception is invited by Jane Austen in her contemporary fiction *Northanger Abbey* (1817–18), whose Catherine Morland takes 'gothic' appearances for reality when reality itself requires her much more vigilant and alert intelligence.

The Novel of Comedy and Transition

In 1817, John Keats wrote to Benjamin Robert Haydon:

> I remember your saying that you had notions of a good Genius presiding over you – I have of late had the same thought. For things which [I] do half at Random are afterwards confirmed by

my judgment in a dozen features of Propriety – Is it too daring to Fancy Shakespeare this Presider?[25]

Keats has in fact been called the most Shakespearean of English Romantic poets, but it was Jane Austen among the English novelists who seems to have been most frequently honoured with the association. Macaulay, in a review of 1843, wrote of her as a prose Shakespeare:

> Shakespeare has had neither equal nor second. But among the writers who [...] have approached nearest to the manner of the great master, we have no hesitation in placing Jane Austen.[26]

Among early nineteenth-century reviewers, Richard Whately, Archbishop of Dublin, wrote in 1821 about Jane Austen's characteristic of 'saying as little as possible in her own person, and giving dramatic air to the narrative, by introducing frequent conversations; which she conducts with a regard to character hardly exceeded even by Shakespeare himself'.[27] The Victorian critic George Henry Lewes also writes of Austen's 'ventriloquism'[28] and of her essentially dramatic creativity. While discussing Shakespeare's 'central power of dramatic creation, the power of constructing and animating character', he remarks that the dramatist 'may truly be said to find a younger sister in Miss Austen'.[29]

In her ability to promote a plot Jane Austen demonstrates a Shakespearean economy. For example, at the end of Chapter 19 of *Persuasion* (1818), she must contrive a crucial meeting between Anne Elliot and Captain Wentworth who, at this point in the novel, has separated from Louisa Musgrove and is therefore once again a marriageable prospect for Anne. Anne, living in Bath, is in conversation with Admiral Croft:

> 'Poor Frederick!' said he at last. 'Now he must begin all over again with somebody else. I think we must get him to Bath. Sophy must write, and beg him to come to Bath. Here are pretty

girls enough, I am sure [...] Do not you think, Miss Elliot, we had better try to get him to Bath?'

And this, at the beginning of the next chapter, is how Jane Austen achieves the potentially complicated business of bringing Wentworth back into the story:

> While Admiral Croft was taking this walk with Anne, and expressing his wish of getting Captain Wentworth to Bath, Captain Wentworth was already on his way thither. Before Mrs Croft had written, he was arrived; and the very next time Anne walked out, she saw him.

In two deftly constructed sentences the plot is advanced and the next 'scene' is ready to proceed.

In *Persuasion*, her last completed novel, Jane Austen seems to have had Shakespeare, the 'presider', prominently in mind, as her theme touches closely upon that of *Twelfth Night*. Shakespeare's setting, Illyria, which ought to be firmly under the direction of the Duke, Orsino and the lady, Olivia, has been allowed, through neglect, to drift to two extremes – on the one hand absolute repression represented by Malvolio and, on the other, total licence and degeneracy in the persons of Sir Toby and Sir Andrew; their names, 'Belch' and 'Aguecheek' suggest it. In *Persuasion*, Sir Walter Elliot, as representative of the gentry, has likewise abandoned his social responsibilities to pursue self-interest, allowing his vanity, extravagance and snobbery to prevail and cause all kinds of unhappiness in his own family. In the first scene of *Twelfth Night*, the self-centred Orsino indulges his private fantasies for a woman whose preoccupation with thoughts of a dead brother makes all else an irrelevance to her. In the opening sequence of *Persuasion* the self-obsessed Sir Walter Elliot scrutinises his favourite book, the Baronetage, for confirmation of his own importance. Orsino's language in the first scene of the play, full of images of surfeit and sickness, reflects his introspection. Life in Illyria has ground to a halt. A healthy sexuality is not only denied by Orsino's self-preoccupation but also by the object of his supposed love, Olivia, who, to mourn her brother's loss, has shut herself away from the world for seven years.

In *Persuasion*, also, seven years becomes a significant time span. Sir Walter is advised that retrenchment and the adoption of a more economical style of life will, in seven years, clear his financial distress. At the beginning of the story, seven years is the amount of time which has elapsed since Anne Elliot had been 'persuaded' into not doing what she had desperately wanted to do, marry Captain Wentworth. Now, aged twenty-seven, she has become an involuntary Olivia, left on the shelf as a faded bloom to observe happiness only in others and to take consolation from the knowledge (so important for Jane Austen) that she had acted prudently and dutifully in following the advice of her guardian, Lady Russell. Anne's missed life opportunity recalls Shakespeare's lines in *Julius Caesar*:

> There is a tide in the affairs of men,
> Which taken at the flood, leads on to fortune;
> Omitted, all the voyage of their life
> Is bound in shallows and in miseries. (IV.iii.218–21)

This is not, of course, to be Anne's fate. She is a figure in romance. But the swiftness of time and the urgency of using it are insistent themes in both *Twelfth Night* and *Persuasion*.

In *Twelfth Night* the character of Orsino is based on that of Narcissus in Ovid's telling of the myth.[30] Orsino cannot see beyond his own preoccupations to a point where he is able to acknowledge the existence and rights of another. It is Viola's task to invite both him and Olivia to think beyond their selves. As young people they should be taking up their rightful places in a world of human relationships, of marriage and children – the world, in other words, of comedy. It is ironic that Anne's extravagant father, Sir Walter, who is reluctantly obliged to let his house, Kellynch, to Admiral Croft, sees it as being positively to Croft's advantage that, as his tenant, he is 'a married man, and without children; the very state to be wished for'. In fact, when Admiral Croft does take up residence, one of his first tasks, as he later tells Anne, has been to send away 'some of the large looking-glasses! Oh Lord! There was no getting away from oneself.' Like Orsino, Sir Walter is Narcissus. His favourite daughter, we are told, is Elizabeth, who 'being very handsome, and very like himself, her influence had always been great, and they had gone on together most happily'.

Jane Austen's heroine, Anne Elliot, may in one sense be a version of Shakespeare's Olivia – the victim seven years previously of a 'little history of sorrowful interest', but she is also Viola, Olivia's dynamic counterpart in *Twelfth Night*. In neither Shakespeare nor Jane Austen is a stagnant and regressive society allowed to prevail, because each moves towards a comic resolution achieved through the agency of individuals whose sensibilities and understanding transform situations existing on the very brink of tragedy. Anne is a less obviously active participant in the events of *Persuasion* than is Viola in *Twelfth Night*, but it is clear that both are pivots on which the respective actions turn. Wentworth's interpretation of Anne's rejection of him as a sign in her character of weakness, of her being easily persuaded, is later replaced by his acknowledgement that in habitually acting as she does, Anne displays real purposiveness; that, instead of being easily led, she has firm 'persuasion' of mind.

In *Twelfth Night* it is Viola who, at the geographical centre of the play and amidst all the disguise and confusion, is a reliable voice: 'By innocence I swear, and by my youth, / I have one heart, one bosom, and one truth' (III.i.159–60). In *Persuasion* Anne Elliot is cast in an identical role. She is the very pattern of integrity and is Jane Austen's moral guide in the midst of all her society's mistakes and stupidity. Time and again we come across statements inviting us to acknowledge Anne's superior wisdom: 'How was Anne to set all these matters to right?' or 'Anne longed for the power of representing to them all what they were about, and of pointing out some of the evils they were exposing themselves to'; or when her sister Mary's little boy has a bad fall, a precursor of Louisa's accident on the Cobb at Lyme Regis, Anne as then, too, takes charge of the entire situation and has 'everything to do at once'.

In both Shakespeare's play and Austen's novel the heroine is empowered by her association with moral values that are invested in the sea. The sea is the element from which Viola emerges in *Twelfth Night*. She has confronted reality in the extreme situation of near-drowning and, with her vigour and purpose, she blows into the affected court of Orsino like a breath of fresh air. Her previous experience in a stark life-and-death situation legitimises her function as mentor to a duke who has altogether taken leave of reality. Similarly, in *Persuasion*, it is the titled landed gentry, Sir Walter, the Dowager Viscountess Dalrymple and the Honourable Miss Carteret, whose hollow affectations are exposed by the 'sea-people' of the novel (Wentworth, Captain Harville, Croft). These are individuals who have earned their titles of 'Captain' or 'Admiral' through individual enterprise in the dangers of the contemporary Napoleonic campaigns (the novel's action is specifically dated in Chapter 1 as 'the summer of 1814'). Jane Austen locates her moral world firmly in the marine landscape at Lyme where the visiting party congregates, just as William Wordsworth invests the scenery of Tintern Abbey with a moral value that transcends its initially picturesque presentation[31] (see Part Three: 'Revolution, Reaction and the Natural World'). As in Wordsworth, Jane Austen's descriptions of Lyme and its environs leave behind the purely picturesque composition of its scenery, and 'The party from Uppercross', we are told, 'soon found themselves on the sea shore […] lingering only as all must linger and gaze on a first return to the sea, who ever deserve to look on it at all' (Chapter 11). Picturesque travel was all about observing, taking up a station and looking at a landscape. But in *Persuasion*, the right to 'look' at the sea is something that has to be earned. The sea is the protean element, full of danger and risk. Its people, like Viola and Sebastian in *Twelfth Night*, are the shape of the future in a new and vigorous society in transition, a society based on generosity, sensibility and integrity instead of on meaningless titles, rank and privilege. It is also a society in which the moral worth of people is determined by their willingness to work for a living rather than having their identity conferred upon them by the dead world of inherited privilege.

Viola's assertion that she has 'one heart, one bosom, and one truth' reminds us of how central is the human heart to Jane Austen's novel.

The role of Anne Elliot and of Viola corresponds with that of another heroine in a novel of the same year as *Persuasion*. In Scott's *The Heart of Midlothian* (1818) it is Jeannie Deans's compassionate heart which eventually replaces the cruel 'values' of the Tolbooth prison, known as the 'heart' of Midlothian. In *Persuasion*, the villain of the story, Mr Elliot, the heir presumptive to Sir Walter's estate who, in the past, has snubbed the family, and into whose grasp Anne almost tragically falls is, as we learn from Mrs Smith, 'black at heart, hollow and black' (Chapter 22). The setting for Wentworth's declaration in a love letter to Anne is, appropriately, 'The White Hart' hotel. One recalls the same wordplay on heart/hart between the essentially 'heartless' Orsino and his gentleman, Curio, in the first scene of *Twelfth Night*:

CURIO: Will you go hunt, my lord?
DUKE: What, Curio?
CURIO: The hart.
DUKE: Why so I do, the noblest that I have.

In *Persuasion* the White Hart hotel is the symbol of a society no longer rooted in landed traditions, but one which is fluid and in a state of alteration. It is the place where the important conversation occurs between the good-hearted Captain Harville ('Heartville') and Anne herself on the relative constancy and inconstancy of men and women, to be examined in the Extended Commentary to follow.

Persuasion, as must all comedy, ends with a marriage, and in *Twelfth Night* Jane Austen seems to have discovered a precedent for her own complex story of love lost and joyfully recovered. That Anne Elliot is given a second chance, that what had apparently been lost to her is found again, suggests that in this, her final novel, Jane Austen looks towards Shakespeare's own last plays, the late romances, to find in them the archetypal pattern of loss, suffering and restoration. In those plays, patience and virtue exercised, often over long periods of time, are rewarded and the sea again becomes, as in *Persuasion*, both symbol and resource in the drama of human fortunes.

On first reading, the Romantic fiction of Hogg, Peacock and Jane Austen may seem to have little in common. Closer examination, however, reveals their shared awareness, not only of the potential, but also of the problems of people coping with a new-found sense of their individualism at the dawn of the modern age.

Extended Commentary: Austen, *Persuasion* (1818), Chapter 23

Anne Elliot finds herself at the White Hart hotel in the company of Mrs Musgrove, Mrs Croft, Captain Harville and Captain Wentworth. The setting is significant in that the hotel represents the changing society of *Persuasion*, which is symbolised by the novel's sea imagery. While Mrs Musgrove and Mrs Croft keep up a conversation together, Captain Wentworth sits at some distance to write a letter, and we become aware of the possibility that he is overhearing the conversations which follow. Captain Harville explains to Anne that Captain Benwick has commissioned his own portrait to be 'properly set' for Louisa Musgrove, whom he is to marry, and that this is the business about which Wentworth is employed in writing the letter. The portrait was originally to have been Benwick's gift to his intended, Captain Harville's sister, Fanny, but she has died and, although Captain Harville is 'not sorry, indeed, to make it over to another', with a 'quivering lip' he cannot help adding, 'Poor Fanny! She would not have forgotten him so soon!'

Earlier in the novel (in Chapter 11), during the excursion to Lyme Regis, Anne had found herself in conversation with Captain Benwick and, in the course of hoping to benefit him in his 'affliction', had engaged with him in a discussion of the relative merits of the contemporary poets Scott and Byron, 'trying to ascertain whether *Marmion* or *The Lady of the Lake* were to be preferred, and how ranked the *Giaour* and *The Bride of Abydos*, and moreover, how the *Giaour* was to be pronounced' (a nice touch). The two latter poems, among the immensely popular verse-tales of Byron, belong to 1813, the year before the events of *Persuasion* itself. Benwick's identification with Byron's 'impassioned descriptions of hopeless agony' is quite funny, in that if Byron is to be thought of as a real-life 'action man', travelling Europe and the Middle East, and fighting in the cause of Greek independence, Captain Benwick must be seen as '*inaction* man'. His relationship with Louisa Musgrove, as described to Anne by Charles Musgrove in Chapter 22, is a parody of what a 'good marriage' (Anne's and Captain Wentworth's) represents: 'I hope you think Louisa perfectly recovered now?', says Anne, to Charles Musgrove;

> He answered rather hesitatingly, 'Yes, I believe I do – very much recovered; but she is altered: there is no running or jumping about, no laughing or dancing; it is quite different. If one happens only to shut the door a little hard, she starts and wriggles like a young dab chick in the water; and Benwick sits at her elbow, reading verses, or whispering to her, all day long.'

Benwick's gift to Louisa of his own 'fixed' portrait symbolises his inertia, his inability to change. In the festive world of *Twelfth Night*, amidst the giving and exchanging which takes place in that play, there are those characters who withhold themselves when they give, and there are equally those who give of themselves with their gifts. Benwick's introspective nurturing of his own sensibilities belongs to this pattern, while his comparative mildness of temperament might be compared with what is observable to Lockwood in the portrait of Edgar Linton when it is pointed out to him by Nelly Dean in Chapter 8 of Emily Brontë's *Wuthering Heights* (1847). Edgar, as depicted, strikes Lockwood as 'soft-featured', the 'pensive and amiable' expression forming a 'sweet picture', his figure 'almost too graceful'. As Benwick contrasts with the 'heroes' of Byron's verse-tales, Edgar Linton, here represented by his 'fixed' portrait, contrasts similarly with the active and dangerous Heathcliff, modelled of course by Emily Brontë on the figure of Byron himself.

Captain Harville's implication that Fanny's place in Benwick's affections has been too easily replaced by Louisa leads into a conversation with Anne about the relative constancy of the sexes. Anne (and presumably within earshot of Wentworth) insists that quickly to forget a former attachment 'would not be the nature of any woman who truly loved'.* Harville asks, 'Do you claim that for your sex?' To which Anne replies:

> 'Yes. We certainly do not forget you, so soon as you forget us. It is, perhaps, our fate rather than our merit. We cannot help ourselves. We live at home, quiet, confined, and our feelings prey upon us. You are forced on exertion. You have always a profession, pursuits, business of some sort or other, to take you back into the world immediately, and continual occupation and change soon weaken impressions.'

It is useful to compare what amounts here to a strongly feminist statement by Anne with Byron's own remarks on the predicament of women in Cantos I and II of his poem *Don Juan*, written for the most part in 1818 and thus contemporary with the publication of *Persuasion*. Here, in Canto I, the married Julia is writing to her lover, Juan, after they have been forcibly separated:

> Man's love is of his life a thing apart,
> 'Tis woman's whole existence. Man may range
> The court, camp, church, the vessel, and the mart;
> Sword, gown, gain, glory offer in exchange
> Pride, fame, ambition to fill up his heart,
> And few there are whom these cannot estrange.
> Man has all these resources, we but one,
> To mourn alone the love which has undone. (stanza 194)

In Canto II, Byron digresses from the story of Juan and Haidée to reflect on man's infidelity to women:

---

* Anne who, as a woman, has no option of declaring her love to Wentworth, resembles the 'sister' who, in the story Viola tells to Orsino, 'never told her love' and 'sate like Patience on a monument, / Smiling at grief' (*Twelfth Night*, II.iv.110, 114–15).

175

for man, to man so oft unjust,
Is always so to women. One sole bond
Awaits them, treachery is all their trust,
Taught to conceal, their bursting hearts despond
Over their idol, till some wealthier lust
Buys them in marriage – and what rests beyond?
A thankless husband, next a faithless lover,
Then dressing, nursing, praying, and all's over. (stanza 200)

In his debate with Anne, Captain Harville is insistent that he 'will not allow it to be more man's nature than woman's to be inconstant and forget those they do love, or have loved'. As the 'argument' continues and Harville exclaims, 'We shall never agree upon this question', a slight noise 'called their attention to Captain Wentworth's hitherto perfectly quiet division of the room'. This turns out to be 'nothing more than that his pen had fallen down'. On a first reading of the novel this apparently insignificant detail might easily be overlooked, but it becomes of great significance symbolically as Harville's conversation with Anne continues. All stories 'prose and verse', says Harville, are against Anne's argument, 'and I do not think I ever opened a book in my life which had not something to say upon woman's inconstancy', although 'perhaps', he adds, 'you will say, these were all written by men'. This is Anne's reply:

> Perhaps I shall. – Yes, yes, if you please, no reference to examples in books. Men have had every advantage of us in telling their own story. Education has been theirs in so much higher a degree; the pen has been in their hands. I will not allow books to prove anything.

The conversation continues until the small gathering in the hotel room, including Wentworth, breaks up and disperses. Under the pretext of returning for his gloves, however, Wentworth places a letter before Anne 'with eyes of glowing entreaty'. This turns out to be his declaration of love for her and is a private letter which all the time he had been penning under the apparent one for Harville. Anne's feelings are 'almost beyond expression', and the written words of Wentworth's letter when she eventually is able to read it are unable to do justice to its overpowering emotional charge. Its direction to 'Miss A. E.' is 'hardly legible', and it begins not with, for example, 'I am writing to you', but instead 'I must speak to you'. It turns out to be a succession of rapid, breathless utterances with references to the heart, to feelings, to hearing and tones of voice.

Jane Austen derived her inspiration from the great English writers of the eighteenth century, from figures such as Jonathan Swift, Alexander Pope and Samuel Johnson, for whom language was more than adequate to its task. But it is a Romantic commonplace to stress the *inadequacy* of language in giving expression to the feelings. For Wordsworth, thirteen books of *The Prelude* were no more than 'Breathings for incommunicable powers' (III.188). His epic poem begins not with a word but with a breath – 'Oh'. Though Byron longed to 'wreak [his] thoughts upon expression' he could do no more than 'live and die unheard, / With a most voiceless thought, sheathing it as a sword' (*Childe Harold*, III.xcvii), while for Shelley the written poem was no more than a feeble attempt to repeat its original inspiration.*

In *Persuasion* the power of the written word for Sir Walter is obvious from page one, where he pores over the entries in the Baronetage confirming his status and family credentials. Unless you are 'written' into this volume, in Sir Walter's eyes, like the unmarried and childless Anne, you are simply 'nobody' (Chapter 1). When, at the end of the novel, Sir Walter is finally convinced that Wentworth will prove to be more than a good match for Anne, we are told that he is willing 'at last to prepare his pen with a very good grace for the insertion of the marriage in the volume of honour' (Chapter 24). The importance earlier, therefore, of Wentworth's dropped pen can now be understood. Symbolically, Wentworth refuses to write Anne's story, in the way that it has been the historical fate of women to have their stories written by men. The marriage of Anne and Wentworth, grounded as it is on

---

* See *A Defence of Poetry*, written as a riposte to Peacock's playing devil's advocate in his *The Four Ages of Poetry* (1820).

feelings, succeeds in escaping the dead inscriptions of Sir Walter's 'pen' and, without being dependent on inherited land and property, establishes a new set of values for a future society. As a 'sailor's wife', Anne will have to pay 'the tax of quick alarm' in any 'future war', but now it is those values symbolised by the sea which inform the 'domestic virtues' and, as in *Twelfth Night*, bring moral redemption to a world of invidious privilege and folly.

Notes

1   See Edgar Allen Poe, *William Wilson*; Elizabeth Gaskell, *The Poor Clare*; Charles Dickens, *A Tale of Two Cities*; *Great Expectations*; Robert Louis Stevenson, *Dr Jekyll and Mr Hyde*; Oscar Wilde, *The Picture of Dorian Gray*; Henry James, *The Jolly Corner*; Joseph Conrad, *The Secret Sharer*.

2   P. B. Shelley, *A Defence of Poetry* (1821).

3   *The Four Zoas*, Night the First, Page 4.

4   S. T. Coleridge to John Thelwall, 14 October, 1797: *The Complete Poetical Works of Samuel Taylor Coleridge*, ed. Earl Leslie Griggs, 2 vols (Oxford: Clarendon Press, 1956), vol. 1, p. 349.

5   Preface to *Lyrical Ballads* (1800).

6   'A Scots Mummy', *Blackwood's Edinburgh Magazine*, xiv, July–December, 1823.

7   *Songs of Innocence* (1789).

8   'Address to Kilchurn Castle, Upon Loch Awe'.

9   'Ode to Psyche'.

10 William Blake, 'Eternity'.

11 S. T. Coleridge, *Biographia Literaria*, ch. 14.

12 Thomas Love Peacock, *The Letters of Thomas Love Peacock*, ed. Nicholas A. Joukovsky, 2 vols (Oxford: Clarendon Press, 2001), vol. 1, p. 152.

13 William Hazlitt, *The Spirit of the Age*, 'Lord Byron'.

14 Peacock, *Letters*, vol. 1, p. 123.

15 Ibid.

16 Ibid., vol. 1, pp. 121–2.

17 *Imitations of Horace*, Epistle II, l. 262.

18 Keats: Letter, 27 April 1818: *The Selected Letters of John Keats*, ed. Lionel Trilling (New York: Farrar, Strauss and Young, 1951), p. 121.

19 Quoted in F. M. Todd, *Politics and the Poet: A Study of Wordsworth* (London: Methuen, 1957), p. 11.

20 Preface to *Prometheus Unbound*.

21 Angela Carter, *The Magic Toyshop* (London: Virago Press, 1987), p. 68.

22 S. T. Coleridge, *Table Talk* (2nd edn, 1836), quoted in Jonathan Bate (ed.), *The Romantics on Shakespeare* (Harmondsworth: Penguin, 1992), p. 161.

23 'I wandered lonely as a Cloud' (Poems of 1807).

24 William Godwin, *An Enquiry Concerning Political Justice*, ed. Isaac Kramnick (Harmondsworth: Penguin, 1976), book IV, chapter 3, 'Of Political Associations', p. 288.

25 *The Letters of John Keats*, ed. H. E. Rollins, 2 vols (Cambridge, Mass.: Harvard University Press, 1958), vol. 1, pp. 141–2.

26 Extract from an unsigned article: 'The Diary and Letters of Mme. D'Arblay', *Edinburgh Review*, lxxvi (January 1843), pp. 561–2.

27 Unsigned review of *Northanger Abbey* and *Persuasion*, *Quarterly Review*, xxiv (January 1821), pp. 352–76.

28 Unsigned article, 'The novels of Jane Austen', *Blackwood's Edinburgh Magazine*, lxxxvi (July 1859), pp. 99–113.

29 From an unsigned review of the anonymous 'The Fair Carew', *The Leader*, 22 November 1851, p. 115.

30 Ovid, *Metamorphoses*, book II, 'Echo and Narcissus'.

31 'Lines Written a Few Miles above Tintern Abbey', *Lyrical Ballads* (1798).

Romantic Travel Writing: Beckford, Byron and Wollstonecraft

Travel writing has existed, historically, both as a literature in itself and as a source from which other literary genres have taken their inspiration. During the Romantic period it achieved great prominence and its influence is to be detected in many forms of writing: aesthetic, political, scientific, religious, imaginative and much more besides. Travel informs some of the most memorable first lines of Romantic poetry: 'I travelled among unknown men', 'Much have I travelled in the realms of gold', 'I met a traveller from an antique land', and in the popular imagination the image of the Romantic poet is best summed up in William Wordsworth's famous opening to 'Daffodils', where the poet presents himself as a solitary traveller, wandering 'lonely as a cloud'.

In *The Prelude*, Wordsworth describes how 'something of the grandeur which invests / The mariner who sails the roaring sea / Through storm and darkness, early in my mind / Surrounded too the wanderers of the earth' (XII.153–6). Taken in the context of the 'Daffodils' lyric, it is important to understand that 'wandering' is being given here a value denied to it in previous centuries. To proceed without direction frequently implied questionable aberration or a dubious straying from rectitude, and 'wanderers' are often 'punished' for their transgression. The *Inferno* of Dante's *Divine Comedy* begins, 'Midway upon the journey of our life / I found myself within a forest dark / For the straightforward pathway had been lost'. In Daniel Defoe's *Robinson*

Crusoe (1719), Crusoe, who persists on his seafaring travels against the wishes of his parents, is shipwrecked and marooned for almost thirty years. Christian and Hopeful, diverging from their road to the Celestial City in John Bunyan's *The Pilgrim's Progress* (1678) and taking the easier route of 'By-Path Meadow', encounter Giant Despair who imprisons, beats and starves them in Doubting Castle.

In Wordsworth's 'Daffodils' the act of wandering leads to a moment of visionary significance, informing the poet's later life and turning his loneliness into 'the bliss of solitude'. Whereas initially he had been simply an observer of them he now, in the course of his recollection, dances *with* the daffodils, heightening the awareness that he is a participant in, rather than excluded from, the 'goings-on' of the natural world.

At the beginning of *The Prelude*, and embarking on the history of his intellectual life, Wordsworth proclaims that 'should the guide I chuse / Be nothing better than a wandering cloud, / I cannot miss my way', adding that 'a twig or any floating thing / Upon the river' might 'point me out my course' (I.17–19, 31–2). In an earlier age, to suggest taking as 'guide' a 'wandering cloud', or relying on a floating twig for one's course, would have indicated both folly and moral danger, and from the way in which the wanderer becomes a recurring motif in all forms of Romantic art, a radical shift in response to this form of travel has clearly taken place. Episodes of special value might now be expected to emerge from discursive, digressive and aimless pursuits.

Varieties of Travel

Travel in the Romantic period extended beyond just the figure of the wanderer to embrace a broad range of meanings. There were travel accounts by voyagers, such as those of Captain Cook (whose first voyage account was published in 1773); explorers, whose quests were primarily scientific; travellers such as Lord Byron, representing individuals who set out in quest of a wider knowledge of other lands, their inhabitants and customs; and tourists, who cultivated a new fashion for travelling as a form of leisure activity. Terms such as 'explorer', 'traveller', 'tourist', though, need further semantic investigation, as historical usages continually changed.

An increasingly pejorative meaning attaches itself to the word 'tourist', whose modern connotation begins to develop during the Romantic period. Yet 'tour' could itself still be used as an interchangeable term for 'travel', as when Wordsworth describes that his lines written 'above Tintern Abbey'[1] were the consequence of revisiting the banks of the River Wye 'during a tour'; or when Percy and Mary Shelley publish their *History of a Six Weeks' Tour* in 1817. Wordsworth exclaims against an early form of recreational tourism at the beginning of his poem 'The Brothers' ('These Tourists, heaven preserve us!'), where he thinks particularly of the cult of the 'picturesque' and its devotees who followed a prescribed set of aesthetic rules in order to appreciate the beauty of a landscape.

Central to this cult, the product of an emerging and prosperous middle class, is the figure of the Reverend William Gilpin, whose 'picturesque tours', beginning in 1782 with *Observations on the Wye Valley*, extended to other parts of the British Isles. These publications were immensely popular. Many tourists followed in his steps, taking up appropriate standpoints from which to view the scenery recommended in his guides. Gilpin's criteria for the 'picturesque' ('that peculiar kind of beauty, which is agreeable in a picture')[2] drew on the work of artists such as the seventeenth-century French landscapists Nicholas Poussin and Claude Lorrain, and in the first lines of 'Tintern Abbey', Wordsworth (who knew Gilpin's *Observations*) constructs his 'scene' to follow their principles of pictorial composition. Below is Anna Seward writing to the Reverend Henry White of Lichfield about a visit to the celebrated Ladies of Llangollen Vale,* where she makes use of identical 'picturesque' principles to form the characteristic foreground, middle and background of her 'composed' description. The open windows provide her with a 'frame' for the landscape:

---

* Lady Eleanor Butler (1739–1829) and the Hon. Sarah Ponsonby (1755–1832) formed a close attachment which lasted for over fifty years. In 1780 they set up a rural retreat together near Llangollen in Wales which became a celebrated place of pilgrimage for the poets Southey, Byron, Wordsworth, Scott and Shelley, among many other notable figures.

[T]hrough the opened windows we had a darkling view of the lawn […] the concave shrubbery of tall cypress, yews, laurels, and lilachs; of the woody amphitheatre on the opposite hill, that seems to rise immediately behind the shrubbery; and of the grey barren mountain which, then just visible, forms the background.[3]

Proceeding through the valley, Anna Seward displays her knowledge of current aesthetic categories in a self-consciously literary performance:

We found the road comparatively dreary during about eight miles; – the mountains were vast, but uniformly barren, and the vales at their feet had little luxuriance; but during the remaining ten miles, that lead us to Dolgelly, romantic Beauty resumed all her empire, with the sublime addition of cataracts thundering down the rocks. These were the present of our late rains. One of them was super-eminent in grandeur and picturesque grace.[4]

In this description of the scenery, the 'beautiful' and the 'picturesque' are prominent, while the ascent on foot uphill, as she goes on to say with a nod to the 'sublime', is undertaken with feelings of 'terror inexpressible'.

Thus, included in what is effectively an account of a 'picturesque' tour is Anna Seward's attempt to bring into her experience 'sublimity', an emotion more usually associated with wilder and more grandiose topographies, and involving feelings of terror which, according to Burke's *Philosophical Enquiry*, is 'the ruling principle of the sublime'[5] (see Part Three: 'Writing in Revolution'). She refers to the 'Alpine steeps' which overhang her road, but the truly 'sublime' landscapes of the European Alps, as witnessed by those who had made the so-called eighteenth-century 'Grand Tour', and by the more intrepid travellers who would increasingly follow its route, were completely unknown to the 'Swan of Lichfield'.[*]

---

[*] Anna Seward (1747–1809) lived in Lichfield for most of her life. As well as conducting an extensive literary correspondence, she was a poet and novelist, and wrote a memoir of the life of Erasmus Darwin.

The Grand Tour

The heyday of the Grand Tour was the first half of the eighteenth century. It had several agendas, but was essentially an expedition for the sons of the aristocracy to acquaint themselves with the various protocols of the ruling class. Using as its principal guide Addison's *Remarks on Several Parts of Italy* (1705), the destination of its route was Rome, the tourist taking in the antiquities and reading the appropriate literatures associated with them at key sites along the way. In an age concerned with raising the art of the 'moderns' to the monumentality of that of the ancient world, the Grand Tour consolidated the elitism of its participants, to whom a knowledge of classical literature was confined. Samuel Johnson's celebrated remark plays up the exclusiveness of those who made the 'tour':

> A man who has not been in Italy, is always conscious of an inferiority, from his not having seen what it is expected a man should see. The grand object of travelling is to see the shores of the Mediterranean.[6]

The journey to Italy took tourists over the alpine regions, where observations of the sublime grandeur of its scenery gave rise to a characteristic hyperbole in their descriptions. Thomas Gray, who travelled with his fellow undergraduate Horace Walpole in Europe (1738–40), wrote of his journey through the Alps: 'Not a precipice, not a torrent, not a cliff, but is pregnant with religion and poetry.' Walpole remarks of his own response: 'This sounds too bombast and too romantic to one that has not seen, too cold for one that has.'[7] But the typical attitude of the Grand Tourist to the sites of Europe was one of restraint, with no display of self-involvement, and reflecting the kind of detached objectivity thought to be necessary for those whose destiny was to govern.

Literature in which emphasis is placed on the feeling of the individual traveller, so much associated with the cult of the personality in

Romantic-period literature, is indebted to Laurence Sterne's influential comedic novel, *A Sentimental Journey through France and Italy* (1768). The minutely analysed social encounters of its traveller-hero Yorick replace the more usual dispassionate reflections on the major sites of the Grand Tour and, as in Wordsworth's *Lyrical Ballads* (1798), 'incidents' in Sterne's novel give way to feelings. In fact, Yorick never makes it over the Alps and into Italy, because he finds that his road, as we read in the final section ('The Case of Delicacy'), is blocked by the fall of a huge boulder. The significant moment of crossing the mountains comes to be displaced by the more delicate possibility of his 'transgression' with another halted traveller, a young lady with whom he is obliged to share a bedroom for the night at a nearby inn.

Throughout his novel, Sterne exploits the strategy of eighteenth-century travellers who endorse the authority of their descriptions by claiming the immediacy of eyewitness experience. Thus, the 'authenticity' of Yorick's own travel writing is pointed up when, in response to the curiosity of two Englishmen at Calais as to what could have set his static chaise in motion ('Preface: In the Desobligeant'), he replies that the cause of the movement was simply the 'agitation [of] writing a preface' to his journey inside the carriage. Although employed here for comic purposes, emotional overpowerings, bursts and rushes of feeling are meant to authenticate the experience of travellers as well as guarantee the virtues of the objects observed on their travels. The spontaneity of Byron's strong physiological response to the Venus de' Medici is an example:

> Away!—there need no words, nor terms precise,
> The paltry jargon of the marble mart,
> Where pedantry gulls Folly—we have eyes?
> Blood, pulse, and breast confirm the Dardan Shepherd's prize.
> 			(*Childe Harold*, IV.447–50)

The emotional disposition of Romantic travel writers is not only significant for the quality of their response but also often the motivation for their travels in the first place. Byron's own disaffections and impulses, expressed through the feelings of his wandering 'Childe', are the occasion of Childe Harold's 'Pilgrimage'. In Thomas Love Peacock's *Nightmare Abbey* (see Part Three: 'Romantic Fiction'), when Scythrop (Shelley) accuses Mr Cypress (Byron) of forsaking his own country, 'to wander among a few mouldy ruins', Mr Cypress replies: 'Sir, I have quarrelled with my wife; and a man who has quarrelled with his wife is absolved from all duty to his country.'[8] To Shelley, the exile, journeying to Italy was important for reasons primarily of spiritual revival. Mary Shelley writes that England had 'caused him to consume half his existence in helpless suffering', but that he was enchanted with the 'first aspect of Italy' and found the 'poetical spirit within him speedily revived'.[9] Italy receives no mention as traditionally the destination of the antiquarian or the Grand Tourist, it is simply a means to alleviate the poet's low spirits. Samuel Rogers, in a prose section of his poem *Italy* (1822), associates travel with the recapturing of what, in a typically Romantic response, has been eroded since childhood: 'Now travel, and foreign travel more particularly, restores to us in a great degree what we have lost.' In travel, 'We surrender ourselves, and feel once again as children.' For Rogers, in this way to reclaim the redemptive power of the child is as though to be reawakened and find that 'All is new and strange'.[10]

Although ability to travel was greatly increased during this period by the construction of our now familiar network of roads, canals and railways, for most people the primary mode of mobility was still to walk. In order to plead with the queen for her condemned sister's life, Jeannie Deans, in Scott's *The Heart of Midlothian* (1818), is obliged to walk from Edinburgh to London. Wordsworth and his college friend Robert Jones journeyed on foot from England to Italy during their summer vacation in 1790. Thomas De Quincey calculated that by middle age Wordsworth had walked 180,000 miles and, as Sir Kenneth Clark writes, 'Even the unathletic Coleridge walked.' Wordsworth and his like, he says, 'thought nothing of walking sixteen miles after dinner to post a letter'.[11]

Pedestrian travel was often thought to distinguish the 'authentic' traveller from tourists or from the more well-heeled who could afford to make use of a carriage. It partly owed its fashionable prominence to Jean-Jacques Rousseau's influential *Reveries of a Solitary Walker* (1782), but in turbulent and revolutionary times it lent itself also to being viewed as a politicised form of activity, in which the radical walker could associate more freely with the body of the people and with those who had no other choice than to walk. Samuel Taylor Coleridge begins his 'Perspiration: A Travelling Eclogue' with 'The Dust flies smothering, as on clatt'ring Wheels / Loath'd Aristocracy careers along', and these lines might be read as being applicable to a figure such as John Clare in the account which he gives of his walk out of Essex:

> I felt so weary here that I [was] forced to sit down on the ground to rest myself awhile and while I sat here a coach that seemed to be heavy laden came rattling up and stopped in the hollow below me and I cannot recollect its ever passing me.[12]

Clare's own hardship, and his situation as a vagrant, is reflected in poems which, taking such figures as their subjects, invite an identification with solitary walkers in their different predicaments and sufferings. Typical examples might be Wordsworth's 'Old Man Travelling', 'The Female Vagrant' and, in 'Resolution and Independence', the old leech-gatherer, 'Wandering about alone and silently'.

Travel locates itself at the heart of the period's literature, not only in the sense of actual geographical travel, but also as a trope used by Romantic writers to present themselves as explorers of their own identities. Such a concept of exploration is central to the purpose of *The Prelude* and is carried by Wordsworth's lines, 'A Traveller I am, / And all my tale is of myself' (III.196–7). The poet, perhaps recalling Christian's companions, Faithful and Hopeful,[13] invites Coleridge on the journey to be 'ever at [his] side' and 'Uphold [his] fainting steps' (III.200–1). His task, as he writes, of undertaking a great new poem of psychological investigation (*The Recluse*), will be like that of the explorer, to 'tread on shadowy ground',[14] a purpose later replicated by John Keats, who turns to a world of 'shadowy thought' in his own determination to build for the goddess Psyche 'a fane [temple] / In some untrodden region of my mind'.[15] In his sonnet 'On First Looking into Chapman's Homer', Keats likens his experience to an astronomer's discovery of a new planet, and to Cortez's (actually Bilbao's) discovery of the Pacific. He demonstrates his awareness of both the older sense of discoverer as scientist, and its more modern sense of discoverer as geographical explorer, when the excitement of both kinds of exploration is felt on his first reading of Chapman's translation. In the 'wild surmise' with which Cortez's men look at each other, 'Silent, upon a peak in Darien', Keats perhaps hints also at the older association of geographical discovery with greed, exploitation and destruction.

'England's wealthiest son': Beckford and His Travels

William Beckford's account of his travels through Holland, Germany and Italy, entitled *Dreams, Waking Thoughts and Incidents*, preceded by three years the publication of the work by which he is best known, his celebrated gothic novel *Vathek* (1786). *Dreams* has been referred to as 'one of the minor masterpieces of English travel literature'[16] and it shares the novel's graphic visual qualities. Beckford was a precociously intelligent child with a mercurial personality who, after the early death of his father, came under the control of his autocratic and domineering mother. He was privately educated by a guardian tutor, the Reverend John Lettice, taught musical composition by no less than Mozart himself, and learned the principles of art from the watercolourist Alexander Cozens. Cozens also encouraged him in his exotic and imaginative fantasies and, throughout his life, Beckford was able to realise them. He had inherited an immense fortune* from his father's sugar plantations in Jamaica, but after sexual transgressions with the eleven-year-old son of Lord Courtenay of Powderham, his reputation was damaged and he went into exile at Cintra in Portugal, where the visiting Byron remembers him in *Childe Harold* as, 'Vathek! England's wealthiest son' (I.270–87).

---

* An estimated £320m in present-day currency.

Beckford's interest in travel began when he visited Switzerland in 1777 to complete his education, and Lettice accompanied him, as then, on the two Continental tours* which would become the subject of his epistolary travel book, *Dreams*. The work itself has a peculiar history in that, on the point of its publication by Joseph Johnson, Beckford recalled it. He then burned the print run of almost five hundred copies, retaining a handful to be privately distributed among friends and for display purposes at Fonthill, the enormous gothic revival 'Abbey' he had built on his estate in Wiltshire. *Dreams* is therefore, in its original form, a very scarce book. Similar in its way to Goethe's *Italian Journey* (1816), made more formal on its publication than the livelier Diary notes (1786) on which it was based, Beckford's book was allowed to reappear with numerous alterations and expurgations, as the first volume of his *Italy; with Sketches of Spain and Portugal* (1834). It is not known for certain why, in 1783, Beckford took a decision to prevent publication, but among the reasons put forward by his biographers are pressures from his family, who may have thought that, as Cyrus Redding suggests, his 'lively imagination' and 'quickness of sensibility' were likely to 'prejudice him in the House of Commons, and make ministers imagine that he was not capable of solid business'.[17]

At the beginning of a series of letters addressed to an unnamed recipient (probably Cozens), Beckford's 'Shall I tell you my dreams?' is an unusual introduction to a work whose apparent purpose is to describe the sights of a European tour. This immediate turning in towards the self anticipates Wordsworth in 'Tintern Abbey' (1798) where, although he is apparently constructing a conventionally 'picturesque' landscape, the poet from the outset directs the reader's attention away from the visual elements of the scene and towards his own 'Thoughts of more deep seclusion'. In a part of that poem where he recollects an earlier stage in the history of his life among natural objects, Wordsworth writes of how 'The mountain, and the deep and gloomy wood, / Their colours and their forms, were then to me / An appetite'. He goes on to distinguish this simpler and more visual response from a later and profounder one which transcends the

---

* June 1780–April 1781 and May–October 1782.

'picturesque' model that has 'no need of a remoter charm, / By thought supplied, nor any interest / Unborrowed from the eye' (ll. 78–83).

In Letter I, Beckford similarly distances himself from the picturesque 'view': 'A frequent mist hovers before my eyes,' he writes, 'and, through its medium, I see objects so faint and hazy, that both their colours and forms are apt to delude me.' He wryly acknowledges that his is not the ideal approach for a tourist to be taking: 'This is a rare confession, say the wise, for a traveller to make; pretty accounts will such a one give of outlandish countries: his correspondents must reap great benefit, no doubt, from such purblind observations.'

'All through Kent did I dose as usual', the letter continues, with Beckford describing how he opens his eyes 'to take in an idea or two' of the scenery through which he is passing, then closing them again, as he is transported back to his 'native hills', peopling his mind with those he 'loved best'. In the environs of Canterbury he misses 'the companions' of his slumbers: 'Where are they?—behind yon blue hills, perhaps, or t'other side of that thick forest.' Any hope the reader may have had for a description of the 'view' is dispelled as Beckford, 'travelling after these deserters' of his imagination, reaches the city, 'vile enough o'conscience, and fit only to be past [sic] in one's sleep'. Expectations of a conventional travelogue are consistently undermined. The reader, instead of being able to share the more usual 'prospect' delivered by the traveller who takes up a 'station' to view a landscape,* is invited to follow the wanderings of Beckford's discursive imagination and focus upon the more substantial 'reality' of his dreams. In *The Prelude*, in a similar passage of thoughtful recollection, Wordsworth seeks the origin of those moments of 'holy calm' when he forgets that he has 'bodily eyes' and remarks that what he saw, 'Appeared like something in myself, a dream, / A prospect in my mind' (II.365–71). Some of Beckford's words and phrasings, such as 'colours and forms' (Letter I), 'wreath of smoke', a rivulet which 'loses itself' (Letter VIII) do seem to anticipate those of Wordsworth (see 'Tintern Abbey', ll. 79, 17, 13), and it is of course possible that Joseph Johnson, Beckford's would-be publisher, and

---

* 'Heavens! What a goodly prospect spreads around, / Of hills, and dales, and woods, and lawns, and spires' (James Thomson, *The Seasons*, 'Summer', ll. 1437–8).

publisher of Wordsworth's *An Evening Walk* and *Descriptive Sketches* (1793), may have retained a copy of *Dreams* which was shown to the poet.

In Canterbury, on his way to embark at Margate, Beckford pays a nocturnal visit to the cathedral. But the venerable building described is not the obligatory sight of a traveller's guidebook. The focus is upon Beckford's melancholy emotions and night thoughts as he wanders in the gothic gloom of its 'lofty pillars, dim ailes, and mysterious arches'. He goes through the motions of being the observing tourist who, 'Pencil in hand and book upon the knee, / Will look and scribble, scribble on and look',[18] but only to note down in his 'pocket book' by 'inspiration' the injunctions of a 'sepulchral voice' that he imagines he hears, for, as he adds '(I could not see)'.

The immediacy of statement, which lends authenticity to the traveller's voice, comes in the first letter, where Beckford pauses momentarily to consider the person to whom he is writing: 'But stop, my good friends; patience a moment!' He announces that 'if —— be contented with my visionary way of gazing, I am perfectly pleased'. Although his training in the visual arts is consistently obvious in the actual powers of description he employs, Beckford implies that Cozens, under whose tutorship he was first taught to 'see', may remain to be convinced of the value which Beckford attaches to the 'inward eye'.[19]

Dreams is not a travelogue of factual information. It belongs more centrally to the kind of visionary pilgrimage we associate with Byron's *Childe Harold* or the Romantic confessional mode of Mary Wollstonecraft's *Letters Written during a Short Residence in Sweden, Norway, and Denmark* (1796). A passage in Letter VIII perfectly illustrates how Beckford's strong emotional responses enhance the details of the colour and forms of a piece of natural description, to reveal the interior world of its author's deepest feelings. Journeying through the Tyrol he hears the roar of a cascade:

> a goats-track [...] conducted me, on the brink of the foaming waters, to the very depths of the cliff, whence issues a stream which dashes impetuously down, strikes against a ledge of grey

rock, and sprinkles the impending thicket with dew. Big drops hung on every spray, and glittered on the leaves, partially gilt by the rays of the declining sun, whose mellow hues softened the summits of the cliffs, and diffused a repose, a divine calm over this deep retirement, which inclined me to imagine it the extremity of the earth, and the portal of some other region of existence; some happy world, behind the dark groves of pines, the caves and awful mountains, where the river takes its source. I hung eagerly on the gulph, impressed with this idea, and fancied myself listening to a voice that bubbled up with the waters; then looked into the abyss, and strained my eyes to penetrate its gloom: but all was dark and unfathomable as futurity.

Descriptions such as this recall the psychological landscapes associated with a mainstream Romantic writer such as Coleridge,[*] and Beckford, 'guided' by the roar of waters to the entrance of 'a wide fissure in the rock', hears an oracular 'voice' emerging from it, expressing, as Wordsworth might say, 'The ghostly language of the ancient earth' (*Prelude*, II.327) and anticipating *The Prelude*'s 'Black drizzling crags that spake by the way-side / As if a voice were in them' (VI.563–4).

Beckford's descriptions bear some interesting comparisons, too, with those of Byron on his 'pilgrimage' among the monuments of Italy's principal cities. Byron's feelings of being overwhelmed by St Peter's in Rome lead him to consider the architectural in terms of the natural sublime, so that contemplation of its 'great whole' (*Childe Harold*, l. 1406) can only be achieved by advancing 'piecemeal' (l. 1405), 'Like climbing some great Alp' (l. 1396). For Byron, the dynamic of the 'ascent' allows him to overcome a sense of his 'littleness' (l. 1420) and identify with the grandeur of the church, 'Till, growing with its growth, we thus dilate / Our spirits to the size of that they contemplate' (ll. 1421–2). Beckford's passage on St Peter's (Letter XXII) is much

---

[*]   See especially 'Kubla Khan' and 'This Lime-Tree Bower my Prison', ll. 1–20. For some interesting connections between Coleridge and Beckford, see John Livingston Lowes, *The Road to Xanadu: A Study in the Ways of the Imagination*, Sentry Edition (Boston: Houghton Mifflin, n.d.), pp. 364, 542.

more fanciful and escapist, although in some ways it prefigures Byron's. He imagines erecting 'a little tabernacle under the dome', so that 'instead of climbing a mountain, we should ascend the cupola, and look down on our little encampment below'. In language which reflects his contemporary taste for the oriental and the exotic, Beckford constructs an imaginary 'pavilion' with 'curtains of yellow silk [...] Lanterns [to] remind us of China, and, depending from the roofs of the palace, bring before us that of the Emperor Ki'. Here we turn away from Byron's mountain vistas to look down and then inwards to an image of Beckford's own heterodox imagination. 'I should desire', he writes, 'no other prospect.' Beckford's disrespectful approach to religion in *Vathek* might reflect an attitude of intolerance towards his mother's teaching. Even the sceptic Byron is suitably reverential within 'this eternal ark of worship' (l. 1386), but Beckford effectively creates a pagan 'pleasure dome' beneath the dome of the very seat of Christianity and where, in usurpation of God's authority, he would have 'a moon at command, and a theatrical sun to rise and set, at pleasure'.

Pilgrimage: Byron, 'Pilgrim of Eternity'

The first two Cantos of Byron's *Childe Harold's Pilgrimage*,[20] based on his travels of 1809–11 and published in 1812, made him famous overnight. Later, after he left England for voluntary exile in Europe, he recommenced work on it, adding a third Canto in 1816 and a fourth two years later. Canto I focuses on Iberia, where the Peninsular War against Napoleon was currently being fought, and Canto II continues the journey, on through the eastern Mediterranean. Byron's travels were on a larger scale than Beckford's. As France and Italy, because of the war, were off-limits to the British, his route had to accommodate these circumstances, and his adventurous itinerary, like the walking tour of Wordsworth and Jones in 1790, was a conscious distinguishing of his travels from the more conventional ones of the 'tourist'. The Iberian peninsula was a war zone, and very few people indeed journeyed into Albania and Greece. The blockade on British travel into the most popular European destinations meant that there was a hunger for the kind of travelogue that Byron was able to supply, and there is much evidence, both in the poem and in the extensive notes that accompanied it, that he is aware of his readership's expectations and tailors his poem accordingly.

The name of Byron's hero, comprising both a medieval word for a knight (Childe) and that of the fallen Saxon king, Harold, suggests that he is both a quester (knight-errant) and a fated soul. From the outset, it is difficult not to identify him with Byron himself, and the opening stanzas of Canto I, dwelling on Childe Harold's boredom, his languor, satiety and excess, deliberately encourage it. But in the dedication of Canto IV to his friend Hobhouse, who had made part of the original journey with him, Byron abandons the 'mask' of the Childe altogether as he has 'become weary', he says, 'of drawing a line which every one seemed determined not to perceive'. Childe Harold had effectively become no more than a vehicle for Byron's own reflections and personal meditations and, as such, is surplus to requirements.

In the title of his poem, Byron consciously recalls the Christian's devotional visit to a shrine or some equivalent 'place' of pilgrimage. This traditional journey always suggests an eventual destination as, for example, the shrine of Thomas Becket is the anticipated place of arrival for Chaucer's pilgrims in *The Canterbury Tales*. The dynamic of *Childe Harold's Pilgrimage*, however, carries its hero on through his travels without any particular sense of an approaching conclusion. The sceptical traveller, Byron (or his alter ego, the Childe), simply responds to a cumulative sequence of locations or situations, the response being sometimes written up with the immediacy of the experiences themselves as they take place. There is no binding narrative thread and no Christian sense of purpose or belief. The poem's cohesiveness, if it has any at all, is provided by the *Weltschmerz** of its hero's reflections, to which the final alexandrine of each Spenserian stanza[†] contributes a cadence of melancholy and resignation.

---

*   A feeling of worldweariness brought on by melancholy reflection.

†   The Spenserian Stanza is so named from the stanza form of Edmund Spenser's *The Faerie Queene* (1590/1596). The stanza has nine lines, and the final line of twelve syllables (an alexandrine) carries an extra stress.

Consistent with the personal inflection given to Romantic travel writing is Byron's use of his journey, not only to work off his private emotions, but also, through the kind of objective analysis which travel makes possible, to obtain a more sound understanding of himself. Much of Canto III conveys his bitterness at being rejected by English society after separating from his wife. He writes to Thomas Moore, 'I was half mad during the time of its composition, between metaphysics, mountains, lakes, love unextinguishable, thoughts unutterable, and the nightmare of my own delinquencies. I should many a good day, have blown my brains out, but for the recollection that it would have given pleasure to my mother-in-law.'[21] The Canto provides a constant expansion and contraction of vistas, outwards towards the geographies of central Europe but then always returning inwards to the 'lonely breast'. It is a sense of his own solitude, and of his difference from them, which leads Byron to say that, even 'in the crowd' of fellow travellers:

> They could not deem me one of such; I stood
> Among them, but not of them; in a shroud
> Of thoughts which were not their thoughts. (III.1054–6)

As Harold visits the battlefield of Waterloo, Byron's gloomy reflections on human life come to centre upon the recently defeated Napoleon, his contemporary rival for status as the most famous man in Europe.* It is as though a consideration of Napoleon's 'spirit antithetically mixt' allows Byron to understand the problems attaching to greatness, more than if he were to focus exclusively on his own predicament. Like the Childe, and like Byron's own notion of himself, 'untaught to submit / His thoughts to others [...] Proud though in desolation', Napoleon shares 'a fire / And motion of the soul which will not dwell / In its own narrow being, but aspire[s] / Beyond the fitting medium of desire' (III.102–3, 108, 371–4).

---

*   Certainly among contemporary European writers there was no one as famous as Byron, and after the death of his mother-in-law, he adopted her name 'Noel', always signing himself 'Noel Byron' and taking pride in his initials being the same as Napoleon's. Even in Russia Pushkin had to insist, 'No, I am not Byron, I am another.'

From the outset, this lonely difference defines Childe Harold who, as he sings 'Good Night' to his 'native land' (I.125), echoes Coleridge's Ancient Mariner: 'And now I'm in the world alone, / Upon the wide, wide sea' (ll. 181–2). The Mariner's 'Alone, alone, all, all alone, / Alone on a wide, wide sea!' (ll. 232–3)[22] might be considered equally appropriate to Byron, especially in the light of John Galt's recollections of their journey, as fellow passengers, en route from Gibraltar to Malta. Galt recalls Byron, near Cagliari in Sardinia, sitting 'aloof [...] amid the shrouds and rattlins [...] almost apparitional, suggesting dim reminiscences of him who shot the albatross'[23] (see Part Four: 'Faith, Myth and Doubt').

Unlike the Mariner, however, for whom the return to his 'own countree' is a 'dream of joy' (ll. 464, 467), Byron, in Canto IV, speculates that he may never come back from his travels: 'and should I leave behind / The inviolate island [Venice] of the sage and free, / And seek me out a home by a remoter sea' (IV.70–2). The lagoon of Venice is not exactly the sea, but the conclusion to Canto IV, with its address to the ocean, returns to the same elemental power with which the Canto begins. Byron expresses his contempt for empires and for war as their instrument. 'Man marks the earth with ruin' but his control 'Stops with the shore' (IV.1605–6). The sea as protean and limitless 'image of Eternity' (IV.1644) not only provides an appropriate 'ending' for this innovative form of 'pilgrimage', but also suitably represents the continuing metaphysical quest of Byron who, as the 'Pilgrim of Eternity',* replaces Childe Harold with himself as hero of the poem.

Travel and Cultural Enquiry

Childe Harold's Pilgrimage established 'Byronism' and reflects the Romantic period in many different ways. But as a work of travel literature it is derivative and, although geographically much wider ranging, it is essentially no more than a latter-day version of a youthful aristocrat's Grand Tour. Sixteen years before it appeared, a book was

---

* Shelley's term for Byron in 'Adonais', l. 264.

published which, as well as being in itself a Romantic spiritual autobiography, opened up new perspectives on the possibility of travel as a form of sociological enquiry. Mary Wollstonecraft was already the celebrated author of *A Vindication of the Rights of Woman* (1792) when, in the summer of 1795, she set out on a four-month-long expedition through Scandinavia, publishing her account of it in the following year.

The full title of this work, widely admired among the circle of her publisher, Joseph Johnson, is *Letters Written during a Short Residence in Sweden, Norway, and Denmark*. Travel accounts by women were rare before 1770, but began to increase thereafter, although they were often confined to manners, customs, details of domesticity and so on. Larger issues to do with politics and society were regarded as the proper domain of men, and Mary Wollstonecraft's travels, as might have been expected from the most prominent feminist writer of her time, are a challenge to this state of affairs. Throughout *A Short Residence*, she engages with all aspects of contemporary life in what was then a little-known part of the world.

Like Beckford's *Dreams*, the book is written as a series of letters but, unlike his, they take on a personal poignancy, being directed by Mary Wollstonecraft to a faithless husband, the father of her one-year-old baby who, together with a maidservant, accompanies her on the journey. She advertises *A Short Residence* in her 'Advertisement' as 'a just description' of what she saw, 'relating the effect different objects had produced' on her mind 'whilst the impression was still fresh' and hoping that, by winning their affections, her readers might wish to become 'better acquainted' with her.

Mary Wollstonecraft's journey into Scandinavia was motivated by more than a traveller's desire to observe foreign parts. *A Short Residence* conceals the fact that she was on a mission, on behalf of her husband, to recover a considerable amount of his money which had been spirited away in the form of a 'lost' treasure ship. The story is intriguing and, because it is so central to Wollstonecraft's state of mind in the book, it needs further explanation.

Mary Wollstonecraft had met her future husband, an American, Gilbert Imlay, in revolutionary Paris. As victors against a common British enemy, Americans were in good standing with the French, and Imlay registered

Mary as his wife to give her some much-needed protection at a time of hostilities between the two countries. After a while they moved to Le Havre, where Imlay became involved in shipping raw materials from neutral countries into France and running the British blockade. In May 1794, a daughter, Fanny,* was born. Mary, finding Imlay faithless, returned to London and made the first of what would be two suicide attempts. Imlay saved her, protesting his devotion, and in an attempt to rescue the relationship, Mary agreed to travel into Scandinavia as his agent in quest of a lost cargo of silver which he had entrusted to a Norwegian, Peder Ellefsen. Ellefsen had absconded with both ship and cargo, and Imlay, it would seem, believed that Mary, with her considerable intellectual powers, would be able to negotiate the recovery of the treasure. Subsequent research has revealed that she did indeed manage to retrieve a portion of it, meeting up with Ellefsen on his home ground of Risør, and even taking up her cause with Count Bernstorff, the prime minister of Denmark, who at that time was also ruler of Norway.

Mary Wollstonecraft's journey, a solitary woman with a one-year-old baby, was an extraordinary undertaking. A traveller himself, Lord Byron is scornful of the female tourists he encounters at Clarens in 1816 for their indifference to, or misunderstanding of, the sublime scenery through which they are passing. He writes to his sister of coming across an English party in a carriage, 'a lady in it fast asleep!':

> —fast asleep in the most anti-narcotic spot in the world—excellent—I remember at Chamouni—in the very eyes of Mont Blanc—hearing another woman—English also—exclaim to her party—'did you ever see anything more "*rural*"' quotha!—Rocks—pines—torrents—Glaciers—Clouds—and Summits of eternal snow far above them—and '*Rural*'![24]

---

* After the death of Mary Wollstonecraft, Fanny Imlay (1794–1816) was brought up in William Godwin's household, together with Mary Godwin (Godwin's child by Mary Wollstonecraft, future wife of Shelley and author of *Frankenstein*) and Claire Claremont, daughter of Godwin's new wife, and mother of Byron's 'love child', Allegra. Fanny took her own life in 1816 at the age of twenty-two. See Janet Todd, *Death and the Maidens: Fanny Wollstonecraft and the Shelley Circle* (London: Profile Books, 2007).

Mary Wollstonecraft's response as a woman traveller is of an altogether different order. At Gothenburg she writes of how she feels the 'picturesque beauty' of the landscape and of how 'the sublime often gave place imperceptibly to the beautiful'.[25] But these are not, for her, simply academic terms in the sense in which Anna Seward might have used them. Their meaning and immediacy is lived out through her first-hand encounter with a landscape described by Richard Holmes as 'almost [...] a boreal wilderness'.* Holmes points out that where the traditional route of the traveller was south, towards the civilisations of the Mediterranean, travelling north to such *terra incognita* as Mary Wollstonecraft did, was to put oneself beyond the reach of Western culture. Only the hardiest of sailors, merchants or diplomats penetrated into the territories of northern Scandinavia and beyond. Of Risør (p. 131), the remote home port of Ellefsen, where Mary is 'prevailed upon to dine with the English vice-consul' (p. 133), Holmes remarks, 'One is amazed to learn such a person existed in such a place' (p. 28).

Throughout the book, Mary Wollstonecraft thinks consistently as someone whose politics and principles have been shaped by her own experiences of the revolutionary period. The preoccupation of her thoughts with notions of imprisonment and freedom is clear from the outset as she describes waiting, after an eleven-day passage, to disembark at Gothenburg. Her frustration seems to be framed by a wider sense of political disaffection, representing the attitude of many of her Romantic contemporaries to the failure of the French Revolution:

> My attention was particularly directed to the light-house; and you can scarcely imagine with what anxiety I watched two long hours for a boat to emancipate me – still no one appeared. Every cloud that flitted on the horizon was hailed as a liberator, till

---

* Boreal: relating to the Arctic or North, from Boreas, the Greek god of the north wind. The quotation is from Holmes's Introduction to *A Short Residence*, p. 17.

approaching nearer, like most of the prospects sketched by hope, it dissolved under the eye into disappointment.*

The tardiness of the local pilots leads her to reflect on how 'Despotism' (p. 63), by providing no financial incentive, 'had here cramped the industry of man', and her determination to make for shore circumvents the captain's hesitation: 'It is a kind of rule at sea, not to send out a boat.' Her feminism and quest for freedom underlines every sentiment as she prevails with the sailors against the captain ('men with common minds seldom break through general rules', p. 64) and then imagines herself, once having reached the rocky headland, making her own way to Gothenburg – 'confinement is so unpleasant'.

Mary Wollstonecraft's delight in the natural beauty of Gothenburg's scenery echoes the tendency of Romantic-period writers to find in the natural world a truer source of emancipation than the political revolution was able to provide:

> How silent and peaceful was the scene. I gazed around with rapture, and felt more of that spontaneous pleasure which gives credibility to our expectation of happiness, than I had for a long, long time before. I forgot the horrors I had witnessed in France, which had cast a gloom over all nature, and suffering the enthusiasm of my character, too often, gracious God! damped by the tears of disappointed affection, to be lighted up afresh, care took wing while simple fellow feeling expanded my heart.
>
> (pp. 67–8)

Mary Wollstonecraft hints here at her personal sorrow for her fading relationship with Imlay, something which underlies her thoughts

---

* The passage is reminiscent of the description Coleridge gives in 'Frost at Midnight' (1798) of waiting, as a boy, to be 'liberated' from his school, Christ's Hospital (ll. 36–43). Richard Holmes points out many probable influences of Mary Wollstonecraft's book on the younger Romantics, as for example, her own situation as 'solitary, outcast woman' on Wordsworth's poem, 'Ruth' (first published in *Lyrical Ballads*, 1800), or as 'woman wailing for her demon-lover' in Coleridge's 'Kubla Khan' (1797). See Wollstonecraft, *A Short Residence*, ed. Holmes, Introduction, Section 6.

throughout the journey, and her concern with freedom inevitably extends beyond her own predicament to the future of her baby daughter:

> I feel more than a mother's fondness and anxiety, when I reflect on the dependent and oppressed state of her sex [...] I dread to unfold her mind, lest it should render her unfit for the world she is to inhabit – Hapless woman! What a fate is thine.* (p. 97)

A Short Residence takes travel writing, and especially women's travel writing, into entirely new territory. Mary Wollstonecraft believes that travelling should mean more than simply paying homage to the past before the monuments of classical antiquity, and must broaden the mind. 'Travellers who require that every nation should resemble their native country, had better stay at home', she writes. The most essential service the traveller can provide is 'to promote inquiry and discussion' (p. 93) so that by 'Mixing with mankind, we are obliged to examine our prejudices, and often imperceptibly lose, as we analyze them' (p. 79).

True to her own precepts, Mary Wollstonecraft considers politics, economics, the role of women, evolution, aesthetics, capital punishment, domestic manners and habits. Hers is a wide-ranging, 'Romantic' intelligence, putting at all times the heart before the head, feeling before understanding, but on the assumption always that 'we reason deeply, when we forcibly feel' (p. 171). *A Short Residence* anticipates the modern travel book, and the measure of Mary Wollstonecraft's difference as a solitary, female traveller from those who have preceded her must, if in anything at all, be located in her intrepidity. At the end of Letter 5, she sets out at night in an open boat to cross the boisterous Skagerrak from Sweden into Norway:

> Wrapping my great coat around me, I lay down on some sails at the bottom of the boat, its motion rocking me to rest, till a discourteous wave interrupted my slumbers, and obliged me to rise and feel a solitariness which was not so soothing as that of the past night. (p. 95)

---

* A particularly poignant moment in the light of Fanny Imlay's fate.

A real-life Coleridgean 'Mariner', she is scornful of fear, as when in Letter 22 before crossing 'The Great Belt' in Denmark, she writes:

> [N]either I nor my little girl are ever attacked by sea sickness [...] I enter a boat with the same indifference as I change horses; and as for danger, come when it may, I dread it not sufficiently to have any anticipating fears. (p. 182)

Drawing on a rich inheritance of travel writing, and exploiting their own opportunities for travel both at home and abroad, Romantic writers produced some of the period's most memorable and innovative literature in poetry, fiction and non-fictional prose.

Extended Commentary: Wollstonecraft, *Letters Written during a Short Residence in Sweden, Norway, and Denmark* (1796), Letters 16 and 17

Making her way by boat down the west coast of Sweden, Mary arrives at Kvistram where she is promised horses to take her forward on the next stage of her journey. Arriving at an inn, she assumes from the crowds of people that there must be a fair in the neighbourhood. So it turns out to be, and she provides a vivid picture of the assembly: 'The boisterous merriment that almost every instant produced a quarrel or made me dread one, with the clouds of tobacco, and fumes of brandy, gave an infernal appearance to the scene' (p. 156). Her remarks on comparative cultural traits extend to the details of popular habits and allow her here to contrast the sobriety of the Parisians, whose fêtes have a gaiety which 'never becomes disgusting or dangerous', with those of the Swedes, where drinking is 'the principal relaxation of the men' (p. 174). Her suspicion of intoxication, 'the pleasure of savages' (p. 174), comes from her witnessing, as a child, the demoralisation of her mother as victim of Mr Wollstonecraft's drunken rage. Yet Mary relies on reason rather than censoriousness to carry a point. She often backs it up with a humorous remark, as in her earlier reflections in Sweden on the tendency of travellers to judge the 'hospitality' of a people in proportion as to how much the bottle is 'pushed about' (p. 73). 'These remarks are equally applicable to Dublin,' she writes, 'the most hospitable city I ever passed through.'

As she leaves Kvistram, she comes across 'a number of joyous groups', and remarks: 'though the evening was fresh, many were stretched on the grass like weary cattle; and drunken men had fallen by the roadside' (p. 156). Her heightened awareness of the contrast between the beauty of the natural scene and the destructiveness of a 'drinking, smoking, and laughing' party of men and women who have damaged some trees to get fuel for their fire, recalls Wordsworth's childhood feeling of pain when he realises that he has destroyed a hazel grove, an event described in the poem 'Nutting'. Wordsworth remembers how, in an innocent quest for hazel nuts, he had devastated the peaceful grove, and had 'dragged to earth both branch and bough, with crash / And merciless ravage'. He describes his 'sense of pain' as he 'beheld / The silent trees and the intruding sky', the episode becoming symbolic of a kind of fall from innocence to a first consciousness of sin. The poem concludes: 'Then, dearest Maiden! Move along these shades / In gentleness of heart; with gentle hand / Touch, — for there is a spirit in the woods'. Mary responds similarly: 'I felt for the trees whose torn branches strewed the ground. – Hapless nymphs! Thy haunts I fear were polluted by many an unhallowed flame; the casual burst of the moment!' Her anxieties about the environmental consequences of thoughtless human activity anticipates, and possibly had some influence on, Wordsworth's own concerns, which, since the Romantic period, have become increasingly urgent and universal ones.

Mary's journey from Kvistram is delayed as the promised horses do not materialise and, in spite of her exhortations, the postilion refuses to continue: 'He even began to howl and weep when I insisted on his keeping his word' (p. 156). In a remark which anticipates *Frankenstein, or The Modern Prometheus*, the famous novel by her other daughter, whom she would never know,* Mary writes: 'Nothing, indeed, can equal the

---

* Mary Wollstonecraft died of puerperal fever ten days after giving birth to Mary, her child by William Godwin.

stupid obstinacy of some of these half alive beings, who seem to have been made by Prometheus, when the fire he stole from Heaven was so exhausted, that he could only spare a spark to give life, not animation, to the inert clay' (p. 156). She has earlier commented on the lack of curiosity and imagination in the male population she encounters in Sweden. Had the men possessed either of these attributes, 'they could not contentedly remain rooted in the clods they so indolently cultivate' (p. 65). However, she applies the Promethean myth more positively when, in describing the beauty of the young women of Strömstad, she wonders 'from whence the fire was stolen which sparkled in their fine blue eyes' (p. 91).

In the graphic account of the night she is obliged to spend at the post-house, polite travel literature becomes only a memory. The following morning, 'not wishing to associate the idea of a pigstye with that of a human dwelling', Mary hastens through her apartment to enquire about the horses, before setting off once again on her journey. She does so, but, typically, not without first commenting on the already faded beauty of young girls, in a country where love seems considered to be 'merely an appetite, to fulfil the main design of nature, never enlivened by either affection or sentiment' (p. 157).

The continuing journey allows Mary Wollstonecraft to construct a 'picturesque' view of the landscape through which she is travelling. The 'purple hue' of the heath harmonises exquisitely 'with the rays of ripening corn', and the people busy in the fields 'continually varied the prospect'. The familiar terminology has now to be considered in the light of Mary's more sociological observations, such as her realisation of an economic situation which obliges the women and children to work to supplement their animals' fodder by cutting off branches from trees. Her implication is that even though it 'injures the trees', such activity is to be distinguished from the wanton destruction described earlier, and that the prospects for such people in society must make the observer think twice about viewing them simply as aesthetic complements to any picturesque 'prospect'.

Letter 16 ends with a description of a happy rural family and a harvest-home, the 'sweetest picture' presented 'for the pencil* and heart'.

---

* A painter's brush.

But its delightfulness as a set piece of pictorial composition is tinged with Mary's all too real sadness. Like Frankenstein's Creature, gazing in on the happiness of the De Lacey family from which he is forever excluded, Mary is led to contrast her own solitude and desertion, while at the same time she fears for her baby's future:

> My eyes followed them to the cottage, and an involuntary sigh whispered to my heart, that I envied the mother [...]. I was returning to my babe, who may never experience a father's care or tenderness. The bosom that nurtures her, heaved with a pang at the thought which only an unhappy mother could feel.
>
> (p. 158)

The mood changes in Letter 17 with Mary's account of her visit to the Trollhättan canal, then under construction. Her admiration for this 'stupendous attempt' to drive a fifty-mile waterway from Trollhättan to Gothenburg, 'a grand proof of human industry' (p. 159), reflects a mixture of pride in Man's endeavour and a regret 'that such a noble scene had not been left in all its solitary sublimity' (p. 160). Mary's response looks on to a typical nineteenth-century ambivalence about such progress, well illustrated in two late sonnets by Wordsworth, both connected with travel, one of which laments the intrusion of the railway on the Lake District,[*] and the other celebrating the wonders of Victorian engineering.[†]

Mary Wollstonecraft observes that in the sublime setting of the cascade of Trollhättan, the activities of the canal construction 'only resembled the insignificant sport of children' and were not 'calculated to warm the fancy'. Like the Romantic poet, she 'wandered about' (p. 159) and in language which particularly recalls the 'mighty fountain' of Coleridge's 'Kubla Khan' (1797), emerging from its 'deep romantic chasm' she describes a torrent issuing from 'a dark cavern' where 'fancy

---

[*] 'On the Projected Kendal and Windermere Railway' (1844): 'Is there no nook of English ground secure / From rash assault?'

[†] 'Steamboats, Viaducts, and Railway' (1835): 'Motions and Means, on land and sea at war'.

might easily imagine a vast fountain, throwing up its waters from the very centre of the earth' (p. 159). Coleridge's 'Huge fragments' of rock vaulting 'like rebounding hail' are prefigured in Mary's description of cataracts 'struggling with huge masses of rock [...] rebounding from the profound cavities'. In such ways, a fascinating mixture of intellectual curiosity, practical observation and poetical sensibility are brought together by Mary Wollstonecraft's *A Short Residence* to create an entirely new genus of Romantic travel writing.

Notes

1   *Lyrical Ballads* (1798).
2   William Gilpin, *An Essay upon Prints* (London, 1768), p. 2.
3   Hesketh Pearson (ed.), *The Swan of Lichfield: being a Selection from the Correspondence of Anna Seward* (London: Hamish Hamilton, 1936), p. 172.
4   Pearson (ed.), *The Swan of Lichfield*, p. 175.
5   Edmund Burke, *A Philosophical Enquiry into the Origin of our Ideas of the Sublime and Beautiful*, Part Two, Section II, 'Terror'.
6   James Boswell, *The Life of Samuel Johnson* (1791).
7   Horace Walpole, *The Yale Edition of Horace Walpole's Correspondence*, ed. W. S. Lewis, 40 vols (London: Yale University Press, 1937–83), vol. 13, p. 182: letter to Richard West.
8   Thomas Love Peacock, *Nightmare Abbey*, ed. Lisa Vargo (Peterborough, Ont. and Orchard Park, NY: Broadview Press, 2007), p. 109.
9   Note on *Prometheus Unbound* by Mary Shelley: P. B. Shelley, *Poetical Works*, ed. Thomas Hutchinson, corrected by G. M. Matthews (Oxford: Oxford University Press, 1970), p. 270.
10 Samuel Rogers, *Italy* (1822), 'Foreign Travel'.
11 Kenneth Clark, *Civilisation: A Personal View* (London: John Murray, 1969), p. 283.
12 John Clare, *Selected Poems*, ed. Jonathan Bate (London: Faber, 2003), 'Recollections of Journey from Essex', p. 262.
13 John Bunyan, *The Pilgrim's Progress* (1678).
14 'Prospectus' to *The Recluse*.
15 'Ode to Psyche'.
16 *Times Literary Supplement*, 3 May 1928.
17 Cyrus Redding, *Memoirs of William Beckford of Fonthill*, 2 vols (London: Charles Skeet, 1859), vol. 1, p. 138.

18   Wordsworth, 'The Brothers', ll. 7–8.
19   Wordsworth, 'I Wandered Lonely as a Cloud'. See also William Blake, 'We are led to Believe a Lie / When we see [*with*] not Thro the Eye', 'Auguries of Innocence', ll. 125–6.
20   All references to *Childe Harold's Pilgrimage* are taken from Byron, *Childe Harold's Pilgrimage and other Romantic Poems*, ed. John D. Jump (London: Dent, 1975).
21   Leslie A. Marchand (ed.), *Byron's Letters and Journals*, 13 vols (London: John Murray, 1973–94), vol. 5, p. 165.
22   S. T. Coleridge, *The Ancient Mariner* (1828 version).
23   John Galt, *The Life of Lord Byron* (1830), ch. 8.
24   Marchand (ed.), *Byron's Letters and Journals*, vol. 5, p. 97
25   Mary Wollstonecraft, *Letters Written during a Short Residence in Sweden, Norway, and Denmark*, ed. Richard Holmes (Harmondsworth: Penguin, 1987), pp. 67–8.

Part Four
Critical Theories and Debates

Imagination, Truth and Reason

As the Romantic period understood the term, the Imagination was a faculty of mind at the centre of human creativity and possessed, at its highest levels of performance, by only the distinguished few. Prior to the celebrated definitions which sound it as the keynote and place it at the heart of Romantic aesthetics, the Imagination was conterminous with the 'imaginary', a capacity in the mind of the artist for invention, and often associated with the inferior 'Fancy', which does no more than decorate or ornament commonly shared perceptions. When Alexander Pope describes the poet's wit (or intelligence), he defines it as an ability to give pleasing expression to universally admitted 'truths':

> True wit is Nature to advantage dress'd;
> What oft was thought, but ne'er so well express'd.[1]

Here the poet reflects what is seen, corresponding with Aristotle's belief that poetry, and indeed all art, has its origin in man's instinct for imitation ('mimesis') or representation.[2] Until the time of Dr Johnson, whose death in 1784 coincided with the beginnings of the mainstream Romantic period, the mimetic is the guiding principle behind all imaginative writing; 'nothing can please many, and please long,' writes Johnson, 'but just representations of general nature'.[3] Insofar as poets are distinguishable only by their ability to please and to make more palatable 'what oft was thought', they are given no special status, and their representational abilities are judged effective or otherwise by their readership or audience.

During the Romantic age, the poet's role changes from a mimetic to an expressive one. Poets continue to reflect the world they occupy, but make a contribution to it from within themselves, altering its aspect in the light of their perceptions. They reveal now a world illuminated by what they have themselves projected into it. This activity of the poet as both reflector (mirror) and projector (lamp) has been investigated through its evolution in critical theory by the American critic M. H. Abrams,[4] and a consequence of the shift from a mimetic to an expressive aesthetics is that the poet takes on an entirely new status. The readership no longer applies its test as to how well poets represent the nature of things. Instead, the test is now of readers' abilities to understand those particular visions, or the versions of reality which poets offer to them. Instead of the reader sitting in judgement on the poet, the poet provides a task of interpretation for the reader.

The lowly status of poets derives from Plato, who had no place for them in his *Republic*. Plato regards poetry as unethical in promoting undesirable passions, as unphilosophical, being remote from truthful knowledge, and as having no pragmatic educational value. Thomas Love Peacock, playing devil's advocate in *The Four Ages of Poetry* (1820), argues accordingly:*

> A poet in our times is a semi-barbarian in a civilized community. He lives in the days that are past. His ideas, thoughts, feelings, associations, are all with barbarous manners, obsolete customs, and exploded superstitions. The march of his intellect is like that of a crab, backward.

* Shelley responds to Peacock in *A Defence of Poetry* (1821).

Shakespearean Precedents

In *A Midsummer Night's Dream*, Theseus, the Duke of Athens, reflects the Platonic view when he describes poets as synonymous with lovers and madmen (V.i.7–8). Their 'imagination', their 'seething brains' and 'shaping fantasies' enable them to 'apprehend / More than cool reason ever comprehends' (V.i.6). 'Apprehension', an instinctive awareness of something intangible, is for Theseus to be distinguished from 'comprehension', the application of reason to promote understanding. For him, the events of midsummer night, as they have been reported, indicate all the characteristics of the poet's dream, the 'antic fables' and 'fairy toys' (I.v.3) of an older and now irrelevant time, leading the clear intelligence 'backward' to the fantasy world of children. Theseus admits no more credibility to the 'reality' of a poet's vision than he would to the apprehensions of a walker at night whose overactive imagination supposes a 'bear' for what turns out to be merely a 'bush' (V.i.21–2).

A Midsummer Night's Dream offers a concept of Imagination completely lost to sight until its re-emergence, in the nineteenth century definitions by Samuel Taylor Coleridge and others, as a faculty central to Romanticism. For a contemporary audience, Athens would have been synonymous with reason, and it is appropriate that its Duke, Theseus, should speak as the rational man. The wood, on the other hand, where the events of midsummer night take place, has all the Burkean qualities of beauty and fear. 'Wood' in Middle English means 'mad', and 'Athens, and a wood near it' suggests that reason is near to madness. The 'genius loci' of the wood is Bottom, who is anything but rational and whose words give expression to his thoughts in an appropriately chaotic syntax. This language contributes to the overall comic effect of the play, but its confusion has crucial significance when, awaking from his dream in Act IV, Bottom tries to make sense of his recent experience. He speaks a muddled version of the following text from St Paul's first letter to the Corinthians: 'Eye hath not seen, nor ear heard, neither have entered into the heart of man, the things which God hath prepared for them that love him.'[5] Bottom's version reads: 'The eye of man hath not heard, the ear of man hath not seen, man's hand is not able to taste, his tongue to conceive, nor his heart to report, what my dream was' (IV.i.211–15). Although Bottom is unable to penetrate the heart of the mystery to his own satisfaction, he realises the folly in attempting to give to a dream a rational prosaic exposition: 'Man is but an ass, if he go about to expound this dream' (IV.i.206–7). His actual experience of 'a most rare vision' dictates to him that his best option is to keep silent about it ('Not a word of me', IV.ii.34). In contrast, Theseus's total lack of any such experience is not enough to prevent him from making his lengthy speech of dismissal.

St Paul speaks of things that, though 'unto the Greeks foolishness', are 'the wisdom of God. Because the foolishness of God is wiser than men.'[6] On these terms, the play invites its audience to reconsider the issues of madness and reason. Bottom, although he gets the words of St Paul muddled, is speaking a form of wisdom when he says that he will 'get Peter Quince to write a ballet of this dream' (IV.i.214–15). Only through art, implies Bottom, can a vision so rare and elusive be adequately communicated. Theseus, on the other hand, a Greek to whom such things are 'foolishness', dismisses their relevance out of hand. Shakespeare's contemporary audience would have detected an inversion of hierarchies. Theseus, a duke, is made to sound foolish, whereas Bottom, a fool, is made to seem wise. In the argument, Theseus goes to the bottom of the class, and Bottom comes out on top.

There is a third party in the 'dialogue' between Bottom and Theseus. Hippolyta, who had previously remarked that the lovers' story was 'strange' (V.i.1), and had provoked Theseus's words in the first place, again adds her voice when his speech comes to an end. Her objection, 'But', is thrown into the well-oiled mechanism of his argument:

> But all the story of the night told over,
> And all their minds transfigur'd so together,
> More witnesseth than fancy's images,
> And grows to something of great constancy;
> But howsoever, strange and admirable. (V.i.23–7)

While not disagreeing with the strangeness of the 'admirable' (astonishing) story, Hippolyta nevertheless detects a consistency in the delivery of those who are telling it. Furthermore, their minds seem to have been 'transfigur'd' (made more noble and beautiful) by their experience. In Theseus's own words, the lover's imagination can see the beauty of Helen of Troy in the brow of a gypsy (V.i.10–11), and love is itself described earlier in the play as a form of imagination, being able to transpose things 'base and vile' to 'form and dignity' (I.ii.232–3).

Hippolyta's even-handed assessment is remarkably like John Keats's notion of 'negative capability', a term of his own invention, by which he attempts to account for Shakespeare's genius. In a letter to his brothers in 1817, Keats writes:

> [A]t once it struck me, what quality went to form a Man of Achievement especially in literature & which Shakespeare possessed so enormously – I mean Negative Capability, that is when man is capable of being in uncertainties, Mysteries, doubts without any irritable reaching after fact & reason.[7]

Hippolyta's response to Theseus illustrates what Keats meant by negative capability. She recognises that there could be more to the story than Theseus will allow, and that Imagination must be admitted as part of the equation if the whole truth of the matter is to be accessed. Keats himself compares the Imagination to Adam's dream, 'he awoke and found it truth',[8] and it is significant that Shakespeare, with the same words he gives Theseus to dismiss Imagination, also contrives to make him celebrate it:

> The poet's eye, in a fine frenzy rolling,
> Doth glance from heaven to earth, from earth to heaven;
> And as imagination bodies forth
> The forms of things unknown, the poet's pen
> Turns them to shapes, and gives to aery nothing
> A local habitation and a name. (V.i.12–17)

The swiftness of the poet's glance reflects a kind of omniscience, comparable in the play to the celerity of Puck's 'I'll put a girdle round about the earth / In forty minutes' (II.i.175–6). In his ability to give a body to unknown forms, and to create something from nothing, the poet takes on the role of God. The poet *is* God. Of course, Theseus does not intend to say this, but his words nonetheless say it for him.

Coleridge: Fancy and Imagination

Over two hundred years later Coleridge, in *Biographia Literaria* (1817), defined what he called 'primary Imagination' in the following terms:

> The primary IMAGINATION I hold to be the living power and prime agent of all human perception, and as a repetition in the finite mind of the eternal act of creation in the infinite I AM.

Coleridge gives to the Imagination a status implicit in the sub-text of Theseus's words. It is essentially a creative faculty, and when the poet or artist 'imagines' a work into being, he (or she) is repeating in the 'finite' mind that original act of creation in the mind of God. When God says 'Let there be light',[9] and there is light, he is not imitating anything, but creating, from within himself, something out of nothing. It is in exactly these terms that Mary Wollstonecraft, echoing Theseus's words, writes her own conjectures on original composition[*] in Letter 9 of her *Short Residence in Sweden, Norway, and Denmark* (1796):

> How often do my feelings produce ideas that remind me of the origin of many poetical fictions. In solitude, the imagination bodies forth its conceptions unrestrained, and stops enraptured to adore the beings of its own creation. These are moments of bliss; and the memory recalls them with delight.[10]

---

[*] *Conjectures on Original Composition* (1759) by Edward Young reflects, as a pre-eminent topic of criticism, the late eighteenth-century preoccupation with genius.

In *Nightmare Abbey* (see Part Three: 'Romantic Fiction'), Marionetta comes across Mr Flosky, Peacock's satirical version of Coleridge, who is made into the embodiment of Shakespeare's poet, 'sitting at his table by the light of a solitary candle, with a pen in one hand […] with "his eye in a fine frenzy rolling"'.[11] Flosky announces (with its allusion by Peacock to 'Kubla Khan')* that he has composed five hundred lines in his sleep and, echoing Bottom's words that a dream can only be communicated through some form of art, tells Marionetta, 'I am now officiating as my own Peter Quince, and making a ballad of my dream.'[12]

In the final act of the *Dream*, Shakespeare makes the small audience of Theseus, Hippolyta and the four lovers apply a misguided rational intelligence to Bottom and his fellows' dramatic performance of 'Pyramus and Thisbe'. A man with a dog, a bush and a lantern, meant to represent 'the man i' th' moon' (V.i.258) should, according to Demetrius, be '*in* the lanthorn; for all these are in the moon' (V.ii.260–1, my emphasis). Such a remark is comparable to an audience at an opera inappropriately querying the physical ability of a dying heroine to deliver a powerful aria. Coleridge, in *Biographia Literaria*, speaks of procuring, for what he calls the 'shadows of imagination', a 'willing suspension of disbelief for the moment, which constitutes poetic faith'.[13] It is this 'poetic faith' which the audience for 'Pyramus and Thisbe' fails to exercise.

Although Theseus apparently concludes the play with his characteristically dismissive 'Lovers, to bed, 'tis almost fairy time' (V.i.364), it is in fact those fairies, Coleridge's 'shadows of imagination' who, in Puck's line, 'If we shadows have offended' (V.i.423), are given the last word. Shakespeare, as a poet-dramatist himself, seems to be reinforcing, by putting his own weight behind it, the credibility of the Imagination in a context where its function is constantly being called into question.

Coleridge's belief in the absolute centrality of the creative Imagination, anticipated so remarkably in *A Midsummer Night's Dream*, seems to have been altogether lost in post-Renaissance literature, and it

---

* Coleridge claimed that his 'Kubla Khan: Or, A Vision in a Dream' was the product of a dream induced by opium, to which he was addicted.

is well over two hundred years before it emerges again in its recognisably Romantic sense.

In the *Biographia*, Coleridge distinguishes clearly between Fancy and Imagination. He writes of Fancy being 'a mode of memory emancipated from the order of time and space, and blended with, and modified by that empirical phenomenon of the will which we express by the word CHOICE'. The fancy receives its materials 'ready made from the law of association'. In 'Shakespeare: A Poet Generally', Coleridge quotes a quatrain from *Venus and Adonis* as an example of Fancy at work:

> Full gently now she takes him by the hand,
> A lily prisoned in a jail of snow,
> Or ivory in an alabaster band:
> So white a friend ingirts so white a foe.[14]

Here the fingers of pale clasped hands might suggest the bars of a jail. The bars, in turn, suggest the hard band of alabaster enclosing ivory, while the whiteness of both brings to mind the 'lily' and 'snow', indicating perhaps the softness of the hands. In other words, the Fancy, which 'has no other counters to play with but fixities and definites',[15] relies on a process of association as the verse is assembled.

As an example of the Imagination at work, Coleridge offers, by way of contrast, a couplet from the same poem: 'Look! how a bright star shooteth from the sky; / So glides he in the night from Venus' eye!':

> How many images and feelings are here brought together without effort and without discord, in the beauty of Adonis, the rapidity of his flight, the yearning, yet hopelessness, of the enamored gazer, while a shadowy ideal character is thrown over the whole.

Operating here is Coleridge's conception of 'secondary' Imagination, which he distinguishes from the 'primary' in being exclusively the preserve of the creative artist. The secondary Imagination 'dissolves, diffuses, dissipates, in order to recreate'. It struggles 'to idealize and to unify' and is 'essentially *vital*, even as all objects (*as* objects) are essentially fixed and dead'.[16] Coleridge's careful preservation of the difference between his two forms of Imagination (primary and secondary) and the Fancy, lies behind the humorous exchange between Marionetta and Mr Flosky when, in *Nightmare Abbey*, Flosky expresses surprise that she should be seeking him out for the purpose of obtaining information: 'No one has ever sought me for such a purpose before.' Marionetta replies hesitantly, 'I think, Mr Flosky—that is, I believe— that is, I fancy—that is, I imagine—'.

To illustrate the different processes by which Imagination and Fancy work, Basil Willey suggests a chemical analogy. The materials of Fancy can be thought of as a mixture of grains of salt and iron filings which, although in close proximity to each other, nevertheless retain their own particular properties. On the contrary, the Imagination at work resembles the reaction of two elements like sodium and chlorine which, in dissolving, diffusing and dissipating, produce a third element, entirely different from both.[17]

Science, Reason and the Imagination

Science is of great interest to writers of the Romantic generation, where the experiments of 'natural philosophers'* who are closely associated with its literature, like Humphry Davy[†] and Joseph Priestley,[‡] provided the scientific context in which Coleridge, Shelley and Keats among others, found analogies for the creative process. For Coleridge, a poet performs an alchemical transformation:

---

*   Natural Philosophy was the term then used for what is now called science.

†   Humphry Davy (1778–1829) met Southey and Coleridge in Bristol in 1798 where he was a member of the Pneumatic Institute, experimenting with the properties of gases for medical use. He saw Wordsworth and Coleridge's *Lyrical Ballads* through the press.

‡   Joseph Priestley (1733–1804), political theorist, scientist and dissenting minister, is usually credited with the discovery of Oxygen and Nitrous Oxide (laughing gas). He also invented soda water, which Edmund Burke objected to on the grounds that its bubbles reminded him of political agitation.

[He] diffuses a tone and spirit of unity that blends and (as it were) *fuses*, each into each, by that synthetic and magical power to which we have exclusively appropriated the name of imagination. This power, first put in action by the will and understanding [...] reveals itself in the balance or reconciliation of opposite or discordant qualities.[18]

Coleridge, who thinks of the Fancy as 'aggregative and associative', describes Imagination as 'shaping and modifying', using the word 'esemplastic', meaning to shape all things into a state of oneness by a 'coadunating' power. The 'discordant qualities' of fire and ice are reconciled and symbolised in the unifying 'dome' image of 'Kubla Khan': 'It was a miracle of rare device, / A sunny pleasure-dome with caves of ice!'

Shelley, for whom 'Poetry, in a general sense, may be defined to be "the expression of the Imagination"',[19] also makes use of the alchemical process in an analogy which, for him, best describes the imaginative function:

[It] subdues to union [...] all irreconcilable things. It transmutes all that it touches, and every form [...] is changed by wondrous sympathy to an incarnation of the spirit which it breathes: its secret alchemy turns to potable gold the poisonous waters which flow from death through life.[20]

Where Shelley, like Coleridge, acknowledges the ability of the Imagination to strip 'the veil of familiarity from the world', he wishes, unlike Coleridge, to transcend the phenomenal world altogether, and expresses in his characteristically erotic imagery his belief in its power to put us in touch with a platonic idealism. The imagination 'lays bare the naked and sleeping beauty which is the spirit of its forms'.

Keats, whose training as a surgeon at Guy's Hospital made him familiar with chemistry,* makes wide-ranging use of its terminologies

---

* Keats took two courses in chemistry during his time at Guy's. See Amy Lowell, *John Keats* (Boston: Houghton Mifflin, 1925), vol. 1, p. 154.

for methods of poetical composition, and sees the Imagination as a kind of heat which, with varying degrees of intensity, can 'evaporate' or 'sublime' whatever it is applied to. He writes that the 'excellence of every Art is its intensity, capable of making all disagreeables evaporate, from their being in close relationship with Beauty & Truth'.[21] The product of the imagination is left as a clear essence, purged of its impurities through the heat of evaporation. In its 'sublime', the Imagination is 'creative of essential beauty'[22] and produces a rarefied work, like the gas created directly from a solid through the process of chemical sublimation.[23]

In all these examples, the creative power emanating from within the poet, or the artist, is given a status, discriminating it from the analytical reason described by William Wordsworth in *The Prelude* as 'that false secondary power, by which, / In weakness, we create distinctions'.[24] For Wordsworth, Imagination 'Is but another name for absolute strength / And clearest insight, amplitude of mind, / And reason in her most exalted mood' (XIII.167–70). Wordsworth refers to Coleridge as one to whom, through his imaginative powers, 'The unity of all has been revealed' (II.226), and it is a higher form of 'reason' which Coleridge himself distinguishes from the limitations imposed upon the mind by materialist philosophy.* Peacock, in getting Mr Flosky to explain to Marionetta that he has 'had a dream of pure reason',[25] makes allusion here to Kant,† whose philosophy Coleridge encountered on his visit to Germany in 1800. Kant's concept of pure reason, largely transmitted into Britain and America through Coleridge's agency, is relevant to the Romantic poet, because it allows to poetry its intimations of what cannot be 'understood' by reason alone. The poet's self-originating vision trespasses beyond the limits of what can be reasonably understood. When Wordsworth writes: 'Oh! Then the calm / And dead still water lay upon my mind / Even with a weight of pleasure, and the sky / Never before so beautiful, sank down / Into my

---

* Coleridge refers specifically to the materialism of Newton, but would also include the 'sensationalist' philosophers such as John Locke (*An Essay Concerning Human Understanding*, 1690) and David Hartley (*Observations on Man*, 1749), for both of whom the mind was simply passive in perception, mechanically responding to sense impressions coming to it from the external world. Coleridge named one of his children after the philosopher Hartley.

† Immanuel Kant, *Critique of Pure Reason* (1781).

heart, and held me like a dream' (II.176–80), while there is nothing by which such a statement can be verified, the veracity of what is being communicated is not in any doubt. In *The Prelude*, Wordsworth privileges the authority of the self as the source of creativity: 'from thyself it is that thou must give, / Else never canst receive' (XI.333–4), a sentiment echoed by Coleridge in 'Dejection: An Ode'* when he writes that 'we receive but what we give, / And in our life alone does Nature live' (ll. 47–8).

Metaphors of Mind

Among the many metaphors for the mind used by Romantics to illustrate creativity in perception† is the so-called Brocken Spectre, a phenomenon Coleridge observed on the Brocken peak in the Harz Mountains in Germany, where the observer's own image appears as a gigantic shadow on the upper surfaces of clouds opposite the sun. Coleridge describes it in his poem 'Constancy to an Ideal Object' (published in *Poetical Works*, 1828):

> And art thou nothing? Such thou art, as when
> The woodman winding westward up the glen
> At wintry dawn, where o'er the sheep-track's maze
> The viewless snow-mist weaves a glist'ning haze,
> Sees full before him, gliding without tread,
> An image with a glory round its head;
> The enamoured rustic worships its fair hues,
> Nor knows he makes the shadow, he pursues! (ll. 25–32)

---

* Coleridge originally wrote this poem as a verse-letter to Sara Hutchinson, and went on to produce several versions. It was first published as 'Dejection: An Ode' on 4 October 1802 in the *Morning Post*. All references to it are to the version which Coleridge produced for his collection of 1817, *Sibylline Leaves*.

† Metaphors such as the Aeolian harp, a small instrument placed in a window and touched into music by the wind sweeping across its strings; or the leaf which creates the atmosphere it assimilates.

It is this phenomenon which in James Hogg's *Confessions of a Justified Sinner* (see Part Three: 'Romantic Fiction') adjusts itself according to whatever happens to be George Colwan's mental disposition at the time. On his early walk to Arthur's Seat one 'calm and serene morning', as it is described in 'The Editor's Narrative', George's initial feelings of good will towards his malevolent brother Robert are reciprocated in the glorious apparition which reflects his frame of mind:

> [H]e beheld, to his astonishment, a bright halo in the cloud of haze, that rose in a semi-circle over his head like a pale rainbow. He was struck motionless at the view of the lovely vision; for it so chanced that he had never seen the same appearance before, though common at early morn. But he soon perceived the cause of the phenomenon, and that it proceeded from the rays of the sun from a pure unclouded morning sky striking upon this dense vapour which refracted them.[26]

Hogg's 'Editor' adds, that such a scene 'would have entranced the man of science with delight', but was one which the 'uninitiated and sordid man would have regarded less than the mole rearing up his hill in silence and in darkness'. The remark calls to mind Wordsworth's Peter Bell, an unimaginative man, for whom 'A primrose by a river's brim / A yellow primrose was to him, / And it was nothing more'.[27] When George Colwan allows darker thoughts of his brother to come 'across his mind' he finds, when suddenly turning his eyes to the right, that a monstrous vision confronts him:

> Gracious heaven! What an apparition was there presented to his view! He saw, delineated in the cloud, the shoulders, arms, and features of a human being of the most dreadful aspect. The face was the face of his brother, but dilated to twenty times the natural size. Its dark eyes gleamed on him through the mist, while every furrow of its hideous brow frowned deep as the ravines on the brow of the hill.[28]

The novel implies that these images are the creations of George himself, a reflection of his own inclination to perceive the world through the perspective of either moral good or moral evil. Coleridge, in 'Dejection', gives to the creative perception this identical power of transformation, making of nature a 'wedding-garment' or a 'shroud':

> And would we aught behold, of higher worth,
> Than that inanimate cold world allow'd
> To the poor loveless ever-anxious crowd,
> Ah! From the soul itself must issue forth
> A light, a glory, a fair luminous cloud
> Enveloping the Earth. (ll. 50–5)

It is important for the Romantic poet to privilege the power of Imagination, replacing the mimetic principle of poetry with an expressive one. In *The Prelude*, Wordsworth recalls how, in the period of his Imagination's impairment, he had been 'even in pleasure pleas'd / Unworthily, disliking here, and there, / Liking, by rules of mimic art transferr'd / To things above all art' (XI.152–5). He refers to 'the eye', the 'most despotic of our senses', being 'master of the heart', and which, at that time, had gained such strength in him 'as often held my mind / In absolute dominion' (XI.172–6). His way out from this 'tyranny' of the sight is to have recourse to moments in his memory which he calls 'spots of time' (XI.258). These are given significance as episodes, perhaps in themselves of no obvious importance, but which are made memorable by being 'Among those passages of life in which / We have had deepest feeling that the mind / Is lord and master, and that outward sense / Is but the obedient servant of her will' (XI.270–3). Wordsworth employs the language of oppression and liberty, transferring the concept of freedom from the political to the imaginative arena, showing how the Imagination is 'Impaired' and how it can be 'Restored' (XI and XII). 'Spots of time' are less significant as narratives than they are as illustrations of the means by which he is assured of his creative power's enduring presence in periods of imaginative dearth. They have 'A virtue by which pleasure is enhanced / That penetrates, enables us to mount /

When high, more high, and lifts us up when fallen' (XI.266–8). In his 'Note' to 'The Thorn' (in *Lyrical Ballads*, 1798), he describes the Imagination as 'the faculty which produces impressive effects out of simple elements', and the 'spots of time', composed of very simple elements, are thus empowered to 'retain / A vivifying virtue' (XI.259–60). If the Imagination has on a former occasion been shown to be powerful and then becomes so again, the process is cumulative, making memory an organic and developing faculty, not something represented simply by a succession of isolated incidents. As Wordsworth puts it: 'So feeling comes in aid / Of feeling, and diversity of strength / Attends us, if but once we have been strong' (XI.326–8).

This emphasis upon process in the Imagination at work is central to Coleridge's thoughts, and finds its earliest expression in his 'Lecture on the Slave Trade'.* 'To develop the powers of the Creator', he writes, 'is our proper employment' –

> and to imitate Creativeness by combination our most exalted and self-satisfying Delight. But we are progressive and must not rest content with present Blessings. Our Almighty Parent hath therefore given to us Imagination that stimulates to the attainment of *real* excellence by the contemplation of splendid Possibilities [...] and fixing our eye on the glittering Summits that rise one above the other in Alpine endlessness still urges us up the ascent of Being, amusing the ruggedness of the road with the beauty and grandeur of the ever-widening Prospect.[29]

Wordsworth's later experience of such imaginative 'Possibilities', but in a literal alpine setting, is described in Book VI of *The Prelude* where, during an episode from his 1790 walking tour to Italy, he learns with disbelief, and some disappointment, that he has already, unknowingly, '*cross'd the Alps*' (VI.524). While in the process, many years later, of writing about an event which did not at the time carry its full significance for him, he finds suddenly that 'Imagination! lifting up itself / Before the eye and progress of my Song' (VI.525–6), reveals its 'Power, / In all

* 16 June 1795.

the might of its endowments' (VI.527–8). Although his crossing of the Alps was complete, his mind continued to be possessed with the grander idea of achieving it, just as he described, earlier, that after his first sight of Mont Blanc he 'griev'd / To have a soulless image on the eye / Which had usurp'd upon a living thought / That never more could be' (VI.453–6). The Imagination confirms for him that

> Our destiny, our nature, and our home
> Is with infinitude, and only there;
> With hope it is, hope that can never die,
> Effort, and expectation, and desire,
> And something evermore about to be. (ll. 538–42)

Coleridge made process an absolute principle of aesthetics in poetry. In his criticism, he describes how the mind is concerned less with the objects created by the Imagination, than with the activity at work in the course of creating them. The reader of poetry 'should be carried forward, not merely or chiefly by the mechanical impulse of curiosity, or by a restless desire to arrive at the final solution; but by the pleasurable activity of mind excited by the attractions of the journey itself'.[30] Such an emphasis on the procedures of composition explains some of the value placed upon the unfinished and the fragmentary, a form especially identified with the Romantic period, and explaining the thinking of an aspiring Romantic artist, such as James Joyce's Stephen Dedalus who, shunning the attainment of a final aim, is content with simply the journey towards it:

> He shrank from the dignity of celebrant because it displeased him
> to imagine that all the vague pomp should end in his own person
> or that the ritual should assign to him so clear and final an office.
> He longed for the minor sacred offices, to be vested with the
> tunicle of subdeacon at high mass, to stand aloof from the altar,
> forgotten by the people, his shoulders covered with a humeral
> veil, holding the paten within its folds or, when the sacrifice had
> been accomplished, to stand as deacon in a dalmatic cloth of gold
> on the step below the celebrant.[31]

William Hazlitt distinguishes Coleridge from William Godwin, who proceeds 'by concentrating his mind on some given object' in order to bring about a conclusion. Coleridge, on the other hand,

> delights in nothing but episodes and digressions, neglects whatever he undertakes to perform, and can act only on spontaneous impulses [...] Mr Coleridge's bark [...] flutters its gaudy pennons in the air, glitters in the sun, but we wait in vain to hear of its arrival in the destined harbour.[32]

Through the satirical persona of Mr Flosky, Peacock (see Part Three: 'Romantic Fiction') has Coleridge distinguish between the kind of 'Analytical reasoning' associated with Godwin's philosophy and his own preferred 'synthetical reasoning, setting up as its goal some unattainable abstraction'. As Flosky goes on to explain to Mr Listless, 'The beauty of this process is, that at every step it strikes out into two branches, in a compound ratio of ramification; so that you are perfectly sure of losing your way, and keeping your mind in perfect health by the perpetual exercise of an interminable quest.'[33]

Coleridge sees the Imagination as synonymous with enfranchisement, and its liberating power being indifferent to physical confinement, as is demonstrated in his poem 'This Lime-Tree Bower my Prison'.* Coleridge's much-anticipated participation in a walk with friends (Wordsworth, Dorothy Wordsworth and Charles Lamb) is curtailed by an accident to his foot, confining him to a lime-tree bower which becomes effectively his 'prison'. The poem is appropriately addressed to Charles Lamb who, because of his employment, is 'many a year, / In the great City pent' (l. 30). Just as prison and the freedom to wander are contrasted with each other, so the ideas of presence and absence are considered together in these more immediate circumstances. Although confined to his bower, Coleridge allows his discursive Imagination to create the situation from which he is excluded. He is able, through an access of joy (always a pre-condition for the Imagination's creative

---

* 'This Lime-Tree Bower my Prison' was first published in the *Annual Anthology* (1800) and then in *Sibylline Leaves* (1817).

presence)* to unite himself with his absent friends: 'A delight / Comes sudden on my heart, and I am glad / As I myself were there!' (ll. 43–5). In the final lines of the poem, this all-inclusive 'coadunating' power ensures not only that Coleridge is 'united' with his friends, but also that he becomes aware of a unity in creation where 'No sound is dissonant which tells of life' (l. 76).

Imagination and Liberty

This emancipating power of the Imagination has far-reaching political implications. In Godwin's *Caleb Williams* (1794), the eponymous hero is impervious to the imprisonment imposed upon him by Falkland's tyranny: 'The mind is master of itself; and is endowed with powers that might enable it to laugh at the tyrant's vigilance.'[34] Although in grimmer circumstances than Coleridge in his bower, Caleb is just as capable of allowing his Imagination the creative licence ('I became myself a poet') to elude 'the squalid solitude of my dungeon'.[35]

The suffering of the incarcerated Caleb Williams becomes, in the Romantic period, almost a pre-condition for imaginative creativity. In Keats's epic fragment, *Hyperion* (1820), Apollo, the god of poetry, can only aspire to poetic maturity through an ordeal involving him in adversity and affliction:

> Soon wild commotions shook him, and made flush
> All the immortal fairness of his limbs;
> Most like the struggle at the gate of death;
> Or liker still to one who should take leave
> Of pale immortal death, and with a pang
> As hot as death's is chill, with fierce convulse
> Die into life: so young Apollo anguish'd. (III.124–30)

---

* In 'Dejection: An Ode', 'distress' and 'afflictions', by cancelling 'joy', suspend for Coleridge 'what nature gave me at my birth, / My shaping spirit of Imagination' (stanza 6).

In *The Fall of Hyperion*,* where Keats himself replaces Apollo as would-be poet, a painful process of ascending the steps towards an encounter with the muse figure, Moneta, is described in similar terms:

> Prodigious seem'd the toil, the leaves were yet
> Burning,—when suddenly a palsied chill
> Struck from the paved level up to my limbs,
> And was ascending quick to put cold grasp
> Upon those streams that pulse beside the throat:
> I shriek'd; and the sharp anguish of my shriek
> Stung my own ears. (ll. 121–7)

Moneta's admonishment, that only by suffering can the true poet be distinguished from 'the dreamer' (l. 175), is taken to heart by Keats in his sonnet 'On Sitting Down to Read *King Lear* Once Again'. Here he bids 'Adieu!' to 'golden-tongued Romance', with its hint of deception, the 'Fair plumèd', but destructive, 'Syren',† and chooses again to 'burn through' Shakespeare's tragedy. It is as though the repeated ordeal of reading *King Lear* involves him each time in a 'fall' from innocence. He will 'once more humbly assay / The bitter-sweet of this Shakespearean fruit', testing its validity as though it were a metal for its preciousness ('assay'), and thus, like Adam and Eve, come to know good by knowing evil. This fall is a kind of *felix culpa*,‡ as once 'consumèd in the fire' of

---

* *The Fall of Hyperion* was begun in July 1819 and 'given up' in September 1821. It was published by R. M. Milnes as 'Another Version of Keats's *Hyperion*' in *Biographical and Historical Miscellanies of the Philobiblion Society 1856–7*.

† See Keats's early poem 'Sleep and Poetry' (1817), where lines 96–125 distinguish between simply decorative 'romance' poetry and the true 'Romantic' poetry, in imitation of Shakespeare, that he wishes to write. See also his letter to Sarah Jeffrey, 9 June 1819 (*The Letters of John Keats*, ed. Rollins, vol. 2, p. 115), where he calls the Italian poet Boiardo (1441–94) 'a noble Poet of Romance' and in contrast to Shakespeare 'not a miserable and mighty Poet of the human heart'. 'On Sitting Down to Read *King Lear* Once Again' was written in 1818 and published in the *Plymouth and Devonport Weekly* on 8 November 1838.

‡ The *felix culpa* or 'happy fault' is a term used in theology to describe the fall of Adam and Eve. It implies that had it not been for their transgression, mankind would never have received Christ's redemptive grace and the greater good which comes from it.

experience, and rising again like the 'Phoenix', he will be able, as a poet, to go beyond the restrictions of romance 'to fly at my desire'.

Keats sees *King Lear* as the child of its parents, Shakespeare ('Chief Poet!') and England ('clouds of Albion'). Together they are the 'Begetters' of 'our deep eternal theme!' His final prayer is to be allowed an escape from the 'barren dream' of romance and become, like Shakespeare himself, a fertile and imaginatively creative poet.

The Privileging Faculty

Although the Romantic period is defined by such testimonies to the centrality of the Imagination, its role becomes increasingly compromised by the advancement of science and the destruction of mythologies which had for centuries provided source materials for poetry. Milton was only able to write the last great epic poem in English, *Paradise Lost* (1667), in the age of Sir Isaac Newton, and of materialist philosophers such as Hobbes,* because the Bible was still widely regarded as the last great repository of truth. It is clear that Milton intends such figures as his personified 'Sin' and 'Death'[36] to be distinguished, as 'inventions', from the biblical truth of Adam and Eve, as well as from the other participators in the story of Genesis.

For the Romantic generation, coming at the end of the Enlightenment, the loss of a mythopoeic world presented particular problems. In 'Lamia' Keats writes of the destructive usurpation of science upon Imagination, alluding specifically to Newton's explaining away of the rainbow as a mere natural phenomenon:

> Do not all charms fly
> At the mere touch of cold philosophy?†

---

* John Hobbes (1588–1679) argued in his most influential work, *Leviathan* (1651), that a social contract is necessary to avoid conflict among peoples whose lives in the state of nature are 'solitary, poor, nasty, brutish, and short'.

† By 'philosophy' Keats means 'science' or 'Natural Philosophy'.

There was an awful rainbow once in heaven:
We know her woof, her texture; she is given
In the dull catalogue of common things.
Philosophy will clip an Angel's wings,
Conquer all mysteries by rule and line,
Empty the haunted air, and gnomèd mine—
Unweave a rainbow. (II.229–37)

In 'Ode to Psyche' (see Part Four: Faith, Myth and Doubt), Keats recognises that a poet can no longer depend, as had once been possible, upon inspiration coming from a world where everything is universally interpreted in terms of a shared mythology. He announces his intention to create, within the de-mythologised nineteenth century ('in the midst of this wide quietness'), 'A rosy sanctuary', and to 'dress' it, through a process of self-originating imaginative effort. Thus, 'branchèd thoughts' and the 'wreathed trellis of a working brain' replace the first stanza's mythical half-dream world, where once such figures as Cupid and Psyche were easily encountered by the 'thoughtlessly' wandering self (l. 7).

For Shelley, visitings of imaginative power are equally undependable. In *A Defence of Poetry* the 'mind in creation' is as 'a fading coal which some invisible influence, like an inconstant wind, awakens to transitory brightness:

> this power arises from within like the colour of a flower which fades and changes as it is developed, and the conscious portions of our nature are unprophetic either of its approach or its departure. Could this influence be durable in its original purity and force, it is impossible to predict the greatness of the results: but when composition begins, inspiration is already on the decline, and the most glorious poetry that has ever been communicated to the world is probably a feeble shadow of the original conceptions of the poet.

Shelley, who believes no less in the transforming, alchemical powers of Imagination, places more of an emphasis on its deficiency, where even the greatest examples of the poet's art are no more than generous or failing attempts to represent a vanished inspiration.

The privileging of Imagination as the source of truth and creativity, together with the pre-conditional 'joy' which accompanies it, gives rise to expressions of despondency at its failure to function. Wordsworth speaks of the 'dejection' which follows 'the might / Of joy in minds that can no further go',[37] Keats of the 'melancholy fit' which falls 'Sudden from heaven like a weeping cloud',[38] and Coleridge of his despair at being able to 'see, not feel' beauty in the natural objects his Imagination seems powerless to transform.[39] In *Childe Harold* III, Byron affirms a therapeutic aesthetic idealism, making Imagination his only escape from a 'world of woe' and explaining why his thought 'seeks refuge' in its creative potential:

> 'Tis to create, and in creating live
> A being more intense, that we endow
> With form our fancy, gaining as we give
> The life we image, even as I do now.
> What am I? Nothing: but not so art thou,
> Soul of my thought! With whom I traverse earth. (III.46–51)

Byron's evocation of the mind's 'lone caves' as the dwelling-place of archetypes, the 'airy images, and shapes which dwell / Still unimpaired, though old, in the soul's haunted cell' (III.43–5), is Coleridgean in its conception; 'we receive but what we give'.[40] Similarly, in Wordsworth's ideal vision of 'a new world', the Imagination 'maintains / A balance, an ennobling interchange / Of action from within and from without',[41] enabling both eye and ear to 'half create' what they 'perceive'.[42]

Coleridge compares the Imagination to moonlight in its ability to alter the aspect of 'a known and familiar landscape'[43] but without substantially changing it. It gives 'the charm of novelty to things of everyday', a capability demonstrated in the Coleridgean 'Custom-House' Preface to Nathaniel Hawthorne's novel, *The Scarlet Letter* (1850). It was through Coleridge that Romantic idealist philosophy was transmitted to the New England writers of the mid-nineteenth century, and Hawthorne reflects its influence when he represents his own predicament as typical of the difficulty artists and other imaginative people often experience with America's more utilitarian values. That he has become 'a tolerably good Surveyor of the Customs'[44] has left Hawthorne's imagination 'a tarnished mirror', inadequate for the composition of the romance (rather than a realist) novel he is aspiring to write. The daily grind affects his walks in nature, and 'The same torpor' attends him home: 'Nor did it quit me, when, late at night, I sat in the deserted parlour, lighted only by the glimmering coal-fire and the moon, striving to picture forth imaginary scenes'; 'If the imaginative faculty refused to act at such an hour,' he continues, 'it might well be deemed a hopeless case.' The passage continues:

> Moonlight, in a familiar room, falling so white upon the carpet, and showing all its figures so distinctly, – making every object so minutely visible, yet so unlike a morning or noontide visibility, – is a medium the most suitable for a romance-writer to get acquainted with his illusive guests. There is the little domestic scenery of the well-known apartment; the chairs, with each its separate individuality; the centre-table, sustaining a work-basket, a volume or two, and an extinguished lamp; the sofa, the book-case; the picture on the wall; – all these details, so completely seen, are so spiritualized by the unusual light, that they seem to lose their actual substance, and become things of intellect. Nothing is too small or too trifling to undergo this change, and acquire dignity thereby. A child's shoe; the doll, seated in her little wicker carriage; the hobby-horse; – whatever, in a word, has been used or played with, during the day, is now invested with a quality of strangeness and remoteness, though still almost as vividly present as by daylight. Thus, therefore, the floor of our familiar room has become a neutral territory, somewhere between the real world and fairy-land, where the Actual and the Imaginary may meet, and each imbue itself with the nature of the other.
>
> (pp. 35–6)

In Hawthorne's novel, Hester Prynne, who has had a secret love child by the Reverend Dimmesdale, is exposed to public shame and, as a mark of her transgression, made to wear the scarlet letter 'A'. Her child, Pearl, as she grows up, rejects the strict Puritan community of Boston and becomes a living embodiment of the Romantic Imagination:

> The spell of life went forth from her creative spirit, and communicated itself to a thousand objects [...] The unlikeliest materials, a stick, a bunch of rags, a flower, were the puppets of Pearl's witchcraft, and, without undergoing any outward change, became spiritually adapted to whatever drama occupied the stage of her inner world. (p. 95)

Like the Romantic poet, her creative vivacity is subject to the familiar episodes of something akin to dejection:

> It was wonderful, the vast variety of forms into which she threw her intellect, with no continuity, indeed, but darting up and dancing, always in a state of preternatural activity, – soon sinking down, as if exhausted by so rapid and feverish a tide of life.
>
> (p. 95)

In a significant passage, Dimmesdale, who cannot bring himself openly to reveal his secret, attempts to assuage the torture of his guilt by, one night, inviting Hester and Pearl to join with him on the 'scaffold' in the town's market place. A meteor, sailing overhead, illuminates the scene where the three figures stand forming 'an electric chain' (p. 153). 'It showed the familiar scene of the street, with the distinctness of mid-day, but also with the awfulness that is always imparted to familiar objects by an unaccustomed light' (p. 154). The meteor, as a symbol of the Imagination's power, makes all visible, 'but with a singularity of aspect that seemed to give another moral interpretation to the things of this world than they had ever borne before' (p. 155). Here the emphasis on the moral power of the Imagination indicates its ability to reveal things in a light different from the one in which it is seen by the Puritan community. Hester's beauty, and her personality, might brand her as a rebel and an individual in a society which only tolerates conformity, yet seen through the perspective of the moral imagination she is perhaps more to be celebrated than condemned. In *The Prelude*, Wordsworth places the same stress on what he considers to be the redemptive powers of natural objects, when informed by the imaginative life emerging from his deepest moral sentiments:

> To every natural form, rock, fruit or flower,
> Even the loose stones that cover the high-way,
> I gave a moral life, I saw them feel,
> Or link'd them to some feeling: the great mass
> Lay bedded in a quickening soul, and all
> That I beheld respired with inward meaning. (III.124–9)

The subjectivism of Romantic writers, making up what Harold Bloom describes as *The Visionary Company*,[45] has become their most distinctive property. The solitary occupant of Milton's 'lonely tower',[46] separated from society by the superiority of his vision and working late into the night, is a recurring figure in Romantic poetry. Coleridge sees Wordsworth as a poet of hope who, 'From the dread Watch-Tower of man's absolute Self' looks 'Far on'.[47] Shelley's Prince Athanase 'sate / Apart from men, as in a lonely tower, / Pitying the tumult of their dark estate',[48] while, later in the poem, as the Prince sits with a teacher in an actual tower,

> The Balearic fisher, driven from shore
> […] saw their lamp from Laian's turret gleam,
> Piercing the stormy darkness, like a star. (ll. 187–90)

Samuel Palmer's etching 'The Lonely Tower' (1879) captures, for the later nineteenth century, the symbolism associated with Romantic writers and their search for undisclosed knowledge, while W. B. Yeats's 'The Phases of the Moon' does the same for the twentieth century.

Yeats's solitary figure has

> chosen this place to live in
> Because, it may be, of the candle-light
> From the far tower where Milton's Platonist
> Sat late, or Shelley's visionary prince:
> The lonely light that Samuel Palmer engraved,
> An image of mysterious wisdom won by toil. (ll. 14–19)

Counter-Voices and Debate

Ever since the Romantic period, the authority given to the writer's perception as 'Sole judge of truth'[49] has encouraged debate on the status of subjective and objective reality, and could be said to emerge with Byron's wry critique of the claims made by Wordsworth in his 'Note' to 'The Thorn'. In an appeal to readers to imagine his poem's narrator as the retired 'Captain of a small trading vessel', Wordsworth had proceeded to ask them to make a whole series of suppositions about him. The Note's favourable evaluation of the Imagination, and the discussion of it as the special endowment of men with 'slow faculties and deep feelings', is persuasive and well-argued, but in his Preface to Cantos I and II of *Don Juan* (1819), Byron takes issue with Wordsworth who, he believes, is asking his readers to 'imagine' too much. In a humorous parody of Wordsworth's rather solemn register, he invites his own readers to imagine for his poem *Don Juan* a similar set of suppositions:

> The reader, who has acquiesced in Mr W. Wordsworth's supposition that [the poem] is related by the 'captain of a small etc.', is requested to suppose by a like exertion of imagination that the following epic narrative is told by a Spanish gentleman in a village in the Sierra Morena on the road between Monasterio and Seville, sitting at the door of a *posada* with the Curate of the hamlet on his right hand, a cigar in his mouth, a jug of Malaga or perhaps 'right sherris' before him on a small table, containing the

relics of an *olla-podrida*. The time, sunset. At some distance a group of black-eyed peasantry are dancing to the sound of a flute of a Portuguese servant, belonging to two foreign travellers, who have an hour ago dismounted from their horses to spend the night on their way to the capital of Andalusia.

The *Preface* continues in this way until Byron remarks: 'Having supposed as much of this as the utter impossibility of such a supposition will admit, the reader is requested to extend his supposed power of supposing so far as to conceive that',[50] only to proceed as before with even more 'suppositions'.

Jerome J. McGann considers Byron's implicit argument to be that if Wordsworth were truly imaginative he would not oblige his readers to imagine anything at all. Instead, everything that is to be 'supposed' in his prosy preface would be included within the body of the poem itself. McGann sees, in Byron, a Romantic counter-voice which puts as much stress upon the validity of the objective world as it does upon the Imagination. In McGann's opinion, the Imagination for Byron becomes not the source of truth but simply one of the tools at a writer's disposal, and the poet is cavalier about this 'godlike' faculty:

> It is the fashion of the day to lay great stress upon what they call 'imagination' and 'invention', the two commonest of qualities: an Irish peasant with a little whiskey in his head will imagine and invent more than would furnish forth a modern poem.[51]

McGann's assessment of Byron's approach towards the Imagination is part of a larger critique developed in his book, *The Romantic Ideology* (1983). He argues that scholarship has uncritically absorbed the ways in which Romantic writers choose to represent themselves and their work, often privileging the Imagination at the expense of political and human social issues which are repressed or evaded by the quest for transcendence. McGann sees Imagination simply as part of the human world and not its defining idea. Where Keats might talk of 'the truth of Imagination', Byron prefers in *Don Juan* to avoid the subject (truth) of poetry as the poetic process itself, and represent 'the human world of men and women in their complex relations with themselves, each other, and their environments, both natural and cultural'.[52]

For Harold Bloom, the archetypal representative of the Romantic Imagination is William Blake, whose consuming vision rejects the natural environment as an impediment: 'Natural objects always did & now do Weaken deaden & obliterate Imagination in me.'[53] In McGann's judgement, the truth of the Imagination, especially in *Don Juan*, is not just poetical imagining 'but actual fact – realities of time, place, circumstance'.[54] He sees Byron as interested in the objectivity of the external world, untransformed by, and often resistant to, the shaping and modifying powers of the mind. For McGann, Byron's strength lies in the fact that his imagination is analytic and critical, rather than creative in the Romantic sense.

Much of the current critical debate focusing on the question of the Romantic Imagination and the pre-eminence of the poet's individual vision involves New Historicist critical approaches, derived from McGann, and emphasising the importance of addressing the historical, economic and social realities of the age. 'The idea that poetry, or even consciousness, can set one free from the ruins of history and culture is the grand illusion of every Romantic poet', McGann writes in *The Romantic Ideology*,[55] and his statement implies some possible resistance from the political sphere, for example, to the Imagination's transforming powers. Although a committed figure politically, Shelley, for example, often struggled to give concrete embodiment to what lay beyond his iconoclasm. Thinking of something better to put in the place of prisons or money is not easy, and sometimes the tensions in his work arise from an urge to reform co-existing with the impulse to escape into 'beautiful idealisms of moral excellence'.[56]

Yet Shelley's critique of the kind of 'natural piety'* associated with Romanticism underlies a line such as 'A people starved and stabbed in the untilled field',[57] hinting at the price the labouring poor have to pay to maintain the more high-minded notions of a commerce between

---

* Wordsworth, 'I could wish my days to be / Bound each to each by natural piety' (from 'My Heart Leaps Up When I Behold').

nature and the Romantic Imagination. The natural world is not always an occasion for tranquil reflection, or something to which the mind can be 'exquisitely fitted'.[58] Shelley points out that fields left untilled when they are not a source of profit to their owners, turn agricultural land into a battlefield when the starving poor dare to challenge so-called natural laws of supply and demand.

The ecological approach in criticism is to argue that the natural world is in fact better off without the intervention of a philosophy of the mind as 'lord and master' and nature as the 'obedient servant of her will'.[59] Jonathan Bate regrets 'a denigration of material nature and an exaltation of human consciousness',[60] and he celebrates a poet such as John Clare (see Part Three: 'Revolution, Reaction and the Natural World') who, rather than invest the world of natural objects with a moral or transcendent significance, is more content to describe than to interpret. A non-subjective poet such as George Crabbe, whose narrative poetry is essentially descriptive of the natural world, might equally fall into this category, or a prose writer like Dorothy Wordsworth who, in her brother's high evaluation of her, 'welcom'd what was given, and craved no more'.[61] Anne Mellor, in her book on Mary Shelley,[62] similarly argues for a more descriptive and 'feminised' approach to the environment, seeing in Frankenstein's quest an extreme version of the Romantic Imagination at work, a kind of masculinised assault on nature for which he is made to pay a terrible price (see part Four: 'Heroes and Anti-heroes').

Shakespeare's Cleopatra acknowledges nature's inadequacy to 'vie strange forms with fancy'. Yet 't'imagine / An Antony', she continues, 'were nature's piece 'gainst fancy / Condemning shadows quite'.[63] Wordsworth, too, speaks of beauty as 'a living Presence of the earth, / Surpassing the most fair ideal Forms / Which craft of delicate Spirits hath composed / From earth's materials'.[64] In both Shakespeare and Wordsworth, the Imagination is seen to inform, with a special creativity, the world in which it operates. Yet that world sometimes answers back, and in such a way as to outshine the greatest triumphs of the Imagination. Literature of the Romantic period celebrates both Imagination's potential and the ordinary world of common appearances, maintaining, ideally, a balance and a harmony which represent, in Wordsworth's words, 'The excellence, pure spirit, and best power / Both of the object seen, and eye that sees'.[65]

Notes

1 *An Essay on Criticism* (1711), II.297–8.
2 Aristotle, *Poetics*.
3 *Preface to Shakespeare* (1765).
4 M. H. Abrams, *The Mirror and the Lamp: Romantic Theory and the Critical Tradition* (New York: Norton, 1953; repr. 1958).
5 1 Corinthians 2:9.
6 1 Corinthians 1:23–5.
7 Letter: 28 December 1817: *The Letters of John Keats*, ed. H. E. Rollins, 2 vols (Cambridge, Mass.: Harvard University Press, 1958), vol. 1, p. 193.
8 Letter: 22 November 1817: ibid., p. 184.
9 Genesis 1:3.
10 Mary Wollstonecraft, *Letters Written during a Short Residence in Sweden, Norway, and Denmark*, ed. Richard Holmes (Harmondsworth: Penguin, 1987), p. 119.
11 Thomas Love Peacock, *Nightmare Abbey*, ed. Lisa Vargo (Peterborough, Ont. and Orchard Park, NY: Broadview Press, 2007), p. 91.
12 Ibid., p. 93.
13 S. T. Coleridge, *Biographia Literaria*, ch. 14.
14 Samuel Taylor Coleridge, *The Literary Remains of Samuel Taylor Coleridge*, ed. Henry Nelson Coleridge (London: William Pickering, 1836), vol. 2, p. 36.
15 Coleridge, *Biographia Literaria*, ch. 13.
16 Ibid.
17 Basil Willey, *Nineteenth-Century Studies: Coleridge to Matthew Arnold* (Harmondsworth: Penguin, 1964), pp. 24–5.
18 Coleridge, *Biographia Literaria*, ch. 14.
19 Shelley: *A Defence of Poetry* (1821): 'the expression of the Imagination' appears to be Shelley's own phrase.
20 Ibid.
21 Letter: 21 December 1817: *The Letters of John Keats*, ed. Rollins, vol. 1, p. 192.
22 Letter: 22 November 1817: ibid., p. 184.

23 See Stuart M. Sperry, *Keats the Poet* (Princeton: Princeton University Press, 1973), ch. 2, 'Chemistry of the Creative Process'. See also Maureen B. Roberts, '"Etherial Chemicals": Alchemy and the Romantic Imagination', *Romanticism on the Net*, 5 (February 1997).

24 *The Prelude* (1805), II.221–2.

25 Peacock, *Nightmare Abbey*, p. 93.

26 James Hogg, *The Private Memoirs and Confessions of a Justified Sinner*, ed. John Carey (Oxford: Oxford University Press, 1981), pp. 39–40.

27 'Peter Bell', Part First, ll. 58–60.

28 Hogg, *Confessions of a Justified Sinner*, p. 41.

29 Samuel Taylor Coleridge, *Collected Coleridge* (Bollingen Series 75; Princeton, NJ), 1: *Lectures 1795 on Politics and Religion*, ed. L. Patton and P. Mann (1971), pp. 235–6.

30 Coleridge, *Biographia Literaria*, ch. 14.

31 James Joyce, *A Portrait of the Artist as a Young Man*, ch. 4.

32 William Hazlitt, *The Spirit of the Age* (1825), 'Mr Coleridge'.

33 Peacock, *Nightmare Abbey*, p. 93.

34 William Godwin, *Things as they Are; or The Adventures of Caleb Williams*, ed. Maurice Hindle (Harmondsworth: Penguin, 1988), p. 195.

35 Ibid., p. 193.

36 *Paradise Lost*, II.648 ff.

37 'Resolution and Independence', ll. 22–5.

38 'Ode on Melancholy', ll. 11–12.

39 'Dejection: An Ode', l. 38.

40 Ibid., l. 47.

41 *The Prelude*, XII.371, 376–7.

42 'Lines Written a Few Miles above Tintern Abbey', ll. 107–8.

43 Coleridge, *Biographia Literaria*, ch. 14.

44 Nathaniel Hawthorne, *The Scarlet Letter*, ed. Brian Harding (Oxford: Oxford University Press, 1990), p. 38.

45 Harold Bloom, *The Visionary Company: A Reading of English Romantic Poetry* (Ithaca, NY: Cornell University Press, 1971; repr. 1983).

46 *Il Penseroso*, ll. 85–8.

47 'To a Gentleman', ll. 41–3.

48 'Prince Athanase: A Fragment', ll. 32–4.

49 Pope, *Essay on Man*, II.17.

50 Byron, *Don Juan*, ed. T. G. Steffan, E. Steffan and W. W. Pratt (Harmondsworth: Penguin, 1973), pp. 38–9.

51 Quoted in Jerome J. McGann, *Don Juan in Context* (London: John Murray, 1976), p. 160.

52 Ibid.

53   William Blake, *The Complete Poetry and Prose of William Blake*, ed. David
      Erdman (New York: Anchor Books, 1988), p. 665.
54   McGann, *Don Juan in Context*, p. 163.
55   Jerome J. McGann, *The Romantic Ideology: A Critical Investigation* (Chicago
      and London: University of Chicago Press, 1983), p. 91.
56   Preface to *Prometheus Unbound*.
57   'Sonnet: England in 1819'.
58   Wordsworth, 'Prospectus' to *The Recluse*.
59   Wordsworth, *The Prelude*, XI.271–3.
60   Jonathan Bate, *The Song of the Earth* (London: Picador, 2000), p. 137.
61   *The Prelude*, XI.207.
62   Anne K. Mellor, *Mary Shelley: Her Life, Her Fiction, Her Monsters* (London:
      Methuen, 1988).
63   *Antony and Cleopatra*, V.ii.97–100.
64   'Prospectus' to *The Recluse*.
65   *The Prelude*, XII.378–9.

Faith, Myth and Doubt

In an essay entitled 'Romanticism and Classicism', the English poet and writer T. E. Hulme set out what he believed to be a prevailing Romantic tendency to secularise religion: 'You don't believe in a God, so you begin to believe that man is a god. You don't believe in heaven, so you begin to believe in a heaven on earth. In other words, you get romanticism', or, in what Hulme calls his 'best definition' of it, 'spilt religion'.[1] The later twentieth-century critic M. H. Abrams, in *Natural Supernaturalism* (1971), announced that his recurrent concern would be with 'the secularization of inherited, theological ideas and ways of thinking', the Romantic 'assimilation and reinterpretation of religious ideas, as constitutive elements in a world view founded on secular premises'.[2] In Abrams's view, the Romantics, confronted by such a world, set out 'to reconstitute the grounds of hope and to announce the certainty, or at least the possibility, of a rebirth in which a renewed mankind will inhabit a renovated earth where he will find himself thoroughly at home'.[3] Abrams's study raised many issues which would later be examined in various social and political contexts by New Historicist criticism (see Part Four: 'Imagination, Truth and Reason'). Although it is certainly true to say that the period witnessed an acceleration in secularism, it was also one of widespread religious belief, and subsequent criticism has done much to make clear the important ways in which radical enthusiasm, millenarian sectarianism, and dissenting ideas and philosophies informed the work of Romantic writers.

At the centre of Abrams's argument that the Romantics were as concerned with inherited tradition as they were with forming new ideas is William Wordsworth's 'Prospectus' (1800) to his ultimately unfinished work, *The Recluse*. Abrams makes it what Frank Jordan calls 'the manifesto of a central Romantic enterprise against which we can conveniently measure the consonance and divergences in the writings of his contemporaries'.[4] The lines which make up the 'Prospectus' come near the conclusion of the only 'Book' of this work to be finished ('Home at Grasmere'). Later they were placed at the beginning of *The Excursion* (also to be part of *The Recluse*) where, in his Preface to that work (1814), Wordsworth states that they 'may be acceptable as a kind of *Prospectus* of the design and scope of the whole Poem'.

Wordsworth begins the Prospectus by echoing Milton's invocation to his Muse, 'fit audience let me find though few' (l. 778).* Although the great achievement of *Paradise Lost* is proof of Milton's 'more gaining than he asked' (l. 779), the scope of *The Recluse* is intended to exceed that of Milton's epic. Wordsworth is to take as his subject the 'shadowy ground' (l. 783) of unexplored territory, 'the Mind of Man— / My haunt, and the main region of my song' (ll. 795–6). In the immediate context of the failure of the French Revolution, Wordsworth held to a belief in the mind's capacity to bring about the transformation which political revolution had been unable to achieve. Writing of the same impetus at work in Samuel Taylor Coleridge, Robert M. Maniquis remarks that 'neither religion nor reason by itself could produce civilized order or allow escape from what had exploded in the French Revolution as a kind of primordial human violence.' Coleridge, he writes, cultivated 'along with every other Romantic writer, his version of a new mental faculty that had to precede any hope in purely rational political or sacramental religious order' and, 'like all other Romantic writers', he called this faculty the Imagination.[5]

As Abrams points out, in the development of the Romantic period, the apocalyptic change in man's condition was no longer anticipated

---

* Milton writes: 'still govern thou my song, / Urania, and fit audience find, though few' (*Paradise Lost*, VII.30–1).

through the agency of fulfilled biblical revelation, or of political revolution, but through the individual imagination and, as Wordsworth's Prospectus describes it, the 'creation' (l. 824) of a new world to be accomplished through the 'blended might' (l. 825) of mind and nature together. In terms which are derivative from the biblical concept of Christ as heavenly bridegroom, whose last words on the cross ('consummatum est') suggest the consummation of his marriage with the 'new Jersusalem' of his people,* Wordsworth will 'chant, in lonely peace, the spousal verse / Of this great consummation' (ll. 812–13). In 'Dejection: An Ode', Coleridge uses the same marriage metaphor: by 'wedding Nature to us' we receive, as our dowry, 'A new Earth and New Heaven, / Undreamt of by the sensual and the proud' (ll. 68–70).† His words echo the Book of Revelation's 'I saw a new heaven and a new earth' (21:1), but in both his and Wordsworth's conception, the biblical promise is secularised and Man becomes his own redeemer.

In the Prospectus, Wordsworth asks why, when we think of paradise, we should always be thinking of something which has been lost:

> Paradise, and groves
> Elysian, Fortunate Fields—like those of old
> Sought in the Atlantic Main—why should they be
> A history only of departed things,
> Or a mere fiction of what never was? (ll. 802–6)

To recall Hulme's words, 'You don't believe in heaven, so you begin to believe in a heaven on earth.' Wordsworth promises to speak in words 'of nothing more than what we are' (l. 814), not in words about what we once were, or about what again we might become, but in words which reveal how paradise, 'A simple produce of the common day' (l. 810), can be established in a world which 'is the world / Of all of us, the place in which, in the end, / We find our happiness, or not at all'

---

* The New Jerusalem is the heavenly city and dwelling place of the saints. It is described in the Book of Revelation as 'the bride, the Lamb's wife' (21:9), and is referred to twice, 3:12 and 21:2.

† *Sibylline Leaves* version, 1817.

(*The Prelude*, X.726–8). His voice, like that of the bridegroom in St Matthew's Gospel,* cries out to 'arouse the sensual from their sleep / Of Death' (ll. 815–16) in expectation of 'the blissful hour' (l. 811).

It is in this way that Wordsworth envisages his epic on the 'mind of man' as going well beyond the remit of Milton's *Paradise Lost*; 'aloft ascending' it will 'breathe in worlds / To which the heaven of heavens is but a veil' (ll. 784–5) and, delving deeper than 'The darkest pit of lowest Erebus' (l. 791), exceed Milton's universe in range, to challenge even God Himself: 'Jehovah—with his thunder, and the choir / Of shouting Angels, and the empyreal thrones— / I pass them unalarmed' (ll. 788–90). Wordsworth's redemptive message for mankind replaces that of God's. His prophetic voice 'proclaims' (l. 817) a truth to which 'the progressive powers perhaps no less / Of the whole species' (ll. 819–20) might be led. This is, essentially, to understand

> How exquisitely the individual Mind
> [...] to the external World
> Is fitted:—and how exquisitely, too—
> Theme this but little heard of among men—
> The external World is fitted to the Mind. (ll. 818–23)

The lordly register of Wordsworth's pronouncements had their negative effects on contemporaries such as William Blake and John Keats,† but the efficacy of his belief in the value of empathising with the

---

* In the parable of the wise and foolish virgins, Christ narrates how 'at midnight there was a cry made, Behold, the bridegroom cometh [...] Watch therefore, for ye know neither the day nor the hour wherein the Son of man cometh' (Matthew 25:6, 13).

† Henry Crabb Robinson records Blake as asking: 'Is Mr W. a sincere and real Christian? [...] If so, what does he mean by "The worlds to which the heaven of heavens is but a veil", and who is he that shall "pass Jehovah unalarmed"?'; 'Does Mr Wordsworth think his mind can *surpass* Jehovah?' He reports that reading the Preface [the Prospectus] to *The Excursion* 'caused him a bowel complaint which nearly killed him': See S. Foster Damon, *A Blake Dictionary: The Ideas and Symbols of William Blake* (Hanover, NH: University Press of New England, 1988), p. 451. Keats implies Wordsworth among 'large self-worshippers' (*The Fall of Hyperion*, 207) and describes him as the 'egotistical sublime' (Letter, 27 October 1818: *The Letters of John Keats*, ed. Rollins, vol. 1, pp. 386–7).

natural world was gratefully acknowledged, later in the nineteenth century, by John Stuart Mill in his *Autobiography* of 1873. Mill's strict education in utilitarian principles, the kind of education satirised by Dickens in *Hard Times* (1854), had led him to the point of mental breakdown. In Chapter 5, 'A Crisis in My Mental History', Mill describes a period of depression caused, not by any sense of God's abandonment, but simply by a feeling of desertion within himself of the value of the principles on which he had been brought up. The 'habit of analysis has a tendency to wear away the feelings', he writes,[6] and it was the imagination's power to reciprocate with the natural world to which it is so 'exquisitely fitted' that Mill discovered in reading Wordsworth. Wordsworth's poems seemed, he writes, 'to be the very culture of the feelings which I was in quest of. By their means I seemed to draw from a source of inward joy, of sympathetic and imaginative pleasure, which could be shared in by all human beings.'[7] Wordsworth, for Mill, did not replace God, as he had convinced himself that there was no God, but the almost 'sacramental' effect of Wordsworth's poetry was clear in that it had enabled him, in what Matthew Arnold calls an 'iron time',[8] to reconnect his feelings in a bond of sympathy with nature.

Religion in the Period

Methodism

Mill describes the mental state to which he had descended as comparable to the one 'in which converts to Methodism usually are, when smitten by their first "conviction of sin"'. Such moments of vision and of heightened self-awareness were a special feature of Methodism; the 'moment of Pentecost', described by its founder, John Wesley, when on 24 May 1738 he felt his heart 'strangely warmed' and experienced the 'sudden assurance' that Christ 'had taken away [his] sins'.[9] Wesley's Methodism was an important precursor of Romanticism, with its return to nature in open-air meetings, and its stress on the authenticity of emotion and personal response. Its 'method', consisting of prayer, Bible reading, academic work and physical exercise, was intended to produce personal holiness and to restore life to an enervated Church of England. But Methodism, like Romanticism itself, went beyond the boundaries of nationalism and, as Coleridge acknowledged, had 'been the occasion, and even the cause, of turning thousands from their evil deeds', making 'bad and mischievous men peaceable and profitable neighbors and citizens'.[10]

F. C. Gill, in *The Romantic Movement and Methodism*, while stressing the emphasis in Methodism on feeling and individual personality, points also to the 'lyricism, sincerity, and spontaneity' of its hymns which, he argues, resemble aspects of *Lyrical Ballads*.[11] Donald Davie regards Wesley's brother Charles as having written in these hymns the outstanding lyric poetry of the eighteenth century, ignored or marginalised not only because it is earnestly Christian, but also because it is intellectually and metrically exacting.[12] According to Stephen Prickett, our familiarity with many of Charles Wesley's compositions* can 'blur our appreciation of a poetic subtlety and compression that lifts him far above most of his contemporaries, and puts him, at his best, in the same class as Herbert or Newman – both of whom had a much smaller range'.[13] T. B. Shepherd in *Methodism and the Literature of the Eighteenth Century* sees connections between Methodism and the Romantic 'love of liberty, a deeper interest in man, a love of Nature, and simple, domestic joys'.[14]

Although Wordsworth in his Prospectus effectively usurps the role of God, being described by Coleridge in a letter of 1796 as 'at least a *Semi-atheist*',[15] and recalled by Henry Crabb Robinson as having once said 'I have no need of a Redeemer',[16] his work nevertheless reflects a strong Methodist influence. Richard Brantley, in *Wordsworth's 'Natural Methodism'*, describes *The Prelude* as a spiritual autobiography following a pattern familiar to Methodism, in which God chastises those he loves. According to Brantley, Wordsworth writes as someone whose faith is strong because, through trials and tribulations, it has come to 'the sanctified vision of maturity'. As he looks back on the growth of his

---

* 'Love Divine, All Loves Excelling' and 'Hark the Herald Angels Sing' are two examples among many.

own mind, Wordsworth 'girds himself for further forward progress, a striving toward perfection through a series of covenant vows, a spiritual yearning sustained at many points, from the dawn of his childhood to his realization of poetic identity, by the fruits of the spirit of God'.[17] The idea of the 'covenant' was important in Methodism. In Book IV of *The Prelude*, Wordsworth recalls the beauty of one particular dawn as he returned from an evening's 'promiscuous rout' of 'dancing, gaiety and mirth' (IV.318, 320). In the language of a religious baptism or an infusion of grace, he describes how 'to the brim / My heart was full' (IV.340–1), and, as a Methodist bonding with a personal God, he enters into his own covenant with nature:

> I made no vows, but vows
> Were then made for me; bond unknown to me
> Was given, that I should be, else sinning greatly,
> A dedicated spirit. (ll. 341–4)

In fact, Brantley reads as ironic Wordsworth's statement in Book X of *The Prelude* that the French Revolution's promise of a new paradise would be fulfilled 'in the very world which is the world / Of all of us, the place in which, in the end, / We find our happiness, or not at all' (X.726–8). It is important to read these lines in context, he argues, in order to understand that Wordsworth is diagnosing the spiritual malaise of France. Far from representing his own mature viewpoint, the sentiment 'epitomizes the blithest and bleakest secularism of the Revolution: in the most general terms of *The Prelude*, a worldly frame of mind, or an attitude that finds no spiritual meaning in the world, can lead to no happy "end"'.[18]

In an article whose title, 'The Party Faithful', reflects an acknowledgement that, in its origins, 'Labour owes more to Methodism than Marxism', Roy Hattersley describes its social as well as its religious dimension:

> The urban industrial working class of the nascent industrial revolution were sheep without shepherds – generally neglected by

the Church of England, which remained with its pew rents and tithes, an essentially rural institution. They found in Wesley's passionate evangelism the emotionally satisfying faith that met their needs. Methodism had the appearance of a poor man's religion.[19]

At the commencement of the Industrial Revolution, the Romantics, focusing upon a new democratic society united in bonds of fellowship and sensibility, and turning to the natural and the commonplace as the basis for their aesthetic principles, inevitably found in Methodism a sympathetic cause. As Hattersley remarks:

> Wesley was a social as well as a religious revolutionary. But instead of liberty, equality, fraternity, he proclaimed piety, probity and respectability. And the search for ready recruits made Methodism crucially influential among the workers who were about to become the indispensable backbone of industrial and imperial Britain.

Unitarianism

Although Coleridge, as mentioned above, would later acknowledge the positive influence of Methodism, his own early conception of Christianity as a philosophy of social reform was enshrined in Unitarianism, a belief which, unlike Methodism, discouraged displays of emotion and piety. Though small in numbers, many members of the Unitarian movement were the leading intellectuals of their day. Unitarianism made its appeal to an educated elite rather than, as Methodism, to the untutored populace. In its stricter forms it saw Jesus as, at most, no more than an enlightened teacher, and sought a simpler moral vision to be found in the conception of one God, as against the doctrine of the Holy Trinity, or three persons in one. Coleridge himself acted briefly as a Unitarian minister until an annuity from the Wedgwood family freed him from the post. He identified completely with many of the more controversial political beliefs of Unitarianism, such as the abolition of the slave-trade, parliamentary reform and the freedom of the press, but unlike many of his contemporaries who espoused the Jacobin cause, he was never an atheist, stressing rather a Christian community and, in the radical years of the early 1790s, the brotherhood, as much as the rights, of man.

The Higher Criticism and Millenarianism

In 1798, Coleridge's intense interest in metaphysics was stimulated by the ten-month visit he paid to Germany. At this time, Germany was the centre of a new kind of biblical scholarship, the so-called Higher Criticism, whose purpose was a reassessment of the scriptures in terms of their textual value. That scripture could now be regarded as a text like any other, to which the instruments of scholarship and literary criticism might be applied, was a crucial development for the following century, with the kind of fundamental effect on Christian belief as powerful in its way as Darwin's later theory of evolution. Anticipating this approach, Robert Lowth's mid-eighteenth-century lectures on the sacred poetry of the Hebrews[*] had examined biblical language, not as revealed truth, but as poetry, the product of the newly created mind of man responding emotionally to nature with all the vivid iconography of a world experienced for the first time. For Lowth, the Hebrew authors of biblical literature were effectively the first poets, whose repetitions and syntactically separated utterances were the expression of their passionately imaginative responses to nature at the dawn of creation. It is in the tradition of Lowth that Wordsworth, quoting from the Book of Judges in his 'Note' to 'The Thorn',[20] describes how apparent tautologies are 'frequently beauties of the highest kind'. He supports his poem's repetitive language by referring to the effective use of repetition in 'innumerable passages from the Bible' and in 'the impassioned poetry of every nation'.

---

[*] Robert Lowth (1710–87) gave his series of lectures, *De sacra poesi Hebraeorum praelectiones*, between 1741 and 1750. They were published in 1753 and translated into English in 1787.

Once released from an obligation to defend the Bible as a record of historical truth, the Romantic period was free to make it the absolute pattern of feeling, and biblical images and references abound throughout its literature.

Coleridge himself was opposed to the Higher Criticism because he believed that it had a false view of the way in which we see the world. Very important for him was the concept of Imagination. To the rationalist mind, aptly demonstrated by Shakespeare's Theseus in *A Midsummer Night's Dream*,[21] the Imagination was the producer of falsehood. It creates things which are not found in nature. Coleridge, although he acknowledges this kind of creativity, espouses a higher level of Imagination. The world produces experiences, but the Imagination has to interpret them. It is a divine faculty, and Coleridge's understanding of the Bible is of a collection of writings which, although imaginative, are nevertheless telling the truth. He calls scriptures 'the living educts of the Imagination' which communicate their meaning in 'a system of symbols [...] harmonious in themselves, and consubstantial with the truths, of which they are the *conductors*'.[22]

The need for human transcendence within the prevalent rationalism, materialism and historical necessity of the revolutionary period is reflected in a spiritual hunger which, in addition to the movements of Methodism and Unitarianism, gave rise to innumerable dissenting religions and sects. Historians such as E. P. Thompson argue that these were probably less important as religious movements than as forms of social protest at a time when the language of democracy and equality was still basically theological.[23] J. F. C. Harrison[24] argues that such millenarian persuasions were, for many, a way of coming to terms with the enormous social upheavals of the age (see Part Three: 'Writing in Revolution'). Change on such an unprecedented scale which might otherwise have seemed inexplicable, could be interpreted theologically as heralding the advent of the long-prophesied apocalypse:

> Living in such a time of acute social change was for many people uncomfortable, bewildering, traumatic. Familiar social landmarks disappeared, assumptions about stability and normality were no

longer unquestioned, the sources of authority to which men looked for guidance were not convincing as they once had been. A new ideology to take account of the disruption or weakening of the old social order and to sanction new aspirations was needed. Millenarianism was that ideology. Although at first it may appear bizarre, in context it has a rationale which makes it intelligible. Millennial beliefs were a response to this period of crisis.

Marilyn Butler, in *Romantics, Rebels and Reactionaries*,[25] detects a coincidence between the rise of very emotional religious cults and the new taste for gothic. To a population which was able to resort neither to the 'officially sanctioned magic' of an earlier naive Christianity, nor to science to explain or protect it from its ills, the formulaic, almost religiously ritualistic, pattern of gothic fiction, she argues, offered a kind of comfort. By allowing its readers to live vicariously through a nightmare which, terrible in sleep, would be even worse in real life, gothic fiction enabled them to face up to fears as an emotionally satisfying way of anticipating the worst. It may be, she writes, that 'in these reiterated adventures by surrogate figures there is reassurance and even the illusion of protection'.[26]

The Evangelical Revival

By the end of the eighteenth century, the emphasis on religious emotion had developed into what is loosely called the Evangelical Revival. Like Unitarianism, Evangelicalism numbered within its ranks many intellectual and reforming members whose organisation was as much directed at social improvement as it was at salvation. Prominent Evangelical figures included the abolitionist William Wilberforce and the philanthropist Lord Shaftesbury,* and the effects of its activities on public and private life were

---

* William Wilberforce (1759–1833) spearheaded the parliamentary campaign which led to the Slave Trade Act (1807) and the Slavery Abolition Act (1833). Anthony Ashley Cooper, 7th Earl of Shaftesbury (1801–85), was a politician and philanthropist behind the Factory Acts of 1847 and 1853, the Coal Mines Act of 1842, and legislation on the protection of Climbing Boys (child chimney sweeps). Shaftesbury's monument is 'Eros' in Piccadilly Circus, London.

far-reaching and enduring. Wordsworth, as well as revealing the influence of Methodism in his poetry, reflects the reformist zeal of the Evangelical in a sonnet of 1807, where he invokes Milton to clean up the 'fen / Of stagnant waters' which is contemporary England.* Many organisations familiar even today, such as the YMCA and the Royal Society for the Prevention of Cruelty to Animals, were founded in Evangelicalism. With its high-minded sense of purpose and its ability to cross class divisions, its influence in England is difficult to overestimate.

The many different denominations which flourished during the Romantic period, whether actively revolutionist or reactionary, demanded an allegiance which often set them against each other. The Methodist's deep faith in a Divinity, for example, lies behind the inspiration of such lines as those in a hymn of Charles Wesley's denouncing the Unitarians, whose conception of Christ was one of a supremely human figure: 'The Unitarian fiend expel, / And chase his doctrine back to hell'.[27] Antinomianism, an extreme version of Calvinism, encouraged a belief that 'justification' by God meant that its adherents could do no wrong. It is under this conviction that the younger Wringhim carries on his persecutions, even to the point of murder, in James Hogg's *Private Memoirs and Confessions of a Justified Sinner* (1824) (see Part Three: 'Romantic Fiction'). The elder Wringhim's hymn denouncing an 'enemy', and sung within earshot of young Wringhim, is typical of the implacable prejudice to which religious sectarianism was prone:

> Let God his father's wickedness
> Still to remembrance call;
> And never let his mother's sin
> Be blotted out at all.
> As he in cursing pleasure took,
> So let it to him fall;
> As he delighted not to bless,
> So bless him not at all.
> As cursing he like clothes put on,

---

* Sonnet: 'Milton! Thou shouldst be living at this hour'.

Into his bowels so,
Like water, and into his bones
Like oil, down let it go.

Hogg's novel describes, with irony, how 'Young Wringhim only knew the full purport of this spiritual song; and went to his bed better satisfied than ever, that his father and brother were cast-aways, reprobates, aliens from the church and the true faith, and cursed in time and eternity.'[28]

While Hogg's *Confessions* describes psychological disseverance, expressed symbolically in the novel by the religious divisions between Cavaliers and Puritans, Episcopalians and Presbyterians, Walter Scott, in *The Heart of Midlothian* (1818), demonstrates how Presbyterianism, divided against itself, could produce both the sympathetic figure of Jeannie Deans and her intractably bigoted father, Douce Davie. In *Letters Written during a Short Residence in Sweden, Norway, and Denmark* (1796) (see Part Three: 'Romantic Travel Writing'), Mary Wollstonecraft, regretting both the 'progress of Methodism' and the 'fanatical spirit which appears to be gaining ground' in England, turned her attention to religious observances among nations and reflected on how the gaiety and gladness of a Sunday, or the 'decadi'* of revolutionary France was, in her experience, 'a sentiment more truly religious than all the stupid stillness which the streets of London ever inspired where the sabbath is so decorously observed'. The Evangelicals' founding of the Lord's Day Observance Society would later consolidate a situation in which, as Mary Wollstonecraft believed, people 'expecting to promote their salvation [...] disregard their welfare in this world, and neglect the interest and comfort of their families'.[29]

---

* In the French Revolutionary calendar, each month was divided into three weeks of ten days. The tenth day, or *decadi*, was the official day of rest which was celebrated in cheerful relaxation.

Atheism and Belief

Mary Wollstonecraft's is one voice among many in Romantic literature that opposes the effects of prohibitive religious authority, but the influence of religion itself was pervasive. Robert M. Maniquis points out that nowhere in the irony of Jane Austen's novels is the value 'of even a superficial layer of religion called into question'. For all his attacks on its representatives, William Cobbett in *Rural Rides* (1822–6) 'defended religion as a guarantee of a free-born Englishman's liberty', while Thomas Paine (see Part Three: Writing in Revolution) was often shunned, 'even by radical friends', not only because of his disagreeable drunkenness but also because some of them detected 'the smell of atheism about him'.[30] Maniquis remarks that, before a period in which it had become a 'common Romantic revolutionary principle', and at least before Percy Bysshe Shelley published *The Necessity of Atheism* (1811), atheism itself was a reason for shame. Shelley's publication of his pamphlet was effectively an 'act of social disorder'.[31] As Richard Holmes points out, this was what could lead even as scandalous a figure as Byron to erase, 'for Shelley's own protection', one of the descriptions Shelley had given of himself in several Swiss hotel registers as 'Democrat, Philanthropist and Atheist'. Holmes remarks that Byron 'immediately felt obliged to cross it out as indelibly as possible', given the reputation of one of the locations, Chamonix, among the travelling English at the time, 'as a natural temple of the Lord and a proof of the Deity by design'.[32] Until his death in 1822, Shelley was in fact more notorious for his profession of atheism than celebrated as a poet.

Belief and atheism come into particular focus in two poems, one by Coleridge, the other by Shelley, both of which take their inspiration from Chamonix and the immediate environs of Mont Blanc. In 'Hymn Before Sunrise, in the Vale of Chamouni' (1802), Coleridge describes how, amidst the 'torrents' (l. 39) and 'Ice-falls' (l. 49) of the Ravine of Arve, and in the presence of the 'dread silent' (l. 13) form of Mont Blanc, he had 'worshipped the Invisible alone' (l. 16). In fact, the setting is fictitious, as Coleridge had never been to Switzerland, yet he gives to the Alpine setting, with its awe-inspiring power, all the familiar characteristics of the Burkean 'Sublime' (see Part Three: Writing in Revolution). As usually interpreted, sublimity, in such a place, pointed to the nature and authority of God, and it is God's name which Coleridge enlists repeatedly as the solution to his questions about Mont Blanc and the nature of its surrounding landscape:

> Who bade the sun
> Clothe you with rainbows? Who, with living flowers
> Of loveliest hue, spread garlands at your feet?—
> GOD! Let the torrents, like a shout of nations,
> Answer! And let the ice-plains echo, GOD!
> GOD! Sing ye meadow streams with gladsome voice!
> Ye pine-groves, with your soft and soul-like sounds!
> And they too have a voice, yon piles of snow,
> And in their perilous fall shall thunder, GOD! (ll. 55–63)

Coleridge works within tradition by viewing his 'sovran BLANC' (l. 3), with its 'kingly Spirit' (l. 81), as a consolidation of God's supremacy. Just as God exercises his rule by right, so too is it appropriate for Mont Blanc, his 'Great Hierarch' (l. 83) and 'dread ambassador from Earth to Heaven' (l. 82), to be 'throned' among its lesser 'hills' (l. 81).

Where Coleridge's 'Hymn' is an imaginative but essentially literary set piece, Shelley's 'Mont Blanc', written during his Genevan period in 1816, is inspired by a landscape of which he had first-hand experience. Just as Mary Shelley, provoking questions on the origin, nature and purposes of the Creator, would make Mont Blanc's glacier, the Mer de Glace at Chamonix, the setting for Frankenstein's meeting with his Creature, Shelley, in the final stanza of his poem, invites an atheist interrogation of the mountain itself. All the elements of the Sublime are there – 'power' (l. 127), 'darkness' (l. 130), the 'infinite' (l. 140), 'Silence' and 'solitude' (l. 144). Yet, as he imagines the deserted summit of Mont Blanc,* Shelley is led to speculate on what conclusions might be drawn, 'If to the human mind's imaginings / Silence and solitude' point not to the presence of God but only, instead, to 'vacancy' (ll. 143–4).

Re-thinking traditional beliefs in a more critical light, Shelley gives Mont Blanc 'a voice' which, although 'not understood / By all' (l. 81–2), can be interpreted and made felt by (presumably including himself) 'the wise, and great, and good' (l. 82). Shelley adopts the role of Romantic poet-prophet, just as Wordsworth in the Prospectus to *The Recluse*, secure in his own vision, encourages its achievement by the 'progressive powers perhaps no less / Of the whole species' (ll. 819–20). For Shelley, the 'wilderness has a mysterious tongue' (l. 76) which, as in his own case, 'teaches awful doubt' (l. 77) or, as in that of Coleridge presumably, 'faith so mild' (l. 77) that, to paraphrase Shelley's meaning, were it not for such 'faith' man might be 'reconciled' (l. 79) with nature. Therefore, if interpreted correctly, Mont Blanc's 'voice' can 'repeal / Large codes of fraud and woe' (ll. 80–1). By large codes, Shelley arguably means the scriptural authority of the Bible, described by William Blake in *The Marriage of Heaven and Hell* as one of the 'sacred codes' responsible for various 'Errors' (Plate 4).

Although he was unknown to Shelley, Blake shares his heterodoxy and makes *The Marriage* a vehicle to criticise, as he sees them, the falsehoods which have been imposed upon religion by its interpreters throughout history. Despite his professed atheism, Shelley's own argument was not with Christ, or the teachings of Christianity. As an activist, he opposed only the great power that traditional Christian morality had over political and social reform. In *The Marriage of Heaven and Hell*, Blake, concerned more essentially with the nature of man, and believing that man was most fully himself when able to give expression to his passions rather than when he was restraining them, took Milton's *Paradise Lost* as an example of how traditional morality had been allowed to distort and misinterpret the truth.

---

* Mont Blanc had been climbed for the first time by Jacques Balmat and Michel Paccard in 1786.

According to Blake,

> Those who restrain desire, do so because theirs is weak enough to be restrained; and the restrainer or reason usurps its place & governs the unwilling.

> And being restrained, it by degrees becomes passive, till it is only the shadow of desire.

> The history of this is written in *Paradise Lost*, & the Governor or Reason is call'd Messiah (Plate 5).

In his own reading of Milton's poem, Blake found it objectionable to have to accept that 'God will torment Man in Eternity for following his Energies' (Plate 4). For Blake, 'Energy is Eternal Delight' and in *Paradise Lost* he saw Satan as its embodiment. God the Father becomes a form of tyrant, and centuries of tradition, Blake believes, have perverted the nature of Jesus Christ, the 'Messiah', into a mockery of his true self. The real imaginative energy that Christ represents has been restrained until it has become simply a 'shadow' of reality. For Blake, a genuine reading of Christ is to understand what he shares with Milton's Satan. He disagreed fundamentally with the division of the universe into good and evil, and rather than have God and the Devil be seen in opposition to each other, he advocated instead of the traditional separation between Jesus and his adversary, their partnership or marriage, made up of those best principles which in his opinion they shared, such as imagination and heroic 'energy'. This essentially is what Blake means by a 'marriage' of heaven and hell. He saw it as his task to free Milton from what he considered to be that false 'Spectre' to which he was in thrall when writing *Paradise Lost*, and to bring into the open the poet's underlying beliefs that gave Satan's presence in the poem more conviction than he was able to achieve in the presentation of his God. In a 'Note' to Plate 5 Blake adds:

> The reason Milton wrote in fetters when he wrote of Angels & God, and at liberty when of Devils & Hell, is because he was a true Poet and of the Devil's party without knowing it.

Faith, Myth and Doubt

Romantic Heterodoxy: Religion and Materialism

Blake's reassessments of inherited religious doctrine are consistent with the radical temper of his times. In France, students of ideas, such as the philosopher and historian Constantin Volney (see Part Three: 'Revolution, Reaction and the Natural World') were, as an ideological arm of the French Revolution, finding the rules for religions in all cultures and beginning to examine them comparatively. In *The Ruins of Empire* (1791)[33] Volney who, after the outbreak of the Revolution, was a member of the Estates-General and the National Constituent Assembly, presented a bleak vision of human history in which successive empires, ruled by despots with the help of small elites, had maintained power by using religion as a tool of the state. In Section VIII of his book he examines the origins of religion. 'Thus the Deity', he writes,

> after having been originally considered as the sensible and various action of meteors and the elements; then as the combined power of the stars, considered in their relation to terrestrial objects themselves, in consequence of confounding symbols with the things they represented; then as the complex power of nature, in her two principal operations of production and destruction; then as the animated world without distinction of agent and patient, cause and effect; then as the solar principle or element of fire acknowledged as the sole cause of motion – the Deity, I say, considered under all these different views, became at last a chimerical and abstract being: a scholastic subtlety of substance without form, of body without figure; a true delirium of the mind beyond the power of reason at all to comprehend. But in this, its last transformation, it seeks in vain to conceal itself from the senses: the seal of its origin is indelibly stamped upon it. All its attributes borrowed from the physical attributes of the universe, as immensity, eternity, indivisibility, incomprehensibleness; or from the moral qualities of man, as

257

goodness, justice, majesty; and its very names, derived from the physical beings which were its types, particularly the sun, the planets, and the world, present to us continually, in spite of those who would corrupt and disguise it, infallible marks of its genuine nature.[34]

Volney's argument here is not unlike Wordsworth's in *The Excursion*, Book IV (1814),* where he, too, writes of myths and religions as having their origin in imaginative readings of the natural world. Wordsworth had lived in France during the revolutionary period, he had mixed with many of its radical figures, and he was familiar with their thought. Volney's argument in the passage above is that no matter how much abstract, theoretical speculation might have evolved over religion, the worship of a Deity was originally no more than the worship of nature. Volney, as a typical intellectual of the first years of the French Revolution, is not interested in what Wordsworth called in *The Excursion* 'The imaginative faculty [as] lord / Of observations natural' (IV.709–10). What interests him more is the ways in which society has manipulated religion, persuading people either that it was their duty to obey, or that another world was more important than this one. He continues:

> Religion, losing its object, was now nothing more than a political expedient by which to rule the credulous vulgar; and was embraced either by men credulous themselves and the dupes of their own visions, or by bold and energetic spirits, who formed vast projects of ambition. Of this latter description was the Hebrew legislator, who, desirous of separating his nation from every other, and of forming a distinct and exclusive empire, conceived the design of taking for its basis religious prejudices, and of erecting round it a sacred rampart of rites and opinions.[35]

* See Wordsworth, *The Excursion*, IV.696–719, 863–79. Book IV was a particular influence on Keats, who called *The Excursion* one of 'three things to rejoice at in this Age': Letter to B. R. Haydon, 10 January, 1818 (*The Letters of John Keats*, ed. Rollins, vol. 1, p. 203).

By the time in which figures such as Wordsworth and Coleridge were moving towards political conservatism and religious orthodoxy, the younger generation of Romantics, including Keats, Shelley and Byron, who had inherited the legacies of the revolutionary period, were becoming more positive about other forms of religion. In particular they tend to celebrate the joyousness, the hedonism, naturalness and innocence, as well as the sexual permissiveness of pantheons, or collections of gods. To believe in more than one God, as in the religion of the Hindus, the Greeks or the Persians (Zoroastrianism) was, during this time, a way of establishing one's radical credentials, and the poetry of Keats, Byron and Shelley is full of gods and goddesses. Those they tend to celebrate are also in line with the materialist tradition of the French revolutionary period: Ceres, Persephone, Pan, Apollo, Bacchus and so on. Deployed throughout the work of the younger Romantics are all kinds of mythologies – materialist, solar, dualistic, pantheistic – deliberately rivalling Christianity. In *Cain* (1821), Byron launches an attack on the God he calls by name, Jehovah. Instead of beginning with the idea of a good God and then trying to accommodate the evils of known circumstances to that conception, he proceeds inductively, starting with the shortcomings of creation and then inferring the nature of the Being who is responsible for them. In *Heaven and Earth* (1823) Byron provides a witty version of Noah's Flood in which God destroys the world because the daughters of Earth are too beautiful and are seducing the angels. For all the above reasons, it is possible to see how Robert Southey, the Poet Laureate, in his Preface to *A Vision of Judgement* (1821), could speak of men of 'diseased hearts and depraved imaginations' (and this was especially pointed at Byron) who had set up in contemporary England what he describes as a 'Satanic school' of infidel poets. These men, writes Southey,

> forming a system of opinions to suit their own unhappy course of conduct, have rebelled against the holiest ordinances of human society, and hating that revealed religion which, with all their efforts and bravadoes, they are unable entirely to disbelieve,

labour to make others as miserable as themselves by infecting them with a moral virus that eats into the soul! […] for through their productions breathe the spirit of Belial in their lascivious parts, and the spirit of Moloch in those loathsome images of atrocities and horrors which they delight to represent, they are more especially characterised by a Satanic spirit of pride and audacious impiety, which still betrays the wretched feeling of hopelessness wherewith it is allied.

In a challenge to biblical authorities which set the age of creation at only a few thousand years previously, Byron, in *Cain*, has the eponymous hero presented with the vision of a universe which has had its beginnings millions of years ago. Cain learns from Lucifer that not only is the earth an insignificant body in an unimaginably vast creation, but that man himself is only one among many life forms:

> many things will have
> No end; and some, which would pretend to have
> Had no beginning, have had one as mean
> As thou; and mightier things have been extinct
> To make way for much meaner than we can
> Surmise, for *moments* only and the *space*
> Have been and must be all *unchangeable*. (II.i.156–62)

Cain, who is obliged to confront a meaningless and indifferent world, finds Abel's piety intolerable. Striking out at Abel is Cain's way of striking at God in a protest against man's predicament, and is a more violent response than that of Frankenstein's Creature who, being allowed the long-time dream of man to have a conversation with his creator, has a more measured, Godwinian response. 'You are in the wrong', the Creature tells Frankenstein, 'and instead of threatening, I am content to reason with you.'[36] In this kind of way, Mary Shelley invites readers to look beyond the immediate story of her novel and speculate, perhaps in broader terms, on the moral superiority of creatures to their creator.

Byron's conception of a heedless and materialist universe is particularly well illustrated in the second Canto of *Don Juan*. En route to Cadiz, Juan with three servants and his tutor, Pedrillo, are shipwrecked and, together with other survivors, take to a longboat. Byron, drawing on various sources, among them an account of the recent shipwreck of the French frigate *Méduse* in 1816,* goes on to present a picture of fallen man at his helpless worst. At one point in the Canto, and keeping the biblical text of Noah's Flood constantly in play, he presents a tragic scene involving the death of two starving children. At this particularly bleak moment in the narrative, a rainbow makes a sudden appearance (II, stanza 91). This is not the rainbow with which God makes the covenant with Noah,[37] nor that with which the 'natural Methodist', Wordsworth, makes his own covenant with nature.† This is Newton's rainbow,[38] which, as 'airy child of vapour and the sun' and obeying its own laws, vanishes as it arrives and simply 'Forsook the dim eyes of these shipwrecked men' (stanza 92). Its description, in Byron's choice of words, is intended to be reminiscent of the Christianity under attack:

> Brought forth in purple, cradled in vermilion,
> Baptized in molten gold, and swathed in dun. (stanza 92)

'Glittering like crescents o'er a Turk's pavilion', goes on to juxtapose Islam with Christianity while, debasing both, the incongruous simile of a black eye, 'blending every colour into one', reflects Byron's own casual indifference to belief and the subject of comparative religion. The appearance of a 'beautiful white bird' (stanza 94) again recalls Genesis, and 'seemed a better omen still'. Byron continues:

---

* Byron's main source is known to have been Sir J. G. Dalzell's *Shipwrecks and Disasters at Sea* (Edinburgh, 1812), but he may have known of the raft of the *Medusa*, notorious for the suffering and cannibalism indulged in by some of the survivors. An account of these events written by two of them (Corréard and Savigny), was translated into English and published in April 1818. A celebrated picture based on the story, *The Raft of the Medusa*, by the French artist Théodore Géricault (1791–1824) is in the Louvre Museum, Paris.
† 'My heart leaps up when I behold / A rainbow in the sky'.

But in this case I also must remark,
'Twas well this bird of promise did not perch,
Because the tackle of our shattered bark
Was not so safe for roosting as a church,
And had it been the dove from Noah's ark,
Returning there from her successful search,
Which in their way that moment chanced to fall,
They would have eat her, olive branch and all. (stanza 95)

The bird recalls the albatross in *The Ancient Mariner*, Coleridge's poem of sin and Christian redemption, as well as the third person of the Trinity,* suggested by the name of Juan's shipwrecked vessel, 'the most holy *Trinidada*' (stanza 24). Not only does Byron make Old and New Testaments the targets of his cynicism but also, by blaspheming against the Holy Ghost, he deliberately commits the 'unpardonable sin'.† Traditionally, in Christian teaching, one of the two sins against the Holy Ghost is Despair. In *The Prelude*, Wordsworth, at a low point in his spiritual history, describes reaching a mental impasse, 'now believing, / Now disbelieving, endlessly perplex'd / With impulse, motive, right and wrong', until he 'Yielded up moral questions in despair' (X.894–5, 901). However, as Nicholas Roe points out, 'Wordsworth's extinction as a Godwinian being carries an intimation of future restoration in its echo of Matthew 27:50, "Jesus, when he had cried again with a loud voice, yielded up the ghost" – but the resurrection was to follow.'[39] By way of contrast, Byron's deceptive rainbow had only 'looked like hope' (II, stanza 93) while, in *The Prisoner of Chillon* (1816), the captive Bonnivard becomes so conditioned to his imprisonment that, abandoning hope altogether, he is made by Byron to sin against it – 'I learn'd to love despair' (l. 374). A later Canto of *Don Juan* echoes Pilate's question:‡

---

* The Holy Ghost is often depicted in art as a white dove.

† The so-called unpardonable sin is referred to by three of the four Evangelists: Matthew 12:31–2; Luke 12:10; Mark 3:28–9.

‡ 'What is truth?' John 18:38.

But what's reality? Who has its clue?
Philosophy? No, she too much rejects.
Religion? Yes, but which of all her sects?

With a characteristic wry scepticism, Byron continues:

Some millions must be wrong, that's pretty clear:
Perhaps it may turn out that all were right.
God help us! Since we have need on our career
To keep our holy beacons always bright,
'Tis time that some new Prophet should appear,
Or old indulge man with a second sight.
Opinions wear out in some thousand years,
Without a small refreshment from the spheres. (XV, stanza 90)

Religion, Myth and Sexuality

To such figures as Byron, Christianity, especially when it came to matters
of sexuality, was an essentially patriarchal system with a repressive moral
code. In the Christian tradition, the serpent, woman and sexuality were
all looked upon suspiciously because, in relation to the moral life of
men, they represented temptation. In *Paradise Lost*, as Milton had
shown, it was Eve who led Adam to the Fall and 'Brought death into
the world, and all our woe'.[40] By contrast, pagan religions were often
admired because they seemed to celebrate joyousness and freedom,
reverencing the feminine and giving equal weight to sexuality and the
female principle. The mythological poems of the younger Romantics
often bring notions of free love into conflict with religious convention.
In the autobiographical 'Epipsychidion' (1822), the married Shelley
takes a young Italian girl, in his imagination, to an island paradise
where, in the erotically charged language and verse rhythm, they become
'one / Spirit within two frames [...] One passion in twin-hearts'
(ll. 573–5). Shelley, in defiance of religious taboos, advocates the

individual's accommodation of loyalty to diverse erotic impulses. From the outset, his ideal was never a marital one:

> I never was attached to that great sect,
> Whose doctrine is, that each one should select
> Out of the crowd a mistress or a friend,
> And all the rest, though fair and wise, commend
> To cold oblivion, though it is in the code
> Of modern morals. (ll. 149–54)

In Canto I of *Don Juan*, Byron's celebration of 'first and passionate love' (stanza 127) contrives to make readers overlook the fact that Juan's relationship is with a woman already married. His poem insists from the outset on the naturalness of sexual desire in women, as well as in men, and depicts the unhappy consequences of society's attempts to repress it or to regard marriage as its only acceptable outlet. Keats, in 'Lamia', avoids any authorial intervention which might give moral direction to his readers' judgements. In Part 1, Hermes's ardent pursuit of a nymph in a rural landscape seems to be implying that to gratify lust is an acceptable thing for a god to do. However, in Part 2, the urban setting is Corinth, a city denounced by the moralist St Paul for its licentiousness.

Keats seems also to be inviting readers to take an unconventional line in their assessment of the female role. A more usual reading of 'La Belle Dame Sans Merci' is to view the female figure as a femme fatale and a threat to the loitering 'knight-at-arms', just as the serpent woman in 'Lamia' can be seen as endangering the male hero, Lycius. However, the 'names' of these women are those conferred upon them by men. 'La Belle Dame' is so named by 'pale kings and princes', 'Pale warriors' (ll. 37–8). 'Lamia', which means a 'vampire', is the name given to the serpent woman by Apollonius, the philosopher and, significantly, the *tutor* of Lycius. Keats seems to be questioning the authority of these male designations and suggesting that it is not the perceived 'dangers' of women that bring about the demise of his male heroes, but rather their own fears and anxieties about sexuality and the female.

In a letter of 1819 to his brother George and wife,[41] Keats takes issue with a view of the world which 'among the misguided and superstitious is "a vale of tears", from which we are to be redeemed by a certain arbitrary interposition of God and taken to Heaven'. Keats prefers to see the world as what he calls 'the Vale of Soul-Making', where each individual is given an identity, to be effected by the three materials of 'the intelligence; the human heart […] and the world'. The letter continues:

> I will call the *world* a school instituted for the purpose of teaching little children to read; I will call the *human heart* the hornbook used in that school; and I will call the *child able to read it* the soul made from that school and its hornbook.
>
> Do you not see how necessary a world of pains and troubles is to school an intelligence and make it a soul, a place where the heart must feel and suffer in a thousand diverse ways? Not merely is the heart a hornbook, it is the mind's Bible, it is the mind's experience, it is the teat from which the mind or intelligence sucks its identity.

Keats's emphasis on the centrality of 'mind' recalls the mind as 'haunt, and main region' of Wordsworth's 'song' (Prospectus, l. 796). His remarks have particular relevance to his own 'Ode to Psyche', written almost contemporaneously. There, he asserts that through 'shadowy thought' and in some 'untrodden region' of his mind (matching Wordsworth's 'For I must tread on shadowy ground'), he will worship the neglected goddess to establish his own identity as a poet. The process of 'Soul-Making', as described in the poem, is an arduous one, but makes up what Keats considers to be 'a grander system of salvation than the Christian religion'.[42]

Keats demonstrates the same kind of interest that earlier figures, such as Volney, had shown in the origins of belief and the varieties of religious experience: 'Seriously, I think it probable that this system of soul-making may have been the parent of all the more palpable and personal schemes of redemption, among the Zoroastrians,* the Christians, and the Hindus.' As the letter continues, Keats makes man the source of his own beliefs, arguing that people invent the religions they need:

> For as one part of the human species must have their carved Jupiter, so another part must have the palpable and named mediator and saviour – their Christ, their Oromanes, and their Vishnu.[†]

He appropriately copies out the 'Ode to Psyche', and writes to his brother:

> You must recollect that Psyche was not embodied as a goddess before the time of Apulieus [sic] the Platonist who lived after the Augustan age, and consequently the Goddess was never worshipped or sacrificed to with any of the ancient fervour – and perhaps never thought of in the old religion – I am more orthodox than to let a hethan Goddess be so neglected.

The main source for Keats in this Ode is Apuleius, in William Adlington's translation of *The Golden Ass* (1566), while another influence was possibly Mary Tighe's *Psyche* of 1805. But Keats replaces the delicate eroticism of Tighe, as well as the furtive and guilty Psyche of Apuleius, with a much more open and sexually charged situation of his own. He first presents himself as an aimless wanderer who is surprised to happen upon Psyche, together with Cupid, pressing down the 'bedded grass' in joyful intimacy. Keats implies that although she has come late in the 'faded hierarchy' of gods and goddesses, she has been fortunate to have escaped not only the trappings of religion, the

---

*   Zoroastrians are followers of the Zoroastrian religion, whose origins were in India and which spread to Persia (modern-day Iran).

†   Oromanes or Ahrimanes, in the dualistic Zoroastrian system, is the evil spirit who is opposed to Mazda, the god of light. Vishnu is the preserver of the universe in Hindu mythology.

'altar heaped with flowers', the 'incense sweet', but also its prohibitions, implicit in the homophonic 'chain-swung censer' and sanctioned by the 'pale-mouthed prophet' to which, as Blake would also have argued, the orthodox have reduced Christ and misrepresented him. Keats substitutes for that of the 'virgin-choir' a more 'delicious moan / Upon the midnight hours', while in the sexual symbolism of a 'bright torch' and a 'casement ope at night / To let the warm love in' he offers his own more libertarian alternative (see Part Three: Romantic Verse Narrative). The 'Ode to Psyche' is typical of the kind of way in which the younger generation of Romantic poets approached the legacy of the past. Keats, like many of his peers, is subversive in his approach to religion, and typically uses myth to communicate truths about human life which traditional beliefs were no longer in a position to supply.

Notes

1   T. E. Hulme, *Speculations: Essays on Humanism and the Philosophy of Art*, ed. Herbert Read (London: 1924; repr. Routledge, 2000), p. 118.
2   M. H. Abrams, *Natural Supernaturalism: Tradition and Revolution in Romantic Literature* (New York: Norton, 1971), pp. 12–13.
3   Ibid., p. 12.
4   Frank Jordan (ed.), *The English Romantic Poets: A Review of Research and Criticism*, 4th edn (New York: Modern Language Association of America, 1985), p. 11.
5   Jon Klancher (ed.), *A Concise Companion to the Romantic Age* (Chichester: Wiley-Blackwell, 2009), p. 23.
6   John Stuart Mill, *Autobiography and Literary Essays*, ed. John M. Robson and Jack Stillinger (London: Routledge, 1981), p. 141.
7   Ibid., p. 150.
8   Matthew Arnold, 'Memorial Verses' (1850).
9   John Wesley, *John Wesley's Journal*, ed. Robert Backhouse (London: Hodder & Stoughton, 1973), p. 56.
10 Robert Southey, *The Life of Wesley; and the Rise and Progress of Methodism*, ed. A. Knox, 3rd edn with notes by the late S. T. Coleridge, 2 vols (London, 1846), vol. 1, p. 184.

11   Frederick C. Gill, *The Romantic Movement and Methodism: A Study of English Romanticism and the Evangelical Revival* (London: Epworth Press, 1937), p. 29.

12   Donald Davie, *The Eighteenth-Century Hymn in England* (Cambridge: Cambridge University Press, 1993).

13   Stephen Prickett (ed.), *The Romantics* (London: Methuen, 1981), p. 127.

14   T. B. Shepherd, *Methodism and the Literature of the Eighteenth Century* (London: Epworth Press, 1940), p. 266.

15   Letter to John Thelwall, 13 May 1796: S. T. Coleridge, *The Collected Letters of Samuel Taylor Coleridge*, ed. E. L. Griggs, 6 vols (Oxford: Clarendon Press), vol. 1, p. 216.

16   Henry Crabb Robinson, *Henry Crabb Robinson on Books and their Writers*, ed. Edith J. Morley, 3 vols (London: J. M. Dent & Sons, 1938), vol. 1, p. 158.

17   Richard E. Brantley, *Wordsworth's 'Natural Methodism'* (New Haven and London: Yale University Press, 1975), p. 88.

18   Ibid., p.108.

19   Roy Hattersley, 'The Party Faithful', *The Guardian*, 14 June 2003, p. 34.

20   *Lyrical Ballads* (1798).

21   See *A Midsummer Night's Dream*, V.i.2–22.

22   S. T. Coleridge, *The Statesman's Manual* (Burlington: Chauncey Goodrich, 1832), p. 38.

23   E. P. Thompson, *The Making of the English Working Class* (London: Gollancz, 1963).

24   J. F. C. Harrison, *The Second Coming: Popular Millenarianism 1780–1850* (London: Routledge & Kegan Paul, 1979), p. 219.

25   Marilyn Butler, *Romantics, Rebels and Reactionaries: English Literature and its Background 1760–1830* (Oxford: Oxford University Press, 1981).

26   Ibid., p. 29.

27   B. L. Manning, *The Hymns of Wesley and Watts: Five Informal Papers* (London: Epworth Press, 1942), p. 17.

28   James Hogg, *The Private Memoirs and Confessions of a Justified Sinner*, ed. John Carey (Oxford: Oxford University Press, 1981), pp. 32–3.

29   Mary Wollstonecraft, *Letters Written during a Short Residence in Sweden, Norway, and Denmark*, ed. Richard Holmes (Harmondsworth: Penguin, 1987), pp. 120–1.

30   Klancher (ed.), *A Concise Companion to the Romantic Age*, p. 17.

31   Ibid.

32   Richard Holmes, *Shelley: The Pursuit* (London: Weidenfeld & Nicolson, 1974), p. 342.

33   C. F. Volney, *Les Ruines, ou méditations sur les révolutions des empires* (1791).

34   C. F. Volney, *The Ruins; or A Survey of the Revolutions of Empires* (London: Freethought Publishing Company, 1881), pp. 117–18.

35   Ibid., pp. 118–19.

36   Mary Shelley, *Frankenstein, or The Modern Prometheus*, ed. M. K. Joseph (Oxford: Oxford University Press, 1983), p. 145.

37   Genesis 9:11–17.

38   See Keats, 'Lamia', ll. 231–8.

39   Nicholas Roe, *Wordsworth and Coleridge: The Radical Years* (Oxford: Clarendon Press, 1988), pp. 220–1.

40   *Paradise Lost*, I.3.

41   Journal-Letter 14 February–3 May 1819: *The Letters of John Keats*, ed. H. E. Rollins, 2 vols (Cambridge, Mass.: Harvard University Press, 1958), vol. 2, pp. 101–3.

42   Ibid.

Heroes and Anti-heroes

Byron begins Canto I of *Don Juan* by searching for an appropriate subject. All epic poems have heroes and this poem is to be no exception:

> I want a hero, an uncommon want,
> When every year and month sends forth a new one,
> Till after cloying the gazettes with cant,
> The age discovers he is not the true one.
> Of such as these I should not care to vaunt;
> I'll therefore take our ancient friend Don Juan.
> We all have seen him in the pantomime
> Sent to the devil somewhat ere his time.

There had been war between Britain and France for almost a quarter of a century as Byron began writing this poem, and Canto I mentions many names involved in the conflict who might have laid claim to heroism. He is generally dismissive of all of them, including the British hero, Nelson, who

> was once Britannia's god of war
> And still should be so, but the tide is turned.
> There's no more to be said of Trafalgar;
> 'Tis with our hero quietly inurned. (stanza 4)

As for Napoleon, his is just another name to be found 'cloying the gazettes with cant':

France too had Buonaparté and Demourier
Recorded in the *Moniteur* and *Courier*. (stanza 2)

Although Byron could not have known the poem, his quest for an epic subject resembles William Wordsworth's in the opening verse paragraphs of *The Prelude.** Here, Wordsworth states a 'determin'd aim' (I.124) to 'grapple with some noble theme' (I.139). Like Milton preparing to write *Paradise Lost*, he has made 'rigorous inquisition' (l. 159) into his own capacities to undertake such a work and lists, as possible subjects, tales of historic struggles for liberty in the great body of traditional epic, as well as the heroic names associated with them. Eventually, 'baffled by a mind that every hour / Turns recreant to her task' (ll. 259–60), he changes direction altogether and resorting to his childhood memories, asks:

Was it for this
That one, the fairest of all Rivers, lov'd
To blend his murmurs with my Nurse's song? (ll. 271–3)

The Prelude, in which he makes himself the hero of the poem, will bring readers back to this very point in Book I, the point from which it now takes up its story. Wordsworth said it was 'a thing unprecedented in literary history that a man should talk so much about himself'.[1]

Byron's and Wordsworth's thoughts on epic heroes have certain implications. Byron is against traditional concepts of heroism and deliberately takes a comic figure from legend as his subject. He turns his back on the idea of heroes as national figures who fight on behalf of king and country. Wordsworth had already been included in Byron's Dedication to *Don Juan* as one of the so-called 'Lake School' of poets:†

---

*   *The Prelude* was first published in 1850.
†   William Wordsworth, Samuel Taylor Coleridge and Robert Southey, who lived in and had associations with the English Lake District.

You gentlemen, by dint of long seclusion
From better company, have kept your own
At Keswick, and through still continued fusion
Of one another's minds at last have grown
To deem, as a most logical conclusion,
That poesy has wreaths for you alone.
There is a narrowness in such a notion,
Which makes me wish you'd change your lakes for ocean.

(stanza 5)

Byron is critical of the kind of privileged sensibility that would lead Wordsworth to write of himself with such earnest conviction in *The Prelude*. By the time he came to begin work on *Don Juan*, he had revised his own judgement on what was important about poets and poetry, and had abandoned the subjective mode of Romanticism, making *Don Juan* a vehicle for his own down-to-earth appraisal of human life and manners:

I perch upon an humbler promontory
Amidst life's infinite variety
With no great care for what is nicknamed glory,
But speculating as I cast mine eye
On what may suit or may not suit my story
And never straining hard to versify,
I rattle on exactly as I'd talk
With anybody in a ride or walk. (XV.19)

The Byronic Hero

By the time he wrote these words, Byron had become a prisoner of his own fame. The so-called Byronic hero, although not entirely his own invention, had attached itself to his name and become famous throughout Europe in the figures of the Giaour, the Corsair and Lara, the heroes of some of the verse-tales with which he followed the enormous success of the first two Cantos of *Childe Harold's Pilgrimage* (1812). In *Don Juan* Byron asserts his determination to make poetry more than simply a reflection of the self.

The Byronic hero would have currency long after the poet's death and is still today a template for its creator in the popular imagination. At the time, it was associated in Byron's mind with the cult of Napoleon. The third canto of *Childe Harold's Pilgrimage* (1816) pauses at one point in order to reflect on Napoleon's fate, and to recognise in him the same kind of spirit 'antithetically mixt' (III.317) as in the hero of the poem, Childe Harold, the alter ego of Byron himself. As Angus Calder remarks, Byron was an 'irresistible combination of beauty, pedigree, sexual challenge, revolutionary heroism',[2] but his Calvinist background also lent to his personality a dark sense of fate and inescapable doom. Byron's contemporaries linked him with his heroes, just as they did with Childe Harold, and it is still difficult not to detect the poet's identity in a hero-figure such as Conrad in *The Corsair* (1814):

Unlike the heroes of each ancient race,
Demons in act, but Gods at least in face,
In Conrad's form seems little to admire,
Though his dark eye-brow shades a glance of fire;
Robust but not Herculean—to the sight
No giant frame sets forth his common height;
Yet, in the whole, who paused to look again,
Saw more than marks the crowd of vulgar men;
They gaze and marvel how—and still confess
That thus it is, but why they cannot guess.
Sun-burnt his cheek, his forehead high and pale
The sable curls in wild profusion veil;
And oft perforce his rising lip reveals
The haughtier thought it curbs, but scarce conceals.
Though smooth his voice, and calm his general mien,
Still seems there something he would not have seen.

(ll. 193–208)

This combination of the attractive and the repellent would make possible the creation of later novelistic heroes who were influenced by Byron's, such as Heathcliff in Emily Brontë's *Wuthering Heights* and Mr Rochester in Charlotte Brontë's *Jane Eyre* (both 1847), while Conrad's detachment from 'the crowd', together with his 'rising lip' of scorn, recalls Byron's rejection of British society, amusingly caricatured by Max Beerbohm in 'Lord Byron, Shaking the Dust of England from his shoes' (1904).[3] Even Conrad's guilty secret inevitably brings to mind the incestuous relationship between Byron and his half-sister, Augusta Leigh, hinted at by Manfred's 'I loved her, and destroy'd her' in the verse-drama of 1816–17 (II.ii.116). The impact of such figures extended well beyond the nineteenth-century literary world to have far-reaching influence, too, within art, music and opera, as well as on popular culture in the twentieth century. Many iconic personalities from cinema and pop music owe their fame in part to the celebrity culture which was arguably initiated by Byron.

Byron replaced Walter Scott as the most popular poet of the day, removing his own heroes from Scott's historical settings to a contemporary one.[*] Marilyn Butler argues that by constructing them also in a Napoleonic image, Byron places them within a present-day theatre of war, and thus 'implies the possibility of effective action in the real world'.[4] It has been suggested that it was during the Napoleonic period that human beings began to have a collective sense of losing control. Historians begin to talk of historical movements and tides of events, where people as individuals seemed to matter less and less. This trend has continued, with contemporary celebrity culture a by-product of it. Butler argues that the popularity of Byron's heroic figures can be explained because they act as 'a focus for contemporary fantasies'.[†] One of these fantasies may have been that the individual still had some sort of prominent role to play. Furthermore, a character such as the rebellious Conrad, Butler writes, 'is sanitized, as far as the English public is concerned, by wielding his sword well away from the

---

[*] Scott's *Marmion* (1808), for example, is a tale of the Battle of Flodden Field (1513).

[†] The popularity of Byron's verse-tales is evident from the sale of 10,000 copies of *The Corsair* on the first day of its publication in 1814.

French proponents of liberty and equality'. In other words, Byron's 'heroes' are not dangerous to society in the real sense that Luddites[*] and other subversives were. Being drained of ideological content, their potential for sparking off revolutionary activity remains confined to the page.

Byron constructed the heroes of his verse-tales from an amalgam of sources. Like many of his contemporaries he was influenced by the eighteenth-century gothic novel, whose male protagonists such as Horace Walpole's Manfred in *The Castle of Otranto* (1764), Mrs Ann Radcliffe's Montoni in her novel *The Mysteries of Udolpho* (1794) and Schedoni in *The Italian* (1797) were much more compelling than the colourless figures which otherwise populate these books. Their secret histories and transgressions anticipate those of characters like Conrad, while Karl Moor, the hero of Friedrich Schiller's sensational play, *Die Räuber* (*The Robbers*),[†] was also influential. Recalling the situation of Edgar in Shakespeare's *King Lear*, Schiller's play involves the schemings of his evil brother which lead to Karl's disinheritance. Karl, who vows vengeance, takes to the Bohemian forest with a band of outlaws but, like Robin Hood, shows himself to be a man of sensibility and conscience in distributing his wealth to the needy. His temperament is in part a reflection of the cult of sensibility, producing fictions such as Henry Mackenzie's *The Man of Feeling* (1771) and Goethe's widely influential novel, *The Sorrows of Young Werther* (1774), a tale of unrequited love which leads eventually to the suicide of its overwrought hero.

However, Byron's own version of the hero required more than these influences alone and, together with his contemporary William Blake, he found inspiration in Milton's presentation of Satan in *Paradise Lost*. The poem was of particular interest to the politics of the Romantic period for the way in which it invited topical questions about oppressors and their victims. Satan is a tyrannical figure, but

---

[*] Luddites, who took their name from the fictive Ned Ludd, worked in the textile industry and broke up modern machinery which they saw as putting them out of a job. Byron's first speech in the House of Lords was against the transportation of Luddites for frame-breaking.

[†] It was published in 1781, translated into English in 1792.

Milton seemed to raise issues about the extent to which it was the responsibility of his creator for making him so. In his Preface to *Prometheus Unbound* (1820), Percy Bysshe Shelley, like Blake, in describing Satan as 'the Hero of *Paradise Lost*', argues that the fallen angel's 'taints of ambition, envy, revenge, and a desire for personal aggrandisement [...] interfere with the interest'. In his own verse-drama, Shelley makes his Prometheus figure wholly good and the adversary, Jupiter, wholly bad and ripe for overthrow. Shelley goes on to argue that, in his judgement, Prometheus is a 'more poetical character than Satan' who 'engenders in the mind a pernicious casuistry which leads us to weigh his faults with his wrongs, and to excuse the former because the latter exceed all measure'.

For Byron and some of his contemporaries, Satan, with all his pride and individuality, is an alluring presence, and his relationship to the eponymous hero, Lara, in Byron's verse-tale of 1814, is evident:

> There was in him a vital scorn of all:
> As if the worst had fall'n which could befall,
> He stood a stranger in this breathing world,
> An erring spirit from another hurl'd. (I.313–16)

Byron: *The Corsair* and *The Giaour*

Where traditional heroes had been admired because they were protectors of their people, Byron seems to invite readers to admire figures who hate the social order. In *The Corsair*, Conrad adopts a seemingly rational policy of a pre-emptive strike against his enemy, 'Stern Seyd' (l. 132). But the scheme quickly turns into an orgy of violence as Conrad's forces, taking on impossible odds, are happy to destroy themselves, just as long as in the process they can pull down the whole fabric of society with them.

On the surface, such 'heroes' were simply criminals. Conrad 'left a Corsair's name to other times / Link'd with one virtue, and a thousand crimes' (ll. 695–6). But Byron's interest in these creations seems to have been provoked by the moral and intellectual issues which they raised. Such figures are too grand, or too evil, or too good to be measured by the standards of convention, and they force the reader to make a more searching enquiry into norms for order and value. Contemporary reviews criticised Byron's 'heroes' for what they saw as the moral confusion they created. Of his verse-drama *Manfred*, for example, the *Critical Review* spoke of how it filled the imagination 'with images of guilt, which cannot at the same time serve as a lesson or a warning'.[5] *Blackwood's* remarked that the hero, Manfred, 'comes at last to have no fixed principles of belief on any subject',[6] while the *British Review* said that Byron seemed to 'bring qualities of a most contradictory kind into close alliance; and so shape them into seeming union as to confound sentiments which, for the sake of sound morality and social security, should forever be kept contrasted, and at polar extremities with respect to each other'.[7] In *Nightmare Abbey*, Thomas Love Peacock makes his fictional version of Samuel Taylor Coleridge, Mr Flosky, condemn the kind of taste which was transforming such dubious figures into heroes:

> That part of the *reading public* which shuns the solid food of reason for the light diet of fiction, requires a perpetual adhibition of *sauce piquante* to the palate of its depraved imagination. It lived upon ghosts, goblins, and skeletons [...] till even the devil himself [...] became too base, common, and popular, for its surfeited appetite [...]. And now the delight of our spirits is to dwell on all the vices and blackest passions of our nature, tricked out in a masquerade dress of heroism and disappointed benevolence: the whole secret of which lies in forming combinations that contradict all our experience, and affixing the purple shred of some particular virtue to that precise character, in which we should be most certain not to find it in the living world.[8]

Mr Flosky's remark is, in fact, a fairly accurate reflection of Coleridge's own thoughts on what, by 1817, he saw as a sympathetic treatment of the outlaw hero in the works of Maturin,* Schiller and Byron. He thought that originality was something writers felt they could produce simply

> by representing the qualities of liberality, refined feeling, and a nice sense of honour […] in persons and classes where experience teaches us least to expect them; and by rewarding with all the sympathies which are due of virtue, those criminals whom law, reason, and religion have excommunicated from our esteem.[9]

By the time he began expressing himself in this way, Coleridge had become part of the conservative tendency, which is evident also in the work and opinions of his contemporaries William Wordsworth and Robert Southey. But Byron, although conscious of his own celebrity, and often tailoring his output to what he judged to be the popular demand,[10] raised in the verse-tales important issues which remove them altogether from the debasement of taste and the sensationalism of which they stood accused. In *The Corsair*, for example, he subtly interrogates the codes of behaviour by which Conrad, the hero figure, conducts himself in war and in his relationship with women.

The Corsair depicts conflict between Western and Oriental values. Conrad emerges from a mysterious past as a pirate ('corsair'), a cruel and implacable enemy preying on Turkish shipping:

> There was a laughing Devil in his sneer,
> That raised emotions both of rage and fear;
> And where his frown of hatred darkly fell,
> Hope withering fled—and Mercy sigh'd farewell! (I.223–6)

However, at the same time, Conrad exhibits a loving fidelity towards his Greek wife, Medora. He is effectively a combination of strong male

---

* Charles Robert Maturin (1782–1824), an Anglo-Irish playwright and novelist, is remembered mainly for his Faustian novel, *Melmoth the Wanderer* (1820) and his play, *Bertram*, which was staged at Drury Lane in 1816 and denounced by Coleridge as 'melancholy proof of the depravation of the public mind'.

prowess and tender sentiment which stereotypically defines heroes so familiar in fiction writing and later in film. Medora is the passive and faithful wife who, expressing herself in tears, belongs in the tradition of eighteenth-century novels of sensibility:

> O'er every feature of that still, pale face,
> Had sorrow fix'd what time can ne'er erase:
> The tender blue of that large loving eye
> Grew frozen with its gaze on vacancy,
> Till—Oh, how far!—it caught a glimpse of him,
> And then it flow'd, and phrensied seem'd to swim,
> Through those long, dark, and glistening lashes dew'd
> With drops of sadness oft to be renew'd. (I.491–8)

Together, Conrad and Medora would seem to enshrine values superior to those of the Turks, who were traditionally represented in literature as cruel and treacherous, while Byron's presentation of the Pasha's court more or less reinforces the conventional picture of the oriental potentate:

> High in his hall reclines the turban'd Seyd;
> Around—the bearded chiefs he came to lead.
> Removed the banquet, and the last pilaff—
> Forbidden draughts, 'tis said, he dared to quaff,
> Though to the rest the sober berry's juice
> The slaves bear round for rigid Moslems' use;
> The long chibouque's dissolving cloud supply,
> While dance the Almas to wild minstrelsy. (II.29–36)

As the story develops, stereotypical assumptions are called into question. The surprise attack which Conrad's corsairs launch on Seyd is a failure because, putting chivalry before military success, Conrad delays in order to rescue the women of Seyd's blazing harem. He is thrown into prison, where Seyd's mistress Gulnare, who has been saved by Conrad and has fallen in love with him, offers to help him escape.

Conrad refuses the offer for the same chivalrous reasons that motivated him to save her life. It would be against fair play towards the Pasha, and would, of course, make him indebted to a woman of dubious status, and a Turk into the bargain. In the continuing story, Gulnare murders the sleeping Pasha and, while sailing back with Conrad to his island, declares her love for him. He gives in to her charms, but on his return home finds that Medora is dead. Her death, seemingly caused by a broken heart after she learned of his fate among the Turks, has a suggestion, too, that it is the result of Conrad's betrayal of her with Gulnare. From this point on, Conrad simply vanishes in a boat and Gulnare is heard of no more.

The Corsair deliberately denies readers a satisfying conclusion, and invites questions about the role and status of its hero. It is in fact Gulnare who takes on the masculine role in the poem, as she is the one who acts on Conrad's behalf to save his life, while Conrad passively acquiesces in the satisfaction of having been true to his own chivalric code. By having Gulnare despatch the sleeping Seyd in cold blood, Byron reverses gender roles and makes her into a redemptive version of Lady Macbeth. As a slave, Gulnare has no conception of Conrad's code of honour and, in the political context of Byron's era, could arguably be construed as an active revolutionary, throwing off oppression and striking a blow against the enslavement of women. Instead of the European Conrad saving Turkish women from their oppressors, the poem puts the emphasis upon a Turkish woman, effectively a prostitute, saving a Christian from death, calling his ineffectual chivalry into question, and taking him away from his wife in the process. It was not surprising that the reactionary Poet Laureate, Robert Southey, should have referred to Byron's as a 'Satanic School' of poetry.[11]

The so-called 'Turkish Tales' are authenticated by Byron's own experience and raise issues of cultural relativism requiring readers to examine their assumptions about heroes and heroism. In *The Giaour* (1813), named as shared reading by Anne Elliot and Captain Benwick in Jane Austen's *Persuasion* (1818) (see Part Three: 'Romantic Fiction'), Byron constructs a tale which is based partly on his being witness to a Turkish punishment for a woman accused of adultery. 'Giaour' is a

Turkish word for an infidel, someone who betrays the Moslem faith, and Leila, who has betrayed Hassan, her master, with the 'hero' of the story, suffers the adulteress's fate of being tied in a sack and thrown into the sea. The un-named Giaour takes a bloody and murderous revenge upon Hassan, but in the final stages of the tale confesses to the Friar:

> Yet did he but what I had done
> Had she been false to more than one.
> Faithless to him, he gave the blow;
> But true to me, I laid him low:
> Howe'er deserved her doom might be,
> Her treachery was truth to me. (ll. 1062–7)

Byron's strategy here is to prevent readers from making a snap judgement and taking as read the moral superiority of the hero. The poem demonstrates that, although passions are shared, creeds divide and turn fraternity into enmity. The poem's fractured structure also encourages the reader to examine the story from multiple points of view, since different perspectives are provided in the individual fragments making up the narrative of what Byron calls this 'broken tale' (l. 1333).

Milton's Satan and Rousseau's 'Discourse on Inequality'

In addition to those readings of Milton's poem which transformed Satan from anti-hero to object of admiration, *Paradise Lost* was also of interest to the Romantics' developing preoccupation with the origins and nature of man. Milton describes both the creation and the fall of man, but ends with the promise of a third stage in human history where Christ, the second Adam, will come to redeem Man's fallen condition. At his second coming, on the Day of Judgement, the Messiah will reward the faithful and, in the Archangel Michael's words,

> receive them into bliss,
> Whether in heaven or earth, for then the earth

Shall all be paradise, far happier place
Than this of Eden, and far happier days. (XII.462–5)

Yet, before he expels Adam and Eve from paradise, Michael provides another perspective on the future, advising Adam that by adding virtues to his new-found knowledge, he will enjoy a much higher form of happiness than was ever his experience in the Garden of Eden:

> only add
> Deeds to thy knowledge answerable, add faith,
> Add virtue, patience, temperance, add love,
> By name to come called charity, the soul
> Of all the rest: then wilt thou not be loath
> To leave this paradise, but shalt possess
> A paradise within thee, happier far. (XII.581–7)

By the dictates of his source in Genesis, Milton could not, of course, suggest any alternative to Christ as man's only hope of redemption. But, as the Romantic period read it, Michael's implication seems to be that Adam's true happiness is not only located within his own mind, but also placed within his own reach. Indeed, earlier in the poem, Milton had made Satan describe the sense of his loss in hell as more one of a mental condition than a physical deprivation.* What interested the Romantics was to read in Milton the prospect of paradise being internalised: 'then wilt thou not be loath / To leave this paradise, but shalt possess / A paradise within thee, happier far'. In his Prospectus to *The Recluse*,[12] Wordsworth would write that the mind 'Once wedded to this outward frame of things' was capable of making its own paradise, and that his own voice, in words which speak 'of nothing more than what we are', would proclaim this very possibility.

The secularisation of the biblical promise had been prepared for much earlier in the work of Jean-Jacques Rousseau, particularly in his *Second Discourse on the Origins and Foundations of Inequality Among Men*

---

* See *Paradise Lost*, IV.18–23 and 73–5: 'Me miserable! Which way shall I fly / Infinite wrath, and infinite despair? / Which way I fly is hell; myself am hell'.

(1755). In Rousseau's hypothetical history of mankind, man's primitive state of nature recalls his situation in the biblical Garden of Eden, while his entry into civil society effectively corresponds with the traditional story of the Fall. However, unlike Milton in *Paradise Lost*, Rousseau does not envisage a third stage of human history. The legacy of his work during the Romantic period was to raise the question: how might the advantages of nature and of civilisation at some future stage be combined? For example, Blake's *Innocence and Experience* lyrics are one such attempt to synthesise into a higher form of organised innocence what Blake himself called the 'Two Contrary States of the Human Soul'.

Rousseau's philosophy encouraged a humanisation of the myth of the Fall. By effectively considering man to be no more than a higher form of animal, he had a much more radically primitive notion than Milton of the original human condition. But where *Paradise Lost* follows Genesis in limiting man's future to God's disposal, Rousseau's reductive vision of man in his original state also made possible later Romantic hopes of his being able to make something better of himself. In other words, man was no longer immutable in terms of his place in the scheme of things, but was capable of improving and developing, advancing into unimaginable territories and perhaps even becoming God-like in the process.

The Figure of Prometheus

In the light of such prospects, therefore, one of the myths the Romantics scrutinised very closely, and which for them became a complex pattern of symbolic meanings, was that of Prometheus. Prometheus had more than one persona. In the better known of his two roles he was the Titan in the Golden Age of Saturn, whose name meant 'foresight', and who being thus able to foresee the outcome of the eventual war between Saturn and his son, Jupiter, saved himself by switching sides. After the deposition of Saturn, the new regime became one of terrible oppression, as Jupiter's tyranny made him oblivious to the sufferings of his subjects.

Prometheus had compassion and brought fire to men by lighting a torch at the chariot of the sun. His gift, however, turned out to be a mixed blessing in that it enabled, for the first time, such things as flesh to be cooked, money coined and weapons forged. In other words, the stories of the Titanic wars and Prometheus as fire bringer ('Prometheus Pyrphoros'), represent mythic versions of man's fall from his state of primal innocence into one of so-called 'civilisation'. Jupiter's response to Prometheus's action was to bind him to a mountain in the Caucasus where every day an eagle (in some versions, a vulture) would eat out his endlessly repairing liver.

Both Byron and Shelley were drawn to the legend, Byron writing his own poem 'Prometheus' (1817), and Shelley, *Prometheus Unbound* (1820), his version of the lost play of Aeschylus. But Mary Shelley, in *Frankenstein, or The Modern Prometheus* (1818), would go on to make use of a later, Roman, account of the myth. In this version, known as 'Prometheus Plasticator', Prometheus is a skilful craftsman, taking earth and water together and moulding the shapes of men from the clay he produces. The myth describes how Prometheus gives animation to these forms with the fire he has stolen, just as Mary Shelley, in the novel, has Frankenstein employ electricity to galvanise what she called her 'hideous progeny' into life.

Prometheus is a multi-faceted symbol for rebellion and suffering, as well as for endurance and creativity, and in the Romantic period his legend provides an appropriate mythic context in which to construct and give definition to heroic figures such as Napoleon. Byron, in his 'Ode to Napoleon Buonaparte' (1814), writes of the exiled emperor in exactly these terms:

> All sense is with thy sceptre gone,
> Life will not long confine
> That spirit poured so widely forth—
> So long obeyed—so little worth!
>
> Or like the thief of fire from heaven,
> Wilt thou withstand the shock?

And share with him, the unforgiven,
His vulture and his rock! (ll. 132–9)

Beethoven, Byron's contemporary, wrote an overture, *Prometheus*, and a ballet, *Die Geschöpfe des Prometheus* (1801), which being mainly about the creation of mankind takes its inspiration from the Prometheus story as a creation myth. A theme from the ballet's finale was later used as the chief subject in the finale of the Eroica ('the heroic') symphony, whose original dedication to Napoleon was withdrawn by Beethoven after Napoleon crowned himself emperor in 1804.

In the Romantic period it was not difficult to enlist the heroic enterprise of Prometheus as a way of understanding the role of the Romantic hero. In the revolutionary climate of the late eighteenth and early nineteenth centuries, the Romantic artist is often seen as a Promethean figure who, resisting the oppressive forms of society and fired by imagination, foresees a future in which all such repression will be overthrown. The great historical movements of the age, the American War of Independence and the French Revolution, were easily construed in terms of the myth as new democratic societies rose, like the forces which had deposed Saturn in the war of the Titans, toppling what had seemed previously unassailable (see Part Three: 'Writing in Revolution'). Even in a Romantic re-reading of *Paradise Lost*, it is possible to fuse Satan with Prometheus in that both, as examples of heroism, supplant passive or repressive orthodoxies with their imaginative energies. In fact, Satan through his name 'Lucifer' or 'bearer of light', becomes another version of Prometheus 'pyrphoros', the 'bearer of fire'. In the dedication of his play *The Fall of Robespierre*, written in collaboration with Southey in 1794, Coleridge writes that he has 'endeavoured to detail [...] the fall of a man, whose great bad actions have cast a disastrous lustre on his name'.[13] Robespierre is described as

Sudden in action, fertile in resource,
And rising awful 'mid impending ruins;
In splendor gloomy, as the midnight meteor,
That fearless thwarts the elemental war.[14]

285

These lines echo the description of Satan in Book I of *Paradise Lost*, where he

> above the rest
> In shape and gesture proudly eminent
> Stood like a tower; his form had not yet lost
> All her original brightness, nor appeared
> Less than arch angel ruined, and the excess
> Of glory obscured. (I.589–94)

Coleridge here presents a heroic version of a Robespierre, like Milton's Satan, unbowed by what he has brought upon himself. His collaborator Southey, in a letter contemporary with the production of the play, writes of how Coleridge had referred to Robespierre as 'the benefactor of mankind'.[15] In Coleridge's mind, it is clear that Robespierre is imaged as both Prometheus *and* Satan, one the benefactor of his race, and the other a rebel who keeps something of his 'original brightness', just as Robespierre's 'great bad actions', described in the Preface, have tarnished, but not entirely obscured, his 'lustre'.

In their own respective versions of the Prometheus myth, Shelley and Byron draw apart, like the figures of Julian and Maddalo in Shelley's poem which opposes Shelleyan optimism to Byronic pessimism (see Part Three: Romantic Verse Narrative). Byron's 'Prometheus' presents the Titan as the unjustly punished would-be benefactor whose 'Godlike crime was to be kind' (l. 35):

> What was thy pity's recompense?
> A silent suffering, and intense;
> The rock, the vulture, and the chain,
> All that the proud can feel of pain. (ll. 5–8)

Byron's concept of Prometheus is like that of one of his own hero figures: a being, part godlike, but with human weaknesses. There is a sense that he identifies personally with the suffering of the outcast victim:

Thou art a symbol and a sign
To Mortals of their fate and force;
Like thee, Man is in part divine,
A troubled stream from a pure source. (ll. 45–8)

Byron's admiration is based on Prometheus's victory, as he sees it. In a metaphysical sense, it is a refusal to submit to 'the inexorable Heaven, / And the deaf tyranny of Fate' (ll. 18–19), and to go to one's grave 'Triumphant' by 'making Death a Victory' (ll. 58–9). In the more political sense, it is to oppose oneself to all forms of oppression and 'The ruling principle of Hate' (l. 20). The ruling principle on which Shelley bases his construction of *Prometheus Unbound* is that hatred narrows perception. Prometheus, in forgiving his oppressor, sets in motion a process which leads to a new world, freed from the oppressions which all along have been ones of his own making. Byron's handling of the myth puts the emphasis exclusively upon defiance, whereas Shelley's version focuses upon transformation, made possible by the act of forgiveness.

Frankenstein, the 'Modern Prometheus'

Myths were the vehicles by which men originally represented archetypal situations and, in the Romantic period, the concept of creation in the Prometheus story was seen to be relevant in a variety of different contexts. Richard Holmes, in *The Age of Wonder*, describes a series of lectures delivered by Humphry Davy to the Royal Society in 1802, and remarks on how Davy's 'Discourse Introductory to a Course of Lectures on Chemistry' became 'a Romantic statement on the progressive role of science in society'. Drawing on previous conversations he had had with Coleridge, Davy presented to his audience a vision of a future for mankind where man, freed from his superstitions and his passive subjection to nature, would become an active agent for scientific development and the improvement of his own condition. As Holmes comments, 'This was in effect Davy's version of the Prometheus myth.'[16]

Mary Shelley, in *Frankenstein, or The Modern Prometheus* (1818), takes the scientist 'hero' as her subject, but instead of celebrating, as Davy had done, the promise of future enlightenment, she explores the dark obverse of Romantic Prometheanism in Frankenstein's chilling potential to destroy worlds and desolate human happiness.[*] (See also Part Three: 'Romantic Fiction'.)

Dr Frankenstein, the scientist-creator or natural philosopher of Mary Shelley's day, is at once both divine and Satanic. His role as a 'modern Prometheus' associates him with the pagan creation myth, while in his ability to give life to his Creature he effectively usurps the role of God. At the same time, Frankenstein is motivated by Satan's pride as well as his ambition for power: 'What a glorious creature must he have been in the days of his prosperity,' writes the character Walton to his sister, 'when he is thus noble and godlike in ruin! He seems to feel his own worth, and the greatness of his fall.'[17] Where Shelley gave to his Prometheus figure a straightforwardly moral part to play, Mary Shelley constructs her modern Prometheus as morally ambiguous and a challenge to the reader's response. Frankenstein has much in common with the Byronic hero, and it is perhaps significant that, as she conceived her novel and worked on it in the Genevan summer of 1816, Mary Shelley was continuously in the company of both Shelley and Byron. Her close experience of two such gifted and creative spirits is likely to have conditioned the ways in which she was thinking about the heroic or exceptional individual. Shelley would give perhaps the most famous definition in Romantic literature to the idea of the 'poet as hero' in *A Defence of Poetry* (1821):

> Poets are the hierophants of an unapprehended inspiration, the mirrors of the gigantic shadows which futurity casts upon the present, the words which express what they understand not, the trumpets which sing to battle and feel not what they inspire: the

---

[*] According to Anne K. Mellor, Mary Shelley probably read Davy's lecture on Monday, 28 October 1816, 'just before working on her story of Frankenstein'. Anne K. Mellor, *Mary Shelley: Her Life, Her Fiction, Her Monsters* (London: Routledge, 1989), p. 91.

influence which is moved not, but moves. Poets are the unacknowledged legislators of the world.

Yet in Shelley's mind there is always a conflict between his dream of perfectibility and his sense of self as a creature trapped in what he called 'the loathsome mask' of the flesh.[18] Anne K. Mellor argues that Mary Shelley embodied in Dr Frankenstein those troubling aspects of Shelley's personality which most gave her concern, his 'emotional narcissism, an unwillingness to confront the origins of his own desires [and] the impact of his demands on those most dependent on him'.[19] These are all recognisable features in Frankenstein's temperament as he pursues, like Shelley, his consuming quest for the realisation of an ideal. Mellor points out that the positive elements of Shelley of which Mary approved, his refined mind, love of nature, fascination with languages and, above all, his capacity for empathy, are all contained in the character of Frankenstein's friend, Clerval. But once Clerval has been murdered, only those elements remained of the things she most feared 'in both her husband and in the Romantic project he served'.[20]

Nicola Trott suggests that Frankenstein's temperamental instability, his 'phases of frenzy and lassitude, intoxication and disgust' are characteristic of Romantic ideas about the moods of creative genius.[21] Frankenstein's elation, too, at the prospect of bringing to fruition a dream he had cherished since childhood, raises additional issues about the link commonly made in the Romantic period between creativity and the imagination of the child.

In Romantic literature the 'child as hero' occurs prominently in Wordsworth's 'Immortality Ode' (1807), where it becomes 'best Philosopher', a 'Mighty Prophet! Seer blest! / On whom those truths do rest, / Which we are toiling all our lives to find'.[22] In Scripture, St Matthew writes of how Jesus 'called a little child unto him, and set him in the midst of them, And said, Verily I say unto you, Except ye be converted, and become as little children, ye shall not enter into the kingdom of heaven.'[23] The Romantic period secularises Christ's theme, and while the period itself did not discover the potential of children to act as mentors to their elders, its literature frequently privileges the visionary capacity of the child as something to be emulated in the pursuit of a better society. The hero of Mary Shelley's novel recounts how 'Curiosity, earnest research to learn the hidden laws of nature, gladness akin to rapture, as they were unfolded to [him]', were 'among the earliest sensations' he could remember. Therefore, by informing Frankenstein's scientific endeavours, the child becomes truly 'Father of the Man'[24] and points towards an unlimited creative potential. Frankenstein describes how, in his earliest days, his passions were turned 'not towards childish pursuits but to an eager desire to learn'.[25] By realising a young dream in bringing his Creature into being, Frankenstein exemplifies the Romantic artist who, as creator, takes inspiration from childhood. However, in his own creative role, he is unable to stand back and admire his handiwork like God in Genesis.* His creation fills him with horror and, instead of facing up to his moral responsibilities, his first instinct is to abandon his Creature and flee from the consequences of what he has produced.

Mary Shelley seems here to be taking a more critical, even a cynical, view of the child as paradigm for Romantic creativity. Frankenstein's preferred option is to carry his childhood fantasies into his adult life and, rather than taking on the role of father in a mature relationship, to avoid procreation in the normal way. By creating life without any need to share in the privilege of parenthood, and thus being able to focus the glory of his achievement solely upon himself, Frankenstein becomes the very type of the self-absorbed Romantic 'hero', raising serious questions about his maturity, as well as the status of the child as role model in Romanticism.

In a passage of the *Defence of Poetry*, about the processes of poetical composition, Shelley describes the gap that exists between the original inspiration of the poet and the disappointing form to which that inspiration is reduced:

> When composition begins, inspiration is already on the decline, and the most glorious poetry that has ever been communicated to

---

* 'And God saw every thing that he had made, and behold, it was very good', Genesis 1:31.

the world is probably a feeble shadow of the original conceptions of the poet.

Frankenstein's experience is exactly analogous. His mind continues to be possessed by 'beautiful idealisms',* and he believes that the success of his Promethean imagination will be measured by its ability to 'pour a torrent of light into our dark world' (p. 54). The hideous form his creation takes, however, is a constant reminder to him of the 'loathsome mask' and limitations of his own flesh.

Critical Perspectives on *Frankenstein*

Feminist Approaches

Anne Mellor's feminist approach to *Frankenstein* examines how the novel shows the consequences of a social construction of gender that values men over women. Mellor, focusing on Mary Shelley's knowledge of the self-indulgent self-image of the poet-writer as hero, argues that Mary's observations of Shelley, Byron and her own father, William Godwin, had given her first-hand experience of how dangerous their neglect in matters of real human concern could be. As one might expect from the daughter of Mary Wollstonecraft, Mary Shelley presents Frankenstein's society as one where men are privileged over women, acting as public servants, scientists, merchants and explorers, with the women reduced to taking a subservient role, such as that of housewife, nurse, servant and child-care provider. Frankenstein's later destruction of the female Creature is, in Mellor's argument, his conscious decision based on a male fear of the power of women. She rehearses Frankenstein's apprehensions about the work he had undertaken, among them, the possibility that the female might refuse to comply with a social contract made on her behalf, and before her birth, by another person, and Frankenstein's fear, too, that her

---

* See P. B. Shelley, 'beautiful idealisms of moral excellence', Preface to *Prometheus Unbound*.

reproductive powers will give her the capacity to generate a race which might then go on to populate the entire earth. Anne Mellor points to the significance of the Oedipal dream in Chapter 5, in which Frankenstein embracing, as he thinks, his future bride Elizabeth, discovers that she has turned into the corpse of his dead mother. The episode anticipates the actual death of Elizabeth on the wedding night, when Frankenstein, sending her alone into their bedroom, puts her at the Creature's mercy. 'I earnestly entreated her to retire,' he says, 'resolving not to join her until I had obtained some knowledge as to the situation of my enemy' (p. 195). In his use of the word, 'knowledge', Frankenstein seems to choose his Creature over Elizabeth and, as Mellor argues, desires his bride only when he knows she is dead. This represents in him a necrophiliac desire to possess the dead female, and thus, by possessing nature (the lost mother) allow Frankenstein himself to become a mother.

From the feminist perspective, Frankenstein is thus the epitome of the male anti-hero whose Creature becomes the instrument by which he can usurp female reproductive power and permit only men to rule. Mary Shelley's language for Frankenstein's experiment is appropriately sexualised. As a student at Ingolstadt University, Frankenstein learns from the lectures of M. Waldman how the modern men of science 'penetrate into the recesses of nature, and show how she works in her hiding places' (p. 47). Accordingly, Frankenstein himself develops into the scientific male 'hero' whose activities represent a usurpation and violent penetration, amounting effectively to nothing less than a rape of nature.

But Frankenstein does not go unpunished for his violations. Nature takes her revenge by reducing him to a physical shadow and afflicting his mental health. He undergoes prolonged periods of sickness and nervous disorder, as well as being made the victim of tumult and upheaval in the elements. Like the poet-hero in Shelley's *Alastor* (1816), Frankenstein is pursued by the consequences of what he has chosen to pursue. Even the electricity with which he gave life to his creation returns as his nemesis in the lightning and storms which, at intervals, rage around him. Far from being the gratuitous effects of a sensational gothic novel, these atmospheric episodes, Anne Mellor argues, 'manifest the power of nature to punish those who transgress her boundaries'.[26]

Mary Shelley's concept throughout the novel is to offset the essentially male impulse to manipulate and control nature with a feminine responsiveness, and to put in place an understanding that is content simply to describe and revere. In *A Defence of Poetry*, Shelley, like Mary in *Frankenstein*, speaks presciently of how 'We want the creative faculty to imagine that which we know' and of how advances in technology have outstripped man's capacity to accommodate them:

> The cultivation of those sciences which have enlarged the limits of the empire of man over the external world, has, for want of the poetical faculty, proportionally circumscribed those of the internal world, and man, having enslaved the elements, remains himself a slave.

Frankenstein: A Modern Parable

Mary Shelley's novel is a warning of the dangers inherent in the mentality directing the grandiose designs of Romantic heroes such as Frankenstein. His monomaniacal obsession with fame and power results, on his own admission, in a haste to complete his creation: 'As the minuteness of the parts formed a great hindrance to my speed, I resolved, contrary to my first intention, to make the being of a gigantic stature' (pp. 53–4). The project results in the creation of something so big that the creator is no longer able to control it. Shelley's 'man, having enslaved the elements remains himself a slave', is called to mind when, later, Frankenstein is led to speak of that 'whole period during which [he] was the slave of [his] creature' (p. 153). As Marilyn Butler writes, 'Mary Shelley's *Frankenstein* is famously reinterpretable',[27] and the tyranny of the nuclear weapon, here anticipated in Frankenstein's conception of becoming the slave to his own monstrous creation, is perhaps a good example of the novel speaking relevantly to times beyond its own. The physicist Robert Oppenheimer's 'Now I am become Death, the destroyer of worlds',* is easily recognised in Frankenstein's own anxiety, expressed over a hundred years previously:

> I had been the author of unalterable evils; and I lived in daily fear, lest the monster whom I had created should perpetrate some new wickedness. I had an obscure feeling that all was not over, and that he would still commit some signal crime, which by its enormity should almost efface the recollection of the past.
>
> (pp. 91–2)

Oppenheimer's remark in a letter to his brother, 'I need physics more than friends',[28] recalls the terrible repercussions for Frankenstein of sacrificing family and friends to an all-consuming quest, and Mary Shelley constructs his admonitory role in relation to Walton, in terms of the Ancient Mariner's to the Wedding-Guest of Coleridge's poem. When Walton says, 'I would sacrifice my fortune, my every hope, to the furtherance of my enterprise' and that 'One man's death were but a small price to pay for the acquirement which I sought', Frankenstein responds, 'Have you drank also of the intoxicating draught? Hear me, – let me reveal my tale, and you will dash the cup from your lips!' (p. 28). The dangerous and unforeseeable consequences of 'thinking big' is one valuable legacy that Mary Shelley's version of the Romantic hero has given to our own vivid and apocalyptic times.

Psychoanalytical Approaches

Frankenstein's predicament also lends itself to psychoanalytical approaches, and Andrew Roberts writes persuasively on the novel in terms of its concept of 'non-separateness and omnipotence'.[29] *Frankenstein* is essentially a work about creativity in its various forms, that of the scientist, the mother and the writer, and Frankenstein's replacement of the natural birth process with his own creativity evokes

---

* Robert Oppenheimer's quotation from the *Bhagavad-gita* after the first atomic test in 1945. Oppenheimer was the director of the project to develop the first nuclear weapons.

the uncanny. According to Roberts it has the effect of making birth itself seem uncanny, and here it might be added that a man's creation of a 'monster' fully formed and with no knowledge of a mother anticipates that of another form of uncanny creation, Heathcliff, in Emily Brontë's *Wuthering Heights*. To all intents and purposes, Heathcliff, a Romantic anti-hero and a kind of 'monster' in his own right, has no family and has had no childhood to speak of. In Nelly Dean's account, his appearance at the Heights was sudden. Mr Earnshaw, back from his journey to Liverpool, 'opening his great coat' in a kind of parody of the birth process, produces a child which 'when it was set on its feet [...] only stared round, and repeated over and over again some gibberish that nobody could understand' (Chapter 4).

In his discussion of Mary Shelley's novel, Roberts examines Frankenstein's own family background as being of crucial importance in forming the response of the creator to his Creature. He identifies in the desexualised marriage of his parents the prototype of Frankenstein's own relationship with Elizabeth, while relationships in the Frankenstein family, in general, are also sentimentalised by a lack of conflict, with aggression being sublimated into such things as 'justice, moral approval, gratitude, worship, reverence and compassion'.[30] In his essay, Roberts draws on the psychoanalytical theory of D. W. Winnicott,[31] who describes both infantile development and adult creative processes in terms of the fantasy of omnipotence. As someone 'whose future lot it was in [his parents'] hands to direct to happiness or misery' (pp. 33–4), Frankenstein develops an identical concept of omnipotence. He comes to believe that he can shape the world according to his own conceptions of it, just as the infant is given a brief experience of omnipotence when all its immediate demands are complied with. Frankenstein, for whom reality depends on his idealistic imaginings, is consequently unprepared for the separateness of his Creature, from whom he expects gratitude. When he is confronted by its reality and human needs, he abandons it, as if he believes it possible to make it disappear by the same act of imagination with which he had brought it into being.

A close analogy here is with Macbeth, for whom the mind becomes the only reality and never ceases working. Macbeth seeks release by intensifying his efforts to make the whole world exactly like his mind: 'Strange things I have in head that will to hand' (III.iv.138); 'The very firstlings of my heart shall be / The firstlings of my hand' (IV.i.147–8). Roberts argues that if we continue to believe at some subliminal level that only our minds give the world meaning then, as Coleridge describes in 'Dejection: An Ode', 'when inspiration is lacking, or when spirits fail, the world threatens to become meaningless'.[32] This is exactly the case with Macbeth, for whom life comes to be no more than 'a tale / Told by an idiot, full of sound and fury, / Signifying nothing' (V.v.26–8). Shakespeare anticipates in *Macbeth* what is often the hero's experience in Romantic literature: isolation, increasing solipsism, ever-intensifying relativism, the sense that man is an irrelevance in the vast reaches of time and space, and an agonising preoccupation with the mind and the self.

In his treatment of *Frankenstein* as a study of 'desire and repression',[33] Roberts describes how the Creature becomes an example of, in Freud's phrase, 'the return of the repressed'. He points out that, although Frankenstein continually opposes the 'beauty, purity, innocence, and harmony'[34] of his family to the ugly deformity of his Creature, the Creature emerges from within his family as a symptom of all that Frankenstein has repressed and believes to have been harmlessly sublimated in his scientific pursuits. Given the sentimentalised nature of his human relationships, the wedding night in *Frankenstein* is 'very dreadful' (p. 194) because it brings tragically to the surface what has so long been repressed in the psyche of its hero. Byron, with whom, as we saw at the beginning of this chapter, the term 'Romantic hero' is most closely associated, clearly saw a fantasy and immaturity in a strand of Romantic literature he had himself encouraged. Like Keats, taking leave of romance to emulate in his poetry the sterner realities of Shakespearean tragedy,[35] he would eventually turn from the heroes of his own creation to find in *Don Juan* a healthier and more recognisable world of 'things existent'.[36]

Notes

1   William and Dorothy Wordsworth, *The Early Letters of William and Dorothy Wordsworth, 1787–1805*, ed. Ernest de Selincourt (Oxford: Clarendon Press, 1935), p. 489.
2   Angus Calder, *Byron* (Milton Keynes: Open University Press, 1987), p. 13.
3   Max Beerbohm, *The Poets' Corner* (1904).
4   Marilyn Butler, *Romantics, Rebels and Reactionaries: English Literature and its Background 1760–1830* (Oxford: Oxford University Press, 1981), p. 118.
5   Donald H. Reiman (ed.), *The Romantics Reviewed: Contemporary Reviews of British Romantic Writers*, 9 vols (New York: Garland, 1972), vol. 2, p. 670.
6   Ibid., vol. 1, p. 119.
7   Ibid., vol. 1, p. 453.
8   Thomas Love Peacock, *Nightmare Abbey*, ed. Lisa Vargo (Peterborough, Ont. and Orchard Park, NY: Broadview Press, 2007), pp. 77–8.
9   S. T. Coleridge, *Biographia Literaria* (Scolar Press, 1971), pp. 271–2.
10   See Philip W. Martin, *Byron: A Poet before his Public* (Cambridge: Cambridge University Press, 1982).
11   Preface to *A Vision of Judgement* (1821).
12   William Wordsworth, *The Poetical Works of William Wordsworth*, ed. E. de Selincourt and H. Darbishire, 6 vols (Oxford: Clarendon Press, 1949), vol. 5, p. 338.
13   Samuel Taylor Coleridge, *The Complete Poetical Works of Samuel Taylor Coleridge*, ed. Earl Leslie Griggs, 2 vols (Oxford: Clarendon Press, 1956), vol. 2, p. 495.
14   Ibid., p. 496.
15   Robert Southey, *New Letters of Robert Southey*, ed. K. Curry, 2 vols (New York and London: Columbia University Press, 1965), vol. 1, p. 73.
16   Richard Holmes, *The Age of Wonder: How the Romantic Generation Discovered the Beauty and Terror of Science* (London: Harper Press, 2008), p. 288.
17   Mary Shelley, *Frankenstein*, ed. M. K. Joseph (Oxford: Oxford University Press, 1983), p. 210.
18   *Prometheus Unbound*, III.iv.193.
19   Anne K. Mellor, *Mary Shelley: Her Life, Her Fiction, Her Monsters* (London: Routledge, 1989), p. 73.
20   Ibid., p. 75.
21   Nicholas Roe (ed.), *Romanticism: An Oxford Guide* (Oxford: Oxford University Press, 2005), p. 498.

22   'Ode: Intimations of Immortality from Recollections of Early Childhood', ll. 110, 114–16.

23   Matthew 18:2–3.

24   Wordsworth, 'My Heart Leaps Up When I Behold'.

25   Mary Shelley, *Frankenstein*, pp. 36, 37.

26   Mellor, *Mary Shelley*, p. 123.

27   Marilyn Butler, 'The first *Frankenstein* and Radical Science', *Times Literary Supplement*, 9 April 1993, pp. 12–14.

28   Robert Oppenheimer, *Letters and Recollections*, ed. Alice Kimball Smith and Charles Weiner (Cambridge, Mass.: Harvard University Press, 1980), p. 135.

29   Roe (ed.), *Romanticism*, pp. 230–4.

30   Ibid., p. 231.

31   D. W. Winnicott, *The Child, the Family and the Outside World* (Harmondsworth: Penguin, 1964).

32   Roe (ed.), *Romanticism*, p. 233.

33   Ibid., p. 230.

34   Ibid., p. 234.

35   Keats, Sonnet, 'On Sitting Down to Read *King Lear* Once Again'.

36   Byron, *Don Juan*, XV, stanza 87.

Forms of Ruin

English literature of the eighteenth century often reflects the optimism and confidence that underpinned a belief that England was coming to have an imperial destiny. Corresponding with the 'Pax Romana' established by the emperor Augustus and prevailing in the first two centuries is the 'Pax Brittanica', celebrated at the conclusion of Alexander Pope's 'Windsor Forest' (1713), where trees, now made into ships, transmit it to the New World, and carry the peace and plenty of the reign of Queen Anne across the Atlantic to 'Earth's distant ends'.

However, as Gibbon's *The History of the Decline and Fall of the Roman Empire* (1776–88)* reminded Britain, wealth and power often prefigure a demise, and the relics of antiquity were still visual evidences of earlier, now fallen, regimes. One of the fashions of the period was the deliberate creation of sham castles, eyecatchers and ruins within great parks and estates, structures often known as 'follies', which seem to have had more significance than simply playfulness in an age of reason, or as a means of adding enchantment to a distant view. To catch sight of a ruined edifice, in the midst of a display of prosperity, would perhaps remind the wealthy patrician that modern empires, if they were to avoid the same fate of many others throughout history, needed the accompaniment of a constant moral vigilance.

---

*   Edward Gibbon (1737–94), historian and MP, published *The History of the Decline and Fall of the Roman Empire* in six volumes between 1776 and 1788.

Reading the Ruins

In 1845 Joseph Severn, the friend of John Keats, painted a portrait of Percy Bysshe Shelley writing his verse-drama, *Prometheus Unbound*, on the ruins of the Baths of Caracalla in Rome. Shelley did in fact write part of the work in that setting, although Severn's is an imaginary picture done many years after Shelley's death. Shelley's radical political persuasions led him to regard the ruins with some optimism. Here was visible testimony to the fact that, no matter how powerful and immovable they seem to be, empires and tyrannies tend not to prevail for ever.

An important contemporary book, well known to Shelley, was *The Ruins* by the French philosopher, historian and politician Constantin Volney (see Part Three: 'Revolution, Reaction and the Natural World'),* whose meditations on history led him to conclude that all human societies are destined to decay. In fact, Mary Shelley ensures that Frankenstein's Creature obtains his 'cursory knowledge of history' by reading Volney's *Ruins*, in which he learns of how, among other things, the 'wonderful virtue of the early Romans' degenerated with the 'decline of that mighty empire'.[1]

In Severn's picture Shelley sits, one hand pointing to his temple, as though to indicate the psychological nature of the drama he is writing, the other holding a pen, poised above the notebook resting on his knee. The painting might be compared with Tischbein's study of Goethe in the Roman Campagna, painted almost a hundred years previously. There Goethe, in a wide-brimmed hat, sits amidst the ruins of ancient Rome musing on the fate of human achievement. His white cloak gives him a timeless sculptural quality and, among the fragments scattered around is a relief with Iphigenia, Orestes and Pylades, a reference to the

---

*   Constantin Volney (1757–1820): *The Ruins, or A Survey of the Revolutions of Empires* (1791, 1792). Volney travelled among the ruins of Egypt and Syria and made a study of comparative religion. His vision of a new, free humanist society in France made him a congenial figure for Shelley, whose programmes for reform were conceived along similar lines.

verse-drama *Iphigenie auf Tauris* on which he was working while in
Rome. The painting is a monument to the neo-classical movement and
Tischbein's depiction of Goethe's posture in the landscape suggests his
reverence for, and deference to, the grandeur of antiquity.

In Severn's painting, the relaxed attitude of Shelley, accentuated by
his large straw hat carelessly thrown to one side, as well as by his
Jacobin's open-necked shirt, suggests the poet's more comfortable
relationship with his own classical source, the lost Prometheus play of
Aeschylus, which he is in the process of 're-creating'. The picture implies
that Shelley looks to a future world freed from its obligations to the
past and from the burden of antiquity.

In a letter to Thomas Love Peacock, Shelley talks of the beauty of
the ruins of the Baths of Caracalla whose 'labyrinthine recesses' are
'hidden and woven over by the wild growth of weeds and ivy'. 'Never',
he says, 'was any desolation more sublime and lovely.'[2] In the Preface to
Prometheus Unbound, he describes his poem being 'chiefly written upon
the mountainous ruins of the Baths of Caracalla, among the flowery
glades, and thickets of odoriferous blossoming trees, which are extended
in ever winding labyrinths upon its immense platforms and dizzy arches
suspended in the air'. Shelley's biographer, Richard Holmes, writes of
how 'external images which express mental states and process, dominate
the language' of *Prometheus Unbound*. 'There is a sense', he writes, 'in
which the whole action is metaphysical rather than physical, and in
which the setting of the drama is not so much the universe at large but
the dome of a single human skull.' Holmes suggests that the ruins of
the Baths would sometimes seem to Shelley 'like an immense cranial
chamber',[3] and the setting itself, in Holmes's view, becomes appropriate
to the position Shelley adopts on the subject of tyranny in general. It is
by internalising responsibility that man becomes the agent of his own
oppression. His 'manacles', in Blake's terms, are 'mind-forged',[4] and the
drama that Shelley writes takes its direction from the act of forgiveness
by which, early in the action, Prometheus is able to unbind himself. As
Shelley writes in *Julian and Maddalo*, 'it is our will / That thus enchains
us to permitted ill. [...] if we were not weak / Should we be less in deed
than in desire?'[5] (see Part Three: 'Romantic Verse Narrative').

The 'cranial' chambers of the Baths make an interesting environment for the composition of Shelley's verse psycho-drama, while the 'Fragment: Rome and Nature', published by Mary Shelley in 1839, indicates how the poet takes heart from the way in which natural growth gradually encroaches on ruins like those among which it is being written:

> Rome has fallen, ye see it lying
> Heaped in undistinguished ruin:
> Nature is alone undying.[6]

A comparison might here be drawn with the final act of *Macbeth*, where the green boughs of Birnam Wood advancing upon the castle of Dunsinane symbolise nature's power to overwhelm the protagonist who, throughout the play, has set himself in opposition to nature, to the values it represents and to the life processes which are made possible by it.

In Canto II of *Childe Harold*, Byron presents his eponymous hero at large amidst the remnants of an earlier civilisation (see Part Three: Romantic Travel Writing). Standing on the Acropolis in Athens, the Childe picks up a skull 'from out the scattered heaps' and, in a traditional form of meditation, Byron is led by the situation to speculate on the puzzling conflict between man's godlike potential and his corrupted remains: 'Is that a temple where a God may dwell? / Why ev'n the worm at last disdains her shatter'd cell!'[7] As the meditation continues, the human skull is presented as a form of architectural ruin where the reader is taken on a conducted tour around, and then into, the bony construction: 'Look on its broken arch, its ruin'd wall. / Its chambers desolate, and portals foul'. The passage continues:

> Yes, this was once Ambition's airy hall,
> The dome of Thought, the palace of the Soul:
> Behold through each lack-lustre, eyeless hole,
> The gay recess of Wisdom and of Wit
> And passion's host that never brook'd control:

Can all, saint, sage, or sophist ever writ,
People this lonely tower, this tenement refit? (II.48–52)

As well as recalling the mysterious occupant of Milton's 'lonely tower' in 'Il Penseroso',[8] the lines obviously allude to Hamlet's speculations on the unearthed skulls of a courtier, a lawyer and the jester, Yorick (V.i), and are written in a mode associated also with the Graveyard Poets of the eighteenth century, in poems such as 'The Grave' of Robert Blair (1743) or James Hervey's 'Meditations Among the Tombs' (1746). As they stand, therefore, the lines are essentially retrospective and derive from a tradition of writings on a time-honoured theme, reflected prominently in the example of Dr Johnson's poem 'The Vanity of Human Wishes' (1749). Later in *Childe Harold*, as the Childe tours the ruins of Rome, Byron presents his hero's reflections on the Coliseum, whose 'colossal fabric's form' (IV.1285) is presented in terms of a human skull. But where Richard Holmes sees in the Baths of Caracalla an 'immense cranial chamber', suggestive of Shelley's innovative handling of his mythic source, and where Shelley himself celebrates nature's triumph over the ruins of empire, the 'garland-forest, which the grey walls wear' (IV.1292) produce from Byron only the supremely commonplace image of 'laurels on the bald first Caesar's head' (IV.1293). The reclamation by nature of Roman remains, for Shelley a symbol of optimism, provides for Byron, in this context, simply an opportunity to reflect on the tragic and cyclical processes of history, where the fates of more recent empires, together with their despots like Napoleon, are foreshadowed in the ruins of much earlier ones. Byron sees Napoleon as at one 'with the Caesars in his fate' (IV.822), while the blood and tears of conflict make up a 'universal deluge, which appears / Without an ark for wretched man's abode' (IV.26–7). This deluge 'ebbs but to reflow!' (IV.28), and the stanza's final prayer is for God to 'Renew [his] rainbow!' (IV.28).

Although it is not certain, J. M. W. Turner, who illustrated several scenes from *Childe Harold*, may have taken these lines as his inspiration for a painting of 1819, *Rome: The Forum with a Rainbow*, in which the rainbow, with its pronounced circular shape, and looking like the section of a wheel, seems to reflect with accuracy Byron's vision of the turning wheel of history. Both visions anticipate that of W. B. Yeats's poem 'The Second Coming' (1920), where it is feared that, in the inescapable cycle of things ('Turning and turning'), a far worse dispensation than that of Christianity's 'twenty centuries of stony sleep' now 'Slouches towards Bethlehem to be born'.

Byron's observations of the remains of the Roman empire in Canto IV of *Childe Harold*, and his conception of the cyclical process of history, owes something also to contemporary theories of geology and palaeontology. The ruins of Rome are 'The skeleton of her Titanic form / Wrecks of another world, whose ashes still are warm' (IV.413–14). Byron looks on the structure of ruins as he would at a fossil or skeleton of an extinct form of life. Catastrophists such as James Parkinson and Georges Cuvier believed that the world was formed over long periods of time and was subject to cycles of catastrophe, of which the last had been Noah's Flood. These cancelled cycles of existence are transmitted to Byron's view of ruins where the Coliseum's 'enormous skeleton' (IV.1281) is here imaged as though it were some form of pre-saurian reptile.

Shelley and 'Ozymandias'

Although the ruins of Greece and Rome were an important source of inspiration for Romantic writings like *Prometheus Unbound* and *Childe Harold*, Napoleon's expedition to Egypt in 1798 and the explorations of figures such as Joseph Ritchie, William Bankes and Giovanni Belzoni were instrumental in opening up another. Egypt was the inspiration for one of the nineteenth century's great sonnet triumphs, Shelley's 'Ozymandias', among the most celebrated of reflections on ruins (see Part Three: Romantic Verse Narrative).

'Ozymandias' was produced by Shelley in competition with a friend, Horace Smith, after their visit to the newly acquired fragments of the pharaoh's statue in the British Museum in 1817. Smith's sonnet was published in *The Examiner* on 1 February 1818, while Shelley's appeared in the same journal a few weeks previously on 11 January. In 'Ozymandias' (the Greek name for Rameses II), Shelley effectively says more briefly what in *Prometheus Unbound* he would go on to say at length. His belief is that the future must not be imposed upon by the past; that mankind must somehow break free from that tragic and endless exchange of power between oppressors and the oppressed which lends such a melancholy register to Byron's perception of history in *Childe Harold*. History showed too clearly what recent events only confirmed, that one form of tyranny is inexorably replaced by another. In France, the Ancien Régime had given way to a democratic revolution, to be superseded in its turn by a new form of imperialism which, after the fall of Napoleon, had resulted once again in the restoration of a monarchical dynasty.

In 'Ozymandias', Shelley hints at the despair-inducing transpositions of power in his hanging phrase, 'the heart that fed' (l. 8). Uncertain of reference, it invites its reader to speculate that the heart belongs either to the sculptor or to his oppressor, while 'mocked' and 'stamped on' suggest that the sculptor may wish to change places with the tyrant and become his oppressor in turn.*

For the atheist Shelley (see Part Four: 'Faith, Myth and Doubt'), the minatory inscription on the pedestal, 'Look on my Works, ye Mighty, and despair', would be likely to recall more familiar prohibitive commandments inscribed on tablets of stone. The pharaoh's self-referential 'King of Kings' is a title often given to Christ. But where Byron might have seen in the surrounding ruins evidence only of Death the Leveller, Shelley's 'lone and level sands' anticipate, in a hopefully more promising and democratic future, the abolition of invidious distinctions between rulers and their subjects. Sand, conventionally associated with the passing of time and the brevity of life, is here endowed with the property of water ('sunk', 'Wreck'), suggesting, more optimistically, the protean and as yet unwritten future which will one day escape from the stony limitations of history.

---

* The word 'mocked', as Shelley uses it here, means 'to imitate', but it also carries its other sense of 'to scorn or despise'. 'Stamped on' is an odd expression to use for an inscription engraved or incised upon stone, so that its more usual suggestion of oppression cannot be detached from it.

The future must not, therefore, in Shelley's scheme, resemble the past. The sonnet suggests that all ideologies and forms of oppression can be undone by a change of heart and mind. As Caleb Williams remarks in William Godwin's novel, the mind is endowed with powers 'that might enable it to laugh at the tyrant's vigilance', and physically empowered by this conviction, Caleb dismantles the prison strong-room in which he is confined, a 'mole hill', as it turns out to be, he says, 'compared with the ruins I had forced from the outer wall'.[9] In this sense ruins lead Shelley, like Caleb, to forward thinking rather than, as in Byron, retrospective musings on how history must inevitably weigh tragically upon the present. For Shelley in 'Ozymandias', the ruins of this particular empire are located not in an 'ancient' but an 'antique land'. Its 'antiquated' belief systems have become simply irrelevant.

Shelley's view of history invites readers to look beyond the confinements of the here and now. Even the unbounded vision of the sonnet's conclusion ('far away'), contrasts with the syntactical limitations imposed by number and tense in the finite opening verb ('I met'). As the poem is structured, the inscription on the fragmented statue's pedestal becomes a traveller's story. This, in its turn, becomes the text of the poem itself. The poem written by the now dead poet, Shelley, is being read by us, ourselves soon to be dead, and in time will be read by others not yet born. Contemporary critical interest in the fragment and the discontinuous, exemplified in the work of Thomas McFarland, Marjorie Levinson and Anne Janowitz,[10] derives in part from post-structuralist theory, and Shelley, it might be argued, here anticipates deconstructionism, by implying that his own text should be free to speak to future readers in whatever way they might choose to read it. He seems even to be inviting, in the violence of the language ('sunk', 'shattered', 'stamped on', 'wreck'), a breaking up of the text of his own poem into fragments which might then be reassembled to suggest new meanings. The limitations of the past, whether conceived in terms of Ozymandias's threats, the prohibitions of biblical commandments, or even the political ideologies symbolised in the Berlin Wall of our own times, can all, in Shelley's vision, be overcome by Imagination as a form of love, a sentiment anticipated by Romeo's 'stony limits cannot hold love out'.[11] With the fragments of the 'colossal Wreck' of Ozymandias's form, Shelley assembles a poem whose range, extending from the distant reaches of antiquity, envisages a future freed from the impositions and tyrannies of the past.

The Giaour and Other Broken Tales

In *The Giaour* (1813), one of the sensationally successful verse narratives of his early career, Byron presents a text which, announcing itself as 'A Fragment of a Turkish Tale', is literally broken into fragments (see also Part Four: Heroes and Anti-heroes). Turner's illustration of *The Giaour* (1822) which shows, in the foreground of the painting, two manacled female Greek slaves under the custodianship of their Turkish guardian, accentuates the fragmented civilisation by its inclusion of a relief from the Parthenon frieze, likely to have been based on a metope depicting the battle of the Centaurs and Lapiths which Turner admired, and one of the Elgin marbles now in London. Accompanying Turner's watercolour is a line, adapted from Byron's poem, ''Tis living Greece no more'.*

The opening passage of *The Giaour*, although a celebration of the magnificent Grecian landscape, describes how its beauty, like that of a person newly dead, is illusory. This once great civilisation, though still beautiful, is beautiful only in its decay. The verse-narrative to follow tells a story from many different points of view, the Giaour's own, that of a Turkish fisherman, those of Hassan and Hassan's mother, and of the Giaour's friend and the Monk. It is as though the ruins of Greece have in some way ensured the 'ruin' which is this poem. Greece, the home of Western culture and source of the epic, the first of poetic 'kinds', has become a slavish victim, and the fractured poem seems to be offering to a culture remote from its magnificent origins the only available form in which poetry can now be written.

The Giaour appears towards the end of the Napoleonic conflict, a period of enormous social and political upheaval, changing the face of Europe forever and ushering in the beginnings of the modern age.

---

* The line reads: ''Tis Greece, but living Greece no more!', *The Giaour* (l. 91).

Byron, in writing it as a second-generation post-war Romantic, might be said to anticipate the twentieth-century modernist poet T. S. Eliot. As a young man experiencing a similar situation at the end of the First World War, Eliot is able in *The Waste Land* (1922) to make no more than an attempt to write an epic poem. Rather than being an organic whole, *The Waste Land* becomes simply a succession of episodes presented by different voices, of which one significantly exclaims, 'These fragments have I shored against my ruins'.[12] In 1813 Francis Jeffrey, editor of the *Edinburgh Review*, writing on *The Giaour*, remarks that 'the greater part of polite readers would now no more think of sitting down to a whole Epic than to a whole ox',[13] and the form of the poem reflects upon the life experience of Byron himself. Unlike William Wordsworth, who traces his history in *The Prelude* as one of a steady growth from childhood and schooltime to what he calls 'The calm existence that is mine when I / Am worthy of myself!', Byron had no experience of such development. He was taken from the obscurity and relative poverty of his Scottish upbringing to be re-invented as an aristocrat and peer of the realm. His ongoing life is episodic, and the range of his work represents the fragmented nature of his story as a man. Byron's approach to poetry is not comparable to Wordsworth's organic conception of his projected epic, *The Recluse*, which is thought of as 'a gothic church', the 'preparatory poem' (*The Prelude*) a kind of 'ante-chapel', and all his other poems the 'little cells, oratories, and sepulchral recesses ordinarily included in those edifices'.[14] Byron proceeds by experimenting with a variety of forms and adopts various voices within them. As such, his work has a strikingly modern resonance, anticipating poets such as W. B. Yeats with his own employment of masks and personae.

The later poets of the 1930s, such as W. H. Auden, found a particularly sympathetic voice in Byron. Their experience as young men had been similar, and they turned a critical attention to the previous generation, which they held to be responsible for the cataclysm of war. While Byron's fragmentary poem, with its statement about the loss of a great culture and its consequences for the present, is relevant to early twentieth-century writers, Shelley's vision, as has been remarked upon, both in its acknowledgement of change and in its invitation to textual deconstruction, is close also to Auden's, especially in its belief that 'the words of a dead man' must be 'modified in the guts of the living'.[15]

Byron and Shelley are typical of the Romantic period's developing engagement with the past, in the way that ruins speak powerfully to them of man's condition. As in the diminutive figures who populate the exaggerated dimensions of the ruins of Rome in Piranesi's etchings,* or in the solitary figure overwhelmed by the grandeur of ancient fragments in Fuseli's sketch,† Byron, in *Childe Harold*, presents himself as 'a ruin amidst ruins' (IV.219), the conventional lonely traveller confronting the mystery of existence. For Shelley, it is for us to transform ourselves by breaking free from those limitations of the past which inhibit the development of individual potential. For Byron, ruins suggest the inevitable triumph of time over the hollow claims of empires. In Peacock's *Nightmare Abbey* (see Part Three: 'Romantic Fiction') the figure of Scythrop Glowry, representing Shelley, debunks Mr Cypress's (Byron's) intention 'to wander among a few mouldy ruins, that are only imperfect indexes to lost volumes of glory':[16]

> You will see many fine old ruins, Mr Cypress, crumbling pillars, and mossy walls—many a one-legged Venus and headless Minerva—many a Neptune buried in sand—many a Jupiter turned topsy-turvy—many a perforated Bacchus doing duty as a water-pipe.[17]

Mr Cypress replies in true Romantic mode, 'The mind is restless, and must persist in seeking, though to find is to be disappointed.'[18] Byron's response to the past in *Childe Harold* is typically interrogative: 'Temples, baths, or halls?' he asks, as he wanders the ruins of Rome,

---

* Piranesi (1720–78) was an Italian artist among whose celebrated works was a series of Vedute or 'Views' of ancient Rome produced in the 1740s.

† Henry Fuseli (1741–1825) was an artist of German-Swiss origin, a friend of the publisher Joseph Johnson and of many of the radical figures in his circle. His sketch, 'The Artist Moved by the Magnitude of Antique Fragments', depicts a figure of indeterminate gender with head in hands and seated by a plinth, above which are situated a gigantic foot and hand, the remnants of a colossal statue.

> Pronounce who can; for all that Learning reap'd
> From her research hath been, that these are walls. (IV.961–2)

If, like the pillar of Phocas ('Thou nameless column with the buried base', IV.983), history withholds its secrets, it is implicitly the function of the poet to try to understand historical process and man's role within it.

Chloe Chard, in *Pleasure and Guilt on the Grand Tour*,[19] examines Byron's responses as part of her chapter 'The Feminine and the Antique', which argues that ruins and the feminine are often elided in travellers' accounts of antiquity as both representing 'the allurements of a mysterious otherness'.[20] While classical scholars often experienced difficulties in investigating the past, an intuitive approach such as Byron's often made it more accessible. As an example, she quotes the section from Canto IV of *Childe Harold*, where Byron's speculations on the obscure life of the occupant of the tomb of Cecilia Metella allow him to form a kind of intimacy with her:

> I know not why—but standing thus by thee
> It seems as if I had thine inmate known,
> Thou tomb! And other days come back on me
> With recollected music. (IV.928–31)

Through this kind of elision, Chard argues, historical time is converted into personal time, and the ruins of antiquity, so often resistant to the urge to know or explain, are 'more easily transportable into a private domain of emotional intimacy'.[21] In *Nightmare Abbey*, exactly this relationship between antiquity and the feminine is apparent in Mr Glowry's remarks on Mr Cypress's pursuit of ruins: 'It is, indeed, much the same as if a lover should dig up the buried form of his mistress, and gaze upon relics which are anything but herself.'[22] The possibility of reconstruction is evident in Laurence Sterne's *A Sentimental Journey* (1768) (see Part Three: 'Romantic Travel Writing'), itself a sequence of fragmentary episodes, where having received only a momentary impression of a woman at Calais, the hero, Yorick, conjures a more complete version of her in his imagination:

I had not seen her face—'twas not material; for the drawing was instantly set about, and long before we had got to the door of the Remise, *Fancy* had finished the whole head, and pleased herself as much with its fitting her goddess, as if she had dived into the TIBER for it.[23]

Chard here argues that an antique becomes a metaphor for 'a combination of the two attractions that women are seen as supplying: on the one hand, a resistance to understanding and, on the other, a promise that this resistance will not be too overwhelmingly daunting'.[24]

The conclusion of *A Sentimental Journey*, an unfinished 'fragment' chapter entitled 'The Case of Delicacy', brings feminine resistance into close relationship with the concept of the Sublime, a central Romantic aesthetic and itself related to the fragment in its resistance to all sense of completion (see Part Three: 'Writing in Revolution'). As Sophie Thomas writes, 'Edmund Burke, in his influential treatise of 1757, identified obscurity, vastness, infinity [...] as key producers of sublime effects.' These categories, she writes, 'particularly relate to situations in which the whole is impossible to see or grasp, where boundaries or limits have been effaced or obscured'.[25] In 'The Case of Delicacy', Yorick's progress across the boundary into Italy has been halted by the fall of a great 'fragment' (p. 121) onto the road, so that he has to spend the night at an inn. The account which is given of the topography suggests his all too familiar acquaintance with the tired rhetoric of the Sublime:

> Let the way-worn traveller vent his complaints upon the sudden turns and dangers of your roads—your rocks—your precipices— the difficulties of getting up—the horrors of getting down— mountains impracticable—and cataracts, which roll down great stones from their summits, and block his road up.

As the story develops, the boundary between Yorick and his actual progress is complemented by the elaborate boundaries he is obliged to set up between his own bed and that of a lady traveller who is obliged to share his room for the night. Just as what lies beyond the geographical division cannot, in such a sublime setting, be grasped but only imagined, so the reader is left to speculate endlessly on what might happen should another, more delicate, boundary be crossed. The narrative 'concludes' with the lady's maid advancing 'so far up as to be in a line betwixt her mistress and me—So that when I stretched out my hand, I caught hold of the Fille de Chambre's END OF VOL. II.' Here an albeit comic situation of 'danger', as well as of possibility, is brought into direct relationship with the dangers and possibilities of the Romantic Sublime, while the fragmentary form and incompletion of Sterne's novel reflects the Sublime's own association with the fragment and the incomplete.

Landscapes of Ruin

The engagement of Romantic-period writers with the ruins of ancient civilisations extends to the natural world, where concepts such as those of sublimity direct attention to the nature of its creator. Mountainous regions, the untamed wilderness, the desert and the ocean all point to the power of the Being which had made them. The emptier the landscape the more evidence it gives of the plenitude of God within it, so that in a world view which 'looks through Nature up to Nature's God',[26] the Sublime in particular becomes a guarantee and protector of the idea of the Deity. The seventeenth-century divine Thomas Burnet argued in his influential work, *The Sacred Theory of the Earth* (see Part Three: Romantic Verse Narrative),* that the kind of topographies which come later to be associated with the Romantic Sublime, were in fact evidence of God's anger with sinful man (see p. 143 footnote above). In Burnet's theory, God's wrath had caused him to destroy a once smooth and perfect creation by a flood whose subsiding waters have left 'the Image or Picture of a great Ruin [...] a World lying in its Rubbish'.[27] The geographical features which, since the time of the Romantics, have come to be appreciated and celebrated were, for Burnet, no more than a sign of man's fallen condition. They are the broken materials of that first

---

* Thomas Burnet's *Telluris Theoria Sacra* or *The Sacred Theory of the Earth* was first published in 1681. An English translation appeared 1684–9.

world, and we now walk upon its ruins. For Burnet, geology provides the key to scriptural truth.

For much of his poem 'Mont Blanc' (1816), Shelley is concerned less with the mountain of the title, and more with the origins of the place which it occupies. The spirit who, in Byron's poetic drama *Manfred* (1816–17), refers to Mont Blanc as crowned 'long ago', and as the 'monarch of mountains',[28] implies that God has established an unchangeable order in which monarchs forever ruling subjects is as 'natural' as it is for some peaks to tower over lesser ones. In 'Mont Blanc', Shelley does refer to 'subject mountains'.[29] But he was no lover of monarchy and his poem goes on to describe how established power relationships might be rearranged. The landscape of the region and, in particular, the glacier of Mont Blanc, are given a political significance. Where 'all seems eternal' (l. 76), the glacier's imperceptible movement has 'overthrown / The limits of the dead and living world' (ll. 113–14) (see Part Four: 'Faith, Myth and Doubt').

Such evidence from nature points to how oppressive and, apparently permanent, regimes might also be changed by the ways in which we choose to think about them. The poem's opening describes how 'the eternal universe of things / Flows through the mind', and when Shelley looks at this particular landscape from his vantage point at 'Pont Pelissier', his knowledge of contemporary vulcanology fuels his speculations about the creation of such a place: 'is this the scene', he asks, 'Where the old earthquake demon taught her young / Ruin? Were these their toys? or did a sea / Of fire envelop once this silent snow?' (ll. 72–5). Unlike Burnet, who sees in the sublimity of such environments an all-round evidence of God's displeasure, Shelley sees in this 'flood of ruin' (l. 108) only a geological phenomenon, but one from which he can derive some optimism. The huge ice formations which 'Frost and the Sun' have created 'in scorn of human power' (l. 104), and which are in the process of being swept away by the moving glacier, are imaged as structures of the established Church and State, 'dome, pyramid and pinnacle' (l. 105). The poem suggests that these, too, can be overthrown. The 'pyramid' recalls the Egyptian setting of 'Ozymandias', whose sands, stretching 'far away' into a future of infinite possibility, find their counterpart in the melting streams of Mont Blanc's glacier, which 'Meet in the vale' to become as 'one majestic river / The breath and blood of distant lands' (ll. 124–5). Shelley's historical sense enables him to construct from ruins, whether natural or architectural, a vision of a transformed future. By contrast, Byron as ever, though in *Don Juan* facetiously, finds in a ruined pyramid an opportunity to express only a characteristic pessimism:

> Let not a monument give you or me hopes
> Since not a pinch of dust remains of Cheops. (I.219)

Fragmented Forms

The great archaeological enterprises of the eighteenth century, the intense interest in antiquarianism, and the historical researches of bodies such as the Society of Dilettanti, make it inevitable that the literature of the Romantic period should reflect a preoccupation with the fragmentary and the ruin. This takes various forms. Prominent large-scale projects in the form of extended fragments, such as Wordsworth's *Recluse* and Keats's *Hyperion* poems, or smaller-scale examples like Samuel Taylor Coleridge's 'Kubla Khan' and *Christabel*, indicate various subjective reasons for incompletion. Others, like Byron's *Don Juan* or Shelley's *The Triumph of Life*, remain fragments because of their author's death. The architectural folly and the sham ruin are reciprocated in fragmentary fakes and forgeries such as Thomas Chatterton's celebrated 'Rowley' poems and James Macpherson's *Fragments of Ancient Poetry*,* while the Romantic

---

* In 1768–9, Thomas Chatterton (1752–70) passed off poems that he himself had concocted as the work of a notional fifteenth-century priest, Thomas Rowley. His suicide, at the age of seventeen, amidst the torn-up pieces of his manuscripts, is the subject of a celebrated painting, *The Death of Chatterton* (1856), by Henry Wallis. He is described by Wordsworth as 'Chatterton, the marvellous boy' in 'Resolution and Independence' (l. 43). James Macpherson (1736–96) published his *Fragments of Ancient Poetry, Collected in the Highlands of Scotland, and Translated from the Galic* [sic] *or Erse Language* in 1760. Their supposed relation to an epic cycle composed by the Bard Ossian and telling of the exploits of Fingal caused a sensation for a time, but their authenticity was eventually dismissed.

emphasis upon isolated moments of spontaneity and immediacy, combined with the encouragement given by uncompleted works for readers to engage with them in acts of imaginative completion, relate the literature back to physical ruins and fragments.

Much of what is associated with the Romantic inflection given to forms of ruin is anticipated in Fuseli's picture mentioned earlier, *The Artist moved by the Magnitude of Antique Fragments* (1778–80). Fuseli's composition has the appearance of being hurriedly sketched in a moment of spontaneity. Perspectives are distorted, and the inscription on the plinth by which the artist sits is dashed off, with little attention given to the kind of accuracy that might enable a student of antiquity to identify a particular historical object. The emphasis falls instead on the emotional intensity demonstrated in the figure. The artist is in tactile relationship with the colossal fragments, but the visual faculty is cancelled as the figure covers its eyes to focus instead upon the inner life and the question of the relationship of genius to the creative imagination, an issue raised also by the fragment forgeries of Chatterton and Macpherson. There is no question in Fuseli's picture of connoisseurship, of historical investigation or an adherence to contemporary rules for pictorial composition. Instead, there is a conscious subversion of such expectations, while the gigantic fragmentary hand in the gesture of blessing seems to be privileging the 'Romantic' figure in its solitude and in its detachment from the esoteric concerns of antiquarian societies.

The pleasures of melancholy, though a particular element of the Romantic period associated with ruins, is long before anticipated in John Webster's *The Duchess of Malfi* (1612–13), where the character Antonio remarks of the Cardinal's dwelling: 'I do love these ancient ruins: / We never tread upon them, but we set / Our foot upon some reverend history' (V.iii.9–11). These 'ruins of an ancient abbey' (V.iii.2), making visible the vanity of human wishes, lead Antonio on to reflect upon past accomplishments and the certainty of their loss: 'But all things have their end: / Churches and cities, which have diseases like to men / Must have like death that we have' (V.iii.17–19). The pattern of Antonio's thoughts is echoed by Mary Wollstonecraft when, in her

Letters Written during a Short Residence in Sweden, Norway, and Denmark (1796), she describes visiting a little recess containing coffins of embalmed bodies in a church at Tønsberg in Norway. Her sentiments initially prefigure Shelley's approach to the fragments of the past as offering an opportunity for hope: 'The contemplation of noble ruins produces a melancholy that exalts the mind. – We take a retrospect of the exertions of man, the fate of empires and their rulers; and marking the grand destruction of ages, it seems the necessary change of time leading to improvement. – Our very soul expands, and we forget our littleness.' These forward-thinking remarks are soon qualified, however, by the disgust she expresses at the attempt to preserve social status in death by embalming: 'Is this all the distinction of the rich in the grave? – They had better quietly allow the scythe of equality to mow them down with the common mass, than struggle to become a monument of the instability of human greatness.'[30]

Melancholy over the ruins of the past is an emotion acknowledged by William Hazlitt as being of almost pathological significance when he describes English students in Rome who, in the presence of ancient wonders, feel their 'sinews of desire relax and moulder away, and the fever of youthful ambition [turn] into a cold ague-fit. There is a languor in the air, and the contagion of listless apathy infects the hopes that are yet unborn.'[31] Gillen D'Arcy Wood, in *The Shock of the Real*,[32] sees in this response a sense of the limitations of the human condition reflected 'in the form of a debilitating melancholia'.[33] The ruin as 'an incomplete and ultimately inscrutable representation of antiquity'[34] evokes what he describes as a sentimental melancholy typical of the age, one that would be destroyed by a complete knowledge of, or identification with, its historical context. He writes that the contemporary Hellenist Winckelmann and the antiquarian Diderot are among the most celebrated figures of a period which tended to displace the authentic objects of antiquity in favour of some mediated representation of them in the form of literary translation, paintings, prints of ruins and travel writing.

The Past Made Present: the Elgin Marbles

Wood argues that this sentimentalisation of ancient Greece is rudely disturbed by the arrival at the British Museum in 1816 of the Elgin Marbles, the first major collection of Greek antiquities in Europe.* The material reality of fragments from the frieze of the Parthenon, shipped by Lord Elgin to London, intruded upon the idealist constructions of Romantic Hellenism and made any future sentimental distancing of antiquity impossible. A writer who registers in a particularly acute way this 'museumizing' of the past is Keats, whose character Oceanus in *Hyperion* links the aesthetics of antiquity to the modern ideology of British imperialism: imagining the new order, destined to replace that of the deposed Saturn, Oceanus states: 'For 'tis the eternal law / That first in beauty should be first in might' (II.228–9). Wood writes that aesthetic wonder ('beauty'), is here made to bear 'the symbolic weight of imperial power' ('might').[35] The Elgin Marbles were not only tangible pieces of evidence demonstrating the realities of cultural imperialism, but also, removed from their historical contexts, irretrievably 'other'. The inseparability of the Parthenon fragments and their culture is a political issue between the governments of Britain and Greece to this day, while the effects of the reality of an ancient culture, brought into stark confrontation with an aesthetic idealisation of the past, is reflected in the troubled responses Keats's poetry registers in its representations of the antique.

In his *Essays on the Nature and Principles of Taste* (1790), Archibald Alison emphasises the advantages of the past's obscurity in allowing to the antiquarian the pleasures of imaginative reconstruction:

---

* Lord Elgin, British Ambassador to the Ottoman Empire (1799–1803), obtained permission from the Ottoman authorities to remove a substantial number of the sculptures of the Parthenon in Athens. Part of the Acropolis was destroyed by the explosion of a magazine during the Venetian siege (1687) and Elgin's ostensible motive was to protect any further damage to the marbles at a time when Greece was under Turkish occupation. The so-called Elgin Marbles were purchased by the British Government in 1816 and placed on display in the British Museum, where they remain.

The antiquarian, in his cabinet, surrounded by the relics of former ages, seems to himself to be removed to periods that are long since past, and indulges in the imagination of living in a world, which, by a very natural kind of prejudice, we are always willing to believe was both wiser and better than the present. All that is venerable or laudable in the history of those times present themselves to his memory. The gallantry, the heroism, the patriotism of antiquity rise again before his view, softened by the obscurity in which they are involved, and rendered more seducing to the imagination by that obscurity itself, which, while it mingles a sentiment of regret amid his pursuits, serves at the same time to stimulate his fancy to fill up, by its own creation, those long intervals of time of which history has preserved no record.[36]

Romantic idealisation of the past is at odds with the feelings of those who actually inhabited it and for whom the resonant names of antiquity carried only familiarity:

No man, however, is weak enough to believe, that to the citizen of Athens, or of Rome, such names ['the Ilyssus, the Tiber, the Forum, the Capitol, &c'] were productive of similar emotions. To him they undoubtedly conveyed no other ideas, than those of the particular divisions of the city in which he dwelt, and were heard of consequence, with the same indifference that the citizen of London now hears of the Strand, or the Tower.[37]

In *The Shock of the Real*, Wood stresses a difference between neo-classical principles of contemporary taste and the 'vivid physicality and expression' of the Elgin marbles as the product of a distant and different culture's 'scientific study of anatomy'.[38]

Keats's own acknowledgement of difference is highlighted in the two sonnets he wrote in 1817 about his visit to the Elgin Marbles at the British Museum in Haydon's company. Both poems, 'On Seeing the Elgin Marbles' and 'To B. R. Haydon, with a Sonnet Written on Seeing the Elgin Marbles', refer to 'these wonders' and to 'these mighty things', respectively, but make no attempt to give the detailed or representational accuracy which their titles' references to 'seeing' seem to be promising. Instead, Keats focuses entirely upon his own emotional responses, his sense of weakness before power, his inadequacy to match such creations, and even his sense of relief that he is not obliged to try. In themselves, the sonnets call to mind Fuseli's picture of the artist moved by the magnitude of antique fragments, but the predicament of the poet, which Keats presents as his own, goes beyond simply a sense of wonder before greatness, the kind of awe-struck response to which Joseph Severn refers when he writes of how Keats 'went again and again to see the Elgin Marbles, and would sit for an hour or more at a time beside them rapt in revery'.[39] It is this kind of enraptured stare which Severn's 1819 portrait of Keats is perhaps meant to reflect, but the sonnets themselves indicate a different response. In the sonnet, 'On Seeing the Elgin Marbles' in particular, Keats's statements about his artistic inadequacy develop into hesitant and broken utterances which register a conception of things so great that they can only be vaguely imagined:

> Such dim-conceivèd glories of the brain
> Bring round the heart an undescribable feud;
> So do these wonders a most dizzy pain,
> That mingles Grecian grandeur with the rude
> Wasting of old Time, with a billowy main,
> A sun, a shadow of a magnitude.

Traditionally, the response of the artist to the sublime object is announced in an inability to give appropriate expression to it. The object is so elevated or overwhelming that fear or rapture is its natural acknowledgment. But Keats's procedure is different. Grant Scott argues that the kind of elliptical disruptiveness found in the sonnet is Keats's way of enacting the marbles' decay in language.[40] In other words, Keats is not describing the Elgin fragments as sublime or beautiful ideals in themselves, objects which he, as an artist, might imaginatively reconstruct into wholes. He is responding to them as no more than the ruins that they are. Gillen D'Arcy Wood argues that Keats, in these sonnets, offers 'a pre-aesthetic image', removing the Elgin Marbles from the sentimentalising designs of the museum and thereby accentuating the political implications that arise when one nation's culture is appropriated by another.

The Romantic poet who most directly engages with the political issues surrounding the activities of Elgin in Greece is Byron who, in *English Bards and Scotch Reviewers* (1809), refers to the enormous expense being incurred by his enterprises:

> Let Aberdeen and Elgin still pursue
> The shade of fame through regions of virtu;
> Waste useless thousands on their Phidian freaks,
> Misshapen monuments and maim'd antiques;
> And make their grand saloons a general mart
> For all the mutilated blocks of art. (ll. 1027–32)

In *Childe Harold* Canto II, Byron also attacks Elgin and his agents for their vandalism, under the semblance of aesthetic concern, in transporting to England a former civilisation's ruins with the actual intent of consolidating Britain's imperial power. The Select Committee's report on Elgin's endeavours in 1816 made no secret of the government's intentions. By securing the marbles from 'further injury and degradation', the committee stressed that they would 'receive that admiration and homage to which they are entitled, and serve in return as models and examples to those, who by knowing how to revere and appreciate them, may learn first to imitate, and ultimately to rival them'.[41] Byron's dismay is registered in his invocation to Pallas Athena:

> Goddess of Wisdom! Here thy temple was,
> And is, despite of war and wasting fire,
> And years, that bade thy worship to expire:
> But worse than steel, and flame, and ages slow,
> Is the dread sceptre and dominion dire

Of men who never felt the sacred glow
That thoughts of thee and thine on polish'd breasts bestow.
(II.3–9)

Byron implies that Elgin and his associates are motivated purely by greed and lack the polish of the true classicist. In 'The Curse of Minerva' (dated 1811), and as a Scot himself, he makes his most direct attack on Elgin who, by his activities, has brought Scotland into disrepute:

Then thousand schemes of petulance and pride
Dispatch her scheming children far and wide,
Some East, some West, some everywhere but North,
In quest of lawless gain they issue forth.
And thus accursed be the day and year!
She sent a Pict to play the felon here! (ll. 143–8)

In Canto II of *Childe Harold*, Byron images Elgin as the sexual ravisher of a defenceless land:

Cold is the heart, fair Greece, that looks on thee,
Nor feels as lovers o'er the dust they loved;
Dull is the eye that will not weep to see
Thy walls defaced, thy mouldering shrines removed
By British hands, which it had best behoved
To guard those relics ne'er to be restored.
Curst be the hour when from their isle they roved,
And once again thy hapless bosom gored,
And snatch'd thy shrinking Gods to northern climes abhorr'd!
(II.127–35)

The consequence of Minerva's curse upon Elgin will be to have his own act of ravishment visited upon him in the transmission of his own faults to his heirs:

First on the head of him who did this deed
My curse shall light, on him and all his seed:
Without one spark of intellectual fire,
Be all the sons as senseless as the sire. (II.163–6)

Ultimately, Elgin becomes himself a form of ruin, left by Minerva's curse to 'stand through ages yet unborn, / Fix'd statue on the pedestal of Scorn' (II.207–8).

In *The Shock of the Real*, Wood argues that Elgin's unusual obsession to possess the Parthenon marbles had a specific pathological cause connected to the break-up of his marriage. A syphilitic condition resulting in the disintegration of his face, and especially his nose, lay behind his wife's adultery with a neighbour, Robert Fergusson, and her trial, with all its attendant publicity, made Elgin's situation notorious. Byron, in a note to *English Bards and Scotch Reviewers*, writes pointedly that Elgin 'would fain persuade us that all the figures, with and without noses, in his stoneshop, are the works of Phidias'.[42] Shelley's cousin, Thomas Medwin, records Elgin's condition in lines he obtains from Byron:

Noseless himself, he brings home noseless blocks,
To show what time has done and what—the [pox].[43]

In his mock-heroic poem, 'The Atheniad', Byron's biographer, John Galt, has Venus employ Cupid, in a symbolic act of castration, to attack Elgin's nose and burn it off. Cupid

Full at his forehead dash'd the flaming torch;
The nose defenceless perish'd with their scorch [...]
The mortal feature was resolv'd to dust,
And left Brucides like an antique bust.[44]

It is clear, too, from 'The Curse of Minerva' that the noses of ruined statuary were not the only parts to intrigue. Byron has

many a languid maid, with longing sigh,
On giant statues [cast] the curious eye [...]
Mourns o'er the difference of now and then,
Exclaims, 'these Greeks indeed were proper men!' (ll. 185–90)

Wood's argument is that an obsession to possess the marbles, together with his intention also to have them restored,* was for Elgin an act of compensation both for the 'loss' of his wife and of his manhood. His activities follow a Freudian psychopathological model whereby mourning for loss 'represents a split in the ego between its diminished present state and the shadow of its former wholeness'.[45] For Wood, both Keats and Elgin venture in their various ways beyond a sentimental response to ruins into what he calls 'an untheorized space – modernity's *lieu péril*'.[46] Elgin becomes a form of ruin, while Keats, in his Elgin Marbles sonnets, as well as in *The Fall of Hyperion*,[47] accentuates not the joy, but rather the pain of experiencing the wonders of antiquity, and registers its resistance to idealisation in terms of his own anguish and sense of disintegration. Wood sees in both Elgin's story and in Keats's poems not only a critique of their age's attempt to embrace antiquity as a form of its own cultural destiny, but also the psychological danger this represents to the Romantic votary of ruins 'who may just get what he wishes for'.[48]

Keats and the Grecian Urn

In the politicised context of the Elgin Marbles, the appropriation of ruins represents, for Byron, an imperialist rape upon the innocent land of Greece. For Martin Aske, in *Keats and Hellenism*, Keats's activity in writing 'Ode on a Grecian Urn' (1820) is a form of 'aesthetic' ravishment. Although not a 'ruin' as such, the Grecian Urn provokes the same kind of imaginative engagement with the past that ruins themselves can invite. In his Ode, Keats confronts the 'bride' / 'foster-child' of antiquity and

---

* Elgin met with both the Italian sculptor Antonio Canova and the English sculptor John Flaxman for advice on restoration.

attempts, in the process of encouraging it to yield up its secrets, to reproduce the urn's 'Fair attitude' (l. 41) in a written form.

For William Hazlitt, himself an artist, 'To put a statue into motion, or to give appropriate, natural, and powerful expression to set features of any kind, is at all times difficult.'[49] For Martin Aske, Keats's ekphrastic* Ode is the poet's frustrated attempt to 'write a Grecian Urn',[50] to 'express' (l. 3) or 'press out' a story from what Aske describes as 'the urn's silent landscape'.[51]

The marble surface's depiction of 'mad pursuit' upon 'maidens loth' described in stanza 1 of the Ode, is reflected in Keats's own pursuit of the urn and its mysteries. His speculations, importunate questionings, and the very intensity of his attempt to articulate the urn's silent eloquence, become a kind of intrusion upon its integrity. In trying to recover in poetic language ('our rhyme', l. 4) the artistic wholeness of its 'silent form' (l. 46), Keats becomes a ravisher of the urn and threatens its imaginative life. As Aske remarks of lines 15–20 of stanza 2, it is as though the poem's rhythm falters and hesitates, while its rhetoric is 'on the point of disintegrating, fragmenting its narrative endeavour and uncovering the inarticulate space between'.[52]

As the Ode develops, it becomes clear through disjunctions, such as that between stanzas 3 and 4, where the embossed figures upon the urn's surface are replaced abruptly by imagined ones from a wholly notional scene, that the text of the Ode is itself a series of broken fragments. Its inability to redeem the urn's 'legend' (l. 5) as a narrative whole is reflected in the internal disruption of the text itself. The last word of the final stanza reflects back upon its first one. What the poet, Keats, wants to 'know' is that 'O', antiquity's silent absence, the teasing vacancy of which the over-represented discourse of his Ode tries, but fails, to bring into some form of articulated existence. Thus the quest for completion and unity, so often associated with the Romantic period, results here in 'an O', or merely a cipher; 'not a rounded whole but a rounded hole, a frame without a middle, a form deprived of content'. Keats's 'Ode on a Grecian Urn' becomes effectively just another form of ruin.

---

* 'Ekphrasis' is a term which describes the written expression of a visual art form.

Notes

1 Mary Shelley, *Frankenstein*, ed. M. K. Joseph (Oxford: Oxford University Press, 1983), p. 119.

2 P. B. Shelley, *The Letters of Percy Bysshe Shelley*, ed. Frederick L. Jones, 2 vols (Oxford: Clarendon Press, 1964), vol. 2, p. 84.

3 Richard Holmes, *Shelley: The Pursuit* (London: Weidenfeld & Nicolson, 1974), pp. 491–2.

4 Blake, 'London': *Songs of Experience*.

5 *Julian and Maddalo*, ll. 170–1, 175–6.

6 P. B. Shelley, *Poetical Works*, ed. Thomas Hutchinson, corrected by G. M. Matthews (Oxford: Oxford University Press, 1970), p. 588.

7 *Childe Harold's Pilgrimage*, II.44–5.

8 'Il Penseroso', l. 86.

9 William Godwin, *Things as they Are; or the Adventures of Caleb Williams*, ed. Maurice Hindle (Harmondsworth: Penguin, 1988), pp. 195, 213.

10 See Thomas McFarland, *Romanticism and the Forms of Ruin: Wordsworth, Coleridge, and Modalities of Fragmentation* (Princeton: Princeton University Press, 1981); Marjorie Levinson, *The Romantic Fragment Poem: A Critique of a Form* (Chapel Hill, NC and London: University of North Carolina Press, 1986); Anne Janowitz, *England's Ruins: Poetic Purpose and the National Landscape* (Oxford: Blackwell, 1990).

11 *Romeo and Juliet*, II.ii.67.

12 T. S. Eliot, *The Waste Land*, 'What the Thunder Said', l. 54.

13 *Edinburgh Review*, xxi (July 1813), p. 299.

14 William Wordsworth, *The Poetical Works of William Wordsworth*, ed. Ernest de Selincourt and Helen Darbishire (Oxford: Clarendon Press, 1949), vol. 5, p. 2.

15 W. H. Auden, 'In Memory of W. B. Yeats'.

16 Thomas Love Peacock, *Nightmare Abbey*, ed. Lisa Vargo (Peterborough, Ont. and Orchard Park, NY: Broadview Press, 2007), p. 108.

17 Ibid., pp. 107–8.

18 Ibid., p. 108.

19 Chloe Chard, *Pleasure and Guilt on the Grand Tour: Travel Writing and Imaginative Geography, 1600–1830* (Manchester: Manchester University Press, 1999).

20 Ibid., p. 133.

21 Ibid., p. 135.

22 Peacock, *Nightmare Abbey*, p. 108.

23 Laurence Sterne, *A Sentimental Journey*, ed. Ian Jack (Oxford: Oxford University Press, 1984), p. 17.

24 Chard, *Pleasure and Guilt on the Grand Tour*, p. 130.

25 Nicholas Roe (ed.), *Romanticism: An Oxford Guide* (Oxford: Oxford University Press, 2005), p. 507.

26 Pope: 'Essay on Man', IV.332.

27 See M. H. Abrams, *Natural Supernaturalism: Tradition and Revolution in Romantic Literature* (New York: Norton, 1971), p. 100.

28 *Manfred*, I.i.61–2.

29 Percy Bysshe Shelley, *The Major Works*, ed. Zachary Leader and Michael O'Neill (Oxford: Oxford University Press, 2003), 'Mont Blanc' (Version B), l. 63.

30 Mary Wollstonecraft, *Letters Written during A Short Residence in Sweden, Norway, and Denmark*, ed. Richard Holmes (Harmondsworth: Penguin, 1987), p. 109.

31 William Hazlitt, *The Complete Works of William Hazlitt*, ed. P. P. Howe (New York: AMS Press, 1967), vol. 17, p. 141.

32 Gillen D'Arcy Wood, *The Shock of the Real: Romanticism and Visual Culture, 1760–1860* (New York and Basingstoke: Palgrave, 2001).

33 Ibid., p. 122.

34 Ibid.

35 Ibid., p. 131.

36 Archibald Alison, *Essays on the Nature and Principles of Taste*, 6th edn, 2 vols (Edinburgh, [1790] 1825), vol. 1, pp. 39–40.

37 Ibid., vol. 1, pp. 106–7.

38 Wood, *The Shock of the Real*, p. 133.

39 See W. Sharp, *The Life and Letters of Joseph Severn* (1892), p. 32.

40 Grant Scott, *The Sculpted Word: Keats, Ekphrasis and the Visual Arts* (Hanover, NH: University Press of New England, 1994), p. 66.

41 *Report from the Select Committee of the House of Commons on the Earl of Elgin's Collection of Sculptured Marbles &c.* (London: John Murray, 1816), pp. 26–7.

42 Byron, *Poetical Works*, ed. Frederick Page, corrected by John Jump (Oxford: Oxford University Press, 1970), p. 869.

43 Quoted in Wood, *The Shock of the Real*, p. 157.

44 Quoted in ibid., p. 166.

45 Ibid., p. 167.

46 Ibid., p. 168.

47 See *The Fall of Hyperion*, I.388–96.

48 Wood, *The Shock of the Real*, p. 169.

49   Quoted in Martin Aske, *Keats and Hellenism: An Essay* (Cambridge: Cambridge University Press, 1985), p. 112
50   Ibid., p. 113.
51   Ibid., p. 111.
52   Ibid., p. 116.

Part Five
References and Resources

Timeline

	Historical Events	Literary Events
1770	England and its colonies ruled by George III (acceded 1760)	Oliver Goldsmith, *The Deserted Village*; (7 April) William Wordsworth born
1771		Henry Mackenzie, *The Man of Feeling*; (15 August) Walter Scott born; (25 December) Dorothy Wordsworth born
1772		William Blake apprenticed to James Basire, engraver; William Gilpin tours the Lake District; (21 October) Samuel Taylor Coleridge born
1773	Boston Tea Party	Samuel Johnson and James Boswell tour Scotland; Goldsmith, *She Stoops to Conquer*
1774	Louis XVI crowned king of France	Johann Wolfgang von Goethe, *The Sorrows of Young Werther*; (12 August) Robert Southey born
1775	American War of Independence begins; Battles of Lexington and Bunker Hill	Johnson, *Journey to the Western Isles of Scotland*; (10 February) Charles Lamb born; (16 December) Jane Austen born
1776	(4 July) American Declaration of Independence; Captain James Cook sails in *Resolution* to find North-West Passage	Edward Gibbon, *Decline and Fall of the Roman Empire*; Thomas Paine, *Common Sense*; Adam Smith, *Wealth of Nations*

Timeline

	Historical Events	Literary Events
1777		Richard Sheridan, *School for Scandal*, first performance at Drury Lane Theatre, London
1778	Cook discovers Sandwich Islands (Hawaii)	Fanny Burney, *Evelina*; (30 May) Voltaire dies, Paris; (2 July) Jean-Jacques Rousseau dies, Paris; (10 April) William Hazlitt born
1779	(14 February) Death of Cook in Hawaii	Sir Joshua Reynolds, *Discourses*; Johnson, *Lives of the Poets*
1780	(2–9 June) Gordon Riots	Thomas West, *Guide to the Lakes*
1781	Sir William Herschel discovers Uranus; (19 October) Cornwallis surrenders to Washington at Yorktown	Friedrich Schiller, *The Robbers*
1782		William Cowper, *Poems*; Coleridge sent to school at Christ's Hospital, London (September); Coleridge meets Charles Lamb
1783	William Pitt, aged 24, becomes prime minister (until 1801); (3 September) Treaty of Paris, confirming US independence; Montgolfier brothers demonstrate first balloon ascent	George Crabbe, *The Village*; William Beckford, *Dreams, Waking Thoughts and Incidents* (suppressed by Beckford)
1784		Charlotte Smith, *Elegiac Sonnets*; Blake writing *Island in the Moon*; (19 October) Leigh Hunt born; (13 December) Johnson dies
1785		Cowper, *The Task*; (15 August) Thomas De Quincey born
1786	Impeachment proceedings against Warren Hastings	Beckford, *Vathek*; Gilpin, *Observations of Picturesque Beauty in Cumberland and Westmorland*; John Boydell's Shakespeare Gallery, London

	Historical Events	Literary Events
1787	American Constitution drafted and signed; Committee for the Abolition of the Slave Trade formed	Wordsworth's first published poem: sonnet addressed to Helen Maria Williams
1788		Robert Burns composes 'Auld Lang Syne'; Blake writing *Tiriel*; Ann Yearsley publishes 'Poem on the Inhumanity of the Slave-Trade'; (28 March) Charles Wesley dies; (22 January) Byron born
1789	(5 May) Estates General meets at Versailles; (14 July) Storming of the Bastille; Washington elected first President of the Republic (till 1797); *Bounty* mutiny	Blake, *Songs of Innocence*; (4 November) Richard Price's 'Discourse on the Love of our Country', address to London Revolution Society, provokes Edmund Burke's *Reflections on the Revolution in France* (published 1790)
1790	(14 July) King of France swears oath to new constitution; Declaration of the Rights of Man and of the Citizen approved by National Assembly of France	Mary Wollstonecraft, *A Vindication of the Rights of Men*; Ann Radcliffe, *A Sicilian Romance*; Helen Maria Williams, *Letters Written in France*
1791	Wolfe Tone founds Society of United Irishmen (leads unsuccessful rebellion in 1798); (22 June) French royal family attempts to reach frontier; captured at Varennes	Burns, 'Tam O'Shanter'; Boswell, *Life of Johnson*; Thomas Paine, *Rights of Man*
1792	Alliance of Austria and Prussia against France; (10 August) Tuileries stormed by Paris mob: king imprisoned; (3–7 September) September Massacres of royalist and other prisoners in Paris; (20 September) French victory	London Corresponding Society formed; Gilpin, *Essay on Picturesque Beauty*; Wollstonecraft, *A Vindication of the Rights of Woman*; Paine charged with sedition, *Rights of Man* banned; (4 August) Percy Bysshe Shelley born

Historical Events	Literary Events
against Prussians at Valmy; National Convention begins: Republic proclaimed; (December–January 1793) trial of the king before the Convention	
1793 Louis XVI sentenced to death (executed 21 January); war between England and France (till 1812); (6 April) Committee of Public Safety formed with Danton, Robespierre, St-Just, Couthon as leaders; (13 July) Marat murdered in his bath by Charlotte Corday; Beginning of Terror; (16 October) Marie Antoinette executed	Wordsworth, *Descriptive Sketches* and *An Evening Walk*; Blake, *The Marriage of Heaven and Hell*; (13 July) John Clare born
1794 Robespierre executed; English radicals, Thomas Holcroft, Horne Tooke, John Thelwall acquitted at Treason trials; Habeas Corpus suspended	William Godwin, *Things as They Are; or The Adventures of Caleb Williams*; Godwin, *Political Justice*; Radcliffe, *The Mysteries of Udolpho*; Blake, *Songs of Innocence and of Experience*
1795 (29 October) King's coach stoned at opening of parliament; Seditious Meetings Act and Treasonable Practices Act passed	Hannah More, *Cheap Repository Tracts*; (31 October) John Keats born
1796 (18 September) Washington's Farewell Address	Austen, *Pride and Prejudice* (completed 1797, published 1813); Coleridge, *Poems on Various Subjects*; Matthew Lewis, *The Monk*; Wollstonecraft, *Letters Written during a Short Residence in Sweden, Norway, and Denmark*; (21 July) Burns dies

	Historical Events	Literary Events
1797	(4 March) John Adams elected second president of USA; (April–June) British navy mutinies at Spithead and Nore	Radcliffe, *The Italian*; (November) Coleridge writes 'Kubla Khan' and first version of *The Ancient Mariner*; (30 August) Mary Godwin (future wife of Shelley) born; *The Anti-Jacobin* first published
1798	French invasion of Switzerland (January) and Egypt (July); Nelson's victory at the Battle of the Nile	Wordsworth and Coleridge, *Lyrical Ballads*; Joanna Baillie, *Plays on the Passions*; Coleridge writes 'Frost at Midnight' and (until April) *Christabel*, and writes *France: An Ode*; Austen writes *Northanger Abbey* (published 1818); Thomas Malthus, *Essay on the Principle of Population*
1799	(9 November) Bonaparte made First Consul under a new constitution; (14 December) Washington dies; Combination Laws (Six Acts) against radical activities	
1800	Act of Union with Ireland	Wordsworth writes 'Prospectus' to *The Recluse*; Coleridge writes *Christabel* Part 2 (October); Wordsworth, Preface to *Lyrical Ballads*
1801	Pitt resigns: end of first ministry; Thomas Jefferson elected third president of USA	*Lyrical Ballads* republished with new second volume
1802	(27 March–16 May 1803) Peace of Amiens, only truce with France; Bonaparte becomes Life Consul	Scott, *Minstrelsy of the Scottish Border*; Coleridge, 'Dejection: An Ode' published in *Morning Post* (later version in *Sibylline Leaves*, 1817); *Edinburgh Review* first published under Francis Jeffrey, editor

Timeline

	Historical Events	Literary Events
1803	Peace of Amiens breaks down; war resumes with France	Mary Tighe, *Psyche* (privately published 1805)
1804	Pitt's second ministry; Bonaparte proclaimed Emperor (May: coronation November); Spain declares war on Britain	Blake, *Milton*; Wordsworth completes 'Intimations Ode', 'Ode to Duty', 'Daffodils'
1805	Battle of Trafalgar, death of Nelson; Russian and Austrian armies defeated by Bonaparte at Austerlitz	Scott, *The Lay of the Last Minstrel*; Wordsworth completes *The Prelude* (19 May) in thirteen books
1806	(23 January) Pitt dies; (14 October) Bonaparte defeats Prussians at Jena; Lord Grenville becomes British Prime Minister	Wordsworth, *Peele Castle* written
1807	Abolition of slave trading in British ships; Duke of Portland becomes British Prime Minister	Wordsworth, *Poems in Two Volumes*; Charles and Mary Lamb, *Tales from Shakespeare*; Byron, *Hours of Idleness*
1808	(January) Africa's slave trade prohibited in USA; Spain invaded by French: Peninsular War begins; British conclude Convention of Cintra betraying Portuguese and evacuating French in British ships	Scott, *Marmion*; Leigh Hunt founds *The Examiner*
1809	(4 March) James Madison elected fourth president of USA; Bonaparte captures Vienna: excommunicated by the Pope; Spencer Percival becomes British prime minister	Blake exhibition with Descriptive Catalogue; *The Quarterly Review* founded (February), editor William Gifford; Byron, *English Bards and Scotch Reviewers*
1810	(December) George III officially declared insane	Scott, *Lady of the Lake*; Crabbe, *The Borough*
1811	(February) Prince of Wales made Regent	Shelley, *The Necessity of Atheism*
1812	Percival assassinated in House of Commons; Lord Liverpool becomes prime minister,	Byron, *Childe Harold* I and II

	Historical Events	Literary Events
	Castlereagh Foreign Secretary, Lord Sidmouth Home Secretary; USA declares war on Britain; (October) Bonaparte invades Russia; Moscow burned by Russians; French retreat with terrible losses; Elgin Marbles arrive in London	
1813	Bonaparte victorious at Dresden, defeated at Leipzig, rejects peace; Mass Luddite trials at York: many hangings and transportations	Austen, *Pride and Prejudice*; Byron, *The Giaour*; Shelley, *Queen Mab*; Southey becomes Poet Laureate
1814	Allied armies enter Paris; Bonaparte exiled to Elba	Byron, *The Corsair* and *Lara*; Scott, *Waverley*; Austen, *Mansfield Park*; Wordsworth, *The Excursion*
1815	Bonaparte escapes from Elba, enters Paris; (18 June) Bonaparte defeated at Waterloo and exiled to St Helena	Austen, *Emma*; Wordsworth, *Poems*
1816	End of Napoleonic Wars, followed in Britain by economic depression and social unrest; (December) Spa Fields riots; Elgin Marbles purchased by British Museum	Byron, *Childe Harold* III, *The Prisoner of Chillon*; Coleridge, *Christabel*, *The Pains of Sleep*; Shelley, 'Mont Blanc'
1817	James Monroe elected fifth president of USA	Coleridge, *Biographia Literaria*; Keats, *Poems*; *Blackwood's Edinburgh Magazine* first published; Byron, *Manfred*; Southey, *Wat Tyler* published
1818	Habeas Corpus restored	Byron, *Childe Harold* IV, *Beppo*; Mary Shelley, *Frankenstein*; Austen, *Northanger Abbey*, *Persuasion*; Peacock, *Nightmare Abbey*; (5 May) Karl Marx born
1819	(16 August) 'Peterloo' Massacre: 11 killed by militia in	Keats writes 'La Belle Dame Sans Merci', *The Eve of St Agnes*

Historical Events	Literary Events
protest meeting at St Peter's Field, Manchester; Passing of the 'Six Acts', including the Seditious Meetings Prevention Act and the Blasphemous and Seditious Libels Act	and *Odes*; Byron, *Don Juan* I and II; Shelley, 'Ode to the West Wind'; Scott, *Ivanhoe*
1820 (29 January) Death of George III, succeeded by his son, Prince Regent since 1811, as George IV; trial of Queen Caroline for adultery; Cato Street conspiracy to kill government ministers fails, leaders executed	Clare, *Poems Descriptive of Rural Life and Scenery*; Keats, *Poems*; Shelley, *Prometheus Unbound* and *The Cenci*; Charles Lamb, *Essays of Elia*; *London Magazine* first published
1821 (May) Bonaparte dies on St Helena	Greek War of Independence begins, Byron sails to Greece; Byron, *Cain*, *The Two Foscari*, *Marino Faliero*, *Sardanapalus*, *Don Juan* III and IV; De Quincey, *Confessions of an English Opium Eater*; Shelley, *Adonais*; Southey, *A Vision of Judgement* (with Preface attacking Byron and the 'Satanic School' of poetry); (27 February) Keats dies, Rome
1822 (12 August) Castlereagh commits suicide	Byron, *The Vision of Judgment*; Shelley, *Hellas*, *Epipsychidion*; Shelley drowns, Bay of Spezia
1823 Lord Liverpool succeeded by George Canning	Byron, *Don Juan*, Cantos VI–XIV published
1824 Combination Act (1799) repealed	James Hogg, *Confessions of a Justified Sinner*; (19 April) Byron dies, Missolonghi; Byron, *Don Juan*, Cantos XV–XVI published posthumously
1825 Opening of Stockton and Darlington railway; John Quincy Adams elected sixth President of USA	Hazlitt, *The Spirit of the Age*

Further Reading

Introductions, Cultural Overviews and Anthologies

Abrams, M. H., *The Mirror and the Lamp: Romantic Theory and the Critical Tradition* (New York: Norton, 1953; repr. 1958)
> Indispensable account of the shift from a mimetic to a Romantic 'expressive' aesthetic

—, *Natural Supernaturalism: Tradition and Revolution in Romantic Literature* (New York: Norton, 1971)
> An important work which examines Romantic literature in terms of its biblical inheritance, tracing developments from an expected apocalypse by divine revelation and political revolution to one brought about by imagination

Bygrave, Stephen (ed.), *Romantic Writings*, Approaching Literature Series (London: Routledge and the Open University, 1996)
> Essays by individual scholars on a variety of topics, including helpful material on women's literature, orientalism, colonialism and the exotic, with many textual close readings

Cox, J., *Poetry and Politics in the Cockney School: Keats, Shelley, Hunt, and Their Circle* (Cambridge: Cambridge University Press, 1998)
> Examines the younger generation which was centred on the Leigh Hunt circle and the implications for its members of the disparaging term 'Cockney School'

Curran, Stuart (ed.), *The Cambridge Companion to British Romanticism* (Cambridge: Cambridge University Press, 1993)
> Important collection of excellent essays by leading scholars. Valuable essay on the sister arts of poetry and painting by Morris Eaves

Donnachie, Ian and Carmen Lavin (eds), *From Enlightenment to Romanticism: Anthology 1* (Manchester: Manchester University Press and the Open University, 2003)
> Useful anthology of primary texts on religion, revolutionary politics, slavery, music and art

Gaull, Marilyn, *English Romanticism: The Human Context* (New York and London: Norton, 1988)
> A detailed compendium of Romantic topics covering the widest range of material

Hepworth, Brian, *The Rise of Romanticism: Essential Texts* (Manchester: Carcanet, 1978)
> A very valuable collection of excerpts from the major philosophy of the pre-Romantic and Romantic periods. Includes e.g. Burnet, *The Theory of the Earth*, Lowth, *Lectures on the Sacred Poetry of the Hebrews*

Jordan, Frank (ed.), *The English Romantic Poets: A Review of Research and Criticism*, 4th edn (New York: Modern Language Association of America, 1985)
> Exhaustive compendium of published work in all areas of Romanticism

Keen, Paul, *Revolutions in Romantic Literature: An Anthology of Print Culture 1780–1832*, Broadview Anthologies of English Literature (Peterborough, Ont.: Broadview Press, 2004)
> Impressive range of primary source material from the period, with lesser known and more canonical writings covering literary criticism, philosophy, politics, science, travel

Klancher, Jon (ed.), *A Concise Companion to the Romantic Age* (Chichester: Wiley-Blackwell, 2009)
> New perspectives on the relationships between literature and culture in a range of excellent essays on religion, historicism, nationalism, politics, law, natural history, the sciences, consumer culture, visual entertainments

Lavin, Carmen and Ian Donnachie (eds), *From Enlightenment to Romanticism: Anthology 2* (Manchester: Manchester University Press and the Open University, 2004)
> Valuable primary source material on industry, nature, science, drama, art and music

McCalman, Iain (ed.), *An Oxford Companion to the Romantic Age: British Culture 1776–1832* (Oxford: Oxford University Press, 1999)
> A huge resource. Essential reference work

Natarajan, Uttara (ed.), *The Romantic Poets*, Blackwell Guides to Criticism (Oxford: Blackwell, 2007)
 Valuable chapters on the six major Romantic poets made up of selections from important criticism from the nineteenth century to the present. A final chapter on 'An Expanding Canon'

O'Neill, Michael (ed.), *Literature of the Romantic Period: A Bibliographical Guide* (Oxford: Clarendon Press, 1998)
 Indispensable guide on most of the major writers

Parker, M., *Literary Magazines and British Romanticism* (Cambridge: Cambridge University Press, 2000)
 Examines the important part played by reviews and magazines in the Romantic period

Pirie, David B. (ed.), *The Romantic Period*, Penguin History of Literature Series (Harmondsworth: Penguin, 1994)
 An excellent survey with many superb essays. Pirie's essay on Keats and Everest's on Shelley are particularly good

Porter, Roy and Mikuláš Teich (eds), *Romanticism in National Context* (Cambridge: Cambridge University Press, 1988)
 A valuable exploration of Romanticism as a phenomenon in England, Wales and eleven other European countries

Prickett, Stephen (ed.), *The Romantics* (London: Methuen, 1981)
 A very helpful collection of essays on the historical context, art, religion and imagination

Roe, Nicholas (ed.), *Romanticism: An Oxford Guide* (Oxford: Oxford University Press, 2005)
 An exhaustive and indispensable compendium of introductory critical essays by leading scholars

St Clair, William, *The Reading Nation in the Romantic Period* (Cambridge: Cambridge University Press, 2004)
 Has become the standard work on writers and their audience

Stabler, Jane, *Burke to Byron, Barbauld to Baillie, 1790–1830* (Basingstoke: Palgrave, 2002)

> A stimulating book, giving equal critical consideration to male and female writers, organised by genre

Wu, Duncan (ed.), *Romanticism: A Critical Reader* (Oxford: Blackwell, 1995)

> A valuable collection of essays

— (ed.), *Women Romantic Poets: An Anthology* (Oxford: Blackwell, 1997)

> Comprehensive anthology of many long-neglected women poets

— (ed.), *A Companion to Romanticism* (Oxford: Blackwell, 1998)

> An excellent introduction to the period, containing over fifty short essays on the period

— (ed.), *Romanticism: An Anthology*, 3rd edn (Oxford: Blackwell, 2006)

> Standard work with lengthy headnotes on biographical and critical approaches to each writer

Literary Genres

Drama

Baines, Paul and Edward Burns, *Five Romantic Plays, 1768–1821* (Oxford: Oxford University Press, 2000)

> A good Introduction to the drama of the times with commentaries on the individual plays, including Walpole, *The Mysterious Mother*, Southey, *Wat Tyler* and Byron, *The Two Foscari*

Bate, Jonathan, *Shakespeare and the English Romantic Imagination* (Oxford: Clarendon Press, 1986)

> An detailed examination of the influence of Shakespeare on the work of the six major Romantic poets

Bate, Jonathan (ed.), *The Romantics on Shakespeare* (Harmondsworth: Penguin, 1992)
> A comprehensive and invaluable selection of Romantic Shakespearean criticism from both English and European figures

Burroughs, C. (ed.), *Women in British Romantic Theatre: Drama, Performance, and Society, 1790–1840* (Cambridge: Cambridge University Press, 2000)
> Essays which explore, in addition to the work of women playwrights such as Elizabeth Inchbald and Joanna Baillie, the contributions of women to the world of Romantic drama as managers, critics and translators

Cave, Richard Allen (ed.), *The Romantic Theatre: An International Symposium* (Totowa, NJ: Barnes & Noble, 1986)
> Timothy Webb's essay on the Romantic poets' ambivalent relationship to the stage is especially interesting in this collection of essays on contemporary drama

Cox, J. and M. Gamer (eds), *The Broadview Anthology of Romantic Drama* (Peterborough, Ont.: Broadview, 2003)
> The anthology contains a very helpful introduction to an understanding of the Romantic theatre

Donahue, Joseph W., *Dramatic Character in the English Romantic Age* (Princeton: Princeton University Press, 1970)
> Analyses the performances of some of the major celebrity actors of the day in the process of discussing the Romantic concept of dramatic character

Howell, Margaret J., *Byron Tonight: A Poet's Plays on the 19th Century Stage* (Windlesham: Springwood, 1982)
> Fascinating account of the Victorian actor-managers who adapted Byron's dramas to the melodramatic and spectacular requirements of the contemporary theatre

Hume, Robert D. (ed.), *The London Theatre World, 1660–1800* (Carbondale, Ill.: Southern Illinois University Press, 1980)
> Series of essays which examine all aspects of the theatre world, audiences, management, scenery, repertory, theatre architecture

Moody, Jane, *Illegitimate Theatre in London, 1770–1840* (Cambridge: Cambridge University Press, 2000)
> An exploration of the significance and range of the drama staged in the minor playhouses of the day

Moody, Jane and Daniel O'Quinn (eds), *The Cambridge Companion to British Theatre 1730–1830* (Cambridge: Cambridge University Press, 2007)
> A collection of essays exploring what made the theatre such an important political, social and cultural venue during the eighteenth and early nineteenth centuries

Richardson, Alan, *A Mental Theater: Poetic Drama and Consciousness in the Romantic Age* (University Park: Pennsylvania State University Press, 1988)
> An exploration of the Romantic poets' innovations in verse-drama

Schiller, Friedrich, *The Robbers* (1792), facsimile edition (Oxford: Woodstock, 1989)

Sillars, Stuart, *The Illustrated Shakespeare 1709–1875* (Cambridge: Cambridge University Press, 2008)
> A complete study of the history and tradition of illustrated editions of Shakespeare. Chapters 5 and 6 are particularly relevant to the Romantic period: 'Ornaments derived from Fancy' and 'The Growth of Feeling'

Fiction

Backscheider, Paula R. and Catherine Ingrassia (eds), *A Companion to the Eighteenth-Century English Novel and Culture* (Oxford: Wiley-Blackwell, 2009)
> Deals with formative influences, engagement with major philosophies of the period, and legacy

Butler, Marilyn, *Jane Austen and the War of Ideas* (Oxford: Clarendon Press, 1975)
> The book argues that Jane Austen was not a figure isolated from the times in which she lived, but was conscious of argument and debate from the range of novels with which she was familiar

Butler, Marilyn, *Peacock Displayed: A Satirist in his Context* (London: Routledge, 1979)
> Butler argues that Peacock has a stronger political awareness than many of his contemporaries, despite his rather minority appeal

Kiely, Robert, *The Romantic Novel in England* (Cambridge, Mass.: Harvard University Press, 1972)
> Twelve essays on major Romantic novels, including Peacock's *Nightmare Abbey*, Mary Shelley's *Frankenstein* and Hogg's *Confessions of a Justified Sinner*

Maxwell, Richard and Katie Trumpener (eds), *The Cambridge Guide to Fiction in the Romantic Period* (Cambridge: Cambridge University Press, 2008)
> Useful sections on women writers and the women's novel, sentimental fiction and fiction of the working classes

Mellor, Anne K., *Mary Shelley: Her Life, Her Fiction, Her Monsters* (London: Routledge, 1988)
> An invaluable study of the work of Mary Shelley by a prominent feminist critic. Especially illuminating on *Frankenstein*

Miller, Karl, *Doubles: Studies in Literary History* (Oxford, Oxford University Press, 1985)
> Examines the theme of the 'Double' in literature, including material on Hogg's *Confessions of a Justified Sinner*

Sedgwick, Eve Kosofsky, *Between Men: English Literature and Male Homosocial Desire* (New York: Columbia University Press, 1985)
> The book is very interesting on the subject of homosocial desire in Hogg's *Confessions of a Justified Sinner*

Poetry and Politics

Butler, Marilyn, *Burke, Paine, Godwin, and the Revolution Controversy* (Cambridge: Cambridge University Press, 1984)
> Valuable primary source material which includes a wide range of those who enter the debate, apart from the main participants such as Price, Burke, Paine and Wollstonecraft

Chandler, James (ed.), *The Cambridge History of English Romantic Literature* (Cambridge: Cambridge University Press, 2009)
> A broad, up-to-date survey of the period. Good essays by John Barrell on London in the 1790s and by Anne Janowitz on rebellion, revolution and reform

Connell, Philip and Nigel Leask (eds), *Romanticism and Popular Culture in Britain and Ireland* (Cambridge: Cambridge University Press, 2009)
> Contains a very useful chapter on politics and the people, as well as helpful chapters on ballad poetry, and on the urban experience

Cronin, Richard, *The Year of 'Lyrical Ballads'* (London: Macmillan, 1998)
> An attempt to re-create and examine the literary culture of 1798

Deane, Seamus, *The French Revolution and Enlightenment in England 1789–1832* (Cambridge, Mass.: Harvard University Press, 1988)
> A key study of the political and intellectual context

Gilmartin, Kevin, *Writing Against Revolution: Literary Conservatism in Britain 1790–1832* (Cambridge: Cambridge University Press, 2007)
> Explores the important literary forms of counter-revolutionary expression in Britain

McCalman, Iain, *Radical Underworld: Prophets, Revolutionaries, and Pornographers in London, 1795–1840* (Oxford: Clarendon Press, 1993)
> Challenges conventional distinctions between 'high' and 'low' culture, revealing links between the literary culture and the political underworld, poverty, crime and prophetic religion

Mee, John, *Dangerous Enthusiasm: William Blake and the Culture of Radicalism in the 1790s* (Oxford: Clarendon Press, 1992)
> Examines the cultural politics of Blake's contemporaries and the currents of sceptical radicalism and dissent within which Blake wrote his Prophetic Books

Roe, Nicholas, *Wordsworth and Coleridge: The Radical Years* (Oxford: Clarendon Press, 1988)
> Examines the radical intellectual world familiar to both Wordsworth and Coleridge, and its influence on them in the years before they emerged as major figures

Roe, Nicholas, *John Keats and the Culture of Dissent* (Oxford: Clarendon Press, 1997)
> Provides new information about Keats's life and shows why his poetry was provocative to his more conservative contemporaries

Stauffer, Andrew M., *Anger, Revolution and Romanticism* (Cambridge: Cambridge University Press, 2005)
> Identifies anger as a central element in the Romantic period and, among others, explores Blake, Coleridge, Godwin, Shelley and Byron in relation to revolution and reaction, terror and war

Thompson, E. P., *The Making of the English Working Class* (London: Gollancz, 1963)
> Definitive study of contemporary working-class consciousness, history and culture

Poetry and Nature

Bate, Jonathan, *Romantic Ecology: Wordsworth and the Environmental Tradition* (London and New York: Routledge, 1991)
> Emphasises the 'green' Wordsworth, examining his sense of community and geography as inherited by subsequent writers such as Hardy, Edward Thomas and Seamus Heaney

—, *The Song of the Earth* (London: Picador, 2000)
> The first ecological reading of English literature, focusing on the link between literature and the environment, grounded in the English Romantic tradition, but exploring also American, Central European and Caribbean poets and engaging theoretically with Rousseau, Adorno, Bachelard and Heidegger

Klonk, Charlotte, *Science and the Perception of Nature: British Landscape Art in the Late Eighteenth and Early Nineteenth Centuries* (New Haven and London: Yale University Press, 1996)
> Examines the complex interactions that took place between artists and scientists focusing on the emergence of a new *phenomenalist* conception of experience around the turn of the century. Excellent illustrations

Perkins, D., *Romanticism and Animal Rights* (Cambridge: Cambridge University Press, 2003)
> Explores the issue of animal rights in the pre-Romantic and Romantic periods, tracing the theme through encyclopaedias, scientific works and literature for children and in the poetry of Cowper, Wordsworth, Coleridge, Clare, and others

Piper, H. W., *The Active Universe: Pantheism and the Concept of Imagination in the English Romantic Poets* (London: Athlone Press, 1962)
> An invaluable book which explores new concepts of the material world as reflected in the work of the major Romantic poets

Roe, Nicholas, *The Politics of Nature: Wordsworth and Some Contemporaries* (Basingstoke: Macmillan, 2002)
> A re-consideration of what 'nature-worship' might mean for Wordsworth and his contemporaries, examining the political context to provide surprising new insights, e.g. 'The Politics of the Wye Valley: Re-placing "Tintern Abbey"'

Thomas, Keith, *Man and the Natural World: Changing Attitudes in England 1500–1800* (London: Allen Lane, 1983; repr. Penguin, 1984)
> Compares and contrasts our present attitudes to the natural world with the attitudes of our forebears

Willey, Basil, *The Eighteenth-Century Background: Studies in the Idea of Nature in the Thought of the Period* (Harmondsworth: Penguin, 1962)
> A helpful survey of the changing attitudes to nature through the century. Especially good on Wordsworth

Travel Writing

Andrews, Malcolm, *The Search for the Picturesque: The Landscape, Aesthetics and Tourism in Britain, 1760–1800* (Aldershot: Scolar Press, 1989)
> An authoritative and engaging account with many superb illustrations

Buzard, James, *The Beaten Track: European Tourism, Literature, and the Ways to 'Culture', 1800–1918* (Oxford: Clarendon Press, 1993)
> Explores Romantic 'anti-tourism'. Especially helpful on Wordsworth and Byron and their influence on later attitudes to travel

Chard, Chloe, *Pleasure and Guilt on the Grand Tour: Travel Writing and Imaginative Geography, 1600–1830* (Manchester: Manchester University Press, 1999)
> An important book on this genre which considers the strategies of description and commentary rather than the social history of travel

Gilroy, Amanda (ed.), *Romantic Geographies: Discourses of Travel 1775–1844* (Manchester: Manchester University Press, 2000)
> Essays by leading scholars on a range of historicist approaches to travel, especially feminist and post-colonial, focusing on 'the politics of location' in writings by well-known and less well-known travel writers of the period

Jarvis, Robin, *Romantic Writing and Pedestrian Travel* (Basingstoke: Macmillan, 1997; repr. 2000)
> Examines the rise of pedestrian travel in the last quarter of the eighteenth century and the relationship between walking and writing in the Romantic period

Leask, Nigel, *British Romantic Writers and the East: Anxieties of Empire* (Cambridge: Cambridge University Press, 1992)
> A discussion of how the rapidly expanding imperialism of Britain informed the work of Byron, Shelley, De Quincey and Coleridge

Littlewood, Ian, *Sultry Climates: Travel and Sex since the Grand Tour* (London: John Murray, 2001)
> The sexual motives of travel from the eighteenth century to 'Club Med'

Thompson, Carl, *The Suffering Traveller and the Romantic Imagination* (Oxford: Oxford University Press, 2007)
> The book examines how the Romantic travellers such as Wordsworth and Byron embraced the concept of 'suffering' as a way of distinguishing authentic from purely recreational travel. It examines branches of Romantic era travel writing such as captivity, shipwreck and exploration narratives

Watson, Nicola J., *Literary Tourism and Nineteenth-Century Culture* (Basingstoke: Macmillan, 2009)
> Essays by leading scholars in this field of travel writing, discussing well-known figures popular on the tourist trail such as Wordsworth and Byron. The introduction provides a useful overview with a back history of associated criticism

Woof, Robert, Stephen Hebron and Claire Tomalin, *Hyenas in Petticoats: Mary Wollstonecraft and Mary Shelley* (The Wordsworth Trust, 1997)
> The catalogue to an exhibition of 1997, with much detailed information and many excellent illustrations on two significant women writers of the period associated with travel. The introductions to Wollstonecraft and Mary Shelley are by Claire Tomalin and Pamela Woof respectively

Verse Narratives

Allen, Graham, 'Romantic verse narrative', in Stephen Bygrave (ed.), *Romantic Writings*, Approaching Literature Series (London: Routledge and the Open University, 1996), pp. 139–59
> A helpful account with close readings of Keats's 'La Belle Dame Sans Merci', *The Eve of St Agnes*, and Shelley's *Alastor*

Jacobus, Mary, *Tradition and Experiment in Wordsworth's 'Lyrical Ballads' (1798)* (Oxford: Clarendon Press, 1976)
> A valuable monograph on what Wordsworth and Coleridge owed to various traditions of poetry and how they transformed them. Useful appendices including poems such as Burger's 'Lenore'

Kroeber, Karl, *Romantic Narrative Art* (Madison: University of Wisconsin Press, 1960)
> Essential reading on this particular branch of Romantic poetry

O'Neill, Michael, 'Romantic Forms: An Introduction', in Nicholas Roe (ed.), *Romanticism: An Oxford Guide* (Oxford: Oxford University Press, 2005), pp. 283–5
> A brief but helpful section on the verse narrative as a significant Romantic poetic form

Key Debates

Fragments and Ruins

Aske, Martin, *Keats and Hellenism: An Essay* (Cambridge: Cambridge University Press, 1985)
    Invaluable readings of Keats's poems in the context of late Enlightenment and Romantic attitudes towards antiquity

Harries, Elizabeth Wanning, *The Unfinished Manner: Essays on the Fragment in the Later Eighteenth Century* (Charlottesville, Va. and London: University Press of Virginia, 1994)
    Discusses the eighteenth-century cultural context and the concept of the Romantic 'fragment'

Janowitz, Anne, *England's Ruins: Poetic Purpose and the National Landscape* (Oxford: Blackwell, 1990)
    Looks at the poetics of fragments and ruins and examines their political and historical implications

McFarland, Thomas, *Romanticism and the Forms of Ruin: Wordsworth, Coleridge, and Modalities of Fragmentation* (Princeton, NJ: Princeton University Press, 1981)
    The argument is that ruin, fragmentation and the unfinished are not only peculiar to Romanticism, but are endemic in all human endeavour

Thomas, Sophie, 'The Fragment', in Nicholas Roe (ed.), *Romanticism: An Oxford Guide* (Oxford: Oxford University Press, 2005), pp. 502–19
    Short helpful sections on the various meanings attaching to the term 'fragment' in Romanticism, with a close reading of Coleridge's 'Kubla Khan'

Wood, Gillen D'Arcy, *The Shock of the Real: Romanticism and Visual Culture, 1760–1860* (New York and Basingstoke: Palgrave, 2001)
    Discusses the variety of ways in which visual culture confronted Romantic 'idealism' with the shock of the real, whether in the form of fragments such as the Elgin Marbles, or in the new images of photography. An absorbing and important book

Woodward, Christopher, *In Ruins* (London: Chatto & Windus, 2001)
  A fascinating study of the history of ruins, and the meanings attached to them, from antiquity to the London Blitz and beyond

Gothic Villains and Heroes

Calder, Angus, *Byron* (Milton Keynes: Open University Press, 1987)
  Section 1, 'Contexts', pp. 1–23, has useful remarks on Byron and the concept of the hero

Cantor, Paul A., *Creature and Creator: Myth-making and English Romanticism* (Cambridge: Cambridge University Press, 1984)
  Particularly useful on *Frankenstein* and the rebellious figures of Byron's verse-tales and drama

Holmes, Richard, *The Age of Wonder: How the Romantic Generation Discovered the Beauty and Terror of Science* (London: Harper Press, 2008)
  An absorbing account of distinguished individuals in the Romantic period in the realms of exploration, astronomy and science and their relevance to the work of the Romantics

Peckham, Morse, *Beyond the Tragic Vision: The Quest for Identity in the Nineteenth Century* (New York: Braziller, 1962)
  Examines the concept of new emerging selfhoods in nineteenth-century philosophy, writing and art as the comforts of religion were rejected

Railo, Eino, *The Haunted Castle: A Study of the Elements of English Romanticism* (London: George Routledge & Sons, 1927)
  Contains chapters on 'The Criminal Monk', 'The Wandering Jew', 'The Byronic Hero' and 'The Young Hero and Heroine' in Romanticism

Thorslev, Peter, *The Byronic Hero: Types and Prototypes* (Minnesota: University of Minnesota Press, 1962)
  Explores the man of feeling, the gothic villain, the noble outlaw, Faust, Cain, Satan and Prometheus as formative prototypes of the Byronic hero figure

The Imagination

Abrams, M. H., 'The Correspondent Breeze: A Romantic Metaphor', in M. H. Abrams, *English Romantic Poets: Modern Essays in Criticism* (Oxford: Oxford University Press, 1960)
> A seminal essay which examines various Romantic metaphors in use to describe the processes of the creative imagination

Beer, John, *Romanticism, Revolution and Language: The Fate of the Word from Samuel Johnson to George Eliot* (Cambridge: Cambridge University Press, 2009)
> The French Revolution called even the authority of language as a cornerstone of knowledge into question. Romantic writers developed new ways of expressing their philosophy of the imagination. Examines a range of writers, including the poets, Blake, Coleridge and Wordsworth, essayists (Hazlitt) and novelists (Jane Austen)

Bowra, Maurice, *The Romantic Imagination* (Oxford: Oxford University Press, 1966)
> Originally a series of lectures on the six major Romantic poets, Poe and the Pre-Raphaelites, which formed the basis of a thesis informing the whole Romantic movement. A helpful introduction

Diffey, T. J., 'The roots of imagination: the philosophical context', in Stephen Prickett (ed.), *The Romantics* (London: Methuen, 1981)
> A clear and accessible introduction

Engell, James, *The Creative Imagination: Enlightenment to Romanticism* (Cambridge, Mass.: Harvard University Press, 1981)
> Lucid, solid, comprehensive and informative discussion of how the Romantics developed ideas already present in the eighteenth century. Examines English concepts in tandem with German ones

Hill, John Spencer, *The Romantic Imagination*, Casebook Series (Basingstoke: Macmillan, 1983)
> Useful extracts from poets and modern critical studies all written before 1970. The poets do not include Blake or Byron

Willey, Basil, *Nineteenth-Century Studies: Coleridge to Matthew Arnold* (Harmondsworth: Penguin, 1964)
> A very useful chapter on Coleridge and his distinctions between fancy and imagination

Religion

Brantley, Richard E., *Wordsworth's 'Natural Methodism'* (New Haven and London: Yale University Press, 1975)
> A persuasive account of the central significance of Methodism in a range of Wordsworth's work

Bush, Douglas, *Mythology and the Romantic Tradition in English Poetry* (Cambridge, Mass.: Harvard University Press, 1937)
> Discusses new ways of thinking and writing about myths in the Romantic period

Harrison, J. F. C., *The Second Coming: Popular Millenarianism 1780–1850* (London: Routledge & Kegan Paul, 1979)
> Discusses the centrality of millennial thought in the Romantic period and the numerous cults and sects associated with it

Paley, Morton, *Apocalypse and Millennium in English Romantic Poetry* (Oxford: Oxford University Press, 2003)
> Describes how the model of history provided by the Book of Revelation, apocalypse and millennium, is interrogated, and sometimes undermined, by the six major Romantic poets

Priestman, M., *Romantic Atheism: Poetry and Freethought, 1730–1830* (Cambridge: Cambridge University Press, 1999)
> A wide-ranging examination of the links between atheism and canonical and non-canonical figures among poet-intellectuals and controversialists in the Romantic period

Ryan, Robert M., *The Romantic Reformation: Religious Politics in English Literature 1789–1824* (Cambridge: Cambridge University Press, 1997).
> Examines the major Romantic poets in the context of the period's debate on religion, politics and society

Thompson, E. P., 'The Transforming Power of the Cross', in *The Making of the English Working Class* (Harmondsworth: Penguin, 1963; repr. 1968), pp. 385–411
> Examines the social significance in the Romantic period of the Methodist movement

—, *Witness Against the Beast: William Blake and the Moral Law* (Cambridge: Cambridge University Press, 1993)
> Examines Blake in the context of dissenting values and nonconformist radicalism

White, Daniel, *Early Romanticism and Religious Dissent* (Cambridge: Cambridge University Press, 2006)
> Explores the dissenting background informing the non-conformity of figures such as Godwin, Mary Wollstonecraft, Coleridge and Southey

Critical Approaches

Copley, Stephen and John Whale (eds), *Beyond Romanticism: New Approaches to Texts and Contexts 1780–1832* (London and New York: Routledge, 1992)
> Collection of essays challenging traditional views on the Romantic period, and opening up new contexts in which to assess the period, e.g. Shelley and magnetism

Ecological Criticism

Kroeber, Karl, *Ecological Literary Criticism: Romantic Imagining and the Biology of Mind* (New York: Columbia University Press, 1994)
> Argues for an ecological approach to literature

Feminism and Materialism

Favret, Mary A. and Nicola J. Watson (eds), *At the Limits of Romanticism: Essays in Cultural, Feminist and Materialist Criticism* (Bloomington: Indiana University Press, 1994)
> Explores how the traditional exclusion of women writers has made cultural issues concerning the marketplace, class and competing cultural discourses easier to ignore

Fay, Elizabeth A., *A Feminist Introduction to Romanticism* (Oxford: Blackwell, 1998)
> Provides a useful introductory survey of feminist approaches to Romantic writings

Mellor, Anne K. (ed.), *Romanticism and Feminism* (Bloomington: Indiana University Press, 1988)
> Alan Richardson's and Stuart Curran's essays in this collection of feminist approaches to Romantic texts have been especially influential

Watkins, Daniel P., *A Materialist Critique of English Romantic Drama* (University Press of Florida, 1993)
> Political readings of major Romantic dramas, including most of Byron's plays, Coleridge's *Osorio* and Baillie's *De Monfort* in an attempt to account for the conditions which, in Watkins's view, caused a decline in the drama of this period

Historicism

Butler, Marilyn, *Romantics, Rebels and Reactionaries: English Literature and its Background 1760–1830* (Oxford: Oxford University Press, 1981)
> Essential reading by the leading historicist critic of Romanticism

Chandler, J., *England in 1819: The Politics of Literary Culture and the Case of Romantic Historicism* (Chicago: University of Chicago Press, 1998)
> Chandler explores ties between Romantic and contemporary historicism, and argues that late twentieth-century practices of cultural history writing have their roots in Romantic historicism in post-Waterloo Britain

Levinson, Marjorie, *The Romantic Fragment Poem: A Critique of a Form* (Chapel Hill, NC and London: University of North Carolina Press, 1986)
> A New Historicist reading of several canonical Romantic fragment poems

Levinson, M., M. Butler, Jerome J. McGann and P. Hamilton, *Rethinking Historicism: Critical Readings in Romantic History* (Oxford: Blackwell, 1989)
> Essays by four of the leading historicist critics

McGann, Jerome J., *The Romantic Ideology: A Critical Investigation* (Chicago and London: University of Chicago Press, 1983)
> A seminal work which argues that Romantic critics have uncritically absorbed the ideas of the Romantic poets themselves

Siskin, Clifford, *The Historicity of Romantic Discourse* (Oxford and New York: Oxford University Press, 1988)
> Argues that almost all of our literary histories of the late eighteenth and early nineteenth centuries are themselves Romantic. Literature is an ideological construction determined by changing social relations, and the critic must historicise such constructions

Psychoanalytic Criticism

Herz, Neil, *The End of the Line: Essays on Psychoanalysis and the Sublime* (New York: Columbia University Press, 1985)
> A study of the central Romantic topic of the sublime, examining Romantic and psychoanalytical texts in tandem

Kirschner, Suzanne, *The Religious and Romantic Origins of Psychoanalysis: Individuation and Integration in Post-Freudian Theory* (Cambridge: Cambridge University Press, 1996)
> Examines Romantic thought as a basis for psychoanalysis

McDayter, Ghislaine (ed.), *Untrodden Regions of the Mind: Romanticism and Psychoanalysis* (Lewisburg, Pa.: Bucknell University Press, 2002)
> Essays which apply psychoanalytical ideas to Romantic writings

O'Neill, Michael, *Romanticism and the Self-Conscious Poem* (Oxford: Clarendon Press, 1997)
> Illuminating new readings of many well-known poems by the major Romantic poets; the book explores the 'self-conscious' poem, that is, a poem concerned with poetry that displays awareness of itself as poetry

Journals

The Byron Journal, published annually by the Byron Society
The Charles Lamb Bulletin, published quarterly by the Charles Lamb Society
European Romantic Review, from 2010 published six times per year
The Hazlitt Review, published annually from 2008 by the Hazlitt Society
The Keats-Shelley Journal, published annually by the Keats-Shelley Association of America
Romanticism, published twice-yearly by Edinburgh University Press
Studies in Romanticism, published quarterly by the Graduate School, Boston University
The Wordsworth Circle, published quarterly

Electronic resources

Romantic Circles

www.rc.umd.edu/
> A major resource with chronologies, a blog, concordances, digital editions of texts, edited by Neil Fraistat and Steven E. Jones

Romanticism on the Net

www.ron.umontreal.ca/
An online *Romanticism* journal (published since 1996) with articles, book reviews and links

Romantic Chronology

www.english.ucsb.edu:591/rchrono/
An immensely detailed chronology of the period

Literature Encyclopedia

www.litencyc.com/index.php
A reference work written by university teachers around the world. There are many good articles available on writings of the Romantic period

Eighteenth-Century Collections Online

www.gale.com/EighteenthCentury/
A hugely ambitious undertaking, claiming to have digitised 'every significant English-language and foreign language title printed in Great Britain during the eighteenth century, along with thousands of the important works from the Americas'

The Age of George III

www.historyhome.co.uk/
A useful resource with a large amount of historical information on government administrations, and events in Britain, Ireland, France, India and America

Periodicals Archive Online

http://pao.chadwyck.co.uk/home.do
Contains the *Edinburgh Review*

The *Quarterly Review* Archive

www.rc.umd.edu/reference/qr/index.html
Contains the volumes published between 1809 and 1831

The William Blake Archive

www.blakearchive.org/blake/
Huge resource of Blake's illuminated books, drawings, paintings, engravings, and more

James Gillray: The Art of Caricature

www.tate.org.uk/britain/exhibitions/gillray/default.htm
The website for an exhibition of Gillray's work at the Tate Britain Gallery, London, in 2001

Index

Index

Index

Index

YORK NOTES **COMPANIONS**

Texts, Contexts and Connections from York Notes
to help you through your literature degree ...

✔ **Medieval Literature**, Carole Maddern
ISBN: 9781408204757 | £10.99

✔ **Renaissance Poetry and Prose**, June Waudby
ISBN: 9781408204788 | £10.99

✔ **Shakespeare and Renaissance Drama**, Hugh Mackay
ISBN: 9781408204801 | £10.99

✔ **The Long Eighteenth Century: Literature from 1660 to 1790**
Penny Pritchard
ISBN: 9781408204733 | £10.99

✔ **Romantic Literature**, John Gilroy
ISBN: 9781408204795 | £10.99

✔ **Victorian Literature**, Beth Palmer
ISBN: 9781408204818 | £10.99

✔ **Modernist Literature: 1890 to 1950**, Gary Day
ISBN: 9781408204764 | £10.99

✔ **Postwar Literature: 1950 to 1990**, William May
ISBN: 9781408204740 | £10.99

✔ **New Directions: Writing Post 1990**, Fiona Tolan
ISBN: 9781408204771 | £10.99

Available from all good bookshops

For a 20% discount on any title in the series visit
www.yorknotes.com/companions and
enter discount code JB001A at the checkout!